The Motor Car and Popular Culture in the 20th Century

The Motor Car and Popular Culture in the 20th Century

David Thoms
Len Holden
Tim Claydon

Ashgate

Aldershot • Brookfield USA • Singapore • Sydney

Published by
Ashgate Publishing Limited   Ashgate Publishing Company
Wey Court East   110 Cherry Street
Union Road   Suite 3-1
Farnham   Burlington
Surrey, GU9 7PT   VT 05401-3818
England   USA

ISBN 978-1-8592-8461-2

British Library CIP Data
The Motor Car and Popular Culture in the Twentieth Century
        1. Automobiles – Social Aspects 2. Automobiles – History – 20th Century
        3. Popular Culture 4. Popular Culture – History – 20th Century
        I. Thoms, D.W. (David William), 1942– II. Holden, Len
        306.4'0904

US Library of Congress CIP Data
Popular Culture and the Motor Car in the Twentieth Century / edited by
        David Thoms, Len Holden, Tim Claydon.
        p.   cm.
        Includes bibliographical references.
        1. Automobiles – Social Aspects – Great Britain – History – 20th Century.
        2. Automobiles – Social Aspects – History –20th Century I. Thoms, David.
        II. Holden, Len. III. Claydon, Tim.
        HE5663.A6M64   1998   97–35619
        303.48'32 – dc21   CIP

MIX
Paper from
responsible sources
FSC
www.fsc.org   FSC® C004959

Printed and bound in Great Britain
by Printondemand-worldwide.com

Transferred to Digital Printing in 2011

Contents

The Car as Image

Entertainment and Leisure

Notes on Contributors

Daryl Adair is Research Officer in the Department of Human Movement Studies, University of Queensland, Australia and a Research Associate with the International Centre for Sports History and Culture, De Montfort University, Leicester. His research has focused on crowd behaviour during public spectacles, risk-taking behaviour in various types of motor sport, and (with Wray Vamplew) Adair is author of *Sport in Australian History*, Oxford University Press, Melbourne, 1997.

Brad Beaven is Lecturer in Social History at the University of Portsmouth. His doctoral thesis was on the establishment and development of the Coventry motor industry to 1939. He has recently published on the development of working-class culture during the nineteenth and twentieth centuries and is currently researching the social history of the British car worker to 1939.

Kathleen Bell is Lecturer in English at De Montfort University, Leicester who has published articles on both twentieth-century poetry and popular literature. She does not drive a car, has never taken a driving test and is a firm supporter and frequent user of public transport.

Dr Tim Claydon is Principal Lecturer in Industrial Relations at De Montfort University, Leicester. He began his academic career as an economic and social historian with a special interest in twentieth century labour history and his doctoral thesis was a study of the early development of trade unionism among motor and aircraft workers. His more recent work has been concerned with contemporary developments in British industrial relations.

Dr Tom Donnelly is Head of Management at Coventry University and has contributed a number of books and articles on the automobile industry.

Ken Gelder is Senior Lecturer in English and Cultural Studies at the University of Melbourne. His books include *Reading the Vampire* (Routledge, 1994) and co-edited with Sarah Thornton, *The Subcultures Reader* (Routledge, 1996).

Duncan Heining is employed as a Senior Probation Officer/Trainer but his first love has always been music. He has written for *Jazz on CD* in the past and is currently writing for a new Jazz magazine *Avant*. He drives a Hyundai Accent 1.5i but dreams of a 'pretty little red Corvette'.

Dr Len Holden is Principal Lecturer in Human Resource Management at Leicester Business School, De Montfort University, Leicester. He has written the *Business History of Vauxhall Motors* and contributed to the *National Dictionary of Business Biography* in the realm of the motor industry. He has had many books and articles published in his specialist academic area, human resource management, but still retains a lively interest in the industrial relations, management and social aspects of the motor industry.

Steve Koerner is currently lecturing at Saitama University in Urawa, Japan. He is a history graduate of the University of Victoria, Canada, and he has recently completed his PhD dissertation, 'The British Motor Cycle Industry, 1935–1975', at the Centre for the Study of Social History at the University of Warwick.

Sebastian Lockwood is professor at Lesley College, Cambridge, USA, where he teaches Anthropolgy, Literature and Business Communications. He holds degrees in Anthropolgy and Education from Cambridge University, UK and spent his early years between North Norfolk and Toronto, Canada. His most recent book is *The Trickster's Tongue*, a collection of poetry.

Steven Morewood is Lecturer in Economic History at the University of Manchester. He is the author of *Pioneers and Inheritors: Top Management in the Coventry Motor Industry 1896–1972* (Coventry Polytechnic, 1990). He has taught at a number of universities.

Sean O'Connell is Research Officer in the Business History Unit at the London School of Economics, where he is working on a history of mail order retailing. His University of Warwick doctoral thesis analysed the 'Social and Cultural Impact of the Car in Interwar Britain. He is the author of *The Car and British Society: Class, Gender and the Car 1896–1939*, (Manchester University Press, 1997).

Tim O'Sullivan is Reader in Media Education and Cultural Studies in the School of Humanities at De Montfort University, Leicester. His recent publications include *Studying the Media* (Arnold, 1994) and *The Media Studies Reader* (Arnold, 1997). He has enjoyed a long-standing and not always harmonious relationship with old cars and motorbikes, including a 1932 Morris and a 1934 Royal Enfield.

Jenny Rice is Programme Leader for the MA Arts and Humanities at De Montfort University, Leicester. She researches and publishes in the area of cultural studies. In particular, her interests focus on cultural forms of consumption and gender issues in news discourse.

Carol Saunders is Acting Head of the School of Humanities at De Montfort, University, Leicester. Her research focuses on academic discourse and she has recently published in the cultural studies area of consumption and nostalgia.

Paul Thompson is Research Professor at the University of Essex, Founder of the National Life Story Collection at the National Sound Archive, and Founder-Editor of Oral History. His books include *The Work of William Morris*, *The Edwardians*, and *The Voice of the Past*.

David Thoms is Professor of Economic and Social History and Head of the Department of Historical and International Studies at De Montfort University. His publications include a *History of the Motor Car Industry in Coventry since the 1890s*.

Dr Paul Wells is Subject Leader in Media Studies at De Montfort University, Leicester. He has made a number of award-winning series for BBC Radio including 'Spinechillers', a six-part history of the horror film. He has recently published *Understanding Animation*, (Routledge, 1997) and edited *Art and Animation* (Academy Group, 1997). He is preparing further books on British Animation and Cartoons and Cultural History.

Nicholas Zurbrugg is Professor of English and Cultural Studies in the School of Humanities, De Montfort University, Leicester. He is the author of *Beckett and Proust, The Parameters of Postmodernism and Critical Vices, The Myths of Postmodern Theory and Positively Postmodern* and *The Multimedia Muse in America: Interviews with the Contemporary Avant-Garde* (forthcoming).

Introduction

David Thoms, Len Holden, Tim Claydon

The motor car has been called 'the machine that changed the world' (Womack et al, 1990). It has brought new concepts and language to the realms of production; it has revolutionised patterns of work, leisure, and residence; it has generated a plethora of changing signs and symbols in all areas of life from the sidewalk to the cinema. Perhaps the greatest testament to the car's cultural significance is, ironically, its contemporary mundanity. Some of us can remember a time when streets were defined by the buildings which formed them; today it is the architecture of the automobile which dominates our sense of public space. Indeed, the car has also become embodied in the very built environment itself – the filling station, the car park and the out of town shopping and leisure complex, not to mention the executive detached house with its two car garage.

This collection of essays explores some of the ways in which the motor car has come to serve as a metaphor for modernity. We have identified three major themes which, while we would not claim them to be exhaustive, seem to us to address some key issues concerning the car's place in the development of twentieth-century culture. The first of these themes concerns the car as image, the way in which the car has come to signify a wide range of meanings which reflect and condition our sense of social reality. The second is the role of the car in the development of entertainment and leisure in the twentieth century. The third deals with a range of social and economic issues related to the production and sale of cars. While these questions, for example labour relations, have received considerable attention from social scientists and historians, our distinctive aim has been to explore them in relation to the development of management thought, popular consciousness and public opinion. While we have divided the book into three thematic sections, it will become apparent to the reader that subtexts flow throughout the book. Issues of identity and self related to nation, class, culture and gender can be discerned, as can social issues which expand beyond the business, production and design concerns of many previous writings.

Section one explores the car as image, and it has long been recognised as a potent symbol of masculinity as a number of writers here attest. In Nicholas Zurbrugg's discussion of the car in modern literature its role as an expression of male auto-erotic fantasy emerges as a strong theme. More generally he discusses how the car has been used in modern literature to express the divisions between pessimistic and optimistic accounts of modernity and its futures. He also touches on the ambiguities and contradictions of the car's social and cultural effects as a force of conformity and constraint, while at the same time offering fantasies of escape and detachment. He concludes by arguing for the emergence of a more detached, possibly ironic, post-modern acceptance of the car as 'something neither threatening nor extravagant, but simply "interesting and unpredictable"'.

As Len Holden states in his exploration of the car as symbol of ideology and culture, 'like clothes and other objects (cars) are outward signs or representations of values, cultural or otherwise, which stretch beyond the object itself'. The poor quality models churned out on soviet production lines served as a metaphor for a failed collectivism, just as the production lines set up to produce the Model T Ford came to represent a system of stifling conformity and alienating work forms. Alternatively they also represent an age of not only mass production but also of mass consumption with echoes of class and status divides in their outward displays, on the one hand, of ostentation, and on the other of modesty. David Thoms explores the theme of ownership and status further and states 'the motor car differentiates on a personal basis; through their particular characteristics cars interact with the individual, perhaps in terms of a status (or inverted status) relationship with the external world, or merely through internalised self identification'. In this sense they are an extension of personality! Sebastian Lockwood develops this personal theme further and in an autobiographical mode reflects on cars as landmarks in the life of the individual. He also sees them serving as dreamscapes through life representing loss of innocence, youthful excitement and ultimately a sense of adult concern and responsibility. As Lockwood states 'we identify with the car that we chose, our parent chose, our lover chose'.

The section ends with an examination of the car in a different context both symbolically and geographically. Ken Gelder's analysis of cars in contemporary Australian road films and narratives explores the metaphorical nature of the *Mad Max* movies which he feels represents a particular Australian white conservatism, evinced through a bleak landscape without Aboriginal presence in which the villains speak with British accents and the police Australian ones. He sees these films as, in essence, a celebration of nationalism which attempts to distinguish Australianism from both its British antecedents and American cultural influence by de-radicalising the US road movie genre.

In section two the theme of the popular image of the motor car as a source of entertainment and leisure is explored. This theme is particularly derived from the car's ability to transport its occupants to the countryside or coast for a day of family revelry. From the 1930s, in particular, motor vehicles became a more flexible alternative to the railways for the enjoyment of British beaches and woodlands, and, like its Victorian counterpart, the family car helped transform people's leisure patterns and sources of entertainment. But as this anthology demonstrates, the car was, and remains, a complex and many faceted source of popular enjoyment. It is represented in sport, the arts, including literature, film and music, and in a variety of more personalised activities and perceptions, some of which blur the edge between imagination and reality.

Although car ownership is higher than ever before, there remains an ambivalence about its social value. Kathleen Bell gives an early example of this when she juxtaposes the attractions of joy-riding, as experienced by Toad in Grahame's *Wind in the Willows*, with the recriminations which attach to those who break the codes of acceptable behaviour. On a related theme, Paul Wells demonstrates that cinematic representations of the car have pointed to the tensions between its desirability as an artefact of the twentieth century and the threat which it poses in terms of environmental and other concerns. In considering the interaction between the car and American culture, he explores how animated film became a medium through which these fears and aspirations were articulated.

Duncan Heining investigates the strong relationship between popular music and the motor car, noting, for example, that 'Rocket 88' by Jackie Brenston and his Kings of Rhythm, perhaps the first Rock and Roll record, has a car as its central feature. He goes on to investigate the thematic representations of the car within popular music, focusing upon gender, and in particular issues of masculinity. Masculinity is also an important aspect of Daryl Adair's analysis of the development of motor racing as a participant and spectator sport. In tracing the gentleman-amateur origins of motor racing, he notes that part of the sport's attraction derived initially from its connections with notions of manliness and heroism. Steven Morewood finds similar attractions in the road-going relative of the racing car, the British sports car, which also had a history of track racing although manufacturers were most likely to invest in these 'sideshows' as a spectacular form of publicity for their production models which sold to the general public. Motor racing soon moved along the spectrum from amateur to professional but the appeal of the sports car was that the dedicated amateur could, as Morewood reminds us, emulate the racing car's 'lively acceleration, high maximum speed and good road holding characteristics', be it at a lesser level.

The motoring public also experienced its own transition in terms of size, taste and purchasing power. Steve Koerner investigates one important aspect of this when he analyses the contrasting fortunes of popular motoring of the two and four-wheeled variety. The theme of mass production for a mass market is further developed by Sean O'Connell's essay in which he establishes the links between cultural factors and consumer behaviour. The motor car became an important mechanism through which people's desire for leisure and entertainment could be satisfied but, as O'Connell reveals, the scope of this was limited in the interwar period by the restrictive practices of the manufacturers and dealers.

Section three develops the theme of sales and production, starting with Brad Beavan's examination of the shop floor experience of car production workers from 1896 to 1920. He argues that the early workers in the motor industry were not motivated merely by reward. They were also concerned to gain degrees of autonomy over their work process. This has usually been seen in terms of the assertion of 'craft' traditions, but Beavan argues that, given the weakness of trade union organisation at this time, and the fact that craftsmen were already a minority in car factories the emphasis on autonomy in shop-floor culture stemmed from more widely solidaristic efforts by car workers to create space and meaning for themselves within the work process. The First World War, by forcing more regular and disciplined work patterns, challenged a number of the defences that car workers had built for themselves. Nevertheless, despite this and moves towards 'scientific management' after the war, Beavan argues that workers 'continued to impose collectively their autonomy within the work process.'

While Beavan examines the influences of the First World War, Tom Donnelly undertakes an analysis of the impact of the Second World War, particularly in terms of the effects which the war had on the culture of the car industry as expressed through relations between employers and the state and management and labour. He picks out two groups for particular attention: trade unions and women. Trade unions gained in terms of membership, security and status, and despite continued limits to trust and cooperation, adapting to wartime pressures forced both management and labour to recognise the need for negotiated agreements. Many observers have made much of the progress of women's status during the war as they substituted for men in a growing variety of occupations. Donnelly's study shows that this must be qualified with a recognition that patriarchy continued to dominate relationships at work, ensuring that women remained subordinate to men. Nevertheless, he concludes that exposure to industrial work raised women's confidence and their capacity to articulate and mobilise in support of their interests as a result of the war.

Tim Claydon continues the historical threads of the previous two chapters by looking at how the image of 'disorder' drawn from media narratives of the motor industry was used to represent British industrial relations as a whole during the post-war period. This representation was influential, not only over popular opinion, but increasingly in the development of debates within British politics. Images of 'disorderly' industrial relations became central to the increasingly negative view of itself that British society was presented with during the late 1960s and 1970s. They fuelled disillusionment with the moves to liberal collectivism that had characterized the British political system since the late nineteenth century and provided a basis for the reassertion of principles of liberal individualism which had been in retreat since the 1870s.

Paul Thompson moves the analysis to a different perspective when he investigates the leisure patterns of Coventry car workers and their families through oral history. His investigation examines the varied forms of leisure activity among car workers and their families in relation to factors such as gender, age and marital status. He explores their richness and diversity and shows how, despite the growing importance of 'passive' forms of entertainment such as television, Coventry car workers and their families were able to maintain and develop active forms of self-expression through leisure. Thompson's essay is both specific and broad ranging, and touches upon many of the issues raised elsewhere in this volume.

The last two contributions return to previously touched on themes concerning the selling of cars and consumerism and brings the historical motif to the present. Jenny Rice and Carol Saunders claim that women have moved from being passengers to drivers in the past 30 years. Nearly 50 per cent of all new cars in the UK are purchased by women. Yet women feel that advertising discourse reflects gendered stereotypes and fails to take account of their purchasing power and life-style changes.

Finally, Tim O'Sullivan explores the ways in which British cars have been advertised in the twentieth century. In particular he examines the shift from early informational modes of advertising to more developed cultural strategies which utilises transformational and life style frames of reference in attempting to establish distinctive brand identities for their models.

References

Womack, J., Jones, D. and Roos, D. (1990), *The Machine that Changed the World*, Maxwell Macmillan International, Oxford.

Part One

THE CAR AS IMAGE

1

'Oh what a feeling!' – The Literatures of the Car

Nicholas Zurbrugg

Perhaps the literatures of the car were born in Paris on 20 February 1909, the day that *Le Figaro* first published the Italian Futurist leader Filippo Tommaso Marinetti's 'The Founding and Manifesto of Futurism', and informed the world:

> A racing car whose hood is adorned with great pipes, like serpents of explosive breath – a roaring car that seems to ride on grapeshot is more beautiful than the *Victory of Samothrace*. We want to hymn the man at the wheel, who hurls the lance of his spirit across the Earth, along the circle of its orbit. (1973a, 21)

One way or another, the motif of the car haunts the twentieth-century imagination, offering a fascinating index of successive dominant social, intellectual and cultural concerns. If it is perhaps the case, as the French cultural theorist Jean Baudrillard argues, that: 'All you need to know about American society can be gleaned from an anthropology of its driving behaviour' (1988, 54), then it is equally probable that much of what one needs to know about the general intellectual temper of twentieth-century society can be gleaned from its 'driving' literature.

Attacking the entropic *fin de siècle* mentality that the futurists associated with the late nineteenth-century's 'millennial gloom', and commemorating the moment when his car's skid into the 'nourishing sludge' of a 'Fair factory drain' revealed how the twentieth century had been 'enriched by a new beauty: the beauty of speed', Marinetti enthusiastically recounts:

> 'Let's go!' I said. 'Friends, away! Let's go! Mythology and the Mystic Ideal are defeated at last. We're about to see ... the first flight of Angels!' ... We went up to the three snorting beasts, to lay amorous hands on their torrid breasts. I stretched out on my car like a corpse on its bier, but revived at once under the steering wheel, a guillotine blade

that threatened my stomach ... And on we raced, hurling watchdogs against doorsteps, curling them under our burning tyres like collars under a flatiron ... 'Let's break out of the horrible shell of wisdom and ... give ourselves utterly to the Unknown!' (973a, 20)

E. M. Forster's novel *Howards End* (1910) rather differently deplores the 'craze for motion' (1969, 316), recording the anguish of those appalled that 'month by month the roads smelt more strongly of petrol' (1969, 102) and offended by both verbal and vehicular acceleration. 'Clever talk alarmed her, and withered her delicate imaginings; it was the social counterpart of a motor-car' (1969, 71).

Whereas futurists such as Boccioni explain that their art rejects the 'fixed *moment*', in order to explore the profundities of '*dynamic sensation* itself' (1973, 107), Forster's 'English to the Backbone' (1969, 9) heroine, Margaret Schlegel, finds the English landscape 'robbed of half its magic by swift movement' (1969, 197), and only when 'penned in by the desolate weather', recaptures 'the sense of space which the motor had tried to rob from her' (1969, 188).

Subsequently witnessing the kind of near road-kill that might have warmed Marinetti's heart, when her friends learn: 'Your car just touched a dog', reflect that their insurance company 'will see to that', and then discover their victim was 'only a rotten cat' (1969, 198–9), she feels that 'their whole journey from London had been unreal' (1969, 200). Anticipating her final wish for 'a civilisation that won't be movement, because it will rest on the earth' (1969, 316), she concludes:

> They had no part with the earth and its emotions. They were dust, and
> a stink, and cosmopolitan chatter, and the girl whose cat had been
> killed had lived more deeply than they. (1969, 200)

As becomes evident from these remarks, the car is associated here with the 'cosmopolitan', and more particularly, with 'cosmopolitan chatter'; an aberration from 'delicate imaginings' that James Joyce's *Dubliners* (1913) evokes as an ambiguous intoxication leaving Jimmy, the protagonist of 'After the Race', 'too excited to be genuinely happy' (1971, 41).

> The car ran on merrily with its cargo of hilarious youth. The two
> cousins sat on the front seat; Jimmy and his Hungarian friend sat
> behind ... The Frenchmen flung their laughter and light words over
> their shoulders, and often Jimmy had to strain forward to catch a quick
> phrase ... Rapid emotion through space elates one; so does notoriety;
> so does the possession of money. These were three good reasons for

Jimmy's excitement. He had been seen by many of his friends that day in the company of these Continentals. (1971, 41–2)

As the English Vorticist leader, Wyndham Lewis, indicates in his autobiography *Blasting and Bombardiering* (1937), the English modernist mentality seems to have been embarrassed by the 'continental' passion of Marinetti's 'craze for motion'. Defending himself against Marinetti's assertion, 'You are a futurist, Lewis!', Lewis delicately replied: 'you Wops insist too much on the machine' (1982, 34). Marinetti's subsequent suggestion that Lewis has doubtless 'never known the *ivresse* of travelling at a kilometre a minute', prompts the exchange:

> 'Never. I loathe anything that goes too quickly. If it goes too quickly, it is not there.'
> 'It is not there! ... It is *only* when it goes quickly that it *is* there!'
> 'That is nonsense ... I cannot see a thing that is going too quickly.'
> 'See it – see it! ... But you do see it. You see it multiplied a thousand times. You see a thousand things instead of one thing.'
> 'That's just what I don't want to see. I am not a futurist ... I prefer *one* thing.'
> There is no such thing as *one* thing ... What a thing to be an Englishman!' (1982, 34–5)

As Forster, Joyce, Lewis and Marinetti demonstrate, literary responses to the car, to speed and to multiplied modes of perception typify the division between those modernists persuaded of the perils of the machine age, and those modernists fascinated by the new sensibility that Marinetti's 'Destruction of Syntax-Imagination without Strings-Words-in-Freedom' manifesto of 1913 defines as:

> Man multiplied by the machine. New mechanical sense, a fusion of instinct with the efficiency of motors and conquered forces. (1973b, 97)

The French novelist Marcel Proust's *Remembrance of Things Past* (1918) has much to say about almost everything, and when discussing the 'motor-car', argues that its very ability to make travel 'more real', 'by following more closely, in a more intimate contiguity, the various gradations by which the earth is diversified', somehow decreases the mystery of locomotion from destination to destination, since,

> the specific attraction of a journey lies not in our being able to alight at places on the way and to stop altogether as soon as we grow tired, but

11

in making the difference between departure and arrival ... as intense as possible, so that we are conscious of it in its totality. (1989, 693)

As Proust's responses to the car indicate, his modernist aesthetic celebrates intense perceptual transitions (in this instance, between past and present locations), and intense perceptual continuities (in this instance, the unchanging quality of each destination), whereas Marinetti's modernist sensibility celebrates mechanised flight from both past and present, towards the future. Like Wyndham Lewis, Proust is not a futurist. Revisiting the Bois de Boulogne of his youth with nostalgic intent, Proust's narrator grimly finds 'nothing now but motor-cars driven by a moustached mechanic' (1989, 459).

How horrible! I exclaimed to myself. Can anyone find these motor-cars as elegant as the old carriage-and-pair? I dare say am too old now ... To what purpose shall I walk among these trees ... if vulgarity and folly have supplanted the exquisite thing that their branches once framed. My consolation is to think of the women whom I knew in the past, now that there is no elegance left. (1989, 460)

One culture's 'vulgarity and folly' are perhaps another culture's 'consolation'. Just one decade later, Sherwood Anderson's *Poor White* (1925) suggested the extent to which 'the mechanical triumphs of the age' (1925, 350) might quite literally overrun America.

When I was in Chicago last month I met a man who has been making rubber buggy and bicycle tires. I'm going in with him and we're going to start a plant for making automobile-tires right in Bidwell. The tire business is bound to be one of the greatest on earth and they ain't no reason why Bidwell shouldn't be the biggest tire center ever known in the world.' Although the car now ran quietly, Tom's voice again became shrill. 'There'll be hundreds and thousands of cars like this tearing over every road in America', he declared. 'Yes, sir, they will; and if I calculate right Bidwell'll be the great tire town of the world. (1925, 351)

Published in the same year as *Poor White*, F. Scott Fitzgerald's *The Great Gatsby* (1925) – which might just as well be titled *Rich White* – suggests the *nouveau riche* world in which cars begin 'tearing over every road in America' – 'a world complete in itself, with its own standards and its own great figures, second to nothing because it had no consciousness of being so' (1974, 11). Offered 'glistening hors-d'oeuvre ... salads of harlequin designs and pastry pigs', Gatsby's guests arrive in his partially ostentatious, partially unpretentious,

12

Rolls Royce, which, 'On weekends ... became an omnibus, bearing parties to and from the city' (1974, 45).

Gatsby's world evokes a curiously American modernism, at times precipitating the pseudo-European elegance of a party invitation delivered by: 'A chauffeur in a uniform of robin's-egg blue' (1974, 47), at times nurturing the more mundane machine age poetry of 'deep summer on roadhouse roofs and in front of wayside garages, where new red petrol-pumps sat in pools of light' (1974, 27).

This is also the machine-age inspiration of artists such as Edward Hopper; of the inimitably twentieth-century detail that in Baudrillard's terms 'makes up odd, everyday America'. Here, the 'extravagance' of new red petrol-pumps 'has passed into things' (and therefore into the 'real'), and does not need to 'lay claim to being extraordinary'. For Americans, Baudrillard argues in *America* (1986), such innovations 'simply are extraordinary', whereas for Europeans their radical unfamiliarity requires aesthetic categorisation (and neutralisation) – as 'surrealistic'; a category 'very European in inspiration' (1988, 86).

Writing half a century before Baudrillard, the French surrealist poet and novelist Louis Aragon's *Paris Peasant* (1924–26), typifies the awkwardness with which the European modernist temper comes to terms with everyday America, as it compulsively mythologises the 'new' as the 'then', rather than accepting it as the 'now'. Observing that 'The nameless sculptors who erected these metallic phantoms were incapable of conforming to a living tradition like that which traced the cruciform shapes of churches' (1971, 131), Aragon hops centuries in order to remedy this omission, offering petrol pumps a more or less 'living' mythological pedigree (and in Baudrillard's terms, accentuating their 'claim to being extraordinary').

> These modern idols share a parentage that makes them doubly redoubtable. Painted brightly with English or invented names, possessing just one long, supple arm, a luminous face, a single foot and a numbered wheel in the belly, the petrol pumps sometimes take on the appearance of the divinities of Egypt or of those cannibal tribes which worship war and war alone. O Texaco motor oil, Esso, Shell, great inscriptions of human potentiality, soon we shall cross ourselves before your fountains. (1971, 132)

Consoling rather than challenging his readers, Aragon concludes that for those distressed by the impact of modernisation, the machine age is nothing less than an age of 'panic terror' (1971, 133).

> Man has delegated his activity to the machines ... And machines certainly think ... they have invented the inconceivable effects of speed

which so modify anyone experiencing them that it would be difficult, indeed arbitrary, to say that person is the same as the one who lived in a world of slowness. (1971, 132)

The Great Gatsby portrays an altogether different domain of modern mythologies and of living gods, such as Gatsby, who welcomes the machine age without 'panic terror', only to find his security shattered when he is assumed to be the driver of 'the "death car" as the newspapers called it' (1974, 144), apparently killing a neighbour 'like you'd run over a dog' (1974, 186). In this respect his story is a parable of American paradise found and American paradise lost, and a celebration of a 'transitory enchanted moment' (1974, 187) born of the reckless hedonism of a jazz-age aristocracy that:

> ... smashed up things and creatures and then retreated back into their money or their vast carelessness, or whatever it was that kept them together, and let other people clean up the mess they had made ... (1974, 186)

In such a culture, the car becomes the dangerous toy of the idle rich; and more than just a hazard to cats and dogs and delicate perception, a threat to self-preservation.

The most obvious English counterpart to such post-war frivolity, Evelyn Waugh's *Brideshead Revisted* (1945), offers another outsider's account of 'magical sadness' (1982, 353) and 'fierce little human tragedy' (1982, 395) played out in a seductively self-parodic world of careless privileged elegance.

> Sebastian entered – dove-grey flannel, white *crêpe de Chine* ...
> 'Charles ... the whole of Oxford has become most peculiar suddenly. Last night it was pullulating with women. You're to come away at once, out of danger. I've got a motor-car and a basket of strawberries and a bottle of Château Peyraguey ...
> It's heaven with strawberries.'
> 'Where are we going?'
> 'To see a friend.'
> 'Who?'
> 'Name of Hawkins. Bring some money in case we see anything we want to buy. The motor-car is the property of a man called Hardcastle. Return the bits to him if I kill myself; I'm not very good at driving.'
> Beyond the gate ... stood an open, two-seater Morris-Cowley. Sebastian's teddy bear sat at the wheel. We put him between us – 'Take care he's not sick' – and drove off. The bells of St Mary's were chiming nine; we escaped collision with a clergyman ... pedalling quietly down the wrong side of the High Street, crossed Carfax, passed

14

the station, and were soon in open country ... open country was easily reached in those days. (1982, 31–2)

'In those days ...' *Brideshead Revisited* offers a 1930s' paradise where bears lounge in cars, clergy pedal peacefully on either side of High Street, strawberries await Château Peyraguey, and open country is never far away. More specifically, as Waugh indicates in his 1959 preface, it displays the nostalgia of those looking back from the 1940s to the 'splendours of the recent past'; splendours that seem still more distant in a mid-century culture of increasingly distant open country invaded by increasingly ubiquitous 'trippers' (1982, 10).

Steering back towards American fiction of the late 1920s and 1930s, and more particularly, to the early detective fiction in Dashiell Hammett's *The Continental Op* (1923–30), one confronts an altogether different world – or more accurately, underworld – of underdogs on both sides of the law, 'tearing over every road in America' (Anderson, 1925, 351) – and over one another, whenever possible. No longer an exclusive symbol of status and wealth, the car becomes the most popular means of rapidly dispatching oneself, or more permanently dispatching one's enemies.

Despite occasional Marinettian references to the car as a 'metal monster', Hammett's lyrically abrupt paragraphs offer an extraordinary new prose-poetry. Interweaving mechanical momentum, physical gesture and immobility and the sporadic glare and glow of gunfire and headlights, Hammett perfects an indisputably *post-modern* narrative, light years away from the writings of Marinetti, Forster, Joyce, Proust, and Waugh, and still without counterpart in any subsequent decade.

> Suddenly a man was in the road ahead – a little beyond the reach of my lights . The lights caught him, and I saw that it was Porky Grout!
> Porky Grout standing facing me in the middle of the road, the dull metal of an automatic in each hand.
> The guns in his hands seemed to glow dimly red and then go dark in the glare of my headlights – glow and then go dark, like two bulbs in an automatic electric sign.
> The windshield fell apart around me.
> Porky Grout – the informant whose name was a synonym for cowardice the full length of the Pacific Coast – stood in the center of the road shooting at a metal comet that rushed down upon him . . .
> I didn't see the end.
> I confess frankly that I shut my eyes when his set white face showed close over my radiator. The metal monster under me trembled – not very much – and the road ahead was empty except for the fleeing red

light. My windshield was gone. The wind tore at my uncovered hair
and brought tears to my squinted-up eyes. (1977, 139)

Something of the raw energy of Hammett's writing subsequently emerges in
the black crime writer Chester Himes' *A Rage in Harlem* (1957), where fast
action and even faster repartee propel both plot and reader into quintessentially
American subcultures.

A cruising taxi came in his direction. He hailed it. He'd have to break
one of the ten-dollar bills . . . but there was no help for it. It was hurry-
hurry.
A black boy was driving. Jackson gave him the address of Imabelle's
sister in the Bronx. The black boy made a U-turn in the icy street as
though he liked skating, and took off like a lunatic.
'I'm in a hurry', Jackson said.
'I'm hurrying, ain't I?' the black boy called over his shoulder.
'But I ain't in no hurry to get to heaven.'
'We ain't going to heaven.'
'That's what I'm scared of.' (1988, 15)

The register of Himes' English contemporaries pales by comparison. Ian
Fleming's *Goldfinger* (1959), for example, unequivocally offers: 'No
resemblance' to 'any real persons living or dead'.

James Bond flung the DB III through the last mile of straight and did a
racing change down into third and then into second for the short hill
before the inevitable traffic crawl through Rochester. Leashed in by the
velvet claw of the front discs, the engine muttered its protest ... Bond
went up into third again, beat the lights ... settled back into second and
let the car idle ... the DB III had ... certain extras which ...included ...
reinforced steel bumpers, fore and aft, in case he needed to ram ...
Bond started motoring again ... following his thoughts as his hands
and feet went through their automatic responses. (1976, 61–3)

Blandly blending travelogue, sports commentary and Heath Robinson
gadgetry, Fleming refines a fantasy world of auto-eroticism in which the
mechanical and the physical, the significant and the insignificant, oscillate to and
fro as cars flex 'velvet claws', spies flex 'automatic reflexes', and boy flexes girl
by penetrating radiator grille with reinforced bumper (the 'ram' position).

Bond glanced in his driving mirror. Well, well! The little Triumph was
only feet away from his tail. How long had she been there? Bond had
been so intent on following the Rolls that he hadn't glanced back since

16

entering the town ... So! ... Something must be done. Sorry, sweetheart. I've got to mess you up. I'll be as gentle as I can. Hold tight. Bond stopped abruptly in front of the butcher's shop. He banged the gears into reverse. There was a sickening crunch and tinkle. . .
The Aston Martin's rear bumper was locked into wreckage of the Triumph's lamp and radiator grille. Bond said aimiably, 'If you touch me there again you'll have to marry me.' (1976, 125)

If it is the case, as Vladimir Nabokov wittily remarks in his notes 'On a Book entitled *Lolita*', that 'in pornographic novels, action has to be limited to the copulation of clichés' (1962, 330), Fleming's narrative typifies the ways in which postmodern pulp fiction inflects (or infects) such clichés with the still more banal clichés of publicity. In turn, J. G. Ballard's *Crash* (1973) suggests that the 'uneasy pleasures' of mid twentieth-century culture increasingly compound the 'nightmare marriage between sex and technology' (1985, 6), in 'a world ruled by fictions of every kind', provoking,

> the increasing blurring and intermingling of identities within the realm
> of consumer goods, the preempting of any free or original imaginative
> response to experience by the television screen. (1985, 5)

As William Burroughs observes, Ballard's *Crash* undertakes a remarkable examination of the 'nonsexual roots of sexuality' (1990, 7) in an 'industrial age' where: 'Sexual arousal results from the repetition and impact of image', and for some, the car crash is not merely 'the most drastic event in our lives' (Ballard, 1990, 7), but also, perhaps, 'more sexually stimulating than a pornographic picture' (1990, 7).
Considered in the contexts of Ballard's and Burroughs' hypotheses, Fleming's *Goldfinger* typifies (rather than criticises) pulp fiction's increasing cannibalisation of advertising imagery; as indeed does Fleming's French contemporary, the 'new' novelist Alain Robbe-Grillet, whose *Jealousy* (1957) offers a curiously cubist variation of the erotic car crash. Like Fleming's thrillers, Robbe-Grillet's cerebral teasers lure the reader into a vacuous cosmos of neutral surface and sexual insinuation; perfect entertainment, perhaps, for fatalistic Europeans sharing Baudrillard's sense that: 'The maximum in intensity lies behind us; the minimum in passion and intellectual inspiration lie before us' (1989, 40).
Leading the reader through a clinical collage of overlapping roadside, bedside, and centipede-side fragments, Robbe-Grillet's narrator observes:

Franck, without saying a word, stands up, wads his napkin into a ball as he cautiously approaches, and squashes the creature against the wall. Then, with his foot, he squashes it against the bedroom floor.

Then he comes back toward the bed and in passing hangs the towel on its metal rack near the washbowl.

The hand with the tapering fingers has clenched into a fist on the white sheet. The five widespread fingers have closed over the palm with such force that they have drawn the cloth with them: the latter shows five convergent creases ...

In his haste to reach his goal, Franck increases his speed. The jolts become more violent. Nevertheless he continues to drive faster. In the darkness, he has not seen the hole running halfway across the road. The car makes a leap, skids ... On this bad road the driver cannot straighten out in time. The blue sedan is going to crash into a roadside tree whose rigid foliage scarcely shivers under the impact, despite its violence.

The car immediately bursts into flames. The whole brush is illuminated by the crackling, spreading fire. It is the sound the centipede makes, motionless again on the wall, in the centre of the panel. (1965, 79–80)

One discovers the same sense of dystopian violence in J. G. Ballard's *Crash* (1973), a novel relentlessly celebrating the 'mysterious eroticism' of those foolish things reminding its narrator of 'Vaughan'; 'Blood-soaked instrument panels' and 'seat-belts smeared with excrement', 'unexpected variations of crushed radiator grilles' and 'complex geometries of a dented fender' (1985, 12).

He dreamed of ambassadorial limousines crashing into jack-knifing butane tankers, of taxis filled with celebrating children colliding head-on ... Vaughan dreamed endlessly of the deaths of the famous, inventing imaginary crashes for them ... His imagination was a target gallery of screen actresses, politicians, business tycoons and television executives. (1985, 13–15)

According to Ballard, *Crash* offers 'an extreme metaphor for an extreme situation' (1985, 6), predicting the worst possible consequences of late twentieth-century culture's increasing confusion of everyday fact and cinematic fantasy. Clearly, *Crash* questions both the initial optimism of modernist culture's futurist impulse, and the unexpectedly utopian register of American 'car' fiction of the 1950s and 1960s.

Reading the beat generation's mile-a-minute monologues of the late 1940s and 1950s, one advances from the fictional underworld of Hammett's gangsters to the auto-biographical overworld of such exuberant petty car thieves and master drivers as Neal Cassady, fast-writing author of *The First Third* (1971) and still faster-driving hero of Jack Kerouac's *On the Road* (1957).

Writing to Kerouac in a letter of 3 July 1949, Cassady sketches his 'brief history of arrests', recollecting that he bought his 'first car' – a Buick – 'for $20', and then followed 'the wisdom of hiking in the day and stealing a car when nite fell', in order 'to make good time' (1971, 127).

> Well, when I returned to Denver this became a habit and every nite I'd sleep in some apt. house bathtub and get up and find some friends place to eat then steal a car to pick up girls at school when they got out … I been arrested 10 times and served an aggravated total of 15 months on six convictions … (1971, 127–9)

It is precisely this sense of unchained mobility that Kerouac celebrates in *On the Road*, in which Kerouac's narrator, Sal Paradise, encounters 'a new beat generation' (1982, 53), and eagerly anticipates 'a new horizon' of 'girls, visions, everything' (1982, 14), inspired by Cassady's counterpart, Dean Moriarty – 'a new kind of American saint' (1982, 40). Moriarty, Paradise explains, is: 'The most fantastic parking-lot attendant in the world'.

> He can back a car forty miles an hour into a tight squeeze and stop at the wall, jump out, race among fenders, leap into another car, circle it fifty miles an hour in a narrow space, back swiftly into tight spot, *hump*, snap the car with the emergency so that you see it bounce as he flies out; then clear to the ticket shack, sprinting like a track star, hand a ticket, leap into a newly arrived car before the owner's half out, leap literally under him as he steps out, start the car with the door flapping, and roar off to the next available stop, arc, pop in, brake, out, run; working like that without pause eight hours a night, evening rush hours and after-theatre rush hours, in greasy wino pants with a frayed fur-lined jacket and beat shoes that flap. (1982, 12)

What seems most distinctive in Kerouac portrayal of Cassady is his evocation of Cassady's extraordinary vitality; the vitality of a mentor not unlike Marinetti, 'tremendously excited about everything that he saw', 'out of his mind with real belief' (1982, 114), who leaves his friends equally elated and equally eager to begin their 'life on the road' (1982, 7).

We were all delighted, we all realized we were leaving confusion and nonsense behind and performing our one and noble function of the time, *move*. And we moved! (1982, 127)

Early sections of William Burroughs' *The Naked Lunch* (1959) somewhat similarly celebrate the fragmentary visions of the back seat junkie, dozing across country as landscapes drift in and out of focus.

Drove all night, came at dawn to a warm misty place, barking dogs and the sound of running water.
'Thomas and Charlie', I said.
'What?'
'That's the name of this town. Sea level. We climb straight up from here ten thousand feet.' I took a fix and went to sleep in the back seat. She was a good driver. You can tell as soon as someone touches the wheel' (1959, 20)

Subsequent sections of Burroughs' novel transmute events into mordant satirical fantasy, suggesting the corruption of both 'Interzone' (its fictional setting) and post-war America in terms of such grotesques as 'Keif the brilliant decadent young novelist', and 'Aracknid', his 'worthless chauffeur, barely able to drive' (1959, 170–71).

On one occasion he ran down a pregnant woman in from the mountains with a load of charcoal on her back, and she miscarried a bloody, dead baby in the street, and Keif got out and sat on the curb stirring the blood with a stick while the police questioned Aracknid and finally arrested the woman for a violation of the Sanitary Code. (1959, 170)

Such incidents acquire a still more fantastic, semi-hard boiled, semi-science fictional register in Burroughs' *Nova Express* (1964); a novel in which 'your reporter' and his sidekick, 'The Intolerable Kid' investigate – and attempt to accelerate America's mutation into a potentially 'burning planet', 'buckling like a bulkhead about to blow' (1966, 17–18).

So the paper has a car there for us and we are driving in from the airport The Kid at the wheel and his foot on the floor – Nearly ran down a covey of pedestrians and they yell after us: 'What you want to do, kill somebody?'
And the Kid sticks his head out and says: 'It would be a pleasure Niggers! Gooks! Terrestial dogs' – His eyes lit up like a blow torch and I can see he is really in form – So we start right to work making our headquarters in The Land of The Free where the call came from

and which is really free and wide open for any life form the uglier the better. (1966, 18)

Like Ballard, Burroughs diagnoses his times as 'an extreme situation' (1966, 6), 'open' to invasion by 'any life form the uglier the better', either of its own making or of such alien extraction as the murderously driving 'Intolerable Kid'.

More recently, younger writers such as the American rock star and underground film star Lydia Lunch, author of *Incriminating Evidence* (1992), have offered even more vitriolic evocation of American culture's decline into gratuitous fetishistic eroticism in texts such as 'Shotgun'; a fantasy describing the plight of a hitchhiker asked if she wants to 'make fifty bucks or what?'.

> I can't seem to remember what came first, the stories or the shotgun, but, he's got it out and aimed directly at my left temple, and ... he goes get out ... get out of the car ... get down on your hands and knees and start worshipping all four of those filthy greasy big black wheels, like you mean it ... and ... in a matter of seconds I'm down there dribbling and kissing that scummy rubber, licking it like I love it ... begging him to end my misery ... shoot me in the goddamn head, do it, do it ... and he says ... get in ... slide in honey, get yourself up here ... that was beautiful ... and he gives me fifty bucks and a ride home, I gave him my phone number and saw him a few times after that, but nothing too memorable, nothing at all ... (1992, 64–5)

If Lunch bleakly assesses American society as a cycle of perversion and delusion adding up to 'nothing at all', her sometime associate, New York film maker Nick Zedd, equally grimly evokes the futility of attempts to disrupt America's general momentum. Describing the last rites and perhaps the 'greatest' achievement' of G. G. Allin, a punk rock singer 'on the verge of becoming famous before he died of an overdose' (1994, 5), Zedd relates:

> Earlier that day in his last performance, G. G. punched out a heckler, took a shit and smeared it all over his nude body, then ... ran into the street nude and blocked a bus full of people before stumbling away ... He vanished as several cop cars arrived, blocking traffic and causing a chaos far worse than his brief performance. The spectacle of a squad of cop cars blocking four lanes of traffic in response to a club manager's complaint over his act ... was G. G.'s greatest achievement. He altered daily life. It was a revolutionary achievement, though a stupid one ... spreading a little more hate and confusion in a world that would never appreciate it. (1994, 9–10)

Describing the narrator's son, Wilder, pedalling across a highway, Don DeLillo's novel *White Noise* (1984) rather more reassuringly hints that even the relentless anonymity of late twentieth-century traffic may at times become 'mystically charged'.

> The women could only look, empty-mouthed, each with an arm in the air, a plea for the scene to reverse, the boy to pedal backwards on his faded blue and yellow toy like a cartoon character on morning TV. The drivers could not quite comprehend. In their knotted posture, belted in, they knew this picture did not belong to the hurtling consciousness of the highway, the broad-ribboned modernist stream. In speed there was sense. In signs, in patterns, in split-second lives. What did it mean, this little rotary blur? Some force in the world had gone awry. They veered, braked, sounded their horns down the long afternoon, an animal lament … Stay, they called, Do not go. No, no. Like foreigners reduced to simple phrases. (1986, 322–3)

At his least reassuring, DeLillo intimates that the mechanical mindset is incompatible with the mystical, and that minds nurtured on 'split-second' cartoon culture, in a world where 'speed' is 'sense', are virtually powerless to verbalise visions of pre-mechanical autonomy. Identifying similar paradoxes in Los Angeles, in *America* (1986), Baudrillard wryly observes:

> If you get out of your car in this centrifugal metropolis, you immediately become a delinquent; as soon as you start walking, you are a threat to public order, like a dog wandering in the road. Only immigrants from the Third World are allowed to walk. (1988, 58)

If, as Cage comments in a letter of 1956: 'Machines … can tend toward our stupefaction or our enlivenment' (1974, 118), it seems evident to Baudrillard that the increasingly stupefied temper of late twentieth-century America is most evident in its 'collective driving' (1988, 54), and in its 'only truly profound pleasure' – 'keeping on the move'.

> Unlike our European motorways, which are unique, directional axes, and are therefore still places of expulsion (Virilio), the freeway system is a place of integration (they even say that there are families who drive around on these roads in their mobile homes without ever leaving). It creates a different state of mind, and the European driver very quickly gives up his aggressive, every-man-for-himself behaviour and his individual relations, and adopts the rules of this collective game. (1988, 53)

Defining this ambiguous 'collective game' as a force neutralising 'individual reactions', Baudrillard concludes:

> This is the only real society or warmth here, this collective propulsion, this compulsion – a compulsion of lemmings plunging suicidally together ... 'Must exit': you are being sentenced. You are a player being exiled from the only – and useless and glorious – form of collective existence. (1988, 53)

Paul Virilio's *The Aesthetics of Disappearance* (1980) similarly argues that in American politics, 'the only true majority is a motorized one, acquiring "good reflexes" along with the driving licence, that is, the habit of reacting to conditioning stimuli' (1991, 73–4). For Virilio, the car offers a dream-like escape from the real world, 'a disappearance into a holiday where there's no tomorrow' (1991, 65), and no particular destination.

> The frantic use of automobiles ... is not, contrary to public transportation, for the purpose of going somewhere in particular ... To go nowhere, even to ride around in a deserted quarter or on a crowded freeway, now seems natural for the voyeur-voyager in his car. On the contrary, to stop, to park, are unpleasant operations and the driver even resents going somewhere or toward someone; to visit a person or to go and see a show seems to require superhuman effort. Able to reach the farthest extremeties, he's not happy except in the narrow cell of his vehicle, strapped into his seat. (1991, 67)

For DeLillo's characters, too, separation from the circulation of cars is a source of anxiety, when nearby traffic ceases to be anodyne, and disconcertingly insinuates 'a remote and steady murmur around our sleep, as of dead souls babbling at the edge of a dream' (1986, 4). Even children seem possessed by this 'murmur', and when observed asleep, with feelings of 'desperate piety', unexpectedly deflate their father's 'search ... for signs and hints, intimations of odd comfort', by chanting:

> Toyota Corolla, Toyota Cecilia, Toyota Cressida. Supranational names, computer generated, more or less universally pronounceable. Part of every child's brain noise, the substatic regions too deep to probe. (1986, 155)

Nowhere is the mind too deep, DeLillo implies, to evade Toyota's 'TV voice' (1986, 155). And yet, on occasion, as DeLillo and others suggest, the threatening or pointless quality of car-travel can be subverted – or converted – into more familiar, more comforting, rituals, such as the waggon train of

vehicles described in the opening paragraph of *White Noise*: 'The station waggons arrived at noon, a long shining line that coursed through the west campus' (1986, 3). Folkloric ritual, one might say, domesticates and de-alienates the 'frantic use of automobiles'.

One confronts similar rituals of de-mystification and re-mystification in Eric Michaels' *Unbecoming: an Aids Diary* (1990), in his entry for 10 August 1988, just two weeks before his death. Faced with the prospect of dying in Brisbane, between unfamiliar walls, Michaels, an American anthropologist working on Aboriginal culture, determined to leave town and ride into the sunset, like any true Western hero.

> Then, after the phone call, I thought: Why not go to Alice Springs? Even if I die getting there, the project still has more style than lying here and being bored to death. ... So I indulged in a fantasy of Buckwell driving me out, lying in the back of the station wagon, watching the desert go by again, getting to Alice Springs and receiving in state for the few weeks left. (1990, 185)

As Stuart Cunningham comments, Michaels' brave idyll is also very much a kind of beat generation, late 1960s' fantasy, partially inspired by popular culture, but still more significantly, motivated by the wish to escape the jingles of the TV voice.

> So here he was, an illegal alien, with a record in the courts, a family on the other side of the world, no way of realising his final 1960s dream of lying in the back of his station wagon and have someone drive him toward Alice Springs ... In another part of the diaries, Eric writes: 'I hesitate to order a television in hospital. One doesn't *watch* TV in hospital, one gives oneself over to it. I don't want to end my days singing "Oh what a feeling, Toyota."' There certainly would have been no such feeling in driving his Toyota. I can assure you. It's also giving up the ghost, lasting only a few weeks more than Eric. (1988, 15)

Taking what Burroughs calls 'a broad general view of things' (1974, 115), one detects a characteristically Australian pragmatism in Michaels' and Cunningham's characterisation of the car as a domestic construction which, as the first paragraph of the late Perth- and Sydney-based American-born poet Allan Vizent's 'I'm busy' indicates, is perhaps just a toy awaiting general 'fixing' for as many greasy Sabbaths as it takes. Vizents' wonderful monologue begins:

I'm going to explain this real simple. I'm busy. I'm real busy with this car here, I'm dirty, greasy, grease under the fingernails, greasy hands, greasy pants, greasy shoes, and I can't come in the house right now and I can't answer the phone 'cause I'm busy and I won't be answering the phone when any granny calls or any mum or dad or Dave, that kind of stuff, 'cause I'm busy and I'm dirty and I'm working on this car and I'm working on the carburettor here, working on the sparkplugs, sparkplug wires and the fan belt, and I'm busy and I've gotta work on the tyres after I finish that, and on top of the bonnet. I'm going to work on top of the bonnet and fix the windscreen wipers so I'm busy and I don't want to hear anything about people phoning me up and all kinds of people comin' over and talking to me and offering me beers and stuff 'cause I'm busy, and I'm going to be busy working on this car and I won't be drinking beers and having breakfast, tea, lunch and all that kind of stuff till I'm finished with this car, you understand? (1990, 21)

Insisting upon the car's priority over the demands of 'all kinds of people comin' over and talking to me and offering me beers and stuff', Vizents amusingly points to its latterday status as an almost ecologically threatened dysfunctional species, requiring the same kind of dedicated attention as the Victorian rural family's household pig.

As the American composer John Cage suggests in the lines below, the sight of cars and the sounds of cars are part of the twentieth-century's collective conscious and unconscious, and if initially a source of disturbance, are best 'fixed' and interwoven within the fabric of our dreams.

I love living on Sixth Avenue. It has more sounds, and totally unpredictable sounds, than any place I've ever lived ... I wouldn't dream of getting double glass because I love all the sounds. The traffic never stops, night and day. Every now and then a horn, siren, screeching brakes – extremely interesting and unpredictable. At first I thought I couldn't sleep through it, then I found a way of transposing the sounds into images so that they entered into my dreams without waking me up. (Cage, 1977, 26)

Cage's comments engagingly exemplify what one might think of as late postmodern culture's mature acceptance of machine culture as something neither threatening nor extravagant, but simply 'extremely interesting and unpredictable', and remind us that the car (like almost any other technology) can be regarded with equanimity and serenity as just another part of the twentieth-century landscape or roadscape, and like the 'little sedan' at the end of Nabokov's *Pnin* (1953), might even lead the writer to 'where there was simply no saying what miracle might happen' (1969, 190).

Bibliography

Anderson, Sherwood (1925) *Poor White* (1924–26), The Modern Library, New York.
Aragon, Louis (1971) *Paris Peasant*, Picador, London.
Ballard, J. G. (1985) *Crash* (1973), Vintage, New York.
Ballard, J. G. (1990) *The Atrocity Exhibition*, new revised edition with annotations and commentary by the author, Re/Search, San Francisco.
Baudrillard, Jean (1988) *America* (1986), trans. Chris Turner, Verso, London .
Baudrillard, Jean (1989) 'The Anorexic Ruins', trans. David Antal, in Dietmar Kamper, and Chritoph Wulf (eds) *Looking Back on the End of the World*, Semiotext(e), New York.
Boccioni, Umberto (1973) 'Futurist Dynamism and French Painting', trans. J. C. Higgitt, in Apollonio Umbro (ed.), *Futurist Manifestos,* Thames and Hudson, London.
Burroughs, William (1959) *The Naked Lunch*, Olympia, Paris.
Burroughs, William (1966) *Nova Express* (1964), Jonathan Cape, London.
Burroughs, William (1974) *Exterminator!,* Calder & Boyars, London.
Burroughs, William (1990) Preface to J. P. Ballard, *The Atrocity Exhibition,* Re/Search, San Francisco.
Cage, John (1970) Letter to Paul Henry Lang (May 22, 1956), in Richard Kostelanetz (ed.), *John Cage*, Allen Lane, London.
Cage, John (1988) Interviews with Michael Zwerin and with Stephen Montague (1982), in Richard Kostelanetz (ed.), *Conversing With Cage*, Limelight Editions, New York.
Cassady, Neil (1971) *The First Third* (1971), City Lights, San Francisco.
Cunningham, Stuart (1988) 'Eric Michaels – Tributes', *Film News*, 18, 10, Sydney.
DeLillo, Don (1986) *White Noise* (1984), Picador, London.
Fitzgerald, F. Scott (1974) *The Great Gatsby* (1925), Penguin, Harmondsworth.
Fleming, Ian (1976) *Goldfinger* (1959), Pan, London.
Forster, E. M. (1969) *Howards End* (1910), Penguin, Harmondsworth.
Hammett, Dashiell (1977) *The Continental Op* (1923–30), Macmillan, London.
Himes, Chester (1990) *A Rage in Harlem* (1957), W. H. Allen, London.
Joyce, James (1971) *Dubliners* (1913), Penguin, Harmondsworth.
Kerouac, Jack (1982) *On the Road* (1957), Penguin, Harmondsworth.
Lewis, Wyndham (1982) *Blasting and Bombardiering* (1937), John Calder, London.
Lunch, Lydia (1992) *Incriminating Evidence*, Last Gasp, San Francisco.
Marinetti, Filippo Tommaso (1973a) 'The Founding and Manifesto of Futurism', trans. R.W. Flint in Apollonio Umbro (ed.), *Futurist Manifestos,* Thames and Hudson, London.
Marinetti, Filippo Tommaso (1973b) 'Destruction of Syntax-imagination without Strings Words-in-Freedom', trans. R.W. Flint, in Apollonio Umbro (ed.), *Futurist Manifestos,* Thames and Hudson, London.
Michaels, Eric (1990) *Unbecoming: An Aids Diary*, EMPress, Sydney.
Nabokov, Vladimir (1962) 'On a Book entitled *Lolita*', in *Lolita*, Corgi, London.
Nabokov, Vladimir (1969) *Pnin* (1953), Doubleday, New York.
Proust, Marcel (1989) *Remembrance of Things Past: 1* (1918), trans. C.K. Scott Moncrieff and Terence Kilmartin, Penguin, Harmondsworth.

Robbe-Grillet, Alain (1965) *Jealousy* (1957), trans. Richard Howard, John Calder, London.

Virilio, Paul, (1991) *The Aesthetics of Disappearance* (1980), trans. Philip Beitchman, Semiotext(e), New York.

Vizents, Allan (1990) *Non Parables: Allan Vizents Performance Texts 1980–86*, PICA Press, Perth.

Waugh, Evelyn (1982) *Brideshead Revisited* (1945), Penguin, Harmondsworth.

Zedd, Nick (1994) 'The Boy Who Cried Wolf', in Kurt Hollander (ed.), *Sampling the City*, *The Portable Lower East Side* (New York), 7, 1.

2

More than a Marque. The Car as Symbol: Aspects of Culture and Ideology

Len Holden

When the Trabants crossed the Berlin Wall in 1989 from East to West Germany their occupants gaped in wonderment at the Western part of the city and revelled in their new found freedom. The cars themselves belching acrid fumes were soon littering the roadsides as many drivers stood by their broken down vehicles and attempted to take in this unique experience. Just as the Berlin Wall had come to stand for the division of, not only a nation, but also two opposing ideologies so too did the 'Trabi' come to symbolise the relative backwardness of East Germany as opposed to West Germany, and, in consumer terms, the Soviet system vis-a-vis Western capitalism. Like the Russian equivalents, the Volga, Moskvitch and the Zaporozitsa, it was made of poor materials, poorly designed and poorly assembled . The Trabis and their Czech counterpart the Skoda became the butt of endless jokes both within and outside the soviet satellites. 'What do you call a Skoda convertible with twin exhausts? A wheel barrow!' 'How do you double the price of a Skoda? You fill it with petrol!' 'Why is the Trabant called Luther? Because Luther once said "Here I stand, I can do no other"' (Benton and Loomes, 1976, 101). They had become the embodiment of a moribund communist system, which Gorbachev had realised would implode if the necessary reforms did not take place (Walker, 1986, 52; Smith, 1991). The irony is that the Trabi ended its life as a symbol of a nostalgic past by becoming a collector's item; and after the last ones were produced at the eastern German town of Zwickau in 1991 these 26 horse power, two stroke engine vehicles with plastic bodies and thin panel doors were selling at twenty times their original price to avid collectors (*Guardian*, 13 October 1995, 22).

The meanings and significations of things thus change with time and at certain periods can come to embody the essence of a mood, a period of rapid change and we argue here – cultural characteristics. Barthes' (1977, 24) notes that 'an object becomes a symbol when it acquires through convention and use a meaning that enables it to stand for something else.' A Rolls Royce can be a symbol of wealth 'and a scene in a play in which a man is forced to sell his Rolls can be symbolic of the failure of the business.' Pierce (1931–38) more precisely distinguishes between an object being an index and symbol. Thus the Rolls Royce is an index of wealth, but a symbol of the owner's social status (Fiske, 1982, 95). Cars like clothes and other objects are outward signs or representations of values, cultural or otherwise, which stretch beyond the object itself. It is when these shared meanings are understood that the symbol becomes significant. But as culture changes so too can the symbolic significance of its meaning. Thus the Trabi once a symbol of totalitarian inefficiency in the 1980s, is stripped of its polluting menace in the 1990s and becomes a symbol of a nostalgic past. The humorous aspect remains but is divested of its original appeal of cocking a snoop at totalitarian authority and instead evolves into a quaint object of fetishist collection.

The powerful imagery of the car is like the car itself – ubiquitous. Inevitably such objects become metaphors and metanyms in which we choose part of reality to represent the whole. Its widespread use in film and literature as a metaphor for freedom, of 'moving on' and starting over is reflective of individualism and the need for control over one's destiny, concepts powerful in the West especially in the USA. In this sense it represents the opposite ascribed values of the Trabi – a failed collectivism.

Nevertheless the name of one of the USA's most well known vehicle manufacturer has come to represent the stifling conformity of modern life. The Ford motor company has spawned the epithet 'Fordism'. Here we see a significant divide between the famous and long lived 'Model T' Ford as a unit of production and as a consumer owned vehicle. The Ford production line developed in Detroit before the First World War become the model for all mass production plants in the twentieth-century (Bloomfield, 1978). 'The automobile industry stands for modern industry all over the globe. It is to the twentieth century what the Lancashire cotton mills were to the early nineteenth century: the industry of industries' (Drucker, 1972, 176). Huxley (1932) in his novel *Brave New World* raises Fordism to a religion in his distopian future. God is replaced by Ford and people proclaim 'thank Ford' instead of 'thank God'. n this controlled and ordered world the production line that began by making Model Ts now produces people through biological engineering which neatly categorises human spermatazoa and eggs into their human potential, from alpha to epsilon. Fordism in this disenchanted and alienating guise came to be recognised by Henry Ford himself. In his latter years he began to attempt to assuage this view by buying up 'arts of "old America", opening folk museums and closing roads to the motor car' (Beynon, 1973, 17).

However, by the 1950s the proximate meaning of Fordism as consumerism and also as display had come into its own. Barthes (1973, 88) came to view cars 'as almost the exact equivalent of the great Gothic cathedrals.' By which he meant that they represented: 'the supreme creation of an era, conceived with passion by unknown artists, and consumed in image if not in usage by a whole population which appropriates them as purely magical object.' This is car celebrated as art object, and mass art object. The post-war years began to witness the emergence of the mass consumer society with cars as a leading consumer totem. As Manning (1995, 33) states:'the automobile myth reached its apogee in the 1950s, when the industry underwent an enormous boom, cars becoming fancier, faster and more fetishised. The car became integral to American courtship rituals, enhancing its perception as a phallic extension.'

The fins and protrusions of the General Motors (GM) range of Cadillacs, Pontiacs, Buicks Chevrolets and Oldsmobiles were the equivalent of the cathedral's flying buttresses and Gothic arches and were mythologised and re-mythologised in movies, art, the novel and music which other authors in this book explore in depth. Nevertheless, some car designers have gained acclaim and have not been consigned to the historical dustbin of anonymity, as Barthes suggests the cathedral stone masons had. Bugatti, Henry Royce, Issigonis and Harley Earl (the designer of those GM 'rocket ships') are known and revered. Soon other American car manufacturers were copying the trend set by Earl, and by 1956 tail fins were on Ford, Studebaker, Hudson and Chrysler models; they had become not only symbols of the 'jet age' (Marsh and Collett, 1986, 118) but also a symbol of American optimism as embodied in consumerism. This found echo in pale British imitations with the Vauxhall Velox, Cresta and Victor and Ford's Consul and Zephyr with its white walled tyres. Harold Macmillan's plaintive election slogan 'You've never had it so good' symbolised the new mass consumption era, which for Americans spelt out that anything is possible. Cars had become grounded spaceships to the final frontier.

This was all in stark contrast to the staidness of British motor car design which had rushed to meet the demands of the export market in the late 1940s and the growing home markets of the 1950s. The 1950s in many ways represented the last phase of the predominance of the middle classes over the car market and the advertisements of the time characterise the laboured and self conscious eulogising of a class not comfortable with itself or its social status in not being quite 'top drawer'. A Morris Oxford advertisement in *The Field* magazine shows a county town street in which two middle class smartly casual couples chat while the car (the object of the advertisement) is partly obscured by their bodies as if they're not quite certain to be seen with it (Stevenson,

1991, 63). The Wolseley 6/90 was advertised by an 'oily pastiche of middle class manners' (Stevenson, 1991, 94) in which Giles and Charles dressed in dinner jackets engage in a stilted dialogue about the merits of their Wolseley's beneath the entrance awning of a nightclub. Their wives in evening dress and fur wraps smile indulgently as they finish their artificial conversation. 'The cars were cheap enough to be afforded by those unable to buy a genuinely exclusive car, but who would not be seen dead in a Vauxhall' (Stevenson, 1991, 6). Here we see car as a true sign of class status, and class status in its very English (English rather than British!) form.

The Rolls Royce epitomised the pinnacle of British social class and its very name has other connotations in keeping with its exclusivity, quality and quiet excellence. 'It altered our ideas of what luxury should be' (Nockolds, 1949, 153). To many like Nockolds it became a symbol of all that was great about Britain, and in the 1990s, about Britain's past. In the 1950s the Silver Cloud cost £5,000 which was equivalent to purchasing a twelve bedroomed house in the stockbroker belt or twelve Morris Minors. As Quentin Willson proclaimed: 'If you owned one – you were somebody', but when it was conceived in 1955 'it was a different world. A world where everything was safe, solid and unquestionable' (BBC Pebble Mill, 1995a). By the end of the 1950s that safe world of privilege was about to be challenged, not by communism or even socialism, but by the very values the Conservative Party claimed to embody – capitalist consumerism in the name of democracy. The swinging sixties forced manufacturers and image makers to acknowledge the importance of the masses as a huge market and the symbol of that decade – 'the Mini'– was to epitomise an affordable car with style. 'No longer would the lower orders doff their caps and cry "God bless the squire and his relations and keep us in our proper stations"' (BBC Pebble Mill, 1995a). The Silver Cloud and Rolls Royce survived this jolt into mass produced style, and its buyers increasingly came from the nouveau riche; the Beatles, Jimmy Tarbuck, Jimmy Saville and Englebert Humperdinck. For them it was perhaps a symbol of ostentatious display but it opened the doors of democratic possibilities to anyone with enough money to feel a small and perhaps fleeting part of something that was previously remote, aloof and unattainable.

Each Silver Cloud took three months to build, weighed two tons and had 12 coats of paint. It was, Quentin Willson asserts, 'a sculptured creation of breeding and privilege ... (It) was styled to look like a stately home and its interior was like a stately throne room ... (It was) a haven of peace in a wild world' (BBC Pebble Mill, 1995a). In the 1960s it took on new connotations, when the romantic novelist Barbara Cartland ordered a white Cloud, much to the initial horror of Rolls Royce executives. Its romantic associations caused white editions to be used for marriages; a symbol of permanence which newly weds hoped would convey some solidity to their relationship. Recently its symbol of Britishness was greatly undermined when Rolls Royce signed a deal with BMW to have the German company's engines installed in all production models by the end of the century. As Barrie (1994, 20) claims 'today's Rolls Royce may symbolise the finest British engineering, but much of the car's sophisticated technology comes from abroad.' It is thus also a symbol of relative British economic decline.

The hope of a new resurgence in Britain's economic fortunes in the 1960s was embodied in the Mini, but it was in Hill's words 'an emblem of false optimism' (1995, 16). The 1970s were to witness industrial strife, managerial ineptitude and an ever declining share of the market for British cars. The one model which epitomised this climacteric in the British car industry was the British Leyland 'Marina', known later as the 'Ital.' Not only were the names appallingly inapt but the car itself was an inferior design. The design was hurried through using parts from the Morris Minor, as Sir John Egan stated 'they were setting out to design cars with resources that were usually a third or half of what their European competitors were putting into designing and developing cars' (Adeney, 1988, 258).

'Marina' suggested foreign exoticism but is, in fact, a boat mooring area and as such appeared to have little relevance to the car! The 'Ital' simply adopted its Italian designer company name, but far from carrying an exotic foreign ring to British ears, it failed to excite. It was foreign sounding but not romantically foreign. It seems to be suggesting Italy but there appears to be some hesitation. The result is one of the worst car model names (with the possible exception of the Ford 'Edsel') ever devised by marketing departments. The marketing briefs even suggested uncertainty as to what kind of animal it was and described it as 'exotic and tending towards the wild but tempered with a high degree of good taste' (Adeney, 1988, 268). The weak name 'Marina' fully reflected the badly designed and badly made car, testified by the number of models returned to the manufacturer for repairs and replacement. It was a symbol of British industry at its worst. The Ital continued in production until 1983 when in the following year the production line and model was sold to the Pakistan government (Baldwin et al, 1987, 338).

The decline of the British car industry caused the motoring press and the press in general to find alternative marques to eulogise as quintessentially British, but Jaguar and Aston Martin were sold to Ford and much of Rolls Royce's technology is foreign and its engines will soon be provided by BMW. A recent edition of the television programme 'The Car's the Star' (BBC Pebble Mill, 1995b) examined the 'Land Rover' in which a proud owner proclaimed: 'it has to be one of the British motor industry's biggest success stories.' Another asserted:'Land Rovers are terribly British. You can plough through anything in them. They don't fall to bits. You see them all round the world.' Its design for rough terrain harks back to colonial times when it was handy for tackling dusty and bumpy Asian and African roads. It evoked nostalgia for the high tide of colonialism but was hurriedly designed by Rover to fill the export market in the post-Second World War years, and ironically became witness to the end of empire.

It found great favour with farmers at home and eventually these rustic associations were spread to the predominantly urban market under the guise of the more comfortable Range Rover. This was a vehicle in which middle class families, preferably with dogs, could don their green wellies and Barbour jackets and play the country squire and lady even if only around surburbia. This British image was not reinforced by its ownership. Rover shared production costs with Honda and was later sold by British Aerospace, its last British owners, to BMW amidst outcries from public and press alike. By the mid-1990s British owned car output was limited to small companies such as Morgan and Reliant. Reliant has moved in and out of bankruptcy several times, and is the producer of the famous 'Robin,' now heavily steeped in humorous mythology, particularly after Del Boy's ownership of one in 'Only Fools and Horses'.

In other countries social divisions such as class can be symbolised by car models and the car, by representing an aspect of social structure, can also signify part of a whole culture. In asking what is, for example, quintessentially Italian, different models can symbolise different aspects of Italian culturality. Like the range of British models discussed above, different models reflect aspects of a culture rather than embody it as a whole. In Italy for example, 'Fiats are for the masses, Lancias for the professional classes, Alfa Romeos for the trendies and Ferraris for the rich' (Marshall, 1989). One stereotype that does persist, however, is that Italian car design is pre-eminent, and this is fully reflected in the classic Bugatti's, Ferraris and Lamborghinis. Wyeth (1994, 34) claims that the three most beautiful cars ever built 'have to be the BAT (Berlinetta Aerodinamica Tecnica) cars, three pieces of pure design extravagance which were built in the 50s by Italian styling house Bertone.' These were the design of Franco Scaglione 'a tale of unjustly forgotten genius.' Here we see an attempt to resurrect one of Barthes' unrecognised stonemasons. Style and élan have always been associated with Italian clothes, films and life style, for both male and female – a style which celebrates the beauty of the human form. In a sense the car is an extension of the human form and the beautiful Italian designs of Ferrari and Lamborghini are evidence to this. Scaglioni's designs combined beauty and practicality. As Wyeth (1994, 38) states:'Scaglione made aerodynamics beautiful. He made stunning shapes which were also models of efficiency.' He also:'produced what is often regarded as the best car Alfa Romeo never made ... the Alfa Sportivo of 1954' (Wyeth, 1994,

39). But such cars are reflective of only one aspect of Italian culture, and the province of the rich and pampered élite.

The Fiat 500, however, reflects another aspect of Italianess-motoring for the masses which inspires affection more than admiration. One British owner of the 'Cinque Cento' described it as the 'smallest car with the biggest personality' (BBC Pebble Mill, 1995c). Its smallness invests it with a sense of humour and as Quentin Willson asserts 'absolutely no sense of machismo' (BBC Pebble Mill, 1995c). It exemplifies the fun loving side of the Italian psyche, its smallness makes it unthreatening and loveable and its popularity has put a generation of Italian families on four wheels. Not a centimetre of space has been wasted, and in this sense it is the perfection of Italian design in the affordable family car. The Americans and most Northern European men would regard it as a joke and its compactness makes it more desirable to women in these countries. In a recent edition of the BBC programme 'The Car's the Star' devoted to the Fiat 500, it was noticeable that the majority of devoted owners were women, many of whom described their ownership as more of a personal relationship. It is ideal for town driving, particularly in the narrow streets of historic Italian towns. It is easy to manoeuvre and easy to park. Designed by Dante Giacosa in 1957, its popularity remains so high that Fiat have resurrected a newer version in the mid-1990s. Although cramped and slow with a maximum speed of 60 mph, its 'a car that's fun to drive ... (and which) you get out of smiling' (BBC Pebble Mill, 1995c). One TV advertisement for the car in the 1970s showed a large happy Italian man emerging from its small frame followed by his wife and then a surprising number of children. The image conveyed was one of humour, family warmth, love and affection. Oliver Le Floch, head of advertising at SEAT in the 1980s, supported this perception and stated that 'the household activity around the (SEAT) Ibiza (the Spanish equivalent of the FIAT) allows the car to figure as a social symbol' (Duprat, 1988, 92).

Just as Italian cars reflect aspects of Italian temperament and style, the Volvo and the Saab are the embodiment of Swedish welfarism with their in-built factors of comfort and emphasis on safety. As Patrick Moyson, the marketing director of Volvo states: 'The Volvo psychology begins with man and goes back to man' (Duprat, 1988, 89). The cars are for people; for their comfort, safety, and welfare. After having tried 'show off' advertisements in the early 1980s which did not really appeal, Moyson has come to the view that 'the Volvo client likes solid things, safety, reliability; he possesses traditional, secure values, and attaches more importance to the quality of his environment than to his status' (Duprat, 1988, 89). The Volvo 780 is described as 'inside ... a streak of polished elm. The scent of soft leather. Quiet comfort ... powerful, trustworthy, never failing. (It has) the virtues of the old world' (*Automobile Year*, 1986, 14).

The car embodies the safety and security of Swedish welfarism which strikes a chord with many of its clients world-wide. The large box-like reinforced frame, the permanent side lights, the adjustable air bags in 1990s models and other safety features reflect the comfort of a secure welfare system. It is not exciting but it will get you, the family and the pets from A to B in one piece. To some it is the essence of Swedish dullness, to others the reflection of a sensible pragmatic society that cares for people and communities.

Recently Saab has tested the bodies of its models against the roof crushing weight of mooses which are prone to dashing in front of vehicles in Sweden. 'Of 20,000 collisions in 1988, 5,400 involved a moose' (Turner, 1995, 64). Car manufacturers are preparing for offset crashes (ones which involve vehicles other than in head-on crash situations) to comply with regulations in 1998. Saab models will pass this test without trouble but Saab asks its owners involved in crashes to return their cars to the dealership so that they can be studied, and details of 5,000 serious road accidents have been kept on a central database. Such is the extent of the regard for safety by Swedish manufacturers (Turner, 1995, 64).

In turning to quintessential Frenchness as mirrored by the car, the chic styling of the Citroën DS 19, eulogised by Barthes, reflects Gallic suavity, sophistication and culture. The DS 19 must be one of the most beautifully designed mass produced cars, and for its time (the late 1950s) was distinctive and breathtakingly sleek. It became a French ministerial car from which one has distinct memories of De Gaulle emerging, after sliding speedily but gracefully into the entrance of the Elysée Palace. With its high front flowing down to a low back, its smooth lines reminded Barthes of a spaceship with 'all the features of one of those objects from another universe which have supplied fuel for the neomania of the eighteenth-century and that of our own science fiction' (Barthes, 1973, 88). However, Barthes' homage to the 'Déesse' over eggs the Gallic pudding when he proclaims ' we are therefore dealing here with a humanised art, and it is possible that the Déesse marks a change in the mythology of cars' (Barthes, 1973, 89). He continues in this vein, praising the tactile quality embodied in design and shape. Nevertheless, the sophistication of Barthes' language and his use of metaphor emphasises the chicness of the vehicle under scrutiny.

Citroën's other famous vehicle, the 2CV, symbolises an entirely different aspect of Gallic culture – the plain simplicity of style in a populist and cheap vehicle. The 'deux chevaux' is a car that represents the values of the alternative; the Left Bank (Rive Gauche), the bereted and corduroyed artist with his bottle of vin du table and French stick. The romance of the poverty stricken artist. Style without affluence. It is not surprising that these images were used in advertisements in the UK where its buyers are perceived to be *Guardian* reading, feminist, vegetarians, with yearnings to live the simple but creative life in a farmhouse in Provence, or a garret in Paris.

The Teutonic aspects of the automobile are quintessentially summed up in the Audi, BMW and Mercedes. These makes became popular in the West with the rising and highly paid executive of the 1980s. But the ultimate 'yuppie' car of that decade was the Porsche. Although produced in numbers, it did not have the mass produced feel of a saloon, with its sports modelling and low slung bullet shape. It was a car to be noticed in, and yet affordable to those who would never really make the Aston Martin or Lotus income bracket. They were fast, efficient, reliable and had to be controlled. Yet the advertisement for a Mercedes makes appeal to the 'tradition' of an essentially recognised 'German' stereotype – the will to achieve excellence. 'Hard work, persistence and an indomitable will to achieve technical and qualitative perfection' describes the attitude towards building the Daimler-Benz AG built in the 1880s. The 1985 advertisement continues by reassuring the consumer that 'today 100 years later this attitude still dominates our company ... these virtues are firmly anchored guidelines for our work' (*Automobile Year*, 1986,15). The use of the words and phrases 'indomitable will' 'dominate' 'firmly' 'hard work' are used to reinforce what some feel about the German character, but it will also give the buyer these 'virtues' on the open road once he owns one, as any experience of the frightening two-lane autobahn in Germany can testify.

The advertising copy-writer uses this awareness of German efficiency to reassure the potential buyer that the machine he is buying (and it is generally a masculine customer) will let you outdo the Germans at their own game by getting you to the beach ahead of time and seizing the sun beds before the Germans themselves. This clever TV advertisement for the Audi appeals to British humour in reinforcing a German stereotype (perhaps a prejudice). The Germans may be efficient and domineering but good old British *nous* wins out in the end. The irony of course is that they have to use German engineering excellence to achieve this, summed up in the Audi advertising slogan 'Vorsprung durch Technik'.

The Volkswagen of course has partly confirmed these prejudices in the mass produced 'beetle' range. This was to be the 'people's car' and was fully endorsed by Adolf Hitler himself, though the lack of materials prevented any being made in quantity before the end of the war. Later the car came to be a symbol of the German 'miracle' in the rebuilding of a strong and vibrant economy from the shattered ruins of the immediate post-war years (Steele, 1995, 2). The British occupying forces in true 'blimp' style saw no great merit in the design and left the VW plant to its own devices, slowly turning it into the best selling model of all time (Baldwin et al, 1987, 511). From the 1930s, when it was designed and first built, through to 1979, when it effectively ceased production, it evolved as the symbol of totalitarian mass consumerism, the symbol of economic rebirth, and from the 1960s the archetypal 'studentmobile', and finally a humanised Hollywood film star in 'Herbie'. Each evolution continued its popularity and sales appeal. To this end it truly was a 'Volkswagen.'

Over the past 30 years we have witnessed the impressive rise of the mass produced car in Japan and the Asia Pacific rim. The car industry, through Toyota, Honda, Nissan and others, has come to represent Japanese efficiency, quality and managerialism. From the 1960s when the first Japanese cars began to enter western markets they were regarded as a joke. By the 1980s the image had evolved to one of respect where they were feared by rival Western manufacturers. This respect and trepidation reached the point where, from the late 1970s, western manufacturers, business and management consultants and even politicians beat a path to the Japanese multinational corporation door to learn the key to its success. This spawned a plethora of management and business literature giving rise to the popularity of quality circles, total quality management (TQM) and various Japanese techniques and methods such as 'kaizen' (continual improvement), used to improve quality and efficiency (Pascale and Athos, 1982; Dore and Sako, 1989). Over the past ten years factories have been established in Britain by Nissan and Toyota, and until recently Honda had a working relationship with Rover, before British Aerospace sold the company to BMW. The result has been a considerable share of the British market being taken by Japanese designed and built vehicles. The philosophy of kaizen has been used frequently in advertising copy of various Japanese makes in western markets. 'Toyota cars have long been world renowned for their quality and reliability' a mid-1980s advert proclaims (*Automobile Year*, 1986, 11). Mitsubishi's advertisements in the same period emphasised the kaizen approach as both philosophy and tradition:

> Ever since we built Japan's first series production automobile back in 1917 our philosophy has been to provide Mitsubishi Motors customers with cars and trucks that are better in every way. This started us on the road to developing automobiles that are making headlines today. We are ... on the road to perfection (*Automobile Year*, 1986, 17).

In keeping with this kaizen approach, models built in the 1960s were based very much on western designs which gradually gave more and more quality and specifications for a competitive price. By the 1990s Japanese companies had moved into nearly all areas of vehicle manufacture from family saloons to top of the range mass produced sports models. In this sense the recent history of the Japanese car symbolises continual improvement by learning from others, and by so doing developing the company, the group and the self. And when they had learnt as much as they could from others they became the master and other companies and their employees, the student. In its development over the last decade, the Toyota Corolla, for example, has embodied this kaizen approach, becoming the winner of the best value for money car in the JD Power survey carried out by the BBC TV programme 'Top Gear' in 1996.

The 'Tuk Tuk' (a three-wheeled taxi), common on the roads of Indonesia, Malaysia, Thailand and other South East Asian countries, symbolises a thrusting and rampant commercialism seen as characteristic of these rapidly growing economies. One writer describes them as a vehicle 'open to the elements and generally regarded as a health hazard to its occupants. Not only do they breathe Bangkok's smog unprotected but Tuk Tuk drivers are notoriously reckless' (Economist Intelligence Unit, 1994, 43). Given the fact that Jakarta, Bangkok and Manila have some of the worst traffic conditions in the world due to the unrestrained and swift expansion of those cities, alternative public transport which is badly needed, such as an underground railway system, is now too expensive to implement because of the high rise buildings which have sprouted up within the last decade. Taxis and Tuk Tuks have thus become the main means of transport around these sprawling conurbations. The Tuk Tuk has evolved from the rickshaw pulled by human beings to a bicycle pulling it occupants in an attached cab to one being powered by a small two stroke motor cycle. It is symbolic of a thrusting, unregulated and chaotic fast growth economy with one foot in the past and the other placed forward into a dynamic future. It is representative of an unbridled and unrestrained new capitalism. We may laugh or be critical of these polluting contraptions but they are an ominous symbol of a globalisation process which will shortly begin to emulate the Japanese challenge to western economic supremacy.

To conclude, most national car producing and consuming nations see cars as representing slices of their own societies, but advertisers have long been aware that different car makes symbolise different aspects of their country of origin, and particular models symbolise a strong vein of that culture. Thus Audi and BMW represent German quality engineering and efficiency through the advertising slogan 'Vorsprung durch Technik.' The Citroën DS 19 represents French chic, elegance and style; Volvo and Saab, Swedish safety and welfarism. Italian élan and style are embodied in the Lamborghini, Ferrari and Bugatti, Italian family values in the smaller Fiats. British aristocratic values are similarly reflected in the Rolls Royce, and the swinging sixties in the Mini.

All of these cars have been sold worldwide and part of their appeal is that they echo a need in the buyer in which the advertiser may utilise a national value of that model's origin to heighten its appeal. Thus those who wish for safety in their cars will be more inclined to believe a Volvo campaign which emphasises their Swedishness. Those who wish for reliability combined with potential power will buy an Audi or BMW, which makes great play of German engineering prowess. Those who wish to register their criticism of mass consumer society will buy into the blue stocking appeal of the 2CV. You do not have to be Swedish, German, or French to enjoy any of these marques, but part of their appeal is embodied in the national characteristics they reflect. The creation of a global car is now being seen as a possibility by some manufacturers, but motor industry pundits are not so sure. The Model T Ford and the Volkswagen Beetle were the two cars which got nearest to that ideal in terms of numbers sold.

As Barthes recognises:

> every object in the world can pass from a closed, silent existence to an oral state open to appropriation by society, for there is no law, whether natural or not which forbids talking about things. A tree is a tree (*or a car is a car*). Yes of course. But a tree as expressed by Minou Drouet is no longer quite a tree, it's a tree decorated, adapted to a certain type of consumption, laden with literary self indulgence, revolt, images, in short with a type of social usage which is added to pure matter (1973,109)

The meaning of things will also change in context and time as Barthes (1973, 110) comments: 'naturally everything is not expressed at the same time: some objects become prey to mythical speech for a while, then they disappear, others take their place and attain the status of myth.' Thus objects can become mythologised according to the stance of those who create the myths and those that perceive them. Car culture compared to other subjects is relatively new but it is a twentieth-century phenomenon which through the rise of a mass literature in magazines, newspapers, advertising and other forms of communication has ensured that they are objects which pass beyond function and enter the realms of fetishism in the continual rediscovery of their distinctiveness in terms of the perception of the mythologisers and the car's significance to culture and ideology.

Bibliography:

Adeney, M. (1988) *The Motor Makers: The Turbulent History of Britain's Car Industry*, Collins, London.
Automobile Year (1986), Edipresse Publishing Group, Lausanne Volvo 780 Advertisement.
Automobile Year, (1986) Edipresse Publishing Group, Lausanne, Mercedes Advertisement.
Baldwin, N., Georgano, G., Sedgwick, M. and Laban, B. (1987) *The World's Guide to Automobiles*, Macdonald Orbis, London.
Barthes, R (1973) *Mythologies*, Vintage, London.

Barthes, R. (1977) *Image-Music-Text*, Fontana, London.

Barrie, C. (1994) 'Germans to be the power behind Rolls', *The Guardian*, Tuesday 20 December, p. 20.

BBC (1995a) *The Car's the Star: Rolls Royce*, presenter Quentin Willson, Birmingham, Pebble Mill, repeat broadcast 21 March 1996.

BBC (1995b) *The Car's the Star: The Classic Land Rover*, presenter Quentin Willson, Birmingham, Pebble Mill, repeat broadcast 21 March 1996.

BBC (1995c) *The Car's the Star: The Fiat 500*, presenter Quentin Willson, Birmingham, Pebble Mill, repeat broadcast 6 March 1996.

Benton, G. and Loomes, G. (1976) *Big Red Joke Book*, Pluto Press, London.

Beynon, H. (1973) *Working for Ford*, Penguin, Harmondsworth.

Bloomfiled, G. (1978) *The World Automotive Industry*, David and Charles, Newton Abbot.

Dore, R. and Sako, M. (1989) *How the Japanese Learn to Work*, London, Routledge.

Drucker, P. (1972) *The Concept of the Corporation*, New York, John Day.

Duprat, F. (1988) 'Launch Campaigns 1987', *Automobile Year*, no. 35, Editions Lamunitiére, Lausanne, pp. 89–94.

Economist Intelligence Unit (1994) 'The Automotive Sector of Thailand: Riding the Tiger', in *International Motor Business,* 4th Quarter, The Economist Intelligence Unit, London, pp. 31–48.

Fiske, J. (1982) *Introduction to Communication Studies*, Methuen, London.

Guardian, The (1995) 'Trabi roars a last hurrah,' 13 October, p. 22.

Hill, D. (1995) 'Rover's Return,' *New Statesman and Society*, 11 August, pp. 16–17.

Huxley, A. (1932) *Brave New World*, Chatto and Windus, London.

Manning, T. (1995) 'Driving along in my automobile,' *New Statesman and Society*, 14 April, pp. 33–35.

Marsh, P and Collett, P. (1986) *Driving Passion: The Psychology of the Car*, Jonathan Cape, London.

Marshall, S. (1989) 'The best of both worlds: why Jaguar and Ford need one another,' *Financial Times*, 11 November, p. 14.

Nockolds, H. (1949) *(Rolls Royce) The Magic of a Name*, G.T. Foulis, London.

Pascale, R. and Athos, A. (1982) *The Art of Japanese Management*, Allen Lane, London.

Pierce, C.S. (1931–38) *Collected Papers*, Harvard University Press, Cambridge, Mass.

Smith, H. (1991) *The New Russians*, Vintage, London.

Steele, J. (1995) 'VW in reverse: How the German economic miracle has run out of road', The *Guardian*, 21 September, Supplement, pp. 1–3.

Stevenson, H. (1991) *Advertising British Cars of the 50s*, Foulis, Sparkford, Somerset.

Turner, L. (1995) 'No moose is good moose'. The *Guardian* Weekend Supplement, 4 November, p. 64

Walker, M. (1986) *The Waking Giant: The Soviet Union Under Gorbachev*, Sphere, London.

Wyeth, P. (1994) 'Mystery and Imagination,' *Top Gear Magazine*, October, pp. 34–41.

3

Motor Car Ownership in Twentieth–Century Britain: A Matter of Convenience or a Marque of Status?

David Thoms

Television images of protestors attaching themselves to trees in a vain attempt to prevent the destruction of woodland associated with the construction of the Newbury bypass graphically highlighted the ambivalent relationship which society has enjoyed with the motor car during the last one hundred years. Although protection of the environment was an issue with which many viewers could sympathise, the Newbury campaign was doomed because of the power of the motor vehicle lobby, including those members of the public who provided tacit support for the extension of the road network. The environmental influence of the motor car is perhaps most obvious in terms of land use with the construction of motorways, ring roads and parking areas. This trend has been particularly apparent in the United States where more land has been sacrificed to the car than to housing. The motor car has been responsible for traffic accidents resulting in millions of deaths and serious injuries, pollution of the atmosphere, extreme examples of aggressive behaviour and rapid depletion of some of the world's most precious natural resources.

The popularity of the motor car is explained in part by its flexibility as a mode of transport. In Britain at the present time (1997) some 86 per cent of passenger miles are by car, while in western Europe as a whole the average distance travelled by car per person per day has increased more than three times since 1965. In the early part of the twentieth century the major motor car manufacturers in Britain directed production towards luxury vehicles. These were high in power, expensive to own and of limited market appeal. The situation changed with the introduction of light cars just prior to the First World War. These were scaled down versions of the larger prototypes and with engine capacity limited to around 1500 cc. These vehicles were fairly comfortable to drive and with a relatively manageable purchase price soon found a market among the more affluent middle classes (Caunter, 1957, 46). Ford quickly dominated sales of light cars, assembling them in Manchester from parts imported from the United States. The Morris Oxford was the cheapest British competitor to Ford, though Singer, Standard and Humber were also active in this embryonic mass market. The era of mass motoring, however, was delayed until the interwar period, especially the 1930s, when the introduction of assembly line techniques and rising real incomes brought the cost of motoring within reach of a broader spectrum of society.

It was predominately the middle classes who had the finances to take advantage of the motoring habit during the interwar years. New owner sales multiplied three times between 1932 and 1937 with the balance moving strongly towards vehicles of up to 10 hp. This reflected the higher purchase cost and running expenses of larger engined cars (Church, 1994, 13). With a growing motoring lobby, road mileage increased but only by 4 per cent between 1899 and 1936. Thereafter, however, the rapid expansion of Exchequer funded 'trunk roads' helped to promote motor car travel for leisure and domestic, as well as business, purposes. The legal framework of motoring also changed significantly during the 1930s. In 1930 the 20 mph speed limit was removed for cars (though a 30 mph was introduced in built up areas in 1935 following a spate of accidents) and in 1934 driving tests became compulsory for all new drivers (Perkin, 1976, 139–141).

In the early post-war period the demand for cars outstripped supply as raw materials were limited and government gave priority to exports rather than the home market. As conditions eased, however, car ownership expanded rapidly reaching a density of 106 vehicles per thousand population in 1960 compared with 42 per thousand in 1938 (Church, 1994, 44). By 1994 the figure had increased fourfold with almost two million new motor cars taking to Britain's roads in that year alone, swelling the total to around 24 million vehicles. By the mid-1990s over half the population of Britain held a driving licence while some 67 per cent of households owned one or more cars. One of the most significant implications of this was the impact on travel to work with around 73 per cent of journeys of this nature being undertaken by car or taxi. By that time, too, the motor vehicle had also come into its own for commercial use, with some 2.5 million cars – 10.7 per cent of the total – owned by businesses (SMMT, 1995). The growth of car ownership over the last four decades is explained partly by an increase in supply, including imports, and partly by a decline in unit costs relative to income. In real terms motor cars now cost approximately one third of their 1960 price, while by the same measure fuel and oil costs have fallen by 50 per cent (*Guardian*, 16 January 1996, 16). In addition, car makers have devised a variety of purchase or leasing arrangements which both facilitate ownership and encourage the regular substitution of vehicles.

The growth of suburban housing estates, and the concomitant problem of ribbon development, may be traced in part to the flexibility of motor travel, particularly for relatively short journeys. The Barlow Report of 1940 on the Distribution of the Industrial Population drew attention to the importance of road transport in the decentralisation of population, noting that 'residential areas beyond easy reach of trains have grown up around most of the big cities'. (Barlow, 1940, 45). Even in areas of rapid population growth, such as Becontree, Dagenham, Romford and Thames Ditton, which were well served by the railway, motor cars proved invaluable in conveying commuters to the local station (Richardson & Aldcroft, 1968, 311). The influence of road transport in the interwar period is also apparent in the appearance of residential and commercial ribbon development, along the main arterial roads. The sprawling and frequently aesthetically unpleasant nature of this type of building reflected the inadequate nature of spatial planning at national level.

Although suburban sprawl was subsequently controlled by tighter planning regulations and methods of enforcement, the motor car has been allowed to dominate the urban environment. One of the earliest initiatives linking road transport with land-use planning was taken in 1936 with the commissioning of a highway development survey for Greater London (Buchanan, 1958, 148). Although the report, which followed, focused principally upon arterial roads and failed to link transport with broader issues of urban development, it did encourage a more systematic approach to town planning which acknowledged the growing and sometimes decisive influence of the motor car. Nevertheless, progress in harmonising motor transport with urban life was slow, often taking the form of modest initiatives such as parking restrictions, rather than a more comprehensive form of planning. In 1971 William Plowden conjectured tentatively that 'It seems likely – though not certain – that in the 1970s it will no longer be possible simply to avoid planning for the motor car' (Plowden, 1971, 407). Yet a quarter of a century later motor transport dominates the urban landscape in a way which Plowden appears not to have envisaged. The growth of out-of-town shopping centres and recreational facilities demonstrate, for example, the omnipotence of the motor car. Planning regulations have become almost the servant of the motorist as we have 'designed cars into our lives'. (*Guardian*, 16 January 1996, 16)

The popularity of the motor vehicle is also explained by its flexibility as an instrument of entertainment and leisure. The lay engineer who enjoyed tinkering with systems of power transmission represented an important source of development for the infant British car industry. At a more sophisticated level, a number of enthusiasts built cars, which had the potential to function effectively as road vehicles but which never went into production, usually for financial reasons. Nevertheless, the presence of the high street motor spares retailer is testimony to the continuing popularity of maintaining, modifying or personalising one's own vehicle.

Despite the economic problems of the 1920s and 30s, this period was characterised by a marked growth in the range of organised leisure activities. Motoring, however, allowed the driver and his family the freedom individually to explore the countryside and the coast for daytrips or holidays. Compared with the train, the motor car enabled travellers to select their destinations unfettered by the limitations of specific routes and timetables. The motor coach, which by 1937 transported some 82 million passengers, had a similarly liberating influence on the choice of leisure destinations, particularly for those on lower incomes. In the post-war years recreational motoring reached new levels of popularity. As Colin Buchanan noted in 1958: 'Invaluable as the car may be for business and domestic purposes, its supreme function is for pleasure and recreation. A fine weekend at almost any time of the year will bring the cars out in tens of thousands making their way to the coast and beauty spots' (Buchanan, 1958, 67). By 1970 a drive in the car represented one of the most popular forms of outdoor leisure, and was shared almost equally by middle and working class motorists. As one observer commented:

> 'Working-class children, who would not have recognised a cow, were piled into the family runabout on a Sunday for a tour around the country lanes where they could stare over the blur of the hedgetops at grazing animals; mum and dad filled the car with children and buckets and spades and trundled off to the seaside for a day of candy floss and a donkey ride on the sand.' (*Sunday Times*, 13 January 1996, 7).

Moreover, the National Recreation Survey of 1967 indicated that class or age made little difference to the nature of the leisure activity with the majority of trippers, 34 per cent of the total, visiting the countryside to enjoy the view, a picnic or to play family games in the open air (Perkin, 1976, 163). The flexibility of the motor car meant that it became widely used to visit family and friends, transport supporters to soccer matches and day trippers to country houses, museums, safari parks and other centres of amusement and recreation. The growth in the number of women drivers has added a further dimension to the relationship between leisure and car ownership. Although this is an area which requires more research, a recent survey found that women most commonly value the car for purposes of shopping, visiting friends and travelling to work. The survey also revealed that image was relatively unimportant in car ownership, though 'researchers suggested that this actually played a bigger role than women were prepared to admit' (*Daily Mail*, 10 February 1996,15).

Although the flexibility of motor travel and the rise of incomes are convincing explanations for the growth and diversification of car ownership, they fail to recognise the presence of a significant cultural dynamic. The motor car differentiates, it has a symbolic quality which takes many different forms. For example, its role as one of the pioneers of motor vehicle engineering gave Britain special status among the world's trading nations. This mood was captured by a *Sunday Times* correspondent who noted that:

> 'By the 1950s, Britain was world leader, exporting more cars than any other nation, including the US, and marques such as Austin and Morris, Jaguar, Riley, Wolseley, Singer, Humber, Standard, Sunbeam, Hillman, Triumph, Vauxhall and Rover were household names' (*Sunday Times*, 13 January 1996, 7).

Thereafter the indicators of national decline followed relentlessly. By the mid-1950s competitors in the United States and Europe outpaced British producers, while the country's share of world exports in cars fell from 52 per cent in 1950 to around 24 per cent at the end of the decade (Church, 1996, 44). In addition, many of Britain's best-known car manufacturers went out of business or were taken over, often by foreign concerns. Of the major car companies with an operating base in Britain, Ford and Vauxhall (General Motors) are both ultimately responsible to executives in Detroit, while Peugeot is a French company and Rover forms part of the BMW group. One of the consequences of this is that even such prestigious marques as Jaguar and Aston Martin are foreign owned, both having been taken over by the Ford Motor Company. By contrast, Rolls Royce, which is part of the Vickers engineering conglomerate, remains under British control, at least for time being. Interestingly, when the proposed sale of Land Rover, 'something as British as the green wellie', to General Motors was mooted in 1986, it brought 'a public eruption of nationalist sentiment' which fatally undermined the deal (*Observer*, 9 March 1986, 37). Even the Thatcher government, with its thirst for privatisation, was unable to overcome the symbolism associated with Land Rover vehicles.

There is reason to believe that motor vehicle manufacture has also played a role in local self-identification. Dagenham, Cowley, Longbridge and Ellesmere Port all draw their national image and reputation in significant measure from their association with car making. However, perhaps the outstanding example in this respect is Coventry where the foundations of the British motor industry were laid in the 1890s and which subsequently came to experience the cold chill of decline throughout its manufacturing base. When Alfred Herbert declared in 1913 that: 'We in Coventry are largely concerned with motors', he was signalling a remarkable transformation that had turned the city from a declining centre of the textile trade to a buoyant engineering centre of national importance (Thoms & Donnelly, 1985, 14). Coventry's reputation rested heavily upon motor vehicles for on the eve of the First World War it accounted for approximately one-third of total British output and included many of the industry's most prestigious marques. One of these was Daimler, the first British public company of any size set up to take advantage of the opportunities offered by the infant motor industry. Although some of the dubious entrepreneurial activities of its founder, Henry Lawson, gave the company a difficult start, under new management its products soon acquired a reputation for quality and desirability. When the Prince of Wales purchased three Daimler cars in 1900 he immediately conveyed a special status on a pioneering engineering initiative which had come to fruition in Coventry. This was given a further twist two years later when the Daimler company received the Royal Warrant. Although the editor of *The Motor* was exaggerating when he claimed that Daimler represented 'virtually the history of the trade', his observation contained sufficient credibility for the kudos to encompass the city as well as the company (Thoms & Donnelly, 1985, 36). During the interwar period Coventry became associated with mass produced vehicles, though its name continued to be linked with high status marques such as Armstrong-Siddeley, Lea-Francis, Alvis, Jaguar and Daimler. During recent decades car production in Coventry has dramatically changed its character with only Peugeot, Jaguar and Carbodies – manufacturing taxicabs – retaining a major presence in the city. The cultural impact of this was captured by the *Coventry Evening Telegraph* when one of its correspondents referred sadly and jingoistically to the car makers of the 1960s falling 'prey to invaders' (*Coventry Evening Telegraphy*, 16 January 1996, 24).

Like other car making towns, Coventry was also associated with car workers, a segment of the labour force which at various times has enjoyed a particular reputation for high incomes and high levels of industrial militancy. To the extent that employment generates specific positions within the social framework, car workers, particularly in the 1960s, enjoyed a special position in the national psyche. The expansion of the motor vehicle industry after 1945 created the conditions for rising incomes for car workers. By 1960, for example, Coventry's engineering workers enjoyed earnings some 35–40 per cent above earnings for comparable labour in other parts of the country. This was based upon a strong demand for labour in motor vehicle manufacture, powerful unions, particularly at shop steward level, and a willingness to take industrial action. With the need to match supply to demand, managers often appeared weak when faced with militant car workers which in turn helped to give the industry a reputation for muscular trade unionism.

Most importantly, however, the motor car differentiates on a personal basis; through their particular characteristics cars interact with the individual, perhaps in terms of a status (or inverted status) relationship with the external world, or merely through internalised self-identification. How else does one explain the purchase of high-powered cars with the capacity to far exceed the maximum legal speed? Similarly, why are 4 x 4 vehicles in such demand when so many of them hardly ever forsake the tarmac? Cars are more than simply a means of transport since for many people they represent an extension of personality. It has been suggested, for example, that:

> 'Cars are often objects of pride and virility, embellished with chrome and the musical roar of a powerful engine. Cars have a strong emotional appeal which goes well beyond their practical use' (*The Motor Car*, 1).

However, the complex socio-psychological basis of car ownership is beyond the scope of this essay. Nevertheless, it is possible to suggest a number of practical reasons for the emergence of the motor car as an icon of twentieth-century culture.

The marketing of motor vehicles, both in terms of research and sales methods, has become a highly organised and expensive operation, Usually, however, manufacturers and their advertising agencies seek to draw a relationship between the product and the personal characteristics, real or imagined, of the customer. Cars are rarely portrayed as merely useful load carriers but as objects of desire, which reflect on the good taste and even technical knowledge of the owner. When Nicole and Papa vie to collect grandmére in the Clio they are appealing to knowledgeable consumers who cross the generation and gender divide. Moreover, advertisements are frequently set in exotic locations and feature glamorous individuals with whom, it is supposed, one would like to identify. Major advertising campaigns normally accompany the introduction of new vehicle models. The annual facelift, which was linked to the marketing possibilities of the motor show, was abandoned by Morris in 1935 on the basis of cost (Rees, 1972, 17). Although other manufacturers followed suit, modest cosmetic changes remain a popular way of injecting new sales life into well established models.

Brand names are a key element in the interaction between car manufacturers and the consumer. The particular associations attached to specific marques are carefully guarded by marketing departments. Model changes are well orchestrated to ensure that reputations for quality, reliability, safety or driver appeal are preserved and yet adjusted, where appropriate, to take account of changing fashions. One example concerns Volvo where the recent introduction of new models has sought to give the company's vehicles a more adventurous image while at the same time projecting their traditional concerns with safety. These dual, and potentially conflicting, objectives are reflected in the well-constructed advertising campaign, which accompanied the appearance of Volvo's new cars. The resurrection of defunct marques is another way in which the marketing strategies of the motor companies seek to exploit image appeal. Examples of this technique include the reintroduction of the Rover and MG nameplates, while BMW is said to be considering a relaunch of the Triumph marque for particular use in the American market where it has a special cache associated with the sports roadsters of the past.

Although the motorist is subjected to a wide variety of driving regulations and bears the burden of numerous forms of taxation, successive governments have been reluctant to impose controls over the use of motor vehicles which would dramatically curb their harmful impact on society and the environment. This is partly for economic reasons, but it also reflects the power of the motorists' lobby. As the Crowther group noted:

> 'A car-owning electorate will not stand for a severe restriction. And even if a severe restriction could be got on to the statute book, it would be almost impossible to enforce' (Plowden, 1971, 407).

It is against this background that controls over the use of the car and the vehicle itself remain relatively modest. Indeed, it may be argued that through the August change of registration – a quarter of all new cars are sold in August – the industry has been allowed to manipulate sales in order to appeal to the vanity of car owners. In a sense, too, the marketing of particular registration plates by the Vehicle Licensing Agency is an attempt to exploit consumer interest in the personalisation of the motor car.

Motor technology has improved enormously since the pioneering days of the early twentieth century. Yet the basics remain essentially the same with progress being built upon improved materials, new production methods and a more sophisticated appreciation of the engineering processes. This has allowed motoring enthusiasts to tune or adjust the operation of their cars bringing a sense of achievement and self-identification. Even the motoring novice may personalise a vehicle with the use of stickers, a change of paint or a cherished registration number. More generally, the growth of a large market in second-hand cars and spares has extended the opportunity to own, modify and personalise motor vehicles to a much broader section of the population than was possible in the austerity years of the post-war period.

It has been suggested that: 'If humans behaved logically, they would drive small fuel-efficient cars with a top speed of around 120 kph' (*The Motor Car* 1995, 1). However, car ownership relates to a whole range of variables of which economics forms only a part. Convenience is clearly an important element, too, but it may also be suggested that studies of the development of the motor vehicle industry and of motoring itself have placed too little emphasis upon cultural factors, particularly the ability of the car to differentiate one individual from another. This is not a new phenomenon but in the early days of motoring was associated with social class and economic power. The middle class car-borne day tripper or holiday maker of the interwar period could visit more remote or less well publicised attractions while their working class counterparts would have little option but to take the train or motor coach to the more traditional destinations. This changed with the advent of mass motoring but the car retains its capacity to individualise, to fragment and to bring together in cultural, as well as practical terms.

Bibliography

Buchanan, C.D. (1958) *Mixed Blessing. The Motor in Britain*, Leonard Hill, London.

Caunter, C.F. (1957) *The History and Development of Light Cars*, HMSO, London.

Church, R. (1994) *The Rise and Decline of the British Motor Industry*, Macmillan, London.

Perkin, H. (1976) *The Age of the Automobile*, Quartet, London.

Plowden, W. (1971) *The Motor Car and Politics 1896–1970*, Bodley Head, London.

Rees, D.G. (1972) *The Motor Industry: An Economic Survey*, Butterworths, London.

Richardson, H.W. & Aldcroft, D.H. (1968) *Building in the British Economy between the Wars*, Allen & Unwin, London.

Royal Commission on the Distribution of the Industrial Population, Barlow Report, (1940) HMSO.

Society of Motor Manufacturers and Traders (SMMT), (1995) *Fact Sheet*, London.

Thoms, D. & Donnelly, T. (1985) *The Motor Car/Industry in Coventry Since the 1890s, The Motor* Car, 'Understanding global issues (UGI) 1995, 9, London Croom Helm, London.

4

'Savage Servility: Cars in the Psyche'

Sebastian Lockwood

It's nineteen fifty-five ... my father says not to get excited, that we probably can't afford it, but here it is ... on the avenue in Brussels, a Facel-Vega: when the salesman opens the door a deep blue light glows as the engine sings a light throaty purr.

It's nineteen fifty-eight and we are driving down the lanes of Norfolk in a brand new Chrysler shipped over for the trip – as we drive, the grass on the banks brushes both sides of the car. When we park at the Quay in Blakeney a scrum of snot nosed kids rub about the car, 'blimey! Coo–er, smashin motor...'. I gaze at them through the windows and feel like Jonah in the whale.

Now we're driving out of London in my uncle's Ford Zephyr, 1964. We stop at the light and he empties urine out of the pipe attached to his cancered penis. When we get up north he finds an abandoned second war airstrip and does 'the ton'. I stare at the gauge as the needle hits the magic 100 mph and feel speed.

There are other cars of youth – so many – a dreamscape of cars that will haunt as psychosis, regret, addiction. In Ballard's *Project for a Glossary of the Twentieth Century* (1992), he enters, 'AUTOMOBILE: All the millions of cars on this planet are stationary, and their apparent motion constitutes mankind's greatest collective dream'. Julian Stallabrass in his *Gargantua* (1996), quotes this and adds: 'In an odd sense the dominance of the car over our environment is so complete that this is true: cars stay put while the planet revolves around them.' Not so odd – what is odd is that so recent a phenomenon can already have had such an overwhelming effect on the internal landscape. We know what cars are doing to the land and the air: but what are they doing to the psyche?

My dream continues: there was the Metallurgic owned by a distant relative who collected cars. This car, as I recall, or imagine, has four cylinders each a thousand cc's. You start one of them, then engage the others. It will do 120 mph at a one to one ratio: thump, thump, thump ... doing the ton, racing from Norfolk to Scotland and back.

For a hundred dollars I bought my first car, an MGA with no roof and no floor. I painted a huge yellow daisy on the hood and felt free and with motor. At an intersection off Avenue Road in Toronto I came to a stop behind a chauffeur driven Chrysler Imperial ... my father gets out of the *Imperial* and walks back to say a polite hello to his long-haired son in the MGA: the mosquito behind the aircraft carrier.

That MGA died in the winter of '67. In London, in the summer of 1968, two Canadian girls gave me their 'clapped out' Morris 1100 ex-post office van. With my wife-to-be I drove that van straight to Morocco, over the High Atlas, and into the Sahara desert. Trying to get home I parked it outside the Casablanca Post Office and went inside to the agony of the telephones and impossible connections only to discover that the friend who was supposed to wire money had vanished to Ibiza. When I came out I could see gas, or petrol (gas has more drive to it – step on the gas ...) dripping on the street and a policeman complaining that I was making a mess. Liquid gold spilling as I lose my temper at the policeman who calls my heroic van junk.

Driving out of Morocco we lose second gear, then third, a hole in the gas tank, the suspension wonky, and feeding water out of empty wine bottles into the hissing spitting radiator. As we arrive back at Blakeney the Morris loses the front suspension just as we stop in front of the house – such bravery! I watch her being dragged off to the knacker's yard. I can get weepy as I write that – anthropomorphising ... you bet: first son conceived in it, the incident with the Spanish police ... the flat outside Tangier where ten Arabs stop and pick it up by hand while I change the tire then give them all cigarettes ... this is a Mount Rushmore car – a car of dreams.

Then there was the battered Renault 4 for the second son – I had to keep it at the top of the hill because the ignition was gone and it had to be roll started for the fateful drive to Norwich hospital and delivery.

Cars have only been around for what ... a hundred years ... a blink in the collective unconscious: but look at the impact on the average life. A terrible beauty indeed and we are changed, changed utterly by the metal internal combustion chariot.

Our dreams, our most basic internal imagery, are now driven by this drive to drive. The pink finned fifty-eight Cadillac, any Jaguar, but particularly the E type that embodies a universal desire to see form and function achieve a spirit-sex unity: our new archetype.

In *The System of Objects*, Baudrillard writes:

> Tail fins were a sign not of *real* speed but of a sublime, measureless speed. They suggest a miraculous automatism, a sort of grace ... cars sprout fins ... features that in other contexts are functional; first they

appropriate the characteristics of the airplane, which is a model object relative to space, then they proceed to borrow directly from nature – from sharks, birds, and so on. (Baudrillard, 1996, 59).

There is a Faustian deal that goes with this bird machine: you can have your personal ego boosting metal chariot but you will not be able to breath the air? We accept. And what do I drive now? An Audi 5000 1983. That was the last year before some wind-tunnel-tested engineer put his lips about the exhaust pipe and blew until a truly handsome car became a bloated blob of its former self. I like those big sedans from the early 1980s. I had a Bavaria ... a Beamer ... '81, had to hot wire it, but oh the sound it made in the tunnel as you downshift. This love/hate is part of the dream relationship: the cars of the unconscious that attack and deliver.

It has come to this then, that in one generation – my father saw first models – our psychic interior is modelled with cars, our romantic memory – much of the sense of achievement: look at me ... look at what I'm finally driving. This is our dreamscape and influences all our thoughts about self and society – yet all so recent that it is raw undigested input that leaves us making decisions on how we build (or rip down) our towns, how we finance our world, what we are willing to sacrifice to achieve the chariot ... and these decisions are made on raw, recent data.

The horse has played its role in the human psyche as: war, sport, art and poetry. The car has replaced it in a neon rush of high speed carbon monoxide. As Baudrillard, in his book *America* (1988), heads out into the heartland he calls driving '... a spectacular form of Amnesia'. It erases the past and consumes the future. We can say that roughly 70 per cent of all the energy put out by humans goes into the making, sustaining and fueling of cars. What on earth were we all doing before? Marshal McLuhan said that we are like drivers heading into the future with our eyes glued to the rear view mirror.

In *For the Union Dead* (1965) Robert Lowell meditates on the sacrifice of Colonel Shaw's 'bell-cheeked Negro infantry . . . Two months after marching through Boston, half the regiment was dead'; Lowell is looking away from St Gaudens' monument as he remembers the aquarium of his youth where now:

> I pressed against the new barbed and galvanized
> fence on the Boston Common. Behind their cage,
> yellow dinosaur steamshovels were grunting
> as they cropped up tons of mush and grass
> to gouge their underworld garage.
> Parking spaces luxuriate like civic
> sandpiles in the heart of Boston.

As he mourns that war and time, he names that 'underworld'
intrusion:
The Aquarium is gone. Everywhere
giant finned cars nose forward like fish;
a savage servility
slides by on grease.

We have become accustomed to that 'savage servility'. We see everywhere
the loss Lowell saw: rivers became natural places to throw down highways –
great roads cut and slash through the heart of once beautiful towns, parks are
ripped up to make parking lots: it is as though any aesthetic sacrifice is worth
the price if it will satisfy the appetite of the car.

Now that it is here, and the damage done, we take it all for granted. We ride
extraordinary cars at extraordinary speed and think it quite ordinary. Here is
the anthropologist, Kenneth Good, describing the first car ride of a
Hasupuweteri man who is both an accomplished hunter and brave warrior: he
has just come out of the Amazon jungle and arrived in Caracas:

Alvaro's car was a big black Ford Crown Victoria, a Conquistador in
Venezuelan nomenclature, the largest luxury automobile sold in the
country. Shori got in hesitantly, already woozy from the throngs of
people and the blaring and honking of hundreds of cars and taxis.
Carefully he lowered himself onto the soft plush seating and sat there
as we pulled out into traffic ... I saw his eyelids flutter when the
windows slid silently up out of the door ... From somewhere behind his
head music suddenly flowed into the air. A cold breeze wafted over
him ... Turning his head slightly to the left, he saw a car pull up and
speed past us... The thing just appeared, noiselessly, moving at a
velocity even more alarming than our own. He put his head back
against the seat ... I hoped he wasn't about to throw up or lose
consciousness. (Good, 1991, 232)

The loss of innocence – the machine in the garden. With the amazing
adaptability of the human, Shori will soon be riding cars with that willing
suspension of disbelief we engage in when we ride airplanes, trains or cars. It is
no wonder that as we put our conscious mind on hold when driving – deny the
miraculous element of the landscape appearing and disappearing at seventy
miles per hour – that our unconscious mind has a great deal of downloading to
do. Shori lived in the jungle beyond the car, now he lives in a universe where
the car, and its effects, will be the overwhelming fact of life.

There is no escape from the car. In Norman Lewis' Naples' 44 (1978), two
eccentric old world lawyers discuss the possibility, as the war is ending, of
drawing a line across Italy just below Rome and banning cars in the south

thereby returning to the idyllic, bucolic, Roman life. Fiat would never allow it. The Tibetans banned the wheel from their world preferring to have wheels for prayer rather than transportation. Oil and car companies conspire to get rid of public transportation and to shelve any inventions that will lead to an electric car. In California the once stringent laws on acceptable pollution levels by 2000 are continually weakened and Americans have given up on high mileage cars and now easily accept fifteen miles to the gallon or less.

As we have moved from foot to wheel what have we lost? Poetry measures its lines in feet – it is the meter of walking. Possibly the last great poet to be raised before the onslaught of the car was Yeats, and in his majestic lines – that read with the certainty of climbing a marble staircase – we hear the last of those rhythms. What has followed has been an age of uncertainty – we've lost our footing as we bow to the wheel. The poetry of the car age is the poetry of the road, the confession at the wheel: it does not compare to Yeats, but has its own furious self-destructive rhythm of concrete and tarmac: the poetry of route 66 and all that re-tread 'beat' work.

Back in Blakeney you could watch the cars arrive at the Quay and line up for the rising tide. From inside their cars couples watch the tide rise, read the papers, drink tea from a thermos – with the full tide the cars, in concert, start and drive away having had their fill of the sea and sunset.

All that lust for a shapely machine – all that sacrifice. It seems so demeaning. And yet it was very much part of the great democratising move of the twentieth century – to be free to drive to wherever: to be on the road. Before the car people were not so free to up and change state, county, city. With the car everyone becomes a restless nomad knowing always that around the next corner the highway will deliver a richer life. Hit the road Jack …

When was the last time a car played in your dreams? I recall a series of dreams in a flat Norfolk Broads landscape criss crossed with roads, but the roads are canals and I'm driving various cars down these canals knowing that this cannot be – but it is – in that absolute concrete reality of dreams.

From this nostalgic dreamscape can we make rational decisions about the future car – will the electric car of our hopes ever growl and catch its breath between second and third? Bosnak (1996), a Jungian analyst specialising in dreamwork, has written a functional, rather than interpretive, guide to the dreams called *Tracks in the Wilderness of Dreaming*. He identifies a semiotics of dreaming – that all we have from that particular reality is tracks in a wilderness of dreaming. The Australian Aborigine dream-worker knows how to follow those tracks. We are just learning as we escape the early Freudian distraction of easy interpretation and instead try to navigate our way in that vast but valid wilderness. For us, the dominant tracks in the wilderness of dreaming are tire tracks.

When we dream cars it is different to the dream of the plane or train because we choose the car – we identify with the car that we chose, our parent chose, our lover chose. As a teen in Toronto I dated a girl whose father managed a Ford dealership and she had at her disposal a brand new Ford Thunderbird. The exquisite sexual feel of that black 1967 Thunderbird! Thunderbird is the strangest of the Native American Trickster figures. Unlike Coyote, Salmon or Spider, Thunderbird does not exist in nature: it is pure vision and of immense potency. Nonetheless Ford had the temerity to appropriate the name for a machine that would destroy the psychic domain of that warrior trickster. In the same way, the strongest malt liquor available in America took its name from a warrior who never drank and fought against his people using alcohol: Crazy Horse Malt Liquor. You can explore the reservation in your Jeep Cherokee.

When I was living in Manhattan, I would pick English friends up at Kennedy Airport in my Oldsmobile Cutlass Supreme with a 350 under the hood, two seater and doors that were half the car. With my left arm out of the driver's window (a left arm more tanned than the right is a road warrior's tan) my left elbow on left knee, little finger on the steering wheel, *Little GTO* on the radio … and say, "Welcome to America …" and floor that sucker in a rubber-laying, G-giving strip of burnt rubber.

This is the love/hate terrain of the automobile. We are aware of the psychic bomb we have released in our minds – but we are too within it, in love with it, driven by it … to truly come to terms with it. Ultimately it will be the future generations – who really suffer the consequences of the internal combustion engine – who will have to deal with it. When all of this is gone to rust they will look back and say: how could you have infected us so? How could you bow so low to that savage servility?

Bibliography

Baudrillard, Jean (1988) *America*, Verso, London
Baudrillard, Jean (1996) *The System of Objects*, Verso, London
Ballard J. G., (1992) 'Project for a Glossary of the Twentieth Century' in *Zone 6*, New York.
Bosnak, Robert, (1996) *Tracks in the Wilderness of Dreaming: Exploring Interior Landscape through Practical Dreamwork*, Delacourt Press, Lausanne.
Good, Kenneth, (1991) *Into the Heart: One Man's Pursuit of Love and Knowledge: Among the Yanomami*, Harper Collins, London.
Lewis, Norman, (1978) *Naples '44*, Pantheon.
Lowell, Robert (1965) *For the Union Dead*, Faber, London.
Stallabrass, Julian, (1996) *Gargantua: Manufactured Mass Culture,* Verso, London.

5

Mad Max and Aboriginal Automation: Putting Cars to Use in Contemporary Australian Road Films and Narratives

Ken Gelder

Australian cinema has produced a small but significant number of 'road movies', the best known of which is George Miller's *Mad Max* (1979) and its two sequels. *Mad Max* itself presents a 'road warrior', a rogue policeman who monitors the roads and cleans up gangs of criminals identified through their 'feral' automobiles and motorbikes and 'savage' attitude. In this first film of the trilogy, the roads themselves are noticeably long and straight: Max himself in a certain sense *keeps* them 'straight', asserting the individuality of his heterosexual manhood over a group of bikers who are also collectively coded as 'gay'. He asserts his Australian-ness over and above these bikers' immigrant Britishness, too: most of them, including the leader, have British accents (at least in the original cut of the film). It may seem unusual for a road movie to take the side of the police since such films generally celebrate outlawry. Certainly *Mad Max* makes the law seem aberrant, but in its relentless cleansing of the roads – along with Max's project of revenge for the bikers' assault on the sanctity of the nuclear family – this film remains a conservative example of the road movie genre.[1]

Let me begin by emphasising these three things about *Mad Max*: the utter straightness of the roads, which seem never-ending; the emphasis on the connection between roads, struggle and vulnerability (the film opens with a warning about deaths on the road); and the absence of Aborigines in this outback battlefield. This latter aspect notwithstanding, *Mad Max* stood apart as an originally Australian narrative (the destruction of those British bikers no doubt helped this along), as something unique in Australian film production.[2] The erasure of Aborigines from the landscape may have even been necessary for this particular kind of identity. It enabled the film liberally to trace its own version of indigenisation, as if the road is 'natural' place for (white) Australians; as if one's claim to the road, built upon struggle and loss and rites of passage, is a claim for white Australians' repossession of country.

This has been a standard feature of much epic literature in Australia (of the kind written by Patrick White or David Malouf, for example), and the *Mad Max* trilogy has its own epic qualities, of course, through its demonstration that white Australians have struggled as well, on a grand scale, that their claim on the landscape can therefore be just as great as Aboriginal claims and that they might even thus deserve an identity that is 'aboriginal' (marking difference only through the shift from a capital to a small 'a'). Ross Gibson has noted how, as we move to the second and third films in the sequel, *Mad Max 2* (1982) and *Max Max Beyond Thunderdome* (1985), the roadscapes give way to settlement (Gibson, 1992, 173). By the third film, the never-ending roads have almost no role to play any more. A town has been built instead, a centre with the leading character Aunty Entity, who oversees Bartertown, celebrating the fact that 'civilisation' has been established at last. The three films therefore chart a trajectory beginning with loss and struggle and closing with (the right to) non-Aboriginal settlement at the heart of Australia. They offer an allegory of colonisation, in other words. Max's automobile, his Interceptor, was foundational to this narrative: in the beginning was ... the car. But it soon becomes redundant; under the logic of this allegory there is no need to drive any more when you are (now) at home: there will be no more road fatalities when settlement is established. A repeated line from the theme song at the end of *Beyond Thunderdome* makes the point absolutely clear. 'We don't need to know the way home', the song tells us, precisely because 'we' (but not 'them') have finally 'arrived'. Not only is there is no Aboriginal presence in these films to unsettle this allegory; in fact, Max dispenses with that presence through his *own* 'aboriginalisation'. Gibson sees this as a mode of 'adaptation', which these films visually celebrate through dress (animal skins, earthy colours) and the outrageous customisation of vehicles. By the third film, Max 'is becoming one kind of native'; he has adapted so well to new conditions precisely because there are no *other* kinds of natives in the picture.

In commentaries on *Mad Max*, it is never noted that Max's Interceptor, customised in a film set located in the underground car park at the University of Melbourne, is in fact a Holden Premier. The Holden is Australia's 'national' car, even though it developed out of post-World War Two agreements and deals with the US General Motors Export Company. Michael Taussig, an Australian anthropologist now based at New York University, has written both affectionately and critically of the genesis of 'the first 'Australian' motor car' (Taussig, 1992, 53–77). The car is designated 'Australian', in inverted commas, because it is already a customised product, an Australian–American industrial hybrid introduced into the country in 1948. General Motors, Taussig notes, had 'australianised the design' in the context (which that design in part effaced) of renegotiated structures of international business, 'making it less flashy and more toughly austere and prim at the same time, hence more in keeping with the older colonial relationship of the Aussie bushman and the British Empire' (57).

Taussig goes on (in anthropological fashion) to trace this conjunction between the imposed design logic of American–Australian capitalism and the local forms of customisation or improvisation which made the Holden 'Australia's Own', building his narrative around an old Australian ex-ANZAC horseman whose Holden Taussig is about to purchase. In a certain sense, Taussig thus talks up the 'australianisation' – the customisation or localisation of the Holden, becoming enthralled enough by it (and by his narrative of it) at the end to make this final comment: 'I drove off newly possessed by Australia's Own' (77). This is, then, another narrative about returning home, about repossession (Taussig buys an 'Australian' car and is himself reconstituted in the process). That final comment is certainly ironic since, as Taussig notes, 'Australia' was never so pure. But in spite of this it also speaks to the exclusivity of that mode of practice he has characterised as 'australianisation'. It helps Taussig, like Mad Max, to become 'one kind of native'.

One aspect of the exclusivity of this practice is built around the ritualised transfer of the Holden from 'father' (the old ANZAC horseman) to 'son' (the young anthropologist, Taussig). The Holden has become iconic not only through its 'australianisation' but also through its precise and spectacular association with white Australian male rites of passage, as shown in Michael Thornhill's film *The F.J. Holden* (1977), for example. Meaghan Morris has noted how, in this film, the Holden promises its young male owner freedom and possibility, while at the same time, its interior spaces 'are so circumscribed, and its social dynamic so circular, that the 'hero's' trajectory is a dead-end drive', in particular because of heavily inscribed gender divisions (Morris, 1989, 126). Thornhill's film is about a boy on the wrong side of the law, which surely explains why the narrative cannot 'progress' in the way that the *Mad Max* films do: the hero in fact shares the positioning of the 'wild' gang members in *Mad Max*, ultimately becoming, like them, a kind of 'fatality'. The circumscription of its interior car-space – with boys occupying one role and place in relation to it, and girls quite another – is another feature it shares with the *Mad Max* films. Max's wife's car looks different and does not travel fast; amongst other things, it is meant to carry a family, and in particular, a child. A woman and child are almost hit by speeding cars driven by competing boys in an opening sequence to the first *Mad Max* film, anticipating the fate of Max's family later on: women, mothers especially are always more vulnerable (on the roads).

In Margaret Dodd's short film *This Woman is Not a Car* (1982), the mother fills her station wagon with children, while the husband goes off to work with a friend in his yellow sports car. Here, the woman – without her man, is shown to be disempowered in the car, subjected to the whims of her children, unable to control them, 'possessed' by the car in quite a different way to Taussig. In David Caesar's documentary *Car Crash* (1996), however, the car is again coded as a means of attaining freedom, especially freedom from the constraints built into a reliance upon public transport and parents. The men interviewed in this documentary relish this freedom most of all, identified as solitary drivers, like Max; but they, too, are shown to be 'possessed' by their cars, overcome by them, unable to keep them under control. The documentary speaks as a narrative about our modern condition: that, now, we have *too much* freedom without responsibility; that, because of the car, the family can no longer cohere and must always define itself through loss (of the children as they drive away or become another road fatality, or – since every one is shown to be equally vulnerable here – of a parent or relative, too).

The narrative trajectory of the *Mad Max* films, which makes the roads – and the car – less and less central as settlement is established, rests on a fantasy of disavowal second only in stature to the accompanying fantasy of a fully-realised white 'aboriginalisation'. In fact, there are now almost 11 million cars on Australian roads: they could not be any *less* central to contemporary life in this country. Over the past twenty years, since around the time the first *Mad Max* film was released, the number of cars on Australian roads has grown by 69 per cent. Australians are more dependant upon their cars than ever before, although this is a feature which rarely translates into popular cultural analysis, with cars barely mentioned at all in such broad-based studies as John Fiske, Bob Hodge and Graeme Turner's *Myths of Oz* (1988) or Verity Burgmann and Jenny Lee's four volume *The People's History of Australia* (1989). The experience of actually *being* on the road, of travelling, is also still underrepresented in Australian popular narratives. There are few cinematic or literary evocations, for example, of how the great distances between cities in Australia, its never-ending roads, are actually negotiated by drivers and passengers, how time is spent, how the journey is perceived, and so on. One exception, however, is a fine horror story by Sean Williams, *Going Nowhere* (1994):

> From Adelaide to Perth by road:
> It didn't look so bad when you broke it down into little bits, which the touring map he referred to did. The stretch of Highway One between Ceduna and Norseman, for example, was just a string of 35s and 101s that crossed the border between SA and WA. It didn't sound like far,

really – not until you added up all the little bits and realised that it totalled one thousand, two hundred and fourteen kilometres.

And that was less than half the total distance – the boring, straight, completely flat half at that, along which the road came to look like a razor's edge, a crack, a tightrope, a hypodermic needle filled with black death, a terrible boundary with nothing one side and nothing the other. (Williams, 1994, 267)

The closing images turn long distance car travel into a Gothic experience, ultimately equating it, as *Mad Max* had done, with fatality. This is the most common way of providing closure, or rupture, to the never-endingness of roads in such narratives: the car crash: death *before* arrival. The documentary *Car Crash*, mentioned above, also presents the crash as its point of narrative closure, allowing a portentous, Gothic tone to overshadow this otherwise 'realistic' account of car use. The Aboriginal author Archie Weller's novel *The Day of the Dog* (1981), based in Perth, ends with a high-speed police chase and a spectacular car crash, all in the midst of an electric storm with rain 'like blood' and the wind 'like a whistling woman crying out to the Devil' (Weller, 1981, 158, 162). This is a pessimistic and highly moralised account, placing an Aboriginal boy with promise firmly on the wrong side of the law – and bearing out Meaghan Morris's concluding remark about F.J. Holden, that 'to be able to drive is a dubious claim to power' (Morris, 1989, 128).

The freedom associated with the car leads inevitably to arrest, closure, fatality: for Archie Weller, this is an available Gothic narrative expressive of modern life. Steve Mickler has looked at newspaper reporting in Perth of Aboriginal youth gangs in the early 1990s to show the other side of this narrative, however: that *The West Australian's* claim that 'more than half the young criminals caught in high-speed chases by the police are Aboriginal' is perfectly consistent with media-orchestrated racism which scapegoats young Aboriginal gangs as urban terrorists (Mickler, 1992, 322–36). The arrangement here may recall the narrative structure of *Mad Max*: white police officers (the rogue officers are always the worst) against gang members coded as 'wild' and 'foreign' who end their careers by dying on the road. There might very well be more of an Aboriginal presence in this film than first realised.

Are there any road narratives told by Aborigines? I can think of only one: Robert Bropho's 'The Great Journey of the Aboriginal Teenagers' (1985). Bropho is an Aboriginal writer and activist living in Perth, founder and leader of the Fringe Dwellers of the Swan Valley Inc. His story is recorded and transcribed for his granddaughter, and tells of 'the days back there in the past' when Bropho and his teenage friends found themselves on the wrong side of the law – the 'long arm of the white man's law, elastic law that stretched so far across the breadth and length of this country' (Bropho, 1990, 164, 165). The

60

story provides a social and historical context of dispossession and boredom for the youths; because there is no work and nothing to do, the Aboriginal boys go stealing. But it is not sensationalist and has no Gothic imagery; in fact, it is mostly comic in its mode. This is because the 'great journey' itself becomes a kind of repossession of country, enabling this particular story to work as a kind of counter-epic to those white narratives of 'aboriginalisation' mentioned above.

Repossession works firstly through the nomination of the Aboriginal gang – a 'mob' of boys, some related to each other – each of them named individually and yet also intimately bound together as a social group. It works secondly, and more spectacularly, through the 'great journey' itself. The boys begin their 'run' from the police by boarding a train, taking them out of Perth into the country. The first stop is at 'my auntie's place': the country is mapped first and foremost in terms of the location of Aboriginal relatives. The boys continue to jump trains; later, they steal 'a Holden ute [utility]' and drive down to the narrator's brother's place. The 'strategy' is to travel at night, heading west: 'travelling through Corrigin, right through to Bruce Rock .... through Merredin .... and pulled right off the road down from Bulla Bulling at the siding just down from Southern Cross' (166–7). The ute gets a flat tyre, so the boys jump another train, stopping to join an Aboriginal man and his wife at a camp. Arriving at Kalgoorlie, they steal another car and head north, later picking up a half-ton International truck: 'through Katherine Valley ... we got to Wiluna ... we went through Yandl station and Roy Hill and Bonny Downs ... we headed for Port Headland' (170–71). The Aboriginal boys use binoculars to watch for the police, 'scanning the area for dust' (169). They are finally caught, however, and locked up at Port Headland, on the north-west coast of Western Australia. The boys escaped in a comic scene which demonstrates the *limits* of 'white law' insofar as it is unable to constrain these Aborigines for very long, and steal a boat and try to row 'to Singapore'. But they are caught again and taken back to Perth, to Fremantle Gaol: 'And that's where the journey of the teenage Aboriginals – that's us – in the late 1940s through the 1950s and early 1960s ended up ...' (172).

The detailed mapping of the 'great journey', with places sometimes identified with other Aboriginal people including relatives, seems to amount to a practice of repossession *in the context of dispossession*. This testifies to the narrative's modernity. The boys are dispossessed enough to entertain the idea of leaving the country altogether by rowing to Singapore. At the same time, the journey makes their social group more coherent than ever through its shared opposition to 'white law' and its movement through a sequence of places which, in the retelling of the story to the granddaughter, become iconic. The route is a kind of modern 'songline', in other words. Sean Williams's horror story had equated long distance travel with boredom. But in Bropho's narrative, the 'great journey' is a way of *overcoming* boredom: it functions as a way of relieving of 'dead-end drive' of dispossession by recovering identity and country. Certainly Bropho's narrative 'ends up' with the Aboriginal boys in gaol, but this is not a 'fatal' ending. In fact, it is quite the opposite: the gaol itself becomes another place in a sequence of places denoting Aboriginal, or pan-Aboriginal, self-identification.

Tom Griffiths, in his book *Hunters and Collectors: The Antiquarian Imagination in Australia* (1996), has noted that, in the midst of contemporary white fantasies about fully-realised settlement, Aborigines by contrast have been considerably *unsettled*: 'They have been dispersed, concentrated, relocated, detached from their land and from one another, and continually kept moving' (Griffiths, 1996, 226). But Griffiths rightly stresses Aboriginal gains, as well as losses, in particular through modes of 'adaptation' in relation to travelling: 'they have survived', he says, 'by continuing to travel lightly in patterned ways' (226). Griffiths traces some aspects of this new 'light' kind of travel, always in the context of Aboriginal relations to white laws (for example, welfare agencies' monitoring of Aboriginal activity; or the taking away of Aboriginal children from their families). Modern Aboriginal travel may at times be evasive, but it is also a means of maintaining social coherence and establishing new identifications with country: 'a crucial map of human affiliations ... and [a] route back to land' (227).

Griffiths' book is about the practice of collecting mostly by amateur historians; but he also comments occasionally on the ways in which collecting can work, productively as he sees it, for modern Aborigines. Aboriginal use of the car is a good example of the business of collection in this context: collection as a means of repossession, a means of providing a 'route back to land'. The anthropologist Tamsin Donaldson has transcribed a song composed by a teenage Aboriginal boy from north eastern Arnhem Land in the Northern Territory, which illustrates this association of the car and (quite literally) the business of collecting. It seems, at first, as if this song is about pelicans (and I present an English translation here, rather than the Aboriginal version):

Two pelicans went along putting (fish) into their fishing nets.
(They) went to Palmi putting fish in (their) pouches.
(They) crept along
putting (fish) into (their) pouches (as they went) to Palmi
Come on! Away (you) go to Wankurr.
(They) went along putting (fish) in their fishing nets.
Then they went scooping up water in their fishing nets.
(They) run to take off...can't
Hey! big brother, fix pelican for us!

(They) went along putting (fish) in their fishing nets, dipping their pouches. (Donaldson 1979; 79–80)

Donaldson notes that the song becomes problematic in the penultimate line: 'Who is big brother, and why is he asked to fix pelican?' (80). It is necessary to know that the Aboriginal boy's father owns a yellow Toyota called 'ka:lumay' (Pelican): all the cars in this community are given names, the same names, Donaldson notes, 'formerly given to canoes' (80). In fact, the song is about a journey the composer made in the Toyota – and perhaps another car – with his older brother. The lines describing the pelicans filling their pouches are also accounting for the way the Toyota stops to collect more passengers. Place names are also mentioned on the journey, evoking a kind of modern 'songline' again. The song may not be about travelling 'lightly' – clearly, the Toyota, now filled with passengers, becomes bogged towards the end! – but it does speak to the repossession of country through the practice of collection. The car becomes central to this practice here, through an 'adaptation' (the car-as-pelican; the easy translation from the canoe to the car) which seems to speak to 'Aboriginalisation' rather than 'aboriginalisation'.

The Aboriginalisation of the motor car requires a particular set of knowledges about the car's function and potential. The car is often taken as a symbol of modernity itself, and early Aboriginal contact ('first contact') with it can be a way of invoking Aboriginal naivety – as in Bill Edward's transcription of a Pitjantjatjara Aboriginal story titled 'Mutuka Nyakunytja – Seeing a Motorcar' (1994), which lifts the car out of any social context by focussing only on one Aboriginal man's responses to it. This transcription at least goes on to note that motor cars 'are now an ever-present and central part of Pitjantjatjara life' (Edwards & Tjupuru 1994, 157). But the sense that Aboriginal use of the car these days is neither naive nor enacted in isolation – like the solitary drivers in *Mad Max* – is well accounted for in Grayson Gerrard's fascinating article, 'Everyone Will Be Jealous For That Mutika' (1989). Gerrard draws on the work of Michael Taussig and A. Appadurai to locate the motorcar ('mutika') in the frame of contemporary Aboriginal social life. The car is a commodity; but in the Arnhem Land community Gerrard describes, 'an active process of de-commoditisation is evident' in relation to it (Gerrard 1989, 97). This is because of what is called 'humbugging', an Aboriginal practice directed at the white Australians in the community (welfare people, anthropologists like Gerrard, teachers, and so on) which means both to 'annoy' and to 'win something to one's own advantage' (99). This practice is used most strongly in relation to cars, not least because Aborigines own very few of them (they are broadly shared across families) compared with white Australians. At the same time, the introduction of the car and road systems in Arnhem Land has, for Aborigines, 'opened up the possibility of fast and relatively cheap movement between scattered kin and between ceremonial centres', as well as enabling goods to be easily transported (100). So there is a dependence upon the car as a means of repossession of country, but a scarcity of resources with which to realise this potential. Gerrard then traces the means by which Aboriginal people 'humbug' whites in order to gain access to their cars: to win the car over to their advantage. He offers an example:

> Peter asks a European for a lift to his outstation but 'just remembers' once he's in the car, that he can't possibly go without picking up something from George's house; and once he's done this he remembers that he has to go to the store, so the car gets turned around; then he remembers that Toby ought to come too and that a visit to Toby's house is necessary, so that car gets turned around again. Toby, once he too has access to the driver and the vehicle, is likely to find errands of his own to multiply. (106)

Gerrard takes this as a typical account of Aboriginal car use: as a means of collecting other Aboriginal people which, in the process, disorients the white driver (until it seems as if his passengers are 'going nowhere'). In the process the driver loses his 'dubious claim to power', in Meaghan Morris's words: he is, to echo an earlier point I have made, 'possessed' by his passengers, 'won over' by them. Gerrard cites his own experiences:

> After first driving into this community, for many hours ... I was descended on by people wanting lifts, angry that I was too tired to stand, let alone drive. The next day I was asked to drive back along that road for five hours to 'drop' someone at a particular destination. One woman asked me if I would 'drop' her at her outstation every barge night, over two hours of hard road. Another asked me to get up at 5 a.m. to take her to the airport. People who borrowed the car, sometimes leaving me to do my work on foot, complained that I had not put enough petrol in it. A friend at the outstation radioed through constantly for me to pick him up on the spur of the moment, ignoring my own schedule and ignoring even the tide times of the open beach I had to drive along to reach him. (110)

The Aboriginal 'de-commoditisation' of the car lies in this causal disregard for white 'schedules' and white notions of distance and directions – for, *proper,* automobile behaviour. One might note that *Mad Max* with his uninterrupted relationship to his car never suffered from these kinds of problems! Gerrard's account thus works as a different kind of allegory: a *post*-colonial allegory. It places us in a context where a white Australian's relationship to his car (which could be re-expressed as: a white Australian's relationship to his *nation*) is liable to be interrupted time and again. And one of the effects of this mode of interruption, this 'humbugging', is precisely to remind those white Australians that they are not 'Aboriginal' with a capital 'A'.

Let me conclude this chapter by noting the serendipitous fact that the acronym of the Council for Aboriginal Reconciliation in Australia, established by the Labour Government in late 1991, is CAR. In a post-colonial nation trying to manage relations between indigenous people and white Australians, there is always a problem of *presence*: of whether one group has enough presence in relation to the other group, or too much, or too little. Can relations between these groups – which are fraught enough – ever properly be settled? Reconciliation is sometimes taken as an impossibility precisely because it promises a mutual settlement that never can be fully realised; it also implies the erasure of differences even as they continually and inevitably return to make their presence felt. The latter implication is often expressed through the kinds of narratives which imagine we could all be 'aboriginal'. But at the same time white Australians are increasingly nervous of Aboriginal 'demands' on resources and land, often regarding 'reconciliation' as a means through which Aborigines can gain power and presence at their expense. In this more negative context, Daniel Lavery's remarks from only a few years ago (which follow the car imagery through) seem optimistic: 'If the membership of the CAR seize the wheel and impose upon it an agenda approximating the demands that the indigenous peoples of Australia are making of the non-indigenous Australian society, then it could be the vehicle for achieving something ...' (Lavery, 1992, 8).

The above discussion has drawn attention to one local instance of 'demands' through Grayson Gerrard's article on the use of the car in Arnhem Land. The fortunes of CAR are also a kind of road narrative: they depend, and will continue to depend, on who is driving and who are the passengers, and in what ways relations between them are 'circumscribed', on the extent to which one might come to feel 'possessed' by the other, and on whether in the light of all this one is then able to move progressively towards a Day of Reconciliation (currently, but unsteadily, identified at some point during 2001) or whether one is ultimately 'going nowhere'.

Endnotes

Thanks to Dominic Pettman for assistance towards the preparation of this chapter.

[1] For a discussion of the 'phobic family' in a number of contemporary Australian films, including the *Mad Max* films, see Morris (1989). Morris convincingly argues that the always-

vulnerable family unit – for example, Max, his wife and his child – 'works as an allegorical displacement of larger historic (national) and geographic (continental) fears' (120).

[2] The *Mad Max* films are seen as 'quintessentially Australian' by Fiske et al (1987: 120). This is because they evoke a 'desire for mobility and the freedom associated with it' in the context of the 'vastness of the continent' (120).

Bibliography

Bropho, Robert (1990) 'The Great Journey of the Aboriginal Teenagers', eds Jack Davis et al (eds), *Paperbark*, University of Queensland Press, St Lucia.

Donaldson, Tamsin (1979) 'Translating Oral Literature: Aboriginal Song Texts', *Aboriginal History*, 3, 1: 62–83.

Edwards, Bill and Tjupuru, Jacky (1994) 'Mutuku Nyakunytja – Seeing a Motorcar: A Pitjantjatjara Text', *Aboriginal History*, 18, 2: 145–58.

Fiske, John, Hodge, Bob and Turner, Graeme (1987) *Myths of Oz*, Allen & Unwin, Sydney.

Gibson, Ross (1992), 'Yondering', *South of the West: Postcolonialism and the Narrative Construction of Australia*, Indiana University Press, Bloomington and Indianapolis.

Grayson, Gerrard (1989) 'Everyone Will Be Jealous For That Mutika', *Mankind*, 19, 2, 95 111.

Griffiths, Tom (1996) *Hunters and Collectors: The Antiquarian Imagination in Australia*, Cambridge University Press, Melbourne.

Lavery, Daniel (1992) 'The Council for Aboriginal Reconciliation: When the CAR Stops on Reconciliation Day Will Indigenous People Have Gone Anywhere?' *Aboriginal Law Bulletin*, 2, 58, 7–8.

Mickler, Steve (1992) 'Visions of Disorder: Aboriginal People and Youth Crime Reporting', *Cultural Studies*, 6, 3, 322–36.

Morris, Meaghan (1989) 'Fate and the Family Sedan', *East-West Film Journal*, 4, 1: pp 113–34.

Taussig, Michael (1992) 'An Australian Hero', *The Nervous System*, Routledge, New York and London.

Weller, Archie (1981) *The Day of the Dog*, Sydney, Allen & Unwin.

Williams, Sean (1994) 'Going Nowhere', Ken Gelder (ed.), *The Oxford Book of Australian Ghost Stories*, Oxford University Press, Melbourne.

Part Two

ENTERTAINMENT AND LEISURE

6

Poop, poop! – An Early Case of Joy-Riding by an Upper Class Amphibian

Kathleen Bell

So far as I can tell, no cultural critic or tabloid journalist has yet ascribed recent spates of joy-riding to the malign influence of a popular work of children's literature and its off-shoots.[1] Indeed, although borrowing and driving fast and expensive motor cars has become a more popular pastime, eventually requiring specific legislation to criminalize this activity,[2] parents have continued to permit their children to read and see dramatisations and adaptations of a classic tale[3] in which a joy-rider eludes the clutches of the law, aided and abetted by friends and acquaintances. The frequency with which the story has been subjected to new adaptations and continuations can point only to the attraction children and adults alike share in observing the prowess of a single, reckless amphibian.

Obviously it would be foolish to exaggerate the influence of Kenneth Grahame's *The Wind in the Willows*[4] on the generations of children who have read it or, more frequently, seen one of the numerous successful adaptations. However its interest in the motor car as the principle instrument of Toad's lawlessness may suggest ambivalence about cars felt not only by the author but also by readers and other audiences from 1908 to the present day. While Grahame's personal concerns about the effects of road-building are absent from the text, the anxieties he does express, clustered around cars, class and crime, persist.[5] This leads to occasional oddities: for instance the road-less Wild Wood with its proletarian inhabitants is presented as far more terrifying than the public highways which are the scene of Toad's manic driving. Nonetheless the motor car becomes a convenient focus for concerns about society, hierarchy and masculinity. These are perhaps demonstrated most clearly in Grahame's treatment of the law, which has formed one of the key areas of difficulty for adapters of the text. Adaptations tend either to deflect attention from Grahame's socio-political views by convenient adjustments to the text or to meet them head on and incorporate direct criticism of Edwardian social hierarchies.

The focus on the motor car in *The Wind in the Willows* seems to indicate a shift in popular anxieties about modes of transport. Mid nineteenth-century works had demonstrated all kinds of concern about the arrival of the railway,[6] as indicated in a wide range of works including Charles Dickens' *Dombey and Son*, Mrs Henry Wood's *East Lynne* and Emil Zola's *Le Baité Humaine*. However, by the end of the nineteenth century and the beginning of the twentieth, this anxiety was diminishing. In the 1892 story *Silver Blaze*, Holmes and Watson travelled happily 'in a first class carriage, flying along',[7] sufficiently secure in their chosen mode of transport to spend most of the journey discussing the case. By 1906, the train appears almost entirely as a force for good in E. Nesbit's *The Railway Children*. Here the by now stock danger of the railway crash can be averted by the simple expedient of turning two red flannel petticoats into flags (Nesbit, 1906, 95–108).

It is not surprising, therefore, that while railway transport is employed in *The Wind in the Willows*, it is one of the least adventurous modes of transport available. Admittedly the engine driver himself has a redeeming streak of lawlessness, regarding the police as enemies rather than friends, but the railway system itself is chiefly functional, the means by which conventional journeys are made, be it the slow train back to Toad Hall after Toad's first encounter with a motor car or the early train by which Toad makes his journey to town for the purpose of buying a car of his own. (Grahame, 1908, 28). Even in the original letters which were a major source for Grahame in writing *The Wind in the Willows*, the excitement the toad (not yet Toad) experiences in his escape by train is closely allied first to his delight at his imminent return home: 'soon they were puffing and rattling through the country, ever so fast, and the toad was jumping up and down with sheer delight, to think that soon he would be home again' (Grahame & Goodeson, 1988, 37), and then to the hot pursuit of policemen 'all brandishing revolvers' (39). It is worth noting that in neither the letters nor the book does Toad, passionate though he is about so many vehicles, ask to drive a railway engine. Only in relatively recent adaptations (notably Alan Bennett's) does the train become as attractive and exciting as the car. For the contemporary audience, of course, the car is no longer a modern danger but a 'veteran,' combined with the steam train to conjure up a nostalgic past.[8]

It is additionally evident from a close reading of *The Wind in the Willows* that many of the distinctive excitements of motor car travel would not be achieved by a train journey. Train drivers require expertise and Toad never claims that he can drive a train, although, in his own opinion, he is able to row a boat, steer a barge, ride a horse and drive a gypsy caravan. In Grahame's day driving remained a pastime permitted to amateurs; the driving test was not introduced until 1934, suggesting a belief on the part of legislators that anyone sufficiently wealthy to purchase a car or impressing an employer as able to drive and care for a vehicle, would have no difficulty in acquiring the necessary skills.

A class distinction may operate here. Railway travel, in Edwardian England as now, was a microcosm of the social hierarchies with travellers separated by income, rank and social role (and, if they wished, by gender). They were served by employees and could expect appropriate deference. The driver, although a vital employee, remained a servant of the railway company and thus of the passengers. By contrast, the motor car was the property of a single individual who would select its occupants and choose whether or not to be driven by a chauffeur. While members of the upper classes on a train journey depended on servants and fellow travellers for a position which reflected their social role, the driver of a motor car was cut off from society and the interactions and obligations which defined class position. Toad's car journeys are particularly suspect because they are solitary adventures in which he surrenders his class position to become 'Lord of the lone trail'.[9] In its solitariness, Toad's driving distinguishes itself from Toad's other social fads which lead him to interact with his friends.

The problem for adult readers of *The Wind in the Willows* at least is that while Toad is plainly condemned by his friends, he remains the most interesting and attractive character. In her book *Not in Front of the Grown-Ups: Subversive Children's Literature*,[10] Alison Lurie declares that Grahame's sympathies lie with Toad 'the motor-car snatcher, the prison-breaker, the Toad who always escapes!' While this may be true of Grahame's *sympathies*, for all his declared opposition to motoring, Lurie seems to tell us more about the way in which the book has most frequently been read than the expressed intentions within it. Such development of plot as there is depends on Toad's continued bad behaviour. However, the plot is a moral one, depending on Toad's reformation and consequent diminution for its closure. The embattled river-bankers are threatened not only by the revolutionary activities of the dangerous wild wooders but also by their own fantasies and desires for solitary travel. Even Mole's solitary adventures are punished as he finds himself at the mercy of the sinister Wild Wooders, and in need of the assistance of Rat and Badger.

Toad's desire for solitary motor-car travel is paralleled by Rat's desire for travel in the chapter 'Wayfarers All'. This chapter, with its heightened language which led to its inclusion in Arthur Quiller Couch's *Oxford Book of English Prose*, at first seems out of place beside the more ordinary language used to tell of Toad's adventures in particular. But in fact 'Wayfarers All' revisits a number of the themes that have already been touched on in *The Wind in the Willows* – nature's parallels with the human environment (especially in the passage about 'Nature's Grand Hotel' (Grahame, 1908, 112); the unsettling effects of change in the environment; the understanding nature of male friendship and, above all, the desire for travel as a means of self-expression which is at odds with social life and its obligations.

In this chapter Rat begins as the defender of home and its values, which is his function for most of the book. He tries to dissuade the swallows from flying south, only to hear the third swallow's account of the dangers of 'disobedience' to nature (Grahame, 1908, 115). For swallows, unrest is something natural that must be obeyed annually as they leave their 'snug homes' (114) and fly southwards to their 'happy holdiay' (115). This sets off Rat's own unrest as he begins to long for escape from 'the great ring of the Downs' which forms his 'simple horizon' (116) and to imagine the world beyond. His meeting with the Sea Rat exacerbates rat's mood of restlessness, even though the Sea Rat's tales do not exactly meet the Water Rat's desire to be 'out of sight of land' with his 'mind communing with the mighty ocean (116.). He ceases to function as an animal but acts mechanically (the word is used twice), 'like a 'sleep-walker' listening to an absent voice, shows 'dogged fixity of purpose' with eyes that are 'glazed and set' (125–6). He is, we are later told, 'under a spell', overcome by 'glamour', not just from the Sea Rat's tales but from 'haunting sea voices that had sung to him'.

While the narrative's acknowledged voice of temptation is that of the masculine, story-telling Sea Rat the 'haunting sea voices' casting their spell seem familiarly feminine, recalling the sirens that in the *Odyssey* lured sailors to their doom. Just as Odysseus had to be bound to the mast while his sailors stopped their ears if he was to listen to the sirens' song and pass unharmed, so Rat has to be saved from his desire for travel by the physical intervention of Mole who throws him to the ground until the fit passes, leaving him significantly prey to the semantically female reaction of 'an hysterical fit of dry sobbing'. The lure of solitary travel, in Rat's case at least, is both a desire for masculine adventure and, paradoxically, a feminine danger which would destroy the cosy masculine world Rat shares with his friends. Mole depicts autumn and winter in masculine terms, stressing size, strength and simplicity. His description of winter's 'hearty joys' which emphasises 'the towering wagons and their straining teams, the growing ricks, and the large moon rising over bare acres dotted with sheaves' (127) opposes as masculine view of nature to the foreign and feminine south of Rat's imagination with its 'purple islands of wine and spice, islands set low in languorous waters!' (117). The eventual cure for Rat is to be through his poetry, even if this is largely a matter of 'sucking the top of his pencil',[11] an activity which is sufficiently masculine to be contained within the River-Bankers' way of life.

To a considerable extent, Toad's adventures following his theft of the motor car provide a vulgar and lengthy parallel to Rat's sickness of longing and cure

72

by his friend in 'Wayfarers All'. After Toad's first encounter with the car he is found 'in a sort of trance', 'breathing short and staring into vacancy' and even 'spellbound'. The arrival of the car even induces hysteria, although this is ascribed to the bird rather than Toad (26–8). Toad's prolonged illness and recovery causes 'violent paroxysms' and 'painful seizures' which leave him 'apparently languid and depressed' (78), just as Rat's 'strange seizure' leaves him with a 'listless air' (126–7). If his recovery is slower that Rat's, this may be ascribed to his lack of 'manly' virtues; by contrast with his friends, he has characteristics which were, in turn of the century debates about women and politics, traditionally ascribed to women. Toad is vain about his dress to the point of absurdity,[12] superficial in his grasp of a series of 'fads', and clever rather than intelligent.[13] Badger's repetition of Toad's father's words – 'He's a good boy, but very light and volatile in character, and simply cannot hold his tongue.' – suggest general and formulaic descriptions of women. Within the text, therefore, one of the motor car's chief functions seems to be to bring Toad's feminine side into the open only so that it can, like the motor car, be dispensed with, reclaiming Toad for proper masculine values.

The motor car, however much it has since come to be seen as an attribute of masculinity, was in some ways highly appropriate for this identification with dangerous femininity. It had not yet attained the phallic shape of the racing cars of the 1930s and could be considered, like the bicycle, as a means by which women could attain independence. At a time when women were coming to the forefront of all kinds of movements for change, from suffrage societies to socialist groups, the car could be linked to an unstable and rapidly approaching future, as Toad put it:

> The poetry of motion! The *real* way to travel! The *only* way to travel!
> Here to-day – next week to-morrow! Villages skipped towns and cities
> jumped – always somebody else's horizon! O bliss! O poop-poop! O
> my! (Grahame, 1908, 26)

David Goodeson, in his introduction to the letters from which parts of *The Wind in the Willows* was drawn, finds it surprising that it was Constance Smedley, 'a feminist who drove a motor car' (Grahame & Goodeson 1988, 11), who first saw the potential of Grahame's letters and whose encouragement brought about the publication of the finished book. Perhaps the association of cars with a feminist played its part in the treatment of cars in Grahame's final anti-feminist and nostalgic version. In the letters 'the Toad', as he is initially called, is markedly different from Toad in the book. He appears abruptly, since the letters are a continuation from a series of bedtime stories told to Grahame's son Alastair, as someone who tricked his friends into believing that he had been taken prisoner by brigands. He is apparently 'a bad low animal' (22) whose main flaw is not his desire to drive motor cars but his insistence on stealing them. As the story told by the letters draws closer to the familiar published version of *The Wind in the Willows*, the emphasis remains on the evils of theft rather than the dangers of driving so that Rat advises the Toad:

> There's no need for you to steal motor cars; you've got lots of money; you can buy a beauty if you like. (93)

It was only as the stories found their way into print that the association of cars with femaleness, the future and danger became complete. In the published text, Toad does not only have to impersonate a woman in order to escape gaol. He is also reminded by Mole that dangerous driving takes him into a world of female authority, the hospital in which he is 'ordered about by female nurses' while the character of the bargee in the letters is transformed into the muscular barge-woman with her 'brawny arm' (Grahame, 1908, 130), enabling Rat to tell Toad that the culminating evidence of his folly is that he has been 'insulted, jeered at, and ignominiously flung into the water – by a woman, too!'

Toad's use of the motor car to jump into the future is in sharp contrast with the continuity represented by the masculine association of Rat, Mole and Badger whose values are associated both with the natural world and the endurance of a heroic, masculine past. It is not surprising that the threats posed by the Wild Wooders are set against the stability and permanence of Badger's home, which is associated with an epic past and the harmony and repetition of Nature's cyclical changes:

> It seemed a place where heroes could fitly feast after victory, where weary harvesters could line up in scores along the table and keep their Harvest Home with mirth and song, or where two or three friends of simple tastes could sit about as they pleased and eat and smoke and talk in comfort and contentment. (44)

Badger's home is linked with the past by more than the impression it gives his friends. It was built for an ancient human civilisation with predominantly masculine values, since its citizens were engaged in feasting, fighting, riding and trading (52). If this past society were not enough, the badgers represent a still greater stability and an older society, since they were there before the men and have remained after the men were gone. By contrast the Wild Wooders are later arrivals, whose appearance follows what is significantly termed 'ruin and levelling and disappearance.' The term 'levelling' may in part refer to the levelling of deserted human cities but it has also, Since the Levellers of the seventeenth century, been associated with what were, by the early twentieth century, termed socialist and communist movements. Later the invasion of Toad

Hall by the Wild Wooders is characterised as 'civil' war and 'a rising' (177), indicating, in the context of English history, that the capture of Toad Hall is to be seen as a revolutionary activity.

Grahame's beliefs, according to his biographer Peter Green, seem to have had a conservative tendency (perhaps influenced by reading of such events as the 1886 Pall Mall riots). It is probable that his attitudes were reinforced by the episode in which, as a senior official of the Bank of England, he was threatened by a deranged man with a gun claiming a socialist justification for his behaviour. Certainly, as critics have recognised, *The Wind in the Willows* demonstrates fear of the activities of the unruly lower orders. Peter Green goes so far as to suggest that Toad represents 'the landed *rentier* squandering his capital on riotous pleasures' and thus 'letting in the enemy' who are represented by the Wild Wooders, 'the stunted, malevolent proletariat of contemporary upper middle-class caricature'. (Green, 1982, 150)

It is hard to resist Green's analysis of Grahame's views. The weasels, ferrets and stoats of the Wild Wood, first encountered when Mole decides on a solitary journey, are inhabitants of a dangerous world with its own complicated set of primitive codes[14] resembling in part the common presentation of working-class industrial cities and dangerous parts of London itself.[15] But although the Wild Wooders are initially seen as lawless, towards the end of the book the law would seem to be on their side since the Chairman of the Bench has found Toad guilty and sentenced him to twenty years in gaol. While the River-bankers declare that this means 'there was no justice to be had in the land nowadays' (Grahame, 1908, 150), the Wild Wooders, in endorsing the sentence on Toad, are, briefly at least, on the side of law and order. Toad's return to Toad Hall is an illegal act which, despite the fantasy element of the story, Grahame works hard to justify. Although Edwardian children's books were beginning to move away from the original role of children's literature as a provision of moral instruction, adherence to an ethical framework was still expected.[16]

Of course, the fantasy element of the story is Grahame's biggest justification. *The Wind in the Willows* uses a variety of kinds of language, from the direct (which is that chiefly used in the letters to Alastair Grahame) to the self-consciously literary in vogue in the early years of the century. When Toad, for his three offences – 'first, of stealing a valuable motor car; secondly, of driving to the public danger; and thirdly, of gross impertinence to the rural police' (Grahame, 1908, 83) is sentenced to twenty years by a lightly parodied Justice of the Peace,[17] the language undergoes a sudden shift to one of exaggeratedly fake archaism, from the point at which: 'The brutal minions of the law fell upon the hapless Toad' to the conclusion of the chapter when Toad is 'a helpless prisoner in the remotest dungeon of the best-guarded keep of the stoutest castle in all the length and breadth of Merry England' (ibid. 84–5). The language here has undergone a shift, in part facilitating the further shift to the stylistically self-conscious chapter that follows, 'The Piper at the Gates of Dawn', but also transforming Toad's imprisonment into the language of children at play.

Grahame's earlier and highly successful children's book, *The Golden Age*, revelled in children's inaccurate parodies of the language of heroic, historical stories.[18] In *The Wind in the Willows* there is a similar use of faked and unlikely archaisms. The helmeted police sergeant exclaims 'Oddsbodikins!' and addresses the gaoler:

> Rouse thee, old loon, and take over from us this vile Toad, a criminal
> of deepest guilt and matchless artfulness and resource. Watch and
> ward him with all thy skill; and mark thee well, grey-beard, should
> aught untoward befall, thy old head shall answer for his – and a
> murrain on both of them! (Grahame, 1908, 85)

Not only is this passage marked by archaisms of language and syntax, it is also used with pleasure in its excesses predominating over concern for exact meaning. Terms like 'loon' and 'murrain' are present because they are as excessive as the policeman's threat to take the gaoler's life should Toad escape. We have moved away from legal reality into the realm of fantasy and play.

Besides moving Toad's punishment into the realms of fantasy, and thus separating it from the mild parody of his appearance in court, Grahame takes us further away from the moral/legal question of crime and punishment by destabilising Toad's identity and, most importantly, his size. The question of Toad's size has always been problematic for illustrators since he interacts with large animals and humans in a way in which no other character in the book does, being capable of driving a caravan and riding a horse as well as talking to humans more or less intelligently. In a sense, by the time he begins to drive a car, it could be said that he is aspiring above his station as an animal as well as failing to live up to his high position as the inheritor and owner of Toad Hall. His punishment is, of course, that people begin to perceive him as a mere animal. The gaoler's daughter sees Toad as an 'animal-friend', although she is too polite to use the word 'pets' (Grahame, 1908, 100) and thus, although Toad misunderstands the gulf between them, he is drawn into her game and dressed up in her aunt's clothes. It is plainly absurd that an amphibian should be gaoled under the English legal system and therefore his escape, as part of a child's game, is perfectly reasonable.

The pursuit by British policemen brandishing revolvers like characters in an early American film is a further child's game, but one in which the Toad has grown to human size. But he diminishes again, into a mere toad, when he identifies himself as such to the barge-woman. Looking closely at him, she sees him for what he is, 'A horrid, nasty, crawly Toad' (134) who can be picked up by a hind-leg and a fore-leg and tossed into the river. Importantly, she laughs at his deception just as she laughed at his failure to do her washing, establishing both her own, human superiority and the comedy of the literal toad passing himself off in human disguise.[19] Toad's size-shifting continues as he escapes from the consequences of his motor car adventure: immediately after the barge-woman's insults he becomes large enough to ride a horse, to trade with a gypsy and drive a car once again only to shrink into a 'fat animal' with short legs under the stress of renewed pursuit (144) until he falls into his natural habitat, the river, from which he can be rescued by the Water Rat.

But despite Grahame's emphasis on the fantasy and animal elements in Toad's story after his criminal escapade, his lawlessness remains sufficiently problematic for Grahame to introduce two further defences of Toad's illegal actions. In the first place 'custom and history' are called into account to sanction Toad's escape from gaol.[20] Secondly, the penultimate paragraph of the story deals with the provision of appropriate economic compensation for those who have assisted Toad and those whom he has wronged (177). The gaoler's daughter receives a gold chain and locket set with pearls, sent with a 'modest, grateful, and appreciative' letter; the engine-driver is 'properly thanked and compensated' while the barge-woman is repaid the monetary value of her horse. Toad, resident in Toad Hall once again, is now acting as the local squire performing his proper role in the social hierarchy by showing favour to his inferiors.

The appearance is of a society bound together by mutual goodwill and advantage in which loyalty to superiors (in this case involving disobedience to the law) is carefully, promptly and exactly rewarded. It might be identified as a bourgeois reformulation of feudalism in which the exact calculation of reward becomes the social glue by which the peasantry's successors are bound to the lord of the manor. The emphasis is not on acts of outstanding generosity but on rewards carefully calculated 'after due consultation with ... friends'. This exactness replaces the workings of justice by leaving the reader with a sense that reparation has been made. But the recipients of the reparation are carefully chosen and judged by their self-appointed superiors; the barge-woman is limited to the value of the horse Toad has stolen, since someone who 'couldn't tell a real gentlemen' does not merit a letter of apology or thanks. It is worth noting too that the recipients of Toad's compensation are all his social inferiors (leaving the animal/human dimension out of the equation). No compensation is offered to the victims of Toad's theft, the owners of the motor car, who are presumably Toad's social equals. Nor is the rural policeman to whom Toad was so rude or the gaoler from whose custody Toad fled granted an apology. Toad has returned to a world in which the state and its laws are replaced by the forces of history as continuum and custom as sustainer of social hierarchies.

Not surprisingly, the problems raised by questions of legality and class have evidently troubled later adapters of *The Wind in the Willows*. A.A. Milne in the play *Toad of Toad Hall*, deals with the problem of legality by making it clear that the trial is rigged; the trial is shifted from the magistrate's court to what is presumably an assize court in which a weasel disguised as a rabbit becomes foreman of the jury, terrorising the other jurors into endorsing his verdict of guilty. By allowing us to see the law as fallible because of the intimidation of jurors, the question of Toad's guilt becomes less problematic.

Willis Hall's adaptation, premiered at Plymouth's Theatre Royal in 1986 prior to a national tour, is notionally derived from Grahame but seems to take Milne's trial scene as the starting point for its own presentation of the trial of Toad. Hall's text seems at times troubled by the class basis of Grahame's book and is unsure of how to deal with it. Toad's role as lord of the manor may have been cleverly undermined by the casting of Terry Scott as Toad but the comic butler still betrays his class origins by dropped aspirates. The play's concern is particularly associated with Toad's trial for theft, dangerous driving and impertinence to a police officer. Badger's Act I song 'Taken in Hand', unlike Grahame's book, places legal justice above social hierarchies:

> An amphibian's accountable like him or me or you,
> For his social class I couldn't give a hoot,
> He's not above the law because he's got a bob or two,
> Be he frog or be he Toad or be he newt! (Hall, 1986, 19)

Nonetheless, when the trial begins, Badger appears as Toad's counsel for the defence, making an affecting plea in mitigation:

> He wouldn't dream of going on to the river without a bag of breadcrumbs for the ducks m'lord, ... One winter, may it please the court, he took a fieldmouse with a broken paw into Toad Hall and kept it safe and snug until the spring ... (38)

This, like the appearance of Rat and Mole as character witnesses for the defence, has the effect of moving the focus of the scene away from the strictly criminal to the audience's enjoyment of Toad's character. However, with a jury of Wild Wooders the verdict is never in doubt and the trial is even further removed from any idea of legal justice by the rather hackneyed comedy of a deaf judge.

Alan Bennett, whose reworking of the play is altogether more sophisticated and thoughtful both in its relation to the original and in its re-readings of history and Englishness,[21] returns to Grahame's original for his trial scene and sets it in a magistrate's court. The offence, however, is the 1968 crime of 'taking and driving away' (Bennett, 1991, 77). Like Hall, Bennett seems concerned lest social class should seem to triumph over the action of the law. However, unlike Hall and Milne, Bennet dispenses with the idea that the trial is rigged by the Wild Wooders, choosing instead to demonstrate a legal system that is fundamentally flawed by class alliances.

While the Wild Wooders in Bennett's version have ceased to be working class[22] and are transformed into 'property speculators and estate agents, spivs and ex-bovver-boys', they remain enemies of the process of law. Ferrets, stoats and weasels attempt to secure Toad's conviction by giving false evidence but the magistrate's class prejudice in Toad's favour is far stronger than their lies. The magistrate points out that Toad 'is a member of the middle classes and has a charming home' and that he 'doesn't have to do his own washing up'. Angling for an invitation to Toad Hall, the magistrate initially proposes that Toad simply be bound over to keep the peace on condition that he does not go near a car again. It is Toad's outburst in response that assures his conviction; he is sentenced to twelve months in gaol for car theft and twenty years for calling the magistrate 'Big Nose'. The conviction is, however, quashed after Toad's escape when the magistrate and constable visit Toad Hall where Toad is holding a garden fête. But while Bennett may be demonstrating an injustice in the operation of the law it is lost in the audience's sympathy for Toad and the carnival of the conclusion.

By contrast, Jan Needle's 1981 children's book *Wild Wood*, shows no more than a passing interest in the trial of Toad. The court scene that other adapters have found so useful is totally omitted. There is simply a reference to Toad's excessive conceit, which prevents him from hiring a barrister or using his wealth to influence the course of the trial and the consequent rejoicing of the Wild Wooders 'that at last and for once justice had been done'. Needle's attempt to counter Grahame's conservatism by ascribing a radical agenda to the Wild Wooders effectively prevents an attack on the justice system (except by vague generalisations) since, in Toad's imprisonment, justice is seen to be done. Instead justice comes into question only when the revolutionary Wild Wooders have turned Toad Hall into Brotherhood Hall and begin to attempt the redistribution of Toad's wealth:

> To us it might seem only justice, and a fine thing indeed to take and share out all the things that Toad had kept from us for so long, but to our parents and others it looked like a plain act of stealing. (Needle, 1981, 144)

Needle's narrator, Baxter Ferret, is a useful counter to Grahame's conservatism since he is presented as a great admirer of motor cars who can both appreciate Toad's Armstrong Hardcastle Morton Special and became its victim, twice losing his job because of Toad's insistence on driving his favourite make of car. The description of Toad's driving in Baxter's narrative has to convince the reader that Toad is not a loveable amphibian but an arrogant dangerous driver as in this description of his collision with the farmer's Squeezer, which Baxter is driving:

> A screaming engine, squealing brakes, a raucous, lunatic poop-pooping
> of a horn. The car hit the lorry at the front, tore off the starting handle,
> the radiator and one mudguard, bounced across the road like a rubber
> ball, glanced off a tree, skeetered back to the centre again – and
> disappeared into the night. (51)

Baxter's account is not, however, an attack on the awfulness of motor vehicles; the absurd sound 'poop-poop' is not identified as the sound of the car (as in Grahame) but linked instead with both the horn and Toad's lunacy. In *Wild Wood*, as in *The Wind in the Willows*, the car seems at times to become the symbol of a rapidly advancing future, understood by some members of the Wild Wood proletariat but dangerous in the hands of the rural upper classes. Significantly, O.B., the revisionist weasel who ultimately assists Toad's escape from gaol, can see only the dangers of drivers. Although parallels with industry are not elaborated, Baxter's dismissal from his second job, as Toad's mechanic, echoes the socialist description of capitalist work practice by which workers are made redundant as soon as they have served their economic purpose.[23]

What Needle's book wittily (and not over-seriously) suggests is that the car can become a useful if incomplete symbol for industrial processes, owned often by the wealthy who do no work but understood, maintained and appreciated by the proletariat. Toad driving his motor car has a role similar to the controlling shareholder in a company who can operate it for his own pleasure regardless of the interests of the employees responsible for its day-to-day running. Of course, these views and the whole of Needle's book seem dated in the post-Thatcher era. Needle's Wild Wooders are predominantly male real ale drinkers with an interest in the finer points of Marxism. Their revolutionary interests have been replaced in the popular consciousness by feminist, anti-racist and ecological concerns and talk of a red–green alliance. Boddington Stoat, Baxter Ferret and their friends would be as out of place in today's left as they would in Tony Blair's New Labour Party.

Nonetheless, of all the recent adaptations, Jan Needle's might offer the reading of *The Wind in the Willows*, which would be most recognizable to Grahame himself. Both view the motor car as the focus of change and the Wild

Wooders as its harbingers. The 'respectful swinging of caps and touching of forelocks' (Grahame, 1908, 51) which Grahame sees as an important outward manifestation of a properly ordered society becomes in Needle's text a compulsory obeisance rightly resented by the smaller woodland animals. And both texts see in Toad's victory as an alternative future successfully averted. In *Wild Wood* the revolutionary attempt is ended, forcing Boddington to flee north with Baxter's sister to found a brewery and continue his revolutionary work. Meanwhile, in *The Wind in the Willows*, an altered Toad gives up his vanity and his motor cars and takes back the high position in the social hierarchy that was occupied by his father before him. The Wild Wood is 'now successfully tamed' by Toad and his friends and the hierarchy restored so that it was, in Grahame's words, 'pleasing to see how respectfully they were greeted by the inhabitants' (Grahame, 1908, 177–8).

Endnotes

[1] Nonetheless, readers looking to chart Dangerous effects of popular culture might wish to note that Alan Bennett's adaptation of *The Wind in the Willows* was premiered at the National Theatre on 12 December 1990. Shortly after, public concern about 'joy-riding' had reached such a peak that new legislation was required to punish it. The Aggravated Vehicle Taking Act was passed into law in early 1992, taking effect from 1 April that year.

[2] Simply taking and driving away a motor vehicle was not an offence under the law until 1968. Previous definitions of larceny, both under common law and under clarifying enactments required an intent 'permanently to deprive' so that merely 'borrowing' a car was not a criminal act. The borrower could, however, be charged with the theft of petrol used in driving the car.

[3] Description on the back of a book-jacket of the Wordsworth edition, 1993.

[4] First published in 1908, page references to 1993 Wordsworth edition (Ware, Hertfordshire).

[5] For instance, while the effects of careless driving by inebriated business men may be quite as drastic as joy-riding by working-class teenagers, public anxieties about the latter are far more developed.

[6] I was alerted to this anxiety by a paper given by Laura Marcus at the 1996 conference *Murder in Bloomsbury!*

[7] In Arthur Conan Doyle (1994), *The Memoirs of Sherlock Holmes*, World's Classics, Oxford.

[8] The train driver in Benett is, however, a modern-day campaigner, declaring 'Railways not roads is my motto' (Bennett, 1991, 51).

[9] Ibid. 83.

[10] Lurie (1990), 25.

[11] Readers acquainted with Freud may wish to offer their own gloss on this phrase.

[12] As demonstrated in the description of Toad dressed for motoring on p. 74.

[13] In his introduction to his adaptation of *The Wind in the Willows*, Alan Bennett suggests that Grahame's characterisation of Toad is based on 'all the faults that genteel Edwardian anti-Semitism attributed to *nouveaux-riches* Jews (Bennett, 1991,xix). While I lack the space

to discuss Bennett's argument in any great detail, it may be helpful to point out that male Jews were often described in popular texts as suspect in part because insufficiently masculine.

[14] These are based on 'pass-words, and signs, and sayings which have power and effect, and plants you carry in your pocket, and verses you repeat, and dodges and tricks you practise' (Grahame, 1908, 36), and suggest simultaneously a primitive society and an epic society, since the plant in the pocket seems to refer to Odysseus' use of herb moly.

[15] The presentation of working-class areas as dangerous and criminal *terrae incognitae* can be found as early as Benjamin Disraeli's *Sybil*, and is considered in detail in Judith Walkowitz, *City of Dreadful Delight*. The idea is continued, belatedly, in the Toff boos of John Creasey.

[16] The moralising element is much stronger in the letters to Alastair Grahame, which include explicit instruction, such as 'Let it be a lesson to us, not to be so puffed up and conceited as the proud Toad' (Grahame & Goodson, 1988, 68).

[17] The sentence is, of course, well in excess of any that could be given by a magistrate's court.

[18] For example, in the narrator's account of a children's game of Knights of the Round Table: 'Once more the lists were dight in Camelot, and all was gay with shimmer of silk and gold; the earth shook with thunder of hooves, ash-staves flew in splinters, and the firmament range to the clash of sword on helm (Grahame, 1895, 31).

[19] Grahame's work is plainly inconsistent here as elswhere. As a human the barge woman is above Toad in the hierarchy and therefore entitled to laugh at him. Nonetheless, disregarding the hierarchy of species, in social terms 9as working-class woman) she is his inferior and therefore her laughter marks Toad's shame.

[20] According to Rat, Mole and Badger defend Toad by arguing 'from history … They said that no criminal laws had ever been known to prevail against cheek and plausibility such as yours, combined with the power of a long purse (Grahame, 1908, 150).

[21] For instance, Toad's feigned illness includes a parody of the conclusion of Ibsen's *Ghosts* in Toad's lines: 'I want the sun. Give me the sun, Ratty, give me the sun.' – lines which not unnaturally spur Rat's departure in search of medical assistance. Toad's conviction also carries echoes of the conviction of Grahame's fellow *Yellow Book* contributor Oscar Wilde with Badger taking the role of Robbie Ross and raising his hat to the condemnd Toad,

[22] Bennett, like Green, reads Grahame's Wild Wooders as representatives of 'the threat to property posed by the militant proletriat' (Bennett, 1991, xvi).

[23] A parallel can be found in Robert Tressell's *The Ragged Trousered Philanthropists*, written at much the same time as *The Wind in the Willows* although published later, in Owen's account of 'The Great Money Trick' (Tressel [1955], chap. 21, 202–16).

Bibliography

Bennett, Alan (1991) *The Wind in the Willows Adapted for the Stage*, Faber and Faber London.

Dickens, Charles (1995) *Dombey and Son*, Wordsworth Editions Ltd, Ware, Herts.

Doyle, Arthur Conan (1994) *Memoirs of Sherlock Holmes*, World's Classics, Oxford.

Grahame, Kenneth (1995) *The Golden Age*, Wordsworth Edition Ltd, Ware, Herts.

Grahame, Kenneth (1993) *The Wind in the Willows*, Wordsworth Editions Ltd, Ware, Herts.

Grahame, Kenneth (introduced by David Goodson) (1988) *My Dearest Mouse: 'The Wind in the Willows' Letters*, Pavilion/Michael Joseph, London.

Green, Peter (1982 – abridged from 1959 edition) *Beyond the Wild Wood – Kenneth Grahame author of The Wind in the Willows*, Webb and Bower, Exeter.

Hall, Willis (1986) *The Wind in the Willows – A Musical*, Samuel French Ltd, London.

Horwood, William (1993) *The Willows in Winter*, Harper Collins, London.

Lurie, Alison (1991 edition – first published 1990) *Not in Front of the Grown-Ups: Subversive Children's Literature*, Sphere Books Ltd, London.

Milne, A.A. (1929) *Toad of Toad's Hall*, Methuen and Co. Ltd, London.

Needle, Jan (1981) *Wild Wood*, André Deutsch, London.

Nesbit Edith, (1975 – first published 1906) *The Railway Children*, Bodley Head, London.

Townsend, John Rowe (1990 – first published 1965) *Written for Children*, Bodley Head, London.

Tressel, Robert (1993 – 1955 edition) *The Ragged Trousered Philanthropists*, Flamingo/HarperCollins, London.

Walkowitz, Judith (1992) *City of Dreadful Delight: Narratives of Sexual Danger in Late Victorian London*, Virago, London.

7

Automania: Animated Automobiles
1950 –1968

Paul Wells

The Oldsmobile can properly be called the first motorised vehicle to really replace the horse and buggy as a popular medium of transportation in American society. It was also one of the first cars featured in an animated advertisement.[1] Simple and affordable, the car still spoke to the folk culture of America while at the same time embodying the progressive spirit of the industrial age. The early pioneers of car-automation in the United States were essentially machinists, toolworkers, mechanics – people struggling with a new medium, not merely in engineering, but of creative expression. In many senses, this echoed the rise of the cinematic apparatus, and the emerging tension between perfecting the mechanism by which progress could be achieved, and monitoring its discernable outcomes and effects. The car harnessed the internal combustion engine to a chassis for passengers; one small step for automotive history, one giant leap for social change. The cinema, in the first instance, erred towards the persuasive novelty of merely recording 'reality'; a documentary tendency that coincidentally monitored the impact of the machine upon mass culture, for example, in Edison's *Automobile Parade* (1905). It was not long before both the car and the camera became subordinated to the twin principles of twentieth century socialisation – used as tools to *reflect and sublimate repressed desires* while encouraging *material consumption and the demands of commerce*. It is at this juncture that the animated film enters the equation, offering insights about the codes and conditions by which the car articulates its culture.

Arguably, live-action cinema offers similar perspectives. Certainly, silent cinema was especially reliant on chases and crashes, and the wholesale destruction of numerous Model T Fords, and hardly could not provide some commentary on American mores.[2] For my purposes here, though, I wish to suggest that animation offers a unique cinematic vocabulary which directly echoes the capabilities and mythic properties of the car. The medium's capacity to represent figurative *and* abstract representational forms, and to extend into non-linear, non-objective, sometimes irrational modes of expression,[3] and thus, literally achieve anything, directly reflected the *projected* potential of the car in terms of speed, adaptability and style, and most specifically, in the ways that it can express and embody dimensions of the human condition unavailable in other cultural forms. Early American cartoons wrestled with the very principles of automated movement, and as Donald Grafton has suggested, are 'comprehensible as images of the turn-of-the-century fascination with self-propulsion' (Grafton, 1993, 32) The principle of 'movement for movement's sake' carried with it an almost spiritual and creative zeal and was clearly common to those working within the new automotive industries and the animation studios.

As early as 1927, Walt Disney had produced *Alice's Auto Race*, a part-live action cartoon, and *The Mechanical Cow*, an Oswald the Lucky Rabbit short – key films in Disney's pre-industrial development, and crucial in the understanding of the increasing impact of *mechanism* itself upon previously simple, normally rural agendas in cartoons. In 1928, *Plane Crazy* finds Mickey Mouse aping pioneer aviator, Charles Lindbergh, while in 1931 he drives an out-of-control taxi in *Traffic Troubles. Building a Building* (1933) and *The Mechanical Man* (1933) also provide further examples of the continuing engagement with the impact of modernity upon everyday cultures of behaviour and expectation.[4] Mickey and his friends become embroiled in a brave new world best epitomised by the developing role of the motor car and the concordant expansion of the city and urban society. Clearly, such shorts reveal that 'humankind', embodied in Disney's anthropomorphism creatures, were ill-equipped to deal with machines.

While such narratives were constructed primarily in the service of creating comic sequences, I wish to suggest that comedy *per se* is a vehicle by which anxiety is dealt with and expressed, and within the animated film works in a way which demonstrates uninhibited models of wish fulfilment and projection. Consequently, Disney's cartoons essentially provide a commentary upon the potential alienatory effects of a newly mechanised society, a theme made explicit in shorts made directly about the automobile by Disney, MGM and Hanna Barbera, in the 1950s and 1960s, which I will address later in this essay. The underlying concern in the *early* shorts is the fear that the individual will not be able to accommodate social change, nor ultimately, be able to cope with the idea that the individual might be subjugated *by* the demands of the industrial mechanism and *to* the inherent conformism of the social paradigm it seemed to create. Perhaps in recognition of this concern, it very quickly became necessary to ally the modernist conception of *function as beauty* to the idea that the car offered greater aesthetic and cultural compensations, and the zenith of this preoccupation, both in the United States car industry and the animation studios was the 1950s.

If the 1930s had been characterised by resilience in the face of economic hardships of the Depression, and the 1940s were inevitably informed by the effect of the necessary sacrifices in the light of the war, the 1950s were effectively the growth period for consumer goods, especially in response to the re-consolidation of the middle-class family, and the rise of youth markets. For the first time since the heyday of the car as the chief symbol of commerce and culture in the 1920s and 1930s, the motor vehicle found prominence as an icon of progress and profit. Immediately after the war, the 'big three' – General Motors, Ford and Chrysler – re-cycled standard models to meet high consumer demand merely in need of transportation. Inevitably, though, it was not long before *style* was once more the key factor in appealing to new buyers; indeed, styling became the determining agenda in the development of car culture in the United States.[5] People even went to observe new stylings in showrooms even if they had little intention of buying.

Perceiving that the public were ready to engage with the car as the mediator of escapist fantasy or entertainment in the same way as television or popular magazines, General Motors initiated the spectacle of the Motorama shows, which featured theatrical performances and the 'Dream cars' of long-time styling guru, Harley Earl.[6] Ironically, Earl created his Dream cars to substantiate and sustain the kinds of feelings he felt were *stimulated* but largely remained *unfulfilled* by Hollywood movies. His cars – essentially, a fairly unsubtle form of production propaganda – were materially 'real', if often commercially untenable as a production model. He, and his fellow designers, made cars which appealed to taste rather than the reassurance of function, and which, therefore, were characterised by almost science-fictional, quasi-aeronautic trappings of tail-fins, chrome-styling, rocket-like bodies and high colour aesthetics.[7] Such excess was inevitably grist to the cartoonal imagination of Tex Avery at MGM. Already acknowledged as one of the greatest animators at 'Termite Terrace' at Warner Brothers, Avery's parodic, joke-making visual style offers a critique of the illusory promise of the over-styled, over-determined automobiles of the period.

In *Car of Tomorrow* (1951), Avery in true Motorama fashion, provides a 'preview of things to come' and embarks upon a series of 'spot-gags' which are essentially visual jokes parodying Earl's design tendencies towards longer, wider, lower, sleeker, highly decorated vehicles, which in themselves sought to encapsulate motion even when static. Avery's principle target was Earl's dream car, Le Sabre, named and partially styled after the F-86 Le Sabre fighter jet, which David Gartman notes, was characterised by state-of-the-art conveniences:

Built in power jacks removed labor from changing a flat tire and the convertible top automatically closed when raindrops struck the central console. All this and more equipment was controlled from a dashboard that was a gadgeteer's delight, containing sixty-three separate switches, buttons and indicators. (Gartman, 1994, 160)

When the principle subject of a possible joke is already informed by excess 'exaggeration' in itself, then over-statement as a comic device is often made redundant. Avery, however, was a pioneer of highly extended jokes in the cartoon, taking cliff-top falls and chases to new extremes of speed and sometimes, surreal incongruity. Avery's knowledge of the animated film enabled him to extend and develop its language. Central to his approach was an anti-Disney spirit, which was fundamentally adult in outlook, and often satiric in nature. Avery sought to poke fun at human foibles, but unusually for the cartoon, and certainly alien to the Disney ethos, his preoccupations were those concerning sex and sexuality, status, power, and personal paranoia. In 1950s car design, Avery, if you'll excuse the pun, found the perfect vehicle by which to play out his cartoonal aesthetics and cultural concerns.

Parodying the sleek symmetries of some models where the hood was similar in design to the trunk, Avery suggests that car culture did not know whether it was coming or going, and presents a car shuffling sideways, an apt metaphor for an industry suddenly concerned with the superficialities of 'look' rather then genuine automotive progress. The trend towards wider cars is satirised by an interior drawn with deep perspective to illustrate a front-seat accommodating a number of passengers. Avery then reveals how this alters the shape of a car, effectively converting it into the winged chassis of an aircraft – his most direct reference to car culture's affectation of aeronautical tropes. Literal gags follow in which 'step-down' models have hidden lift-shafts, 'bugs' (insects) are found in the motor, and 'deep, soft cushions' completely consume the passenger. Quick to conflate related conceptual ideas (a mode of *condensation*, a narrational strategy I discuss elsewhere[8]), Avery then mixes the conventions of the catwalk, the perceived gender of the car as 'feminine',[9] and the anticipated material aspects of the middle class home,[10] into a car design he cites as a 'Paris Creation'. In 'Seychelle pink', the car appeals to women in the new suburbia, with its Louis IV criss-cross curtains. Its 'fender panties' are gathered white lace, the front grill reveals a 'plunging neckline' while the rear end has a 'flattering bustle effect'. The design is offset with potted Peruvian poppies. Avery effectively targets the absurd lengths car manufacturers will go to reach certain markets – markets created and maintained by the promise of material pleasures articulated through the ideologically charged concepts of 'family' and 'home'.

Avery locates his satire in the way that status is measured through middle class values and the new (albeit sexualised) femininity of post-war 'monism'. From a contemporary perspective, it is clear that this 'sexism' was part of a regressive strategy after the war to re-locate women back into domestic roles after their previous freedoms and functions during the conflict. Arguably, though, the reassertion of the role of the automobile in the United States, however, is both a reassertion of masculinity, and also a compensatory recognition of the emergent status of women. Avery's imagery in the 'Paris Creation', and later jibes at the mother-in-law and the indecisiveness of women drivers, is an ambivalent acknowledgement of this position.

Clearly, too, such imagery uses cultural stereotypes that inform quick, easily constructed, visual jokes. Avery, for example, illustrates a 'convertible' by showing how a vehicle transforms into an Indian tee-pee; a 'roadster' is actually a chinaman pulling a Coulee; while a 'super-thrifty Scotchman model' is a Scotsman on a bike. Avery is at his sharpest, though, when satirising the automotive industry's promotion of accessories. For example, highlighting that the industry is only concerned with speed and style, and not safety, Avery invents the glass-bottomed car, so after knocking down a pedestrian, you can 'look down and see if he was a friend of yours'. Adjustable seats are available to automatically draw a couple together for 'that bashful date'; an autoshaver is also present for drivers who are late and need to shave on the way to the office. A bumpy road results in the severance of the driver's head. These darker edged jokes reveal the inherent anxieties of motoring in the modern world, and significantly inform Avery's principle satiric point that the (blue collar) driver is being commercially exploited. The film's final image shows a car costing $545 costs $8432.69 with accessories. Self-evidently, such accessories ultimately re-define the motorist's *identity*, and seduce the new consumer by fulfilling desire rather than guaranteeing safety.

As Julian Stallabrass has noted, however, 'identities are fluid in the matter of driving but this is not based on *subjectivity* but on pure *activity*' (Stallabrass, 1996, 121–2, my italics). Avery clearly plays this out by using the fluidity and dynamism of animation itself to address the subject through the excesses of car design culture, with explicit function allied to the implied *mythos* of activity. Disney, on the other hand – some would say, inevitably – uses its animation style to address the subject and subjectivity by creating narratives looking at social conduct and moral dilemmas. *Motor Mania* (1950), made by Jack Kinney, like *Car of Tomorrow* seizes upon the post-war auto-boom, only to warn that 'the motor car in the hands of the average man is facing extinction'. Far from extolling the virtue of the car at the moment when it was subject to some of its most profound social prominence and commercial exploitation, this short concentrates upon the driver. In this instance, this turns out to be a highly re-constructed Goofy, stalwart of many Mickey Mouse cartoons, and Kinney's exemplary 1940s *How to ...* series in which Goofy is featured as a gullible oaf falling foul of sporting etiquette, rules and regulations, and equipment for slapstick effects. In the 1950s, Goofy plays a typical 'Mr Suburbia', but Flora O'Brien cites some unease at his role in *Motor Mania:*

> Is it too much to suggest that ... Goofy is hinting at a darker side to the American dream? If suburban man feels trapped in a conformist lifestyle, he may struggle comically in its grasp. But may he not also feel a destructive rage, an invisible urge to break through the barriers of inhibition? (O'Brien, 1985, 54)

O'Brien's anxiety partly comes out of an inability to accept that the previously amicable and wholly innocent Goofy may be the mediator of complexity in the cartoon, and further, a bleaker, more sinister view of American culture, than he, and for that matter Disney usually offer. The real concern of the cartoon, though, is the automobile as the arbitrator of urban power relations, and in broader terms, how this fits within Disney's ideological stance about the individual's response to the democratic ethos in American society. If Avery locates the individual as a function of American capitalism, Disney still sees 'individuality' (ironically) as wholly determined by social responsibility. Goofy plays the archetypal good citizen, 'Mr Walker', who when driving becomes 'an uncontrollable monster, a demon driver' – 'Mr Wheeler' – who abuses other motorists and road users, claiming 'I own the road'. The issue of ownership is inevitably bound up with aspects of control, and intrinsically relates to Disney's preoccupation with social order and the consequences of transgression.[11] Here 'Mr Walker' is arguably the American super-ego trying to come to terms with the American id, 'Mr Wheeler' as it is mediated through the ego-object of the the car and its environment.

Mr Wheeler puts the roof down on his car, and puts his hat down in a similar gesture, which echoes the action of the roof (a man at one with his car), puts on some music, and slows down. He becomes a 'road hog'. The animation here, unlike Avery's speed and pace, stresses the control of time and space through slow motion. In a similar narrational premise to Avery's, however, *Motor Mania* plays out 'spot-gags' as examples of Wheeler's increasingly poor road practices. At traffic lights, he prepares to race other motorists, only to crash into the lights themselves. He deliberately soaks a pedestrian by driving through a puddle, only to be similarly soaked by another driver. Where Avery's drivers employed an expanded bumper to make sure that they hit pedestrians, Goofy's car is equipped with a gunsight as a hood-ornament. Like a World War Two pilot, he stamps a victory sign on the side of his vehicle. The newspaper reports 'Accidents Increase', and the voiceover, a significant quasi-documentary device in determining the ideological authority of the film, suggests that Goofy, at once a model citizen and a pathological miscreant, embodies the lack of empathy between the motorist and the pedestrian.

Only by fostering sensitivity and understanding, it is implied, can road users create a car culture, which is not merely safe but *civilised*. In other words, Disney seeks to recall the 'humanity' back to the subject, and the sense of order to 'activity', an aspect that the language of animation almost in itself refutes. Disney presses home the moral lesson, though, by using emphatic means to punish transgressors. Mr Wheeler inevitably crashes; 'You've broken your toy' stresses the authoritarian voiceover, castigating the apparently childish attitude, which characterises Goofy's behaviour. It concludes by saying, 'Let this be a lesson, Mr Wheeler, drive safely, give the other fellow a break...', but surprisingly, is interrupted by Goofy directly addressing the implied camera, and saying 'Shut up!'. Little wonder that O'Brien feels unease. Disney heightens the idea of a 'moral panic' by dehumanising one of its most amiable and appealing characters. The implication is that by being a *selfish* motorist, seduced by the empowerment, status, and pleasure offered by the car, Goofy, a ready symbol for Americans, is no longer capable of the 'populist' notions of good neighbourliness, honour and duty so necessary to the possible fulfilment of a dream of suburban utopia.

Alternatively, and more radically, (and evidently feared by O'Brien), Goofy's actions become a model of resistance to the ways in which, as Stallabrass suggests, 'the modern car becomes the expression of the mass-produced personality' (Stallabrass, 1996, 128). Here the car is a symbol for a model of 'individuality' which stands outside social order, and Avery's economic constraints, and legitimises indeterminate social freedoms. Animation, arguably an unregulated, perhaps *unregulatable* language of expression, actually illustrates these freedoms. One might suggest that however ideologically determined an animated film is thought to be in its construction, its very language legitimises a 'leakage' of alternative meanings. The cartoonal 'jokes' created by Avery and Kinney in their cartoons reveal a complex discourse in which the car is half-revered, half-feared, but perhaps, more importantly, imply an underlying anxiety which informs the way that the car necessarily offers fantasy, escapism, or plainly, liberation, from an increasing sense of social imposition and jurisdiction.

The Disney studios embarked on a series of motor-linked animations from 1957 through to 1965, which sought in earnest to educate the American motorist. *The Story of Anyburg, U.S.A.* (1957) creates a courtroom drama in which the car is actually on trial for its misdemeanours on American roads. Anthropomorphised cars are interrogated and chastised by an angular, brutal prosecutor, who lists accidents, fuel consumption, pollution, speeding, and mass production as the ills of contemporary driving. Half-aping the minimalist UPA (United Productions of America) style, and using rhyming couplets as a narrative tool, the film once more emphasises the impact of the car on 'a great, enlightened and *civilised* country' (my italics), and stresses 'homicide on the highways was increasing at a startling rate'.

The use of the word 'homicide' is crucial, and perhaps a little surprising, in the sense that it sees the actions of the car/motorist as in some way 'murderous', and not far short of deliberate. The 'Tin Lizzy', the Sports Car, and the 'Wreck' are all brought to the witness stand as evidence for the demise of motor culture, yet the scientists, engineers and town planners are all absolved of any responsibility, the film stressing the positive effects these people have had upon the progress of motor culture as 'helpmates' to the car.[12] Sirus P. Sliderule, of the Bureau of Highways, has built super-highways and produced helpful signs, but the car has wilfully abused them. The prosecutor recommends that the automobile must be banned, but the defence lawyer coolly rounds on his opponent, and in a way that animation proves most effective shows that by absenting the car from the very scenarios the prosecutor highlights, what one is left with is 'the speeding man'. The motorist is accused of causing accidents, being drunk, and always likely to endanger himself and others, and actually be the cause of death. Though 'the car' is acquitted, and the motorists temporarily bring 'safety and sanity' to the roads, car culture once more collapses into inevitable excess and transgression. Even the quasi-utopian Disney outlook cannot reconcile the likelihood of this occurring, nor resolve humankind's seemingly inevitable drive towards self-destruction; a death wish played out in the *fantasy* of the car.

I might usefully conclude by indicating that Disney continued its project to educate the motorist in Les Clark's *Freewayphobia: The Art of Driving the Super-Highway* (1965) and *Goofy's Freeway Troubles* (1965), schematic narratives seeking to teach drivers safe practice in a good humoured way. The former features the characters of Driverous Timidicus (the over-cautious driver), the Motoramus Fidgetus (the impatient driver) and Neglecturus Maximus (the inattentive driver), who are articulated as more detailed versions of 'Mr Wheeler', and perpetually cause accidents. Inevitably, these shorts reflect the change in American auto-culture, and show the implications of the shift from the excess of styling in the 1950s to the excess of horsepower in the 1960s. In appealing to an increasingly irrational marketplace, the 'muscle car' – a Pontiac GTO, a Chevrolet Camaro, a Ford Mustang, a Dodge Challenger – fulfilled the fantasies of the young, the image-conscious, the thrill-seeker, and the prestige buyer.

Motoring itself had little to do with the appeal of the car. It is no accident then, that in 1968 Hanna Barbera created *Wacky Races*, the animated fulfilment of every car fantasy, and a direct response to the 'muscle car' era. Based on two live-action films, *The Great Race* (1965) and *Those Magnificent Men in their Flying Machines* (1965), *Wacky Races* included eleven drivers whose cars had an array of devices for additional speed and aesthetic interest (Sennett, 1989, 153). Designed by Iwao Takamoto, they included Peter Perfect's 'Turbo Terrific', the vehicle most self-evidently styled on a racing car, yet also the car most frequently breaking down. Despite this, and common to all the cars in the race, is the fact that it remains indestructible, versatile, easily repaired and capable of coping with all weathers and terrains. Whether highly accessorised, like Professor Pat Pending's 'Converter car' (capable of becoming a rocket, a pogo-stick, a giant drill, a snowplough or a pancake-flipper to roll-up rubber roads!) or Penelope Pitstop's 'Compact Pussycat' (equipped with a number of highly feminine beauty aids like a hairdryer and lipstick applier), or primitive, like the Arkansas Chug-a-Bug (based on a backwoods cabin) or the Creepy Kook (essentially a mobile Gothic tower), these vehicles demonstrate an intrinsic faith in technological progress, which is further festishised by the versatility of the animation medium to illustrate 'fantastic' advances. *Wacky Races* was essentially a fantasy of the drag-strip, hot-rod culture taken to its logical extreme – an uninhibited expression of anarchy projected across a named American terrain. From the 'ice and snow in Idaho' in *The Ski-Resort Road Race* to the 'swamplands of Louisiana and Alabama' in *Traffic Jambalaya* to the Hawaiian islands in *Overseas Highway Race*, the racers represent a self-absorbed, ascendent culture, wholly dedicated to the fantasy of the car, and the revolt against Fordism. In many ways, however, this was the zenith of auto-mythology, for as David Gartman suggests, 'the social costs of auto consumption had so undermined the ideology of consumer individualism that most Americans were demanding social solutions to the problems of safety, congestion and pollution' (Gartman, 1994, 210). The safe context of an animated series like *Wacky Races* offered the escapism of enjoying the car as an aesthetic and technological dream without having to consider its social effects.

Though always dismissed as an undemanding children's entertainment, and often marginalised as an important contemporary artform, animation enjoys its anonymity in offering alternative, and sometimes subversive versions of the world. In whatever event, animation reflects social and cultural trends in the same way as many art-forms, and between 1950 and 1968, offered an often insightful view of the car's impact upon American culture, showing that like the car itself, it could accommodate expressions of desire and dread unable to be articulated elsewhere.

Endnotes

[1] During the Depression era, Paramount created a scheme by which advertisers could promote their goods in short films which would be shown in all the studio's 100 theatres, and thus be seen by over three million potential customers. Advertisers would pay $15,000 for this privilege, of which $7,500 would be dedicated to the production of the film. The Fleischer studios created three motor-orientated shorts – *In My Merry Oldsmobile* (for Oldmobile), *Step On It* and *Tex in 1999* (both for the Texaco Company), all made in 1930. In *My Merry Oldsmobile* is almost a prototypic Fleischer film in that it prefigures the aesthetics and thematics of their later Betty Boop and Popeye short films. The story, as far as it goes, is a mini-melodrama in which Lucille, the film's heroine, is spied upon as she is undressing by a villain, harassed for her attentions, then saved by hero, Johnny Steele, who takes her away in his Oldsmobile. Lucille prefigures Betty Boop in design and potential allure, but more readily anticipates Olive Oyl in being the subject of conflict between a large villain and a little hero (later Pluto and Popeye). The Fleischers' highly sexualised themes are clearly played out in the villain's voyeurism as Lucille removes numerous striped petticoats, and in the way that the villain offers her a stick of rock which she duly licks. The ambiguities of the Oldsmobile 'jingle' are also played upon – special emphasis is placed on the line 'you can go as far as you like with me in my Merry Oldsmobile' in the animated version of the lyric that appears on the screen. The 'jingle' lyric itself, actually based on a popular song, appears on the screen, firstly over live-action footage of the Oldsmobile, then in cartoonal form, after the main story. A bouncing white ball moves along the lyric as it is sung, operating in a similar way to the 'Cartune' series the Fleischer studios had made in the late twenties, as illustrations of popular songs which were then sung out-loud to the accompaniment of an organist in the cinemas. The same strategy was applied to the Oldsmobile advertisement, which was clearly appealing to couples, and working in a nostalgic way. The animation creates surreal effects with moving paintings and ornaments in Lucille's room and illustrates literal aspects of the lyric, for example, 'stealing away' is accompanied by the presence of a thief, and ultimately, concludes the story of Johnny and Lucille in a church, where they marry, and begin a life of fighting in a boxing ring. Highly successful, the animated auto-ad became a staple of production, particularly in the television era of the 1950s, and after.

[2] Raymond Lee's picture essay (1969) *Fit for the Chase: Cars and the Movies*, (A. S. Barnes & Co Inc, New York, 1969) offers some broad thematics within which the car has been used in Hollywood cinema. These include comedies, gangster films, romances, and movies based on races. Lee shows how certain models of car have been deployed.

[3] For a full address of the dynamics of the animated film, see the author's (1996) *Understanding Animation*, Routledge, London, in which he discusses definitions of animation, its diverse forms, aspects of narration, theories of comedy and representation, and models of audience response.

[4] These issues are more fully explored in the author's (1997), *Cartoons to Computers: Animation in the United States 1896–1996*,University of Keele Press, Keele.

[5] In an article from *Time* magazine, 25 January 1954, entitled 'Answer from the Hustlers', it is reported that Ford and Chrysler mobilised in the face of General Motors design agendas. It is noted that Chrysler's 'conservative styling has not helped its sales', while 'Ford is planning a complete changeover of body styles for 1956, then will revive its famed Continental'. Nash and Hudson merged to form the American Motor Corps to boost its production and place in the market, while Studebaker, Kaiser Motors and Packard struggled. The article concludes that the US car buyer 'will be able to buy increasingly better cars at a

lower price.' (Information from *Time Almanac of the 20th Century*, Soft Key International CD-ROM, Time Inc. Magazine Company, 1994).

[6] Alfred Sloan, President of General Motors, recognised that his cars needed to have different associations from those of the Model T Ford, with its utilitarian efficiency during the Depression era. In the late 1920s, therefore, he created the first design division in the car industry, led by the flamboyant and highly creative Harley Earl, who was responsible for the styling of all General Motors cars. Earl established an efficient, commercially aware Art and Color Unit that developed the innovative techniques of using full scale blueprints and full-scale three-dimensional clay models to create innovative designs.

[7] Dale Carter (1988), in his book *The Final Frontier*, Verso, London & New York, suggests that post-war America was constituted as a 'Rocket State,' where the contemporary media 'used an expanding stockpile of mythological apparatus to dramatise contemporary existence as an extreme extension of established frontier myth' (94). Further, he details the rapid expansion of rocket technologies at the moment when 'between 1947 and 1957 automobile credit multiplied eightfold' (97–9). Clearly, the idea of 'progress' in a Rocket State' became available to ordinary people through the everyday automobile, its futuristic design, and the commercial culture than made it affordable.

[8] See *Understanding Animation* (Routledge, London & New York, 1996).

[9] For a full discussion of the various ways in which objects may be gendered, see the essays (1996) in *The Gendered Object*, edited by Pat Kirkham, Manchester University Press, Manchester & New York, which also includes a piece by the author on the gendering of cartoon characters, Tom and Jerry.

[10] For an interesting and related discussion of how middle class consumer values were created and disseminated, see Mary Beth Haralovich's essay (1988), 'Suburban Family Sit-Coms and Consumer Product Design: Addressing the Social Subjectivity of Homemakers in the 50s', Phillip Drummond & Richard Paterson (eds), *Television and its Audience: International Research Perspectives*, BFI, London, 1988, 38–61.

[11] Disney's feature films often include 'conscience' figures or caring companions who attempt to warn the central protagonist not to transgress from what is right, or into dangerous situations. These include Jimmy Cricket in *Pinocchio* (1940), Timothy Mouse in *Dumbo* (1941), and Thumper in *Bambi* (1942).

[12] A far more paranoid vision of car culture was made by the Halas and Batchelor studio in Britain in 1963. The science-fictional *Automania 2000* wholly blames scientists, industrialists and capitalists for the way in which the car has brought the world to an apocalyptic end. Families are confined in cars which are merely stacked on top of each other, and have not moved for five years; special custom built cars, echoing Tex Avery's exaggerated functionalism and decoration are made for particular occasions; cars stack up and submerge the Empire State Building, Big Ben, St Pauls cathedral and the Taj Mahal; 'Universal Immobility occurs, ironically preventing wars, but creating difficulties of survival; new social hierarchies form, but all is ultimately destroyed by 'the ultimate in automation', the self-producing car. Mass production consume the ivory tower of scientific progress, and like mangled, monsters, cars brutally engulf each other until the implied point of complete social breakdown. A far cry from Halas and Batchelor's earlier film, *The Moving Spirit* (1951), a Shell-sponsored history of the motor car, both nostalgic and educational, which nevertheless warns of too many cars, but ultimately endorses science driven notions of progress.

Bibliography

Gartman, David (1994) *Auto Opium: A Social History of American Automobile Design,* Routledge, London & New York.

Grafton, Donald C. (1993) *Before Mickey: The Animated Film 1898–1928,* University of Chicago Press, Chicago and London.

O'Brien, Flora (1985) *Walt Disney's Goofy: The Good Sport,* Ebury Press, London.

Stallabrass, Julian (1996) *Gargantua: manufactured mass culture,* Verso, London.

Sennett, Ted (1989) *The Art of Hanna Barbera: Fifty Years of Creativity,* Viking Studio Books, London and New York.

8

Cars and Girls – The Car, Masculinity and Pop Music

Duncan Heining

From Elvis Presley's pink Cadillac to John Lennon's white Rolls Royce, from Brian Wilson's *Little Deuce Coupe* to Prince's *Little Red Corvette* the car keeps appearing in pop music. In fact what is arguably the first rock and roll record, *Rockett* 88 by Jackie Brenston and his Kings of Rhythm, is about a car. Most car songs, though not all, are written by male writers. As is often the case in pop music, the use of a metaphor or symbol, here the car, finds its first significant expression in Black Music. This article is first and foremost about gender, specifically masculinity, but it is also about the debt owed by pop music and culture to Black Music.

This is a debt not always honoured by white commentators. Credit often goes for a song to the white artist who produces a cover version rather than its black originator. Marsh and Collett (1986) provide a classic example of this in attributing *Crazy 'bout an Automobile (Every Woman I Know)* to Ry Cooder. The irony here is that as a champion of Black Music, Ry Cooder would never make such a mistake. We will need to go back in time shortly to Robert Johnson and others, but William 'Billy the Kid' Emerson's song is in fact a good place to start our journey.

The song is a plaintive moan, the title of which says it all. The singer is himself carless and unable to attract women as a result. This sorry state of affairs finds the hero a victim of a change in circumstances. No longer are women prepared to be walked home, now they expect to be driven in style (Marsh and Collett, 1986). The writer-performer is clearly making assumptions about what women want. Herein lies its paradox. Every woman he knows wants a man with a fancy car but as a result of his lack of the same he no longer knows that many women. One is already beginning to lose any sense of the singer proving an expert witness in support of his case. It is in the final verse that the crux is reached and the link between the car and sex is made:

Ridin' and lovin' can't be beat
You and your woman on your own front seat
Now she can play with your keys shift your gears
Turn on your radio just loud enough to hear
Turn on your heater and flip on your fan
Then you start a'rollin' just as fast as you can

Wilson Pickett's *Mustang Sally* comes at this from a different point. The singer has bought her a car but Sally shows her gratitude by running round all over town. All she wants to do is ride. The double meaning here is an obvious one, as is the clear inference that women cannot be trusted. In a sense the singer has been duped. The car has turned Sally on, as he had hoped, but not towards him. In *Maybellene* Chuck Berry is driving along in his V8 Ford when he sees the object of his desire with another man in a Cadillac Coup de Ville. His response to this betrayal is to give chase, finally overtaking the Cadillac and leaving it 'sittin' like a ton of lead'. The message to Maybellene and her new beau is clear he may have the money but it's what's under the hood that counts. Marsh and Collett note rightly that the song has several layers of meaning that would not be lost on his audience. There is the issue of class and status represented by the Cadillac and the Ford. Then in his victory over the Cadillac the audience would note this as representing a win for the ordinary Joe over the rich usurper. It would further see this as a slap in the face for the fickle Maybellene. However, there is more to this than a simple tale of Rich Man, Poor Man and Female Infidelity. Chuck Berry is making clear assumptions about what women want – they want money, sex and male potency. In this as in other car songs, the car operates as a signifier for these signifieds (Barthes 1981; Hawkes, 1992). Further to this the song assumes that male and female desires focus on the same things with the essential difference lying in the fact that in her fickleness a woman would always put money first. Men know what women want.

The suggestion of a link between the car and sex in popular song hardly represents a major insight. We are all familiar with the facile notion that the car can be seen as a phallic symbol. That it would fulfil a similar symbolic function in pop music would in itself be hardly worthy of note. However, it is proposed that the examples given are not solely concerned with a simple car-sex signification. More than that they are instructive because they start to tell us something about how men define their own sexuality and also how they attempt to understand female sexuality.

So far we have looked at examples by black writers and performers. However, when we look at the work of white artists we see similar assumptions being made. In *I Get Around*, a song about drag racing, Brian Wilson tells us:

We always take my car 'cause it's never been beat
And we've never missed yet with the girls we meet
None of the guys go steady 'cause it wouldn't be right
To leave your best girl home on a Saturday night.

Again cars get you girls and to the winner the spoils. However, to this we can add another male notion about women – they must always be peripheral in the world of male things. There is even a hint here in the juxtaposition of girl and home and in the general theme of the song that if he had a 'best girl' her ultimate aim would be to get him to settle down. The 'cars get you girls' theme can be seen in the importance that the hero in Eddie Cochran's *Summertime Blues* attaches to the loss of the use of the car on Saturday night because he 'didn't work a lick'. In *Somethin' Else* alternate verses explore two objects of desire, a 'fine-looking' girl and a 'brand new convertible', both of which are 'somethin' else'. Here the hero gets the girl but has to make do with second best as far as the car is concerned. In *Brand New Cadillac*, Vince Taylor revisits Chuck Berry territory. His baby is leaving him for a richer model and what is more 'she ain't never comin' back'. This song is an unusual one in being a British car song. Released in 1959 when car ownership was not widespread and did not extend to working class youth, it is forced to rely on the American image of the Cadillac to give it authenticity and in doing so it unintentionally but successfully emphasises the extent of the loss and that this is insurmountable. Taylor's audience would only ever see a Cadillac on the cinema screen. Ownership would be an impossible dream. In 1959 British youth aspired more to a bicycle than a car culture.

This question of male perceptions of female desire can also be found in the Blues. From this side of the Atlantic the notion that the car might prove a recurring symbol in the Folk music of an oppressed minority is a surprising one. At the same time it is not necessary to produce statistics of car ownership among black Americans to recognise that even though owning a car might be out of the question, along with poor white Americans, the aspiration to possess the ultimate consumer object would be a powerful one. Similarly, the car would hold the same symbolic power to convey status and confer dignity for the black as for the white Community.

The Robert Johnson song *Terraplane Blues* recorded in 1936 uses the imagery of the car to convey both male and female sexual desire. The Terraplane was a popular make of car at that time:

I got a woman that I'm loving' way down in Arkansas
Now you know the coils ain't even buzzin,' your little generator
won't get the spark,
All in bad condition, you gotta have these batteries charged

I'm cryin' please don't do me wrong
Who's bin drivin' my Terraplane now for you since I been gone?

Despite the suggested infidelity the hero is still willing to 'keep on tangling' with her wires till her 'spark plug will give me fire'. This seems to be saying that a woman whose man does not pay her the right sexual attention is likely to find that she will seek it elsewhere, another example of male assumptions about female sexual desire. The song also conveys the same sense of male sexual power we found in Chuck Berry's song Maybellene; here it is allied to the skill of the mechanic. (Staats, 1979)

Paul Oliver (1990) in his classic work 'Blues Fell This Morning: Meaning in the Blues' has suggested that the use of imagery derived from the world of machinery and the factory to signify the sexual act represents a new development in the Folk song lyric. Whilst he is perhaps overstating his case (examples from nineteenth century England abound), we may still share Oliver's enthusiasm when we confront the complexity of imagery in Robert Johnson's song. We may also note that this was one of his most successful releases and therefore assume that his audience appreciated and understood the imagery he was using. In Lightnin Hopkins' *Black Cadillac* the car appears to be used to signify both his woman and the sexual act with her:

Wah Baby! Come on back
You got somethin' I sure do lack
And that's that black Cadillac
That blacks Cadillac in the mornin'
Yeah that black Cadillac
That's what I lack
She's built up pretty
Kind of like a Ford
But it makes no difference
It sure can hold the road.

Other examples of the use of the car for sexual imagery can be found in *Car Machine Blues*, Lightnin Slim's *My Starter Won't Work*, Charlie McCoy's *Valves Need Grinding* and Sonny Boy Williamson's *My Little Machine*. This tradition continues through the history of Black Music, from the Blues through Chuck Berry and Rock and Roll, through Soul and on to Prince and *Little Red Corvette*.

Before leaving the Blues I want to begin to examine this article's central thesis, namely that car songs have something to tell us about masculinity and the different ways in which men and women perceive the world. In Memphis Minnie's *Me and my Chauffeur Blues*, Minnie tells us:

Won't you be my chauffeur (Repeat)
I want someone to drive me
Downtown.
Baby driver so easy, I can't turn him down.
But I don't want him (Repeat)
To be ridin' these girls (Repeat)
A-round
You know I'm gonna steal me a pistol
Shoot my chauffeur down.

Staats (1979) suggests that the singer is portraying herself as the car. This is not my reading of the song. In fact the crucial difference between this example and *Terraplane Blues* is the degree of distance between subject and object of desire. In Robert Johnson's song the mechanical metaphor serves to create distance. The performance of the act is central to the song, the relationship of secondary, if any, importance. We are to admire the hero's performance. Even the suggestion of infidelity is treated differently in the two songs. Johnson is hardly bothered, Memphis Minnie has reached for a gun. In her song the car signifies the sexual act, not her. The distance between her and the chauffeur, despite any reversal of power relations implied, is minimal. The implied freedom in *Terraplane Blues* is there for the hero not his lover. In the second song his freedom is seen as a threat to their relationship.

Deborah Tannen (1993), a psycholinguist, has described women as speaking and hearing a language of connection and intimacy. Men on the other hand speak and hear a language of status and independence. It is not only that we understand and explain things differently, we even use the same words to convey different meanings. In a study of divorcees Catherine Kohl Riessman (1994) notes that when women refer to the freedom arising from divorce they do so in a positive sense of gaining autonomy. Men on the other hand refer to freedom in the sense of freedom from obligation, i.e. in the negative, as an absence of restraint. Harding (1975) suggests that due to their different social needs men and women have developed different cultures of communication, with each sex learning a different set of skills for the manipulation of words and language. Studies of children referred to by Maltz and Borker (1982) note that girls learn to use words to create close and equal relationships, involving mutually acceptable criticism and accurate interpretation of others' communication. Boys on the other hand use words to establish dominance, attract an audience and assert oneself in the face of competition. Referring to the differences between all female and all male groups, Coates (1986) notes that women share a great deal more information about themselves and talk about their feelings and relationships. Men on the other hand use language competitively, changing the subject frequently and using anecdotes centred around themes of superiority and aggression with the purpose of demonstrating themselves to be the best informed, most experienced or knowledgeable.

Hudson and Jacot (1995) refer to the different relationship that the sexes have with the world and their different experiences of socialisation. For men this involves them in the world of things, machines and technology. Ideas are also important in the male world, as is the holding and articulation of opinion. As with the studies noted above, Hudson and Jacot note the significance of concepts such as status and independence and the role of hierarchy and competition in establishing precedence. Indeed Hudson is something of a pioneer in this area. His 1968 work *Frames of Mind* looked in some depth at gender differences in ability, perception and self-perception in the Arts and Sciences.

It is my suggestion that Memphis Minnie and Robert Johnson deal with a similar subject matter in ways, which reflect the discussion above. The former concerns herself with the relationship, the latter with the activity. Memphis Minnie focuses on connection and intimacy, Robert Johnson on status and independence. Her song is unusual in being a song by a woman using the car as a central signifier. Cars are more often seen as being part of the male world. Where women writers such as Nanci Griffiths and Tracy Chapman write songs using the car as a signifier, they do so in ways that would seem to confirm the research referred to above. Male writers, in turn, do so in ways that emphasise status, freedom and independence. It is further my contention that male writers are far more likely to use the car as a signifier in a song. Bob Dylan has used the car as a powerful satirical image in *Talkin' World War III Blues:*

Well, I seen a Cadillac window up town
And there was nobody aroun'
I got into the driver's seat
And I drove down 42nd Street
In my Cadillac
Good car to drive after a war.

Dylan's lyric has several layers of imagery. He simultaneously uses the image of the Cadillac to satirise the triviality of advertising (One could imagine the slogan – 'Buy Cadillac! A good car to drive after a War'), the shallowness of the song's hero in being concerned with such trivialities in the face of a nuclear holocaust and in the use of such everyday imagery emphasises the enormity of the tragedy that nuclear war would mean (Gray, 1972). Again we see the car being used to signify status. One wonders what image would have been chosen in a similar song by a woman writer. A woman writer might also use a status image to make a satirical point; however I would suggest in this context it would be unlikely that she would select a car or other piece of machinery to make that point. Frank Zappa has also used the car to satirical effect in *Bow Tie Daddy* to emphasise the vacuousness of the Middle American male:

> Don't try to do no thinkin'
> Just go on with your drinkin'
> Just have your fun, you old son of a gun
> Then drive home in your Lincoln.

Elsewhere he uses the sign of the car to pour scorn on teenagers and in his view their mindless activities. In *Dog Breath* we find 'Fuzzy dice/ Bongos in the back' and in *Cruising for Burgers* 'In daddy's new car/ My phoney freedom card/ Brings to me/ Instantly/ *Ecstasy'*. I would suggest that a woman writer would be unlikely to use a car as a kiss-off in that way to convey the subject's straightness. Nor would she concern herself with trappings such as 'Fuzzy dice' in any satirical intent. It is worth noting here that once again those issues of status and freedom can be seen to be significant in these lyrics. In fact the car occurs frequently in Zappa's work and can be seen as an example of his 'conceptual continuity' (Watson, 1995).

If we contrast this with Joni Mitchell's road song *Coyote*, the narrator tells of the experience of being picked up as a hitchhiker by the philandering Coyote of the title. The tune drives the lyrics along, conveying both the sense of the motion on the road and the pace at which the heroine moves from being just 'a hitcher/ A prisoner of the white lines of the freeway' to entanglement with Coyote. Mitchell conveys both the dalliance and the subsequent disengagement. In her reflections on the different worlds they inhabit – 'I'm up all night in the studio/ And you're up early on your ranch'– she succeeds in communicating both closeness and distance. This is the language of connection and intimacy, used here with humorous and even satirical intent.

Again in Laurie Anderson's distopian and apocalyptic *O Superman (for Massenet)* the consequences of disaster are conveyed in terms of its impact on the most primal relationship, namely that of mother and child. Mother becomes a satirical metonymic for the nation state:

> So hold me mom in your long arms (repeat)
> In your automatic arms. Your electronic arms.
> In your arms. So hold me mom in your long arms
> Your petrochemical arms. Your military arms.
> In your electronic arms.

Though not a car song, *O Superman* does demonstrate a very different handling of a similar theme to that evident in *Talking World War III Blues*.

There were a fair number of car songs written in the 1950s and 1960s. Most of these celebrate youth and masculinity. Both Chuck Berry and Brian Wilson made the car a central feature in their lyrics. Both were clearly addressing a particular audience and its concerns. Wilson can be seen as a troubled individual who chose his subject matter from a vicarious position, his brother Dennis providing source material about cars and surfing from personal experience. Berry on the other hand was a confirmed car freak. His autobiography (Berry, 1996, 45) makes frequent reference to cars and speaks lovingly of the 27 he has owned. With reference to his song *No Money Down*, he notes that while his 'broken down ragged Ford' had served him well, the switch to a 1933 Plymouth provided advantages in terms of its lengthy front seat. 'I had learned there was too much opportunity for rejection when moving to the back seat was suggested.' In *Little Deuce Coupe* Brian Wilson tells us 'Little Deuce Coupe you don't know what I got!' The first line of the first verse throws down a challenge and with its 'babe' we can presume that this challenge is in some way directed towards women in general:

> I'm not bragging babe so don't put me down
> But I've got the fastest set of wheels in town

Information follows as to her attributes. She's just a little deuce coupe but she has got a 'flat head mill', she will do 140 at the top in fourth' and has a 'competition clutch with a 4 on the floor'. In *Shut You Down*, which is an account of a race, there are references to 'power-shifts' and 'pressure plates'. Although the 413 gives the hero's Stingray a run for its money in the end it is no match for the 'fuel-injected engine sitting under the hood'. The amount of detail about the cars as well as the race is essential rather than peripheral to these songs. Similarly when Chuck Berry refers to a car in a song or in his autobiography he notes the name, model and year.

While we should not lose sight of the competitive elements in these examples and will have noted these in relation to earlier comments about the use of language by men to establish status, there actually seems to be something far more fundamental going on here. One can add here Ray Peterson's *Tell Laura I Love Her*, in which the hero is killed in a stock car race that he has entered to buy his beloved a wedding ring, and Jan and Dean's *Dead Man's Curve*, another death disc that seems to celebrate the very thing it purports to be condemning. These songs present a world-view, a window into the world of the young (American) male. What other explanation can there be for the mechanical detail in Brian Wilson's car songs? Someone other than Chuck Berry must be interested in whether it was a '53 or '54 Olds. Death by stock car is not something which the average teenager is likely to experience, yet it must have some other resonance not immediately apparent. In a sense with Wilson, Berry and also Eddie Cochran, it is almost as if they are addressing a constituency rather than an audience. This a point made well by Wicke (1990) in relation to 'Mod' groups such as The Who and their relationship with their audience.

These songs and others like them, describe a world of cars, girls, fun and excitement. They speak a language, which is shared with the audience, for whom 'competition clutches and pressure plates' will be readily understandable terms. They will identify with Chuck Berry's frustration in *No Particular Place To Go*:

> Riding along in my calaboose
> Still trying to get her belt unloose
> All the way home I held a grudge
> But the safety belt it wouldn't budge.

They will appreciate the exciting but potentially dangerous world of *Dead Man's Curve* and the difficult but honourable requirements of manhood expressed in *Tell Laura I Love Her*. It is not so much that women are excluded from this discourse. There are after all expressions of masculinity in these songs, which might well, meet with the approval of a female audience. Rather women are peripheral to the discourse. They are outside it looking in. Their role is primarily to observe and applaud maleness.

Horrocks (1995) notes the impact of Lacanian psychology within the field of cultural studies. Lacan challenges the traditional relationship between subject and object and hence that between subject and text. Instead of the subject reading the text or creating it in the act of reading, it is rather the case that the text creates the subject. In what we read, listen to or watch, we glimpse ourselves. Through the identifications we make with the text we find ourselves. Identification is for Lacan the means by which the ego discovers itself. For the purposes of this article it is not necessary to go into the wider implications of Lacan's theory. It is, however, important to note that his work has had a significant impact on the study of language and that central to this thesis is the idea that language is not seen as an expression of the human subject but rather as the means by which the subject must define itself.

Language is the 'given' in this situation and is the means whereby the infant moves from the pre-symbolic to the symbolic phase, which is marked both by the separation from the mother and the acquisition of subjectivity. For Lacan this separation is experienced as a 'loss' and as a result the subjectivity realised is a split subjectivity (Kaplan, 1987). What is interesting here is its implications in terms of the use of the car as a signifier in pop music. Approached from this perspective, the essentially male audience discovers itself and its maleness in these songs through a process of identification with the text. The language in a

Chuck Berry or Brian Wilson song presents a symbolic representation of masculinity. This is what it is like to be a man. These are the kind of things of which the male world is comprised. Kaplan uses the term 'social-imaginary' to emphasise the cultural and historical 'embeddedness' of both language and imagination. We should not lose sight of the given world of male–female relations and their power imbalances and their consequent impact on thought and word.

However, I think there is a further process at work here. Language for Lacan is prior. If this is so, then this applies to the author as well as to their audience. Just as the listener discovers himself or herself in the text, so too does the author. They do not create images of masculinity. Rather they too are created by them. This suggests almost a Chinese Box effect of multiple identifications, emphasising again the split nature of subjectivity. This indicates the possibility of alternative identifications. I think this enables us to begin to consider the impact of Black Music on white popular music in a different way. Chambers (1993) describes the influence as leading to the breaking up of the 'facile intimacy of sentimental romanticism in pop music', thereby enabling the transferral of the 'erotic narcissism' of the Blues to white popular music. Reynolds and Press (1995) note the very different meanings that Bo Diddley's *I'm A Man* may have in a black American context in contrast to its meanings when performed by white adolescents. In the former it is an assertion of manhood in the face of a white supremacy that denied full humanity and manhood to black men. In the latter it became a rant against parental authority, denying manhood to its male youth. Is it too much to suggest that the identification with Black Music amongst white male youth is more to do with the way in which it is able to express male sexuality than it is concerned with youth rebellion or the attraction of its otherness?

The influence of black on white popular music is well known. It is also well documented that Chuck Berry was a major musical influence on the young Brian Wilson. It seems likely that there was also a lyrical influence in terms of subject matter and song structure. Marcus (1977) points out that Elvis' version of *Let's Play House* was in fact originally written and recorded by a black singer Arthur Gunter, though Elvis added the Pink Cadillac reference. The Beatles, one car song *Drive My Car* was influenced musically by George Harrison's love of the music on the Stax label. Lyrically, it finds its precedents in the Blues and Chuck Berry. Much has been written about the ways in which the Blues and other black musical forms provided source material for white artists. The car as a signifier of masculinity or male sexuality is, as we have seen, another case in point.

Reynolds and Press (1995) have written of the 'special utopian resonance' in American culture of the freedom to 'just up and move somewhere else'. They have also located the restlessness often expressed in songs by male artists as having its origins in the Beat writings of Kerouac filtered through Bob Dylan. As they point out, the rock rebel is constantly making a break for freedom. 'Commitment and closeness quickly become enclosure.' (Reynolds & Press, 1995, 49) This reiterates my earlier comments in relation to Deborah Tannen's work. Apart from the example above, Dylan rarely uses the image of the car in his songs, though the title of *From a Buick 6* conveys the distance or even the alienation of the narrator from his subject matter. Nevertheless, as Reynolds and Press point out, he frequently uses the images of the road and travelling, which appear so often in the work of his 'first idol' Woody Guthrie and which surface in so many Blues songs, such as Big Bill Broonzy's *Key to the Highway* or Robert Johnson's *Ramblin' on my Mind*.

These images are quintessentially male and signify a masculinity that is concerned with presenting itself in terms of freedom from the restrictions of family, relationships and social constraint. It is hard to think of the early Dylan or Guthrie or the Delta Bluesmen without seeing a picture in your mind of a lone male figure walking away down a never-ending road with just a rucksack and guitar for company. It is not important that we are in the territory of the myth and what is more one with eighteenth century origins in Romanticism. The picture is still a powerful and abiding one. Reynolds and Press make another valuable point here. They note that the things that are being left behind are the female. The man-child is escaping mother's apron strings or breaking loose from the safe, seductive trap that the girl-woman offers him and who would have him settle down to the domestic life. The image of the car in pop music is a signifier of a similar kind and part of a similar mythology.

It is interesting to note that the car song largely disappeared around the Summer of Love (1967). Jefferson Airplane's *She has Funny Cars* has nothing beyond its title to do with automobiles. Detroit's finest, the MC5, never bothered to mention their hometown's main industrial product. Even those Texan Good Ol' Boys Doug Sahm and Steve Miller passed on the subject. In fact the only car song that springs to mind from this period is Steppenwolf's wonderfully lumpen *Born to be Wild*. This song contains all of the elements discussed in the previous paragraph. Motor running ... out on the highway ... and we are born to be wild. Never mind its association with Biker culture, an association for which the film *Easy Rider* is only partly responsible. Who amongst us can fail to turn the volume up when John Kay's anthem of the road plays on the car radio? And who amongst us does not push the throttle a little further to the floor?

One needs to bear in mind here the range of symbolic functions the car performs. It crosses distances and also creates distance. It is a means of exploring space or territory. It is a means of escape. All of these things it can actually achieve at both real and metaphorical levels. As I have outlined, it can represent or signify maleness or male sexuality of particular types. With the arrival of the hippie, a different kind of masculinity and associated images began to emerge. This did not mean that the male hippie proved to be any less sexist than any of his predecessors. If anything it meant that as well as being obliged to continue to perform to existing expectations, the female hippie was also obliged to put up with her 'old man' being sensitive and commend him accordingly.

Nevertheless there was a shift in priorities. The territory that now needed exploring was the 'self and the space to be explored was 'inner space'. Steppenwolf, their name taken from the quasi-mystical writer Hesse, may have been born to be wild but they also took a *Magic Carpet Ride*. The Airplane sang on *Fat Angel* of flying 'TransLove Airways', while the Byrds were *Eight Miles High*. The MC5, as well as singing *Motor City is Burning*, also covered *Starship* on the same album, this track being jointly credited to the group and avant garde jazz musician Sun Ra. As for Brian Wilson, in his article *The Last Beach Movie Revisited* Nick Kent (1994) quotes the group's one-time press agent Derek Taylor:

> I also recall having ... a conversation with Brian and Dennis about the Beach Boys never having written surf music or songs about cars; that the Beach Boys had never been involved in any way with the surf and drag fads.

Such things were no longer credible musically or intellectually. One is reminded of St Paul: '... when I became a man, I put away childish things' (Corinthians I). However, there was to be yet another sea change in the world of masculinity. It would again become possible for men to define themselves in terms of the external rather than the internal and okay for them once again to return to childish things. Play was to become a compulsory and therefore serious activity. So in the 1970s the car song made a comeback. However, with consciousness expanded, if not raised, it would never again have quite the innocence that Brian Wilson or Chuck Berry gave it.

If we look at three different songs with the same title – *Roadrunner* – we can see this transformation clearly. In Bo Diddley's original, written at the turn of the 1950s, the hero boasts both of his sexual prowess and his 'love them and leave them philosophy'. No woman can tie him down. The song and performance is underpinned by machismo and one has a sense of controlled violence. The Pretty Things' 1965 version of the song by contrast succeeds in placing the emphasis as much on the sexual threat implicit in the original as on the hero's avoidance of emotional entanglement. Junior Walker's 1966 song of the same name continues the theme, stressing the hero's independence:

All my life has been like this
If you love me it's your own risk
When the dust hits my shoes
I get the urge to move.

The performance is confident and self-assured but there is none of the violence that we see in the Bo Diddley song. Walker's is instead both lyrically and musically more sophisticated. The impression is also that the hero himself is similarly a more sophisticated individual. By 1976 and The Modern Lovers' *Roadrunner*, a great deal had changed. Jonathan Richman's song presents a hero who is 'in love with Rock and Roll' and who drives around Boston late at night with the radio on' because that way he does not 'feel so alone'. The song is full of references to girls, cars and driving and presents a superficial picture of innocence. The performance too is quite simple with a solid repetitive beat and with the Farfisa organ (a real early 1960s sound) to the fore in the mix. However, as a whole, the song and its performance are too knowing, too camp to convince. We are into familiar post-modernist territory here – pastiche, ambiguity and nothing is quite as it seems. Richman is playing with styles and positions and instinctively we know this.

In her study of pop videos on MTV, Kaplan (1987) categorises these according to five types: romantic, socially conscious, nihilist, classical and post-modernist. Clearly there are problems involved in taking concepts that derive from a perspective that applies to a particular medium, such as film and television. How, for example, can the concept of the 'gaze' be applied to a song? Nevertheless, categorising car songs in a similar way throws up some interesting insights. Kaplan explores two specific themes in relation to her identified categories – Love/Sex and Authority. For example, in the classical category she defines the authority theme as male as subject/ female as object. In terms of the socially conscious category the view of authority involves the presentation of a cultural critique of parent and public figures. This approach is central to Kaplan's argument and it is impossible to do it justice here. Of the categories she uses, I would suggest that few car songs fall within the nihilist category; perhaps Gary Numan's CARS, Steppenwolf's *Born to be Wild* and definitely Sammy Hagar's *I Can't Drive At 55*. I would further suggest that most of the songs so far considered would fall into the classical or romantic categories with their emphasis on traditional views of authority and of male/female relationships. It is, however, the socially conscious and post-modernist categories that are most useful in considering car songs written from the 1970s onwards. As Kaplan points out, categories can rarely be discrete and overlap is inevitable. Indeed most of the songs still to be considered contain elements that can usefully be described as post-modernist.

108

It is worth considering why this should be. Post-modernism can hardly be described as a movement such as Surrealism or Expressionism or even Popism. It is perhaps best seen as a sign of the times – a reflection of uncertainty. During the 1960s a new set of certainties confronted the old. A belief system built on patriotism, the family and respect for authority faced a new ideology basing itself on love, peace, revolution and rock and roll. As the 1960s turned into the 1970s neither belief system held sway. Indeed neither could really sustain their simplistic ideology in the face of a far more complex reality of unsuccessful foreign wars, oil crises and increasing urban crime. At one level, the growth of both the New Right and the Greens can be seen to represent the attempt to re-establish moral certainty in a world which appeared to be losing it.

After Chuck Berry, the person most associated with the car song in pop music is of course Bruce Springsteen. So many examples exist in his work one can only select a few to include here. Springsteen's sense of the rock tradition has always been impeccable. It has been both a strength and weakness in his work. At times he has produced precisely the 'Boys Own' Rock and Roll that has resulted in critical opprobrium.

The album *The River* is littered with examples that justify the accusation. In *Sherry Darling*, the singer complains of having to drive his mother-in-law around. In *Hungry Heart* the singer goes out for a ride and never returns, leaving his wife and kids behind. In *Stolen Car*, separated from his wife, the singer drives his stolen car hoping he won't be stopped by the police. It is, however, wrong to confuse the artist with the view expressed in their work. In the title track of *Born to Run*, the hero asks Wendy to – 'Just wrap your legs round these velvet rims/ And strap your hands across my engines'. The use of the car as a sexual image here harks back to the Blues. In *Thunder Road*, from the same album, the hero says to Mary – 'All the redemption I can offer girl/Is beneath this dirty hood'. He is inviting her to escape:

> They scream your name at night in the street
> Your graduation gown lies in rags at their feet
> And in the lonely cool before dawn
> You hear their engines roaring on
> But when you get to the porch they're gone
> On the wind so Mary climb in
> It's a town full of losers
> And I'm pulling out of here to win.

The song *The River* also refers to a Mary. There, however, you get the sense that that relationship is doomed and the car that took them both away will soon carry the hero away alone. The language in all these songs is concerned with escape from entanglement and therefore echoes earlier songs referred to in this article. The difference in *Born to Run* and *Thunder Road* lies in the hero's desire to take Wendy/Mary with him. The language in the other songs noted, for example *Hungry Heart*, is therefore more in keeping with my comments on this theme.

These songs could almost fit Kaplan's classical and romantic categories but not quite. Springsteen's artistic sense is sufficiently well developed to allow him to play with styles. He is also well aware of the problematic nature of relationships. A good song to reveal this contrast is *Racing in the Street*. It begins with references to a '69 Chevvy, Fuelie Heads and a 'Hurst on the floor'. Think back to Chuck Berry and the Beach Boys. He and his buddy race for money and in the first chorus we learn:

> Tonight, tonight the strip's just right
> I wanna blow 'em off in my first heat
> Summer's here and the time is right
> For racin' in the street.

Again think back to the Beach Boys' *Shut You Down* and *Little Deuce Coupe* and Chuck Berry's *Maybellene*. The difference here is that Springsteen's hero is not doing it for fun or male braggadocio. Further on in the song we are introduced to his partner who cries herself to sleep worrying whether he will make it home. The final verse closes:

> Tonight my baby and me, we're gonna ride to the sea
> And wash these sins off our hands.

Those two lines from *Thunder Road* about redemption are echoed here. Beneath that 'dirty hood' lies the car's heart and soul, its engine. Beneath that 'dirty' exterior lies the heart and soul of the man. The use of religious imagery here is complex and profound. The body is dirty and sinful but the soul can still be redeemed. We can wash the dirt and sins off our hands. Cars may appear to perform similar functions in Springsteen's songs to those previously discussed. However, even in his most apparently simplistic songs those male images of escape, independence and freedom are located by their heroes in a blue-collar world of betrayed dreams and aspirations. Springsteen does not condemn but he certainly does not praise the men in his songs that run away from responsibility. Here freedom is as much concerned with the struggle for autonomy as with freedom from responsibility. Love is a problematic relationship and is presented as such in what amounts to a well considered cultural critique. This in my opinion locates Springsteen clearly in Kaplan's socially conscious category.

With the pop song interpretation can sometimes require as much attention to the performance as to the lyric. With pop music, however, interpretation and understanding can often be complicated by the artist's public image or persona on the one hand and the knowledge/sense that the gap between that persona and reality may be wide indeed. This question becomes still more crucial in the postmodern period, where styles are adopted and meanings conveyed in contexts that seem to suggest that truth or reality will always be found in the next Chinese doll that we open. Meaning, belief, reality, style, truth and intention are all prisoners of the continuous present. The past and future represent merely wardrobes of styles to be ransacked or phases we will go through.

It is for these reasons that it is difficult to locate the moral or political centre of Springsteen's *oeuvre*. Questions continue to dog us. What do these songs tell us about Springsteen's viewpoint on masculinity? What precisely is his position on maleness? Will the real Bruce Springsteen please stand up? This lack of certainty illustrates Kaplan's point (Kaplan, 1987) that the categories she has identified are blurred by post-modernist elements.

Tom Waits is another singer-songwriter who uses the car as an image in his lyrics. His work, unlike Springsteen's, is more openly and deliberately theatrical. Springsteen's 'man of the people' is clearly an image important in his marketing. It has been adopted, however, in a way which seeks to locate that image in a sense of the artist's personal integrity, ie that image and reality are close companions. With Waits there is less of a problem. We know that he is not really the Beatnik tramp who finds himself at the end of a three day drink pounding the mission hall piano and growling his monologues of lowlife and Bohemia. He just writes his songs. He does not have to live in them.

For these reasons I would locate Waits more or less in the post-modernist category. The car is a recurring image in Waits' songs. An early number OL '55 appears to speak lovingly of a trip to the singer's hometown. 'His' first car an OL '55 takes him away too soon but he cannot stay. It drips with nostalgia and the image of the car creates that sense of distance between where he has been and where he is now. There is a strong impression that past and present are both compartmentalised in this song. In *Looking for the Heart of Saturday Night* the singer tells us:

> You've gassed her up
> You're behind the wheel
> Cruisin' with your sweet one
> In your Oldsmobile
> Tearin' down the boulevard
> Lookin' for the heart of Saturday night.

The image here is almost iconographic – car, girl, bright lights, big city, Saturday night. Again it oozes nostalgia. The car gives access to that whole world and is central to that search for the elusive and intangible perfect

Saturday night. As with OL '55 it matters not whether Waits knows of whence he speaks. These are powerful myths and even though they attach themselves to memories and half-remembered feelings, they reify both subject and object to the extent that they provide a male code or language for dealing with one's past and youth.

On the later album *Foreign Affairs* Waits' ability to place himself in different worlds is still further developed. *Burma Shave* is in James M. Cain territory. A young man drives into town and leaves with the young woman who fills his car with gasoline. She wants to escape the small-town world of 'Marysville' to Burma Shave, a mythical place born of Waits' childhood misunderstanding of an advertising hoarding. Their dreams crash, however, when the hero makes a mistake attempting to overtake:

> Why don't you have another swig
> And pass that car if you're so brave
> I wanna get there before the sun comes up in
> Burma Shave.
>
> And the spider web crack and the Mustang screamed
> Smoke from the tyres and the twisted machine
> Just a nickel's worth of dreams and every wishbone
> that they saved
> Lie swindled from them on the way to
> Burma Shave.

Jack and Neal takes us to another myth, here that of the Kerouac and Cassady. Waits offers us his Kerouac. Not the real one, just his own version. We find ourselves on the road and the car figures largely on our journey from New York to California. Waits conveys beautifully the sense of freedom and movement that we associate with the Beats. Images of sex and Jazz and the 'Road' catch us wishing we were along for the ride. But it is a myth for all that and Waits' engagement with his subject is ultimately ironic and knowing. This is no different really from the myth that Hollywood made of the Wild West. If anything it is more honest. However reluctantly we may admit it, we know that Waits is acting out this scenario for us. Elsewhere Waits plays with the images of Vaudeville and the Carnival. His songs are like the little vignettes that go on behind the curtain as Waits the carnival barker calls us to pay our money and enter. As a writer Waits has a range and depth that few can match but these songs seem to me to focus on the same representations of maleness that we have seen elsewhere. Women by and large play ancillary or support roles. Relationships where referred to simply exist and do not require examination. Freedom from constraint combines with a desperate searching for something that lies always beyond reach, whether it is the heart of Saturday night, our lost youth, 'the Road' of Jack and Neal or the Eldorado of Burma Shave.

Nevertheless, Waits' irony, distance from his subject and his ability to play with styles mark him as a post-modernist. *Frank's Wild Years* from the album *Swordfishtrombones* offers a final glimpse of the car and masculinity. Waits later used the song as the basis of a musical, which emphasises the consciously dramatic aspect of his art. This song tells how Frank has settled down to domesticity with his wife, 'a spent piece of used jet-trash' who made good Bloody Marys and 'kept her mouth shut'. One day he buys a can of gasoline, douses the house and sets light to it. He sits in his car drinking beer and watches the house burn with his wife's pet Chihuahua inside. He then drives North for the big city with the pay-off line – 'Never could stand that dog'.

In this song the hero destroys not only the house but also everything female in his life. The car offers a sanctuary and an escape from the apron strings Frank has found so constraining. The last words echo with the image of a man who experiences difficulty expressing emotion or in articulating his needs or desires. He is the suburban counterpart of Dylan's hobo, of Kerouac's hero Dean Moriaty and Bo Diddley's Roadrunner. He is not Waits. He is just Frank, a character in a play. That is the big difference. He is not presented as an ideal of masculinity but simply as a character for our entertainment.

Tom Robinson has added two numbers to the canon of car songs. His first hit *2–4–6–8 Motorway Song* still delights despite its moronic chorus and lumpen lyric. His other car song *Grey Cortina* is by contrast a mess. The latter seems to be an attempt to explore Chuck Berry/Brian Wilson territory from an English perspective and it fails to convince. Robinson assures us on the LP sleeve of his desire to own 'a smoke-grey silver fox supercharged 1600E J registered furlined four door Ford Cortina'. The song describes the merits of the car somewhat clumsily but in a form that is not a million miles away from Berry, but we are simply not able to suspend disbelief. In contrast to Waits and Springsteen, the acting is not good enough to sustain our attention. It lacks glamour, wit or charm and we have no involvement with its subject matter.

Robinson's other example does succeed in engaging us precisely because we have had or can imagine the experience of driving along a motorway with the radio playing Springsteen at full volume. What appeals here is the way in which Robinson speaks to the male desire for freedom and movement. There should be nothing surprising in a gay man seeking to address issues of masculinity. Indeed this has essentially been Robinson's subject matter during a long and interesting career. He has written better songs than *2–4–6–8 Motorway Song* but few as enjoyable. Robinson has also produced work more genuinely falling within Kaplan's socially conscious category. In terms of his early material he appears more a parody of that style.

Shortly I want to bring this article to a close with two final examples that perhaps best illustrate pop's ability to address issues of masculinity within the scope of the car song. First I want to provide a contrast to what has gone before with a song by Tracy Chapman. In *Fast Car* Chapman provides a picture of a woman wanting to escape the drabness and poverty of her existence. She speaks it seems to a male lover:

> You got a fast car
> I want a ticket anywhere
> Maybe we can make a deal
> Maybe together we can get somewhere.

Clearly the car represents escape but here that escape is based upon notions of co-operation between the song's two protagonists:

> You got a fast car
> And I got a plan to get us out of here.

Their venture requires them both to succeed:

> You got a fast car
> But is it fast enough so we can fly away
> We gotta make a decision
> We leave tonight or live and die this way.

As noted earlier women in their speech and in their art emphasise relationships and connection as against men who speak more in terms of abstracted notions of freedom and individualism. Another song worthy of note here is *Ford Econoline* by Nancy Griffiths. The heroine packs her kids and belongings in the car, leaves her worthless husband and heads off for a new life. She does not dump the kids and though the car provides the escape, it is not a flight from commitment or to autonomy. Rather she flees to a life where personal fulfilment becomes a reality within the context of her relationships.

These examples reiterate the points made earlier and it is important to note this as an ongoing issue in male/female perceptions of the world. It is not merely in the context of 1950s or 1960s patriarchy that the car song should be seen. Its continuing presence reveals both how much and how little has changed. How different after all is the male world portrayed by Springsteen and Waits from that revealed by Berry and Wilson?

So far I have covered pop's adolescence and its young adulthood. It remains to be seen if the car song can be used to take a more mature view of masculinity. Two songs suggest it can – Don Henley's *Boys of Summer* and

Prefab Sprout's *Cars and Girls*. Henley's song presents a rather mixed experience, with its somewhat obsessive aspect of the hero's pursuit of the object of his desire. That said, it does offer a sense that his pursuit is based on the understanding that in order to get her back 'after the Boys of Summer have gone' requires that he must demonstrate that he is worthy of her – 'I'm gonna show you what I'm made of'. The cars in this song create a sense of movement at odds with that in previous examples. Here they keep her at a distance, constantly on the move and always unreachable.

We are still dealing with a 'man as subject, woman as object' situation. However, here the difference is that the car gives her control over the distance between them rather than him. What is more he is unable to bridge that gap. Ultimately, what sets this song apart and gives it a degree of emotional maturity not present elsewhere in the examples already given are the lines:

> Out on the road today
> I saw a Deadhead sticker on a Cadillac
> A little voice inside my head said
> Don't look back you can never look back
> I thought I knew what love was
> What did I know
> Those days are gone forever
> I should just let them go but
>
> I can see you
> Your brown skin shinin' in the sun
> You got the top pulled down
> Radio on, Baby
> I can tell you my love for you
> Will still be strong
> After the Boys of Summer have gone.

The lines about the Deadhead sticker on the Cadillac represent a mature and ironic comment. Henley is contrasting the values of the Summer of Love represented by the Grateful Dead with those of the Cadillac owner. The narrator is caused in turn to reflect on his own life changes. How far has he moved? How far has he aged? This song is in fact as much about the loss of youth and of the ideals of that period in one's life as it is about a lost love. The Cadillac and the convertible driven by his love are contrasted in a way that emphasises the distance between them but also between what he was and what he is now. *Cars and Girls* is in part writer Paddy McAloon's riposte to Bruce Springsteen:

Brucie dreams life's a highway too many roads bypass my way
Or they never begin. Innocence coming to grief
At the hands of life – stinkin' car thief, that's my concept of sin
Does heaven wait all heavenly over the next horizon?

The hook line in the chorus is – 'some things hurt more much more than cars and girls' is used to point up the trivial nature of Springsteen's frame of reference. McAloon is suggesting there is more to life and subjects more worthy of attention. The remark about car theft and original sin delights in view of the many religious references in Springsteen's work. If cars are so important, McAloon is saying, then car theft is surely a crime deserving damnation. Does Heaven wait over the horizon? This is McAloon's comment on the car song and the endless searching of its heroes for some new and better experience, that need to move on and that escape from entanglement. But he goes further, adding irony upon irony to reflect on the very nature of masculinity as posed by the car song:

Little boy got a hot rod, thinks it makes him some kind
of new God Well this is one race he won't win, cos life's no cruise
with a cool chick Too many folk feeling car sick, but it never pulls in.
Brucie's thoughts – Pretty streamers – guess this world needs its
dreamers may they never wake up.

Cars and girls are at the heart of pop. The car song tells us much about the ways in which men make sense of their maleness. McAloon is well aware of this but subverts the form to give a different take on the subject. Much of his writing fits most easily into a post-modernist frame. In this song despite its post-modernist elements he presents a socially conscious version of the car song and by implication a mature and reflective view of masculinity.

To summarise, I have attempted here to do several things. Firstly, I have tried to use the car song to explore the ways in which masculinity is revealed in pop music. The pop song is after all primarily concerned with gender as its subject matter. Secondly, I have sought to examine the different ways in which men and women writers use language in the car song and compared this with research about gender differences in language use. Thirdly, I have attempted to reveal the clear and continuing link between Black Music and pop music and the ways in which the latter finds inspiration in the former. Finally, I have reflected in passing on how far relationships between men and women have changed with over thirty years of debate and discussion behind us. In the unlikely event that the car song can provide some kind of road map for changes in how we understand gender differences, I think it might tell us that things have changed, although perhaps less than we imagine. For real change to take place it must be necessary for men to learn how to talk about sexuality and not just sex. Some things really do hurt much more than cars and girls!

Bibliography

Barthes, R. (1981) Mythologies, Granada, St.Albans.

Berry, C. (1996) The *Autobiography*, Faber, London.

Chambers, I. (1993) *Popular Culture – The Metropolitan Experience*, Routledge, London.

Coates, J. (1986) *Women, Men and Language: A Sociolinguistic Account of Sex Differences in Language*, Longman, Harlow.

Gray, M. (1972) *Song and Dance Man: The Art of Bob Dylan*, Granada, London.

Harding, S. (1975) 'Women and Words in a Spanish Village', in R. Reiter, (ed.), *Towards an Anthropology of Women*, Monthly Review Press, New York.

Hawkes, T. (1992) *Structuralism and Semiotics*, Routledge, London.

Horrocks, R. (1995) *Male Myths and Icons*, Macmillan, Basingstoke.

Hudson, L. (1968) *Frames Of Mind – Ability, Perception and Self-perception in the Arts and Sciences*, Penguin, Harmondsworth.

Hudson, L. and Jacot, B. (1995) *The Way Men Think: Intellect, Intimacy and the Erotic Imagination,* Yale University Press, New York and London.

Kaplan,E.A. (1987) *Rocking Around The Clock – Music Television, Postmodernism and Consumer Culture*, Routledge, London.

Kent, N. (1994) 'The Last Beach Movie Revisited: The Life of Brian Wilson' in N. Kent, *The Ark Stuff*, Penguin, Harmondsworth.

McHale, B. (1992) 'Making (Non)sense of Postmodernist Poetry in Language' in M. Toolan (ed.), *Text and Context: Essays in Stylistics*, Routledge, London.

Maltz, D.N. and Borker, R.A. (1982) A Cultural Approach to Male–Female Miscommunication, in J.J. Gumperz (ed.), *Language and Social Identity*, Cambridge University Press, Cambridge.

Marcus, G. (1977) *Mystery Train*, Omnibus, London.

Marsh, P. and Collett, P. (1986) *Driving Passion – The Psychology of the Car*, Jonathan Cape, London.

Oliver, P. (1990) *Blues Fell This Morning: Meaning in the Blues*, Cambridge University Press, Cambridge.

Reynolds, S. and Press, J. (1995) *The Sex Revolts – Gender, Rebellion and Rock and Roll*, Serpent's Tail, London.

Riessman, C.K. (1994), *Divorce Talk: Women and Men Make Sense of Personal Relationships*, Rutgers University Press, New Brunswick.

Staats', G.R. (1979) 'Sexual Imagery in the Blues', *Journal of Jazz Studies,* Spring/Summer.

Tannen, D. (1993) *You Just Don't Understand – Women and Men in Conversation*, Virago, London.

Watson, B. (1995) *Frank Zappa: the Negative Dialectics of Poodle Play*, Quartet, London.

Wicke, P. (1990) *Rock Music – Culture, Aesthetics and Sociology*, Cambridge University Press, Cambridge.

Discography

w. = writer; p. = publisher/record label

Anderson, Laurie, O SUPERMAN (FOR MASSENET) (1982: w. Anderson, p. Difficult Music).

Beach Boys, I GET AROUND (1964: w. Wilson, p. EMI Music Publishing Ltd.)

Beach Boys, LITTLE DEUCE COUPE (1963: w. Wilson/Christian, p. EMI Music Publishing Ltd).

Beach Boys, SHUT DOWN (1963: w. Wilson/Christian, Screen Gems/Emi Music Publishing Ltd).

Beatles DRIVE MY CAR (1965: w. Lennon/ McCartney, p. Northern Songs).

Berry, Chuck MAYBELLENE (1955: w. Berry/Fratto/Freed, p. Jewel Music).

Berry, Chuck NO MONEY DOWN (1956: w. Berry, p. Jewel Music).

Berry, Chuck NO PARTICULAR PLACE TO GO (1964 w. Berry, p. Jewel Music).

Borrom, William CAR MACHINE BLUES (1930).

Brenston, Jackie and the Kings of Rhythm ROCKET 88 (1955?: w. Turner?, p. unknown).

Chapman, Tracy FAST CAR (1987: w. Chapman, p. SBK April Music Inc/ Purple Rabbit Music).

Cochran, Eddie SOMETHIN' ELSE (1959: w. Sheeley/Cochran, p. Burlington Music Co Ltd).

Cochran, Eddie SUMMERTIME BLUES (1959: w. Cochran/Capehart, p. Cinephonic Music Co Ltd).

Diddley, Bo ROADRUNNER (1960: w. McDaniel, p. Jewel Music).

Dylan, Bob FROM A BUICK 6 (1965: w. Dylan, p. Blossom Music).

Dylan, Bob TALKIN' WORLD WAR III BLUES (1963: w. Dylan, p. Blossom Music).

Emerson, William CRAZY 'BOUT AN AUTOMOBILE (EVERY WOMAN I KNOW) (1956?: w. Emerson, p. unknown).

Griffiths, Nanci FORD ECONOLINE (1987: w. Griffith, p. Warner Bros Music Ltd/ Bug Music Ltd.)

Hagar, Sammy I CAN'T DRIVE AT 55 (1984: w. Hagar, p. Geffen Records).

Henley, Don BOYS OF SUMMER (1984: w. Henley/Campbell, p. Warner Bros Music Ltd).

Heining, Duncan POP MUSIC.

Hopkins, Lightnin' BLACK CADILLAC (1960?: w. Hopkins, p. Prestige Music).

Jan and Dean DEAD MAN'S CURVE (1963: w. Christian/Berry/Kornfeld, p. unknown).

Johnson, Robert TERRAPLANE BLUES (1936: w. Johnson, p. unknown).

Minnie, Memphis ME AND MY CHAUFFEUR BLUES (1941: w. Lawler p. MCA Music Ltd).

Mitchell, Joni COYOTE (1976: w. Mitchell, p. Crazy Crow Music).

Numan, Gary CARS (1979: w. Numan, p. Beggars Banquet/Momentum Music Ltd).

Peterson, Ray TELL LAURA I LOVE HER (1960: w. Raleigh/Barry, p. MCPS/EMI Music Publishing Ltd).

Pickett, Wilson MUSTANG SALLY (1966: w. Rice, p. Fourteenth Hour).

Prefab Sprout CARS AND GIRLS (1988: w. McAloon, p. Kitchen Music Ltd/ SBK Songs Ltd).

Presley, Elvis LET'S PLAY HOUSE (1957: w. Gunter, p. unknown.)

Prince, LITTLE RED CORVETTE (1982: w. Prince, p. Controversy Music/Warner Bros Music Ltd).

Richman, Jonathan and the Modern Lovers ROADRUNNER (1976: w. Richman, p. Modern Love Songs/Warner Bros Music Ltd).

Robinson, Tom GREY CORTINA (1978: w. Robinson, p. EMI Music Publishing Ltd).

Robinson, Tom 2-4-6-8 MOTORWAY SONG (1978: w. Robinson, EMI Music Publishing Ltd).

Springsteen, Bruce BORN TO RUN (1975: w. Springsteen, p. Zomba Music Publishers Ltd).

Springsteen, Bruce HUNGRY HEART (1979: w. Springsteen, p. Zomba Music Publishers Ltd).

Springsteen, Bruce RACING IN THE STREET (1978: w. Springsteen, p. Zomba Music Publishers Ltd).

Springsteen, Bruce SHERRY DARLING (1980: w. Springsteen, p. Zomba Music Publishers Ltd).

Springsteen, Bruce THUNDER ROAD (1975: w. Springsteen, p. Zomba Music Publishers Ltd).

Steppenwolf BORN TO BE WILD (1968: w. Bonfire, p. Duchess Music Corp).

Taylor, Vince BRAND NEW CADILLAC (1959: w. Taylor, p. Carlin Music Corp).

Waits, Tom BURMA SHAVE (1977: w. Waits, p. Intersong Music Ltd).

Waits, Tom FRANK'S WILD YEARS (1983: w. Waits, p. Jalma Music).

Waits, Tom JACK AND NEAL (1977: w. Waits, p. Intersong Music Ltd).

Waits, Tom LOOKING FOR THE HEART OF SATURDAY NIGHT (1974: w. Waits, p. Intersong Music Ltd.)

Waits, Tom OL '55 (1973: w. Waits, p. Intersong Music Ltd).

Walker, Junior ROADRUNNER (1966: w. Holland/Dozier/Holland, p. Jobete Music).

Zappa, Frank BOW TIE DADDY (1967: w. Zappa, p. Frank Zappa Music).

Zappa, Frank CRUISIN' FOR BURGERS (1969: w.Zappa, p. Frank Zappa Music).

Zappa, Frank DOG BREATH (1969: w. Zappa, p. Frank Zappa Music Ltd).

9

Spectacles of Speed and Endurance: The Formative Years of Motor Racing in Europe

Daryl Adair

Because human body movement is limited by anatomical and physiological constraints, the movement *of* bodies by secondary means has, over time, assumed enormous significance. The practical value of all sorts of conveyances, from animals to machines, is readily apparent; more puzzling is a fascination with speed that has often accompanied such innovations. Competitive racing has, in fact, been part of human existence since the chariot races of Ancient Rome, so contests of speed hardly seem novel. What is different about the modern age, though, is that the pace of human movement has increased exponentially because of advances in technology (Marsh & Collett, 1986, 189). While steam and coal-driven forms of transport were developed during the Industrial Revolution, it was the invention of the internal combustion engine in Germany in 1885 which allowed for the practical possibility of speeds well in excess of those that had been achieved previously.[1] The motor car was, to use a pun, the experimental vehicle by which powered human movement accelerated. Other motorised conveyances via land, sea, and air followed, but it was the car that sparked the speed revolution. And, like the chariot events of yore, competitive rivalry was central to the development and performance of speed. So the sport – and indeed the business – of motor racing was to be expected.

Motor racing, social position, and economic power

When motor sport began in Europe in the mid-1890s it was not only a by-product of technological innovation, it was also a creation of dominant social groups and economic interests. Motor racing was not an accessible sport; rather, it was an unashamedly socially exclusive pastime – successfully so. The early motor sport 'scene' in Europe was basically the preserve of two affluent groups, aristocratic enthusiasts and experimental car manufacturers. This élitism was, however, no surprise; ownership of an automobile, which was very expensive, presupposed wealth. Moreover, involvement in motor sport, a precarious and capricious venture, required financial means to repair or replace a damaged vehicle. Hence racing was a prestigious preoccupation, with wealthy private enthusiasts and entrepreneurs displaying their affinity for motoring before thousands of spectators who assembled to witness their exploits. (Villard, 1973, 21)

It is significant, too, that pioneer racing drivers were seen as 'adventurers' risking life and limb simply by participating, let alone striving to win. Motor sport, therefore, was not a leisurely or timorous social promenade. Indeed, although racing was a contest of machines and a display of technology, it was also a celebration of human gallantry, fortitude, and achievement. Manliness was central to this glorification of the driver, and this was not just because motor sport was essentially the preserve of men. The heroic qualities ascribed to racing drivers, such as bravery, courage, and composure, epitomised 'character-building' traits that were prized by many contemporary educators and writers as a way of 'making' men out of boys. In the élite public schools of Victorian England, for example, organised sport for boys was taken very seriously as a training ground for life and leadership. While racing drivers adopted more of a 'dare-devil', cavalier approach to their sport than did schoolboy cricketers or rowers, their enterprising spirit, self-reliance, and stoicism were admired widely. Moreover, although drivers were acclaimed for their 'artistry' and 'style' behind the wheel, this was described emphatically as a manly virtue (Villard, 17, 1972; Setright, 1981 34).[2] In the guise of the racing driver (and other aristocratic sporting 'adventurers'), gentlemen were thus able to deflect criticism that they were becoming effeminate and sedentary in a less physically demanding modern age.[3]

While motor sport was made possible by technological innovation, it was made practical by economic interests – in other words, by commercial manufacturers. Amateur drivers relied on private companies to sell them vehicles and components for races, and these manufacturers used motor sport to advertise their products. The races were, after all, not only contests of speed, they were also tests of endurance and reliability – features that were important to potential car buyers outside of motor sport. Winning was, however, still the best publicity of all: companies soon realised that in order to advertise their products effectively through motor sport they needed to employ drivers and mechanics to compete on their behalf. This development ushered in commercialisation and professionalism to motor racing in a short time, despite complaints that 'firms with the most money would always win because they could give their drivers an advantage over pure sportsmen' (Rendall, 1991, 35). Indeed, as early as 1906, just twelve years after the first organised road race, the British amateur driver Charles Jarrot lamented that 'only men who make it their business to drive these cars can hope to be successful ... the curse of commercialism is the ruin of every sport' (Rendall, 1991, 35).

Prize-money and sponsorship had, however, been part of motor sport from its inception. When Pierre Giffard, a writer with the Paris newspaper *Le Petit Journal*, organised a motoring trial for 'voitures sans chevaux' (horseless carriages) between Paris and Rouen in 1894, a first prize of 5,000 francs was offered by the paper. This was supplemented by a 'private' donation of a further 5,000 francs to the placegetters offered by Monsieur Marinoni, the owner of *Le Petit Journal*, who wished to associate himself personally with the spectacle (Rendall, 1991, 35; Villard, 1972, 28–9). This seventy-eight mile event was an exhibition of automobile technology more than a race, because competitors left at different intervals and were judged by factors such as reliability, manoeuvrability and design simplicity. Speed was only one part of this motoring equation. The first competitor to reach Rouen was Count (later Marquis) de Dion, driving a steam-powered conveyance, but he was not awarded first prize because his vehicle required the attention of two crew in order to function, it was difficult to handle, and it was too expensive to be considered practical. Instead, the more practical petrol-driven automobiles entered by two French car manufacturers, Peugot and Panhard, were declared the victors jointly (Setright, 1981, 11,14; Villard, 1972, 30). So the enterprising Count de Dion had not only forgone first prize, the eventual winners were representatives of car companies rather than titled amateur enthusiasts like himself.

It appears, at first glance, that amateurs' competing for prize-money in motor racing was contradictory. However, this particular use of the term amateur was reminiscent of the men of social position who took part in sport as a leisure pastime rather than as an occupation during the eighteenth and early nineteenth centuries, but who were not opposed to prize-money and gambling. These sportsmen were called gentlemen, rather than amateurs, with the latter term coming into use from the mid-nineteenth century as a contradistinction to the widespread emergence of sporting professionals, who were paid to take part in sport as their *occupation*.[4] Gentlemen drivers raced for both prize-money and pleasure, but could still be considered amateur because they competed as part-time sporting enthusiasts rather than as full-time salaried professionals.[5] Such a liberal interpretation of the term amateur was, however, unusual by the turn of the century: a puritanical middle-class amateur code had, by this time, eschewed monetary reward or speculation in sport generally. Middle-class amateurs argued that monetary gain corrupted sport because competitors were not only paid to win, they could also be paid to lose – particularly where prize-money, stake-money, or gambling proliferated. What was more, the staunchest advocates of amateurism argued that there should be a separation of social classes in sport. Some sportsmen gained physical fitness or expertise in their chosen sport simply by going about their ordinary work, such as scullers who plied their trade on rivers. This made it difficult for middle-class sportsmen, who tended to be employed in sedentary occupations, to compete against them effectively (Halliday, 1990, 81–4).

In motor racing, however, there does not seem to have been any suggestion that chauffeurs, for example, had a decided advantage over those who drove for pleasure (although some chauffeurs certainly did race). The major point of contention was not with those who gained their motoring skills routinely; rather, as we saw previously, amateur enthusiasts like Charles Jarrott complained that they were disadvantaged by competing against men whose occupation was a *racing* driver, and who were in turn sponsored to pursue their career by car manufacturers. The winner of the 1906 Targa Florio, for example, was the Italian Allesandro Cagno, who was employed at the time by Itala; while the champion grand prix driver at Le Mans in 1906 was the Hungarian Francois Szisz, who represented the Renault motor company (Setright, 1981, 65; Rendall, 1991, 61).

There was, however, counter-evidence that social position rather than sporting ability remained a basis for involvement in early motor racing. For the prestigious Gordon Bennett race of 1903, for example, the Automobil Club von Deutschland entered a team of three Mercedes cars, to be managed by Emil Jellinik, a 'distinguished gentleman'. While Jellinik moved in the 'highest circles' his peers considered that he was prone to 'unfortunate lapses of taste' – in this case his selection of drivers Wilhelm Werner and Otto Hieronymous. These men were talented but not titled: the result was that the ACD, acting on 'social grounds' refused to allow them to compete (Setright, 34–6). Setright explains that:

> The honour of Germany could only be represented by gentlemen who were *hochwohlgeborene* (of high birth) – and by some curious process of elimination this meant ... two Belgians, the Baron Pierre de Caters and Camille Jenatzy, and the Englishman Mr Foxhall Keene. (Setright, 1981, 36).

Alternatively, several aristocratic motoring enthusiasts started up car companies of their own, or bought into existing enterprises. The Marquis de Dion, for example, had a prominent role in French motor racing as founder of the Automobile Club of France, but he was also president of the De Dion–Bouton Motor Corporation. This was a partnership with Georges Bouton, a

Parisian mechanic who ran a modest engineering company. In order to develop racing cars Bouton required de Dion's capital, while the Marquis needed the mechanic's technical knowledge. They were involved in racing for different reasons, and socially they were opposites, but a relationship of mutual dependence was forged by their shared interest in motor sport (Andrews, 1964, 15; Villard, 1972, 33–4). So while automobile manufacturers were in the 'driving seat', as it were, in terms of developing motor cars for racing, aristocratic investors and patrons were part and parcel of this endeavour, which brought two powerful groups – men of social position and middle-class entrepreneurs – together in a common cause. Moreover, as we are about to see, given the variety of races in early twentieth-century Europe there were numerous opportunities for private enthusiasts to remain personally involved in motor sport at some level.

Early spectacles of speed and endurance

The Paris–Rouen trial of 1894 had stimulated interest in motoring, but competitors now wanted genuine races, not just an exhibition. Two aristocrats, the Count de Dion and Baron de Zuylen de Nyevelt, asked *Le Petit Journal* to sponsor a full-scale competitive event. But the newspaper was mortified:

> No one could complain at a competition in which reliability was the chief factor; but a long race in which speed was the be-all and end-all is quite another thing. Supposing an accident were to take place – and if these automobiles could really attain the terrifying speed of fifteen or twenty miles an hour ... a catastrophe was more than likely to happen. (Setright, 1981, 14)

Undaunted, the count and baron convened a committee to organise a motor race over 732 miles from Paris to Bourdeaux and back (1895), and this was followed by a 1063 mile race between Paris and Marseilles and back (1896). Prize-money and promotion for these events improved considerably: the 1895 contest boasted a total of 75 000 francs to placegetters, while the 1896 race was championed by the new motoring magazine *La France Automobile* (Rendall, 1991, 45). However, as *Le Petit* had predicted, there were numerous accidents. The 1896 race, for instance, was marred by boggy conditions after the narrow and dusty roads were drenched by rain. This made braking and steering particularly difficult, with a result that telegraph poles were struck, two cars collided with carts, another two were attacked by 'furious' bulls, and several cars ended up in ditches (Setright, 1981, 16). But *Le Petit's* fears of a catastrophe had not emerged: this was only early days, though, where cars were not particularly powerful and speed was hampered by poor road conditions.

By the beginning of the twentieth century, European manufacturers such as Renault and Mercedes had developed racing cars that could travel at eighty or more miles per hour. Their engine power was, however, far more advanced than their handling or braking, which created special problems for some of the heavy car models, weighing in at almost 3000lb (Setright, 1981, 19). Although France was the centre stage of European motor sport, neither the French government nor the police were enthusiastic about road racing, expressing fears of calamity that were reminiscent of *Le Petit Journal*. Indeed, the Paris–Madrid race of 1903 proceeded despite the reluctance of the French government to endorse it, although the Spanish leg of the contest did receive the sanction of King Alfonso (Boddy, 1977, 46–51). It was this event, however, that was to spell the demise of road racing in France.

The Paris–Madrid race promised to be one of the biggest sporting spectacles in history, with a crowd of perhaps three million people lining the road to Bordeaux alone. According to historian Henry Villard, though, 'therein lay the certainty of distaster'. This was because the masses of spectators were largely ignorant about the difficulties faced by drivers trying to control speeding motor vehicles, while the small contingent of police responsible for public order was woefully inadequate to contain undisciplined or unrestrained spectator behaviour (Villard, 89). On this evidence there seemed to be a catastrophe in waiting. However, according to Monsieur Tampier, the official timekeeper for the race, 'safety measures would be fully effective', and 'the drivers were all skilled and well qualified'. The French government's nervousness about the contest was surely justified, though, for Tampier nevertheless predicted 'We do not anticipate more than four deaths, onlookers or drivers' (Villard, 1972, 89). Despite this inglorious admission that fatalities were expected, neither the organisers nor the drivers saw any reason to modify the event, which contained 221 entries representing all the major car firms of Europe. It was very difficult politically for the French government to stop the race: at that time France was the leading manufacturer of automobiles in the world, with an industry valued at some 16 million francs in 1901 (Villard, 1972, 88). So the economic imperative behind motor sport was very powerful. As the entrepreneurial Marquis de Dion argued: 'A great yearly test is indispensable for the automobile industry. The livelihood of twenty-five thousand workers depends on that test' (Villard, 1972, 88). Yet it did not seem to dawn on the Marquis that race fatalities might, in fact, sour public confidence in motor vehicles.

The gamble of Paris–Madrid ended in disaster – and we only need a glimpse at the problems facing drivers to appreciate why. At Versailles, for example, some 100,000 people assembled to witness the start of the race, even though it began at 3.30am. Many of them carried Chinese lanterns to light the morning sky, but others scrambled onto the roads to try to obtain a view. Charles Jarrott's mechanic, Cecil Bianchi, recorded in his memoirs that 'the crowd hadn't the least idea what motor car speed was' (Villard, 1972, 93), while Jarrott recalled: 'It seemed impossible that my swaying bounding car could miss the reckless spectators. A wedge-shaped space opened out in the crowd as I approached ... I tried slowing down, but quickly realised that the danger was as great at 40 miles an hour as at 80' (Setright, 1981, 21). While the milling spectators appeared to be collectively mindless or irrational, the absence of crowd management techniques, such as race marshalls or barricades, together with public ignorance about the dangers of racing, were the fundamental reasons for safety problems. On the first leg of the race to Bourdeaux there were numerous casualties among drivers, their mechanics (who travelled with them on the side-step of the car), and spectators. In addition to the injured, though, two drivers, one mechanic, and five spectators were killed – as were numerous animals strewn along the roads. This was too much for the French government, which stopped the race at Bordeaux, demanding that the cars return to Paris aboard trains. Racing on open public thoroughfares was now basically finished in France, with racing now moving to closed circuits (Boddy, 1977, 51; Rendall, 1991, 48).

New styles of racing, new modes of participation

French car-makers had clearly dominated the early years of motor racing, so much so that a new style of motor race was promoted by James Gordon Bennett, an American newspaper entrepreneur resident in Paris. His plan was for national motor racing teams, rather than car manufacturers, to compete against each other: the cars and components would have to be built solely by individual countries, their drivers would have to be members of their country's auto club, and the cars would race in national colours. Bennett was alarmed that his own country lagged so far behind Europeans in motoring, so he suggested sporting rivalry between nations as a way of sparking development across the Atlantic. Moreover, because the focus of competition was countries, rather than manufacturers, this was a way of challenging French dominance of motor sport – particularly as each nation was restricted to only three cars. French manufacturers could have entered ten times that number if they were allowed to. The Gordon Bennett races, as they were called, began in 1900 but attracted only fleeting interest from American racing teams; what was more, France dominated the competition for the next six years, with the exception of an unlucky loss to Britain in 1902. French car manufacturers were, however, incensed by the nationalistic format of the race, which, they argued, prevented a contest between the best cars and drivers. In 1904, for example, France had to run an elimination race in order to select three cars for the Gordon Bennett from a total of twenty-nine nominations. While there were eighteen other countries represented in the race, none of them could claim this kind of depth. It was no surprise, therefore, that the French came up with their own racing format – the Grand Prix, a battle between the best drivers and a contest between the leading manufacturers (Rendall, 1991, 51–55).

The first Grand Prix, held at Le Mans in 1906, was notable because it was staged on a closed triangular circuit, rather than a point-to-point public route, which made it easier to manage both vehicles and crowds. For example, although the race cars travelled near St Calais, this traffic was diverted via a specially made wooden bridge. Hence for the first time competitors could race without 'control' areas restricting their speed through towns and villages. What was more, some forty miles of wooden barricades were erected to create a safe distance between performers and audience, while a tunnel was dug underneath the track to allow spectators to cross the area without danger. This modernised racetrack structure was completed by the erection of a grandstand to accommodate thousands of paying spectators. The Grand Prix format was also distinct in that, unlike earlier types of races, it was restricted to car manufacturers. This made it impossible for amateurs to enter their car in the Grand Prix as private enthusiasts – which had been a custom in the early point-to-point contests. The Grand Prix, therefore, was a race for car-making entrepreneurs (Boddy, 1977, 60; Villard, 1972, 144–5).

While France controlled early Grand Prix racing alternative types of motor sport, with more liberal rules of participation, were being introduced in Europe. Motor racing in Italy, for instance, was promoted very seriously in the early 1900s, where Italian manufacturers were rivalling their French competitors in developing racing cars. Unlike their Parisian counterparts, however, the Italians were not renowned for staging great races – although the Coppa Florio, a 231-mile road race in northern Italy in 1904, was a start. This event was organised by Count Vincenzo Florio, the son of a prominent Palermo merchant, who dreamed of staging a motor race to rival the forthcoming French Grand Prix. Florio had his first experience of race driving at Brescia earlier that year, and was now smitten with the sport. In order to entice Europe's best drivers to Italy, the Count commissioned French craftsmen to make a solid gold plate – the Targa Florio – for which race entrants would compete. Ever the patriot, Count Florio wanted the contest to take place in his native Sicily, so he selected a 92-mile circuit in the Madonie Mountains on the north coast of the island. This was to be a severe test of machine and driver: cars were to begin at sea level, ascend along narrow and winding roads to a height of 3600 feet, and then descend to sea level again for the finish (Owen, 1979, chapters 1–2; Villard, 1972, 153; Rendall, 1991, 58).

With rather cheeky timing the first Targa Florio was staged on 6 May 1906, some six weeks before the inaugural Grand Prix race at Le Mans. It began as a modest affair; there were only ten starters and six finishers, with little in the way of opposition to the Italian car-makers. By 1907, though, the demanding Targa circuit had attracted forty-three entries from nineteen different countries, including several of Europe's leading drivers, so its place on the racing calendar now seemed assured. The Fiat and Itala companies dominated the finish, so the reputation of Italian motor racing continued to grow, as the Count had hoped. Unlike Grand Prix racing, though, the Targa Florio was not restricted to car manufacturers. What was more, it allowed the entry of Vouiturettes, the small and light sports cars which were becoming popular as an alternative to the 'monstrous' Grand Prix cars of the early 1900s which, as Rendall puts it, 'were far removed from the touring cars the manufacturers were supposed to promote' (Rendall, 1991, 67). This all made the Targa Florio especially popular among private enthusiasts, the rich men (and a handful of women) who could afford to buy and maintain a suitably swift and reliable car. Indeed, while Italian car maker Bugatti dominated the Targa in the late 1920s, its drivers winning the event between 1927 and 1929, the company was also kept busy supplying cars to numerous amateur drivers who were keen to take part (Rendall, 1991, 83, 98).

This Italian tradition of providing racing opportunities for both professional and recreational drivers was continued in a new event, the Mille Miglia, founded in 1927 by the Auto Club di Brescia. To encourage all comers, organisers introduced a 'utility class' entry in the 1930 race which, as Rendall explains, 'limited … engine size and price to make sure that the entries represented the kind of car which could be bought in the showroom' (Rendall, 108). Not surprisingly, the entry list for that year doubled to 135 cars. A second innovation was a staggered start separating amateurs and professionals. The recreational drivers in 'utility class' were given an eight-hour head start over the élite-level contenders for this 1000 mile test of endurance, although the sports cars driven by the professionals had little trouble out-performing the rest of the field. But the charm of the Mille Miglia was that both groups took part in the same event, while for young Italian males, the race became something of a 'test' of their manhood (Rendall, 1991, 110).

By contrast to France and Italy, motor racing in Britain was poorly developed in the early 1900s, largely because road racing had been banned there by state authorities. The erection of the Brooklands racetrack in England in 1907 – the first purpose-built motor racing arena in the world – was thus a particularly welcome initiative. It was soon obvious, though, that Brooklands had a more exclusive code of participation than either the Targa Florio or various Vouiturette events. Indeed, a striking feature of Brooklands was that it revived aristocratic power in motor sport at the very time it had fallen with the introduction of Grand Prix racing on the Continent. Rendall describes racing at Brooklands as akin to socially prestigious English sporting events like Royal Ascot, Henly Regatta, and Wimbledon. Indeed, entry fees to the enclosure were deliberately high, this 'ensuring that the sport was beyond the pockets of most working people' (Rendall, 1991, 101). The Brooklands Committee consisted of members of the British aristocracy who presided over a programme that was broadly similar to a horse-racing event. Drivers were obliged to wear coloured uniforms, cars were handicapped by performance, and bookmakers took bets. Rendall concludes that 'Brooklands was a club run by a particular social group for its own pleasure; the technical advance of motor cars was not its primary concern' (Rendall, 1991,101). The arena did become a venue for world speed record attempts, this giving it some utility in terms of motoring development, but it was not really an ideal track for high performance racing and, by 1933, it was superceded by the new Donington Park raceway.

The early 1900s also featured endurance motor events over, what was then, fantastic distances. Races had previously been conducted within Europe between national capitals, but intercontinental motor sport was unprecedented. It was therefore big news, which helps to explain why the French newspaper *Le Matin* came up with the idea of organising and sponsoring a race from (of all places) Peking to Paris in 1907. *Le Matin* argued that circuit racing had done little to develop the car other than to 'make it go round in circles'. What was needed, insisted the paper, was a type of racing that had practical value for motorists: 'The supreme use of the automobile is that it makes long journeys possible. Its effect is to make man the master of distance ... [completing] journeys hitherto undreamed of' (Villard, 1972, 14). What *Le Matin* failed to acknowledge was that racing was restricted to circuits for reasons of public safety, and long distance driving was not really practical because the road system was poorly developed. Yet this realisation only seemed to inspire the competitors. The ubiquitous Marquis de Dion, for example, announced: 'The roads [from Peking to Paris] are abominable, and often only exist as lines on a map. However, it is my belief that if a motor-car can get through, the de Dion-Bouton will get through.' As the Marquis saw it, therefore, this was an opportunity to advertise his company's motor vehicle and to try to show that it was superior to competitors. Predictably, though, a chance for personal glory also underpinned de Dion's interest. He claimed: 'This is a Jules Verne undertaking, a Mayne Reid adventure. But nothing is impossible' (Villard, 1972, 15).

Given the cost of transporting cars by steamer to Peking, plus the daunting task of making the return journey by car, there were only five entries for this intercontinental motor sport marathon. Predictably, the drivers encountered all sorts of hazards, with bogs and quicksand in the deserts of Asia their most common obstacle. For much of the journey they were towed by oxen through terrain barely fit for walking, let alone driving. Yet two months to the day after their start from Peking on 10 June, a winner was welcomed into Paris by exultant crowds. The victor was Prince Scipione Borghese, driving an Itala, which he had ordered for the race to his personal specifications. The Marquis's de Dion-Boutons came in next, twenty-one days later, so it was a dual triumph for aristocratic 'adventurers' and manufacturing interests.

Further intercontinental races were soon planned. In the United States, where speed events on closed circuits were popular, such as with the Vanderbilt Cup and the Indianapolis 500, there had already been a transcontinental endurance trial across North America, where in 1903 Tom Fetch made the journey in sixty-one days (Villard, 1972, 167–8). As in Britain, speed events on public roads had never been accepted by American authorities, but marathon trials, with a slower pace and an emphasis on reliability, were tolerated. Since American and European car makers and drivers largely operated in separate spheres, the suggestion in 1908 of a race between New York and Paris seemed a way of stimulating trans-Atlantic rivalries. It would, of course, also sell newspapers for the co-sponsors – *Le Matin* and the *New York Times*. There were six entries – five European and one American. Against these odds the lone American car – Thomas Flyer, a standard road car – scored an unexpected victory after a horrendous 170 days of driving, which included a journey over the frozen Bering Strait, between Alaska and Russia.[6] This win had immense symbolic value to American motoring interests: at an Automobile Club luncheon in New York speakers confidently predicted that 'the American car was at last equal to a foreign machine', and the victory by an American driver spelled 'the beginning of the end of European supremacy' (Villard, 1972, 174). These sentiments underscored the longstanding primacy of car makers in Europe, as well as the leadership of European drivers and manufacturers during the formative years of motor sport.

Endurance racing of a different kind began in France in 1923. The 24-hour Grand Prix d'Endurance was conceived as 'the ultimate test of the stamina of touring cars' on a closed circuit (Rendall, 1991, 101). Predictably, this event was attractive to automobile manufacturers as a display of their cars' handling and reliability – particularly as this was a contest for touring cars. Many car makers in the early 1920s had pulled out of the European Grand Prix racing circuit owing to its increasing expense, but also because the types of cars now being developed for these high performance events were far removed from conventional roadsters. The Le Mans 24-hour race was also notable because, as a one-off annual event, a small team of manufacturers could put together a car specifically for this contest. By contrast to the Grand Prix circuit, therefore, the Le Mans 24-hour race could better accommodate minor car makers, and there was even a place for part-time gentlemen drivers.

Perhaps the best expression of this came in 1924 when Englishman John Duffy entered his British-made Bentley car at Le Mans, taking victory against 39 French rivals. William Owen Bentley, the car's manufacturer, had not been interested in the race, but soon changed his mind after this win, which gave his car a public profile he could not have imagined. Bentley thus entered a team in subsequent years, winning Le Mans from 1927 to 1929 – even filling the first four placings on the last of these occasions. The affluent gentlemen who produced and drove these cars were labelled affectionately as 'The Bentley Boys', and they rode on the crest of a wave of public approbation. It was a dream come true: 'British cars, in British racing green, with British drivers, beating foreign competition on its own ground' (Rendall, 191, 101). However, the cost of racing car development and manufacture had escalated, and this, coupled with the economic impact of the Depression, forced Bentley to withdraw from Le Mans in 1931. The company was taken over subsequently by Rolls Royce. Le Mans continued, of course, still featuring a smattering of private entries and gentlemen drivers among the works' teams. But Le Mans, like Grand Prix racing more generally, proceeded mainly as a contest between high profile manufacturers.[7]

Motor sport and the development of motoring

Motor racing, particularly the Grand Prix format, developed as a commercial display by car manufacturers who, through the medium of sport, colluded to provide themselves with spectacular and dramatic product displays. For some car makers, though, the rising cost of motor racing did not appear to reap sufficient commercial benefit; others complained that, especially with Grand Prix events, the racing cars had become too different from family saloons to have a tangible advertising connection. Endurance and reliability events, though, certainly helped to convince governments that road-building ought to form a greater proportion of capital expenditure: the economic benefits of road transport, while uncertain in the early 1900s, were therefore at least being considered by policy makers. Transportation was, after all, a topical issue at this time, particularly as air travel had developed significantly in the wake of World War I. Through the motor car and the aeroplane, therefore, the potential for rapid human movement over long distances loomed larger than ever before –

and Europe was taking a leading role in applying both these technologies to civilian life.

As a sport, though, motor racing was somewhat unusual, involving as it did a contest between both manufacturers and drivers. Performance-enhancing equipment was at the heart of motor sport from its inception, and while governing bodies brought in new rules every year to regulate or curb its impact, motor racing certainly remained a technology-driven sport. The individual skill of drivers was, of course, still central to a car's performance, but the winning edge was also gained by mechanical or technical innovation – as is still true of motor racing today. To some 'purists', however, this contest between machines, not just men, was contrary to the 'value' of sport, an activity which, they claimed, was founded on the idea of an equal chance for all participants. As a recent critic of sport has put it: 'if technology is a factor in the result, is the competition fair?' (Rintala, 1995, 72). What was more, some of the pioneering motor companies had greater resources than others to spend on research and development: this gave them an advantage in terms of improving their cars before they even made the track on race day. Yet there is a sense in which motor racing was the most honest of sports during the early twentieth century: this is because it was at least open about the economic and technological differences that sustained it. Most sports were shielded from such public scrutiny, which only perpetuated myths about 'level playing fields' during the formative years of modern sport.[8] Aside from economic factors there was, of course, also considerable social prestige associated with participation in motor sport. This helps to explain why affluent private enthusiasts spent personal fortunes in order to drive by the seat of their pants, risking life and limb in a quest for racing 'glory'.

Significantly, though, such perils of participation in motor sport weighed against both its entertainment value and its commercial potential. Spectator injuries and fatalities were, however, significantly reduced by the introduction of closed racing circuits, spectator barricades, and grandstand seating. Despite these modernising reforms, the rising speed of cars still presented potential for distaster if drivers lost control and a vehicle left the track. There were several tragic incidents of this kind at Italian road-racing circuits, where crowd safety measures were not as well developed as at small arenas like Monza or Donnington Park. For the most part, though, spectator safety improved considerably during the first three decades of the twentieth century. Drivers, instead, faced the greatest danger. While a full statistical analysis of driver injuries and fatalities has yet to be attempted, it is well known that there were numerous casualties in motor sport – particularly during its formative years when the handling of cars was suspect and drivers were not provided with protective helmets or fire-proof suits. Historian William Court has listed more than seventy of the most famous Grand Prix drivers killed in motor sport this century, but this type of study needs to be supplemented by an analysis of driver mortality rates across the board.[9]

The formative years of motor racing in Europe were, therefore, a time in which the development of the motor industry and motor sport were closely aligned. However, as racing at the élite-level became more specialised by the 1920s and 1930s, this symbiotic relationship began to break down. In particular, many car makers left Grand Prix competition, unable to justify the cost of maintaining their involvement, and uncertain whether the performance of Grand Prix cars had a deciding influence on sales of a company's passenger cars. Another characteristic of this early period was the modernisation of tracks upon which motor cars raced. Increasingly, small-scale, enclosed circuits were preferred to open roads, both for the safety of spectators, and for economic reasons – it was far easier to charge spectators for watching a performance if they entered through a turnstile in a closed arena. Finally, the formative years of motor racing saw the declining influence of gentleman amateurs, although some of them – such as the Marquis de Dion – took up an entrepreneurial role in the sport. This suggested a new role for these enthusiasts: monetary gain had, in the past, assumed little importance in terms of their involvement in motor racing. Motor sport, in other words, had become big business all round.

Endnotes

[1] It is worth noting, however, that steam-powered cars also achieved impressive speeds in these early years. The 'Stanley steamer', for example, was rated in 1906 at more than a hundred and twenty miles per hour over a 'flying mile'. H. S. Villard (1972), *The Great Road Races 1894–1914*, Arthur Barker Limited, London, 24.

[2] For film footage of the brazen driving feats of early Formula 1 drivers (1906), see the video recording *The Saga of Formula 1: Vol. 2, The Legendary Drivers*, Southern Star/Roadshow.

[3] For wider discussions about sport, 'adventure', and manliness in the late nineteenth and early twentieth centuries, see the various essays in J.A. Mangan and J. Walvin (eds), (1987) *Manliness and Morality: Middle-Class Morality in Britain and America, 1800–1940*, Manchester University Press, Manchester; and J. Nauright and T.J.L. Chandler (eds), (1996) *Making Men: Rugby and Masculine Identity*, Frank Cass, London.

[4] See R. Holt (1989), *Sport and the British: A Social History*, Oxford University Press, Oxford, chap. 2.

[5] Rendall refers to such drivers as 'gentlemen professionals', but this phrase is surely misleading because he acknowledges that 'they did not rely on driving for a living', having the financial wherewithal to take part in racing as an 'indulgence'. (Rendall, 1991, 98). They accepted prize-money as did *gentlemen* in sports like horse-racing; they were certainly not professionals in the sense of relying on racing for their livelihood.

[6] For fuller discussion, see D. Cole (1991), *Hard Driving: The 1908 Auto Race from New York to Paris*, Paragon House, New York.

⁷ See P. McKay and B. Naismith (eds) (1984), *24 Heures du Mans*, Garry Sparke and Associs, Glen Waverley Vic.

⁸ For wider discussions, see chapter 6, 'Stretching the Limits: Science and Technology', in D. Adair and W. Vamplew (1997), *Sport in Australian History*, Oxford University Press, Sydney.

⁹ An interesting comparison could also be made with pioneer aviators during the early twentieth century, see D. Adair (1995)'"Wings Across the World": The Heyday of Competitive Long Distance Flying in Australia, 1919–34', *Sporting Heritage*, 1, 73–90.

Bibliography

Andrews, A. (1964) *The Mad Motorists: The Great Peking–Paris Race of 1907*, Harrap, London.

Boddy, W. (1977) *The History of Motor Racing*, Orbus, London.

Cole, D. (1991) *Hard Driving: The 1908 Auto Race from New York to Paris*, Paragon House, New York.

Court, W. (1992) *Grand Prix Requiem: A Celebration of Motor Racing Greats. Paid Speed's Ultimate Price*, Patrick Stephens Ltd, Sparkford.

Halliday, E. (1990) *Rowing in England: A Social History*, Manchester University Press, Manchester.

Marsh, P. & Collett, P. (1986) *Driving Passion: The Psychology of the Car*, Jonathan Cape, London.

Owen, D. (1979) *Targa Florio*, Haynes, Sparkford.

Rendall, I. (1991) *The Power and the Glory: A Century of Motor Racing*, BBC Books, London.

Rintala, J. (1995) '"Sport and Technology": Human Questions in a World of Machines', *Journal of Sport and Social Issues*, 19, 1, February.

Setright, L.J.K. (1981) *The Pirelli History of Motor Sport*, Frederick Muller Ltd, London.

Villard, H.S. (1972) *The Great Road Races 1894–1914*, Arthur Barker Ltd, London.

10

Classic and Desirable: The Mystique of the British Sports Car

Steven Morewood

The mystique and desirability of classic British sports cars

There is a mystique attached to classic British sports cars, which possess an allure that defies description. The story goes that on an overseas trip William Morris, later Lord Nuffield, was introduced to a foreign businessman as the manufacturer of Morris cars. A look of incredulity appeared across the latter's face, but following the revelation that Morris also produced MG Cars a smile of instant recognition resulted (Adeney, 1988, 127). A recent survey in Japan, which has been notoriously unreceptive to Western manufactured imports, found that motorists considered the home-bred Mazda to be the top sports car, followed by the British MG, confirming its endurance as one of the world's most famous specialist marques (Eason, 1995). When Lord Montagu, founder of the National Motor Museum Trust and head of the National Motor Museum at Beaulieu, selected the 12 British models which had 'made a profound impact on motoring history' in terms of 'design, technology, or production techniques', no less than five sports cars made the list: the Bentley 4.5 litre supercharged (1930), MG TC Midget (1946), Jaguar XK120 (1950), Aston Martin Vantage (1977) and McLaren F1 (1994) (Montagu, 1995a).

While sports cars are not exclusive to Britain, the 'Britishness' associated with the best of the breed and their distinguishing handling characteristics mark them out. The increasing rarity and coveted status of classic British sports cars has seen their monetary value increase astronomically over the post-1945 period. As one commentator remarked: 'in 1936, a 10-year-old 3 litre [Bentley] could be had for £40. Today, you cannot get a good example for a thousand times that' (Montagu, 1995b). Jaguars dominate the classic model market. At the height of the 1980s boom in classic cars, a Jaguar E-Type fetched £100,000 while the going rate for an Austin Healey 3000 was £40,000 (Williams, 1996). In 1996, on its thirty-fifth anniversary, an E-Type Jaguar was acquired by the New York Museum of Modern Art. By the mid-1990s good examples of the Aston Martin DB5 were fetching between £35,000 and £60,000. Even the Daimler Dart, the famous marque's solitary venture into the sports car market which proved so disastrous that it exposed the company to a takeover from Jaguar, now enjoys a rarity and desirability value, fetching up to £15,000 for well preserved examples (Selby, 1996a). In fact, the British vintage car industry is now a near £1 billion a year industry, earning millions in exports (Copps, 1996). The mystique of past British sports cars is kept alive by owners' clubs and motoring magazines such as *Classic Cars, Thoroughbred and Sports Car, Classic and Sportscar, Performance Car, Top Marques* and *Top Gear*.

To define a sports car is no easy task. Doug Nye said it best when he wrote: 'Perhaps a sports car is largely indefinable, but those who seek it will recognise it when they see it...'(Nye, 1980, 9). One publication suggested that the features normally associated with the type are 'lively acceleration, high maximum speed, and good roadholding characteristics' while convertible status, the capacity for two passengers only and minimum luggage space were also likely ingredients (Whistler, 1995, 11–12). Of all these features, perhaps the most important are a sleek appearance, rapid acceleration and the ability to take corners at speed, which combination give sports cars an air of superiority over conventional models. On open highways, other road users are soon aware of the fleeting presence of a sports car in their rear view mirrow and have no sooner cast admiring and envious glimpses in its direction than it has sped past them, weaving in and out of slower traffic and quickly disappearing from their vision into the distance. As one journalist lucky enough to drive a test E-Type Jaguar recalled: 'We returned on the A5, where the E-type's ability to leap past groups of cars and lorries with a deep-throated growl in second or third gear was ... impressive' (Langley, 1996).

There is an argument for suggesting that modern day sports cars have lost the lustre and character, which imbued the classic models of yesteryear. Today, it is usual practice for new high-performance models to be designed by computer and made by robots which takes the human element out of the equation. In many ways, vintage sports cars of yesteryear reflected the personalities of their owners and, by extension, the managing directors and designers who commissioned and conceived them in the first place. As one authority notes,

> ... the motor men gave a 'sporting' look to their products. The image of a car as some kind of latter-day four legged charger has largely devolved from the products designed by these men. (King, 1989, 139)

Vintage British sports cars were more individualistic in appearance and performance as a result. One entrepreneur, Sir William Lyons, founder of Jaguar, was acutely aware of the appeal of the specialist British sports car – 'particularly high standards of design, manufacture and performance', seeing his audience as 'the connoisseurs of motoring who were invariably prepared to pay a considerable premium for such vehicles' (Adeney, 1988, 127).

Volume producers often turned to the production of semi-specialist sports cars as a means of supplementing their sales. Morris established the MG Car Company while in 1944 Sir John Black, managing director of Standard Motor Company, bought the bankrupt Triumph Motor Company, thereby creating Standard-Triumph in a blatant attempt to add lustre to his company's somewhat dour products range. Black's sports car connections went back a long way: it was he who helped to design the original Morgan three-wheeler. The Austin Healey was born at the 1952 Earls Court Motor Show when Austin's supremo, Leonard Lord, decided he needed a sports car and conceived the new name after Donald Healey, a rally driver and engineer, had approached him the previous year to supply engines for him.

While the British motor industry has had a chequered history (indeed, volume producers are now all in foreign hands and most specialist producers like Aston Martin and Lotus have gone the same way), the consistent selling power of British sports cars, which have retained their appeal at home and abroad from their inception to the present day, has been remarkable. If anything, their allure to foreign customers was often stronger than home demand. For instance, the *Guinness Book of the Car* states that of 101,000 MGAs produced between 1955 and 1962, no less than 94 per cent of them found overseas buyers.

Once the concept, image and desirability of the sports car was established, there was a cluster effect with specialist British marques, such as Aston Martin, Lagonda, Lotus and MG emerging that devoted their energies exclusively to fulfilling the dream car motoring fantasies of the élite to whom they appealed. Models, which are launched today inevitably, draw comparisons with their illustrious predecessors. For example, the Lotus Elise and the Jaguar XK8, both launched in 1996, received rave reviews, the first as a purist sports car in the finest Lotus tradition (Hutton, 1996), the second as 'a spiritual successor to the E-Type' (Chapman, 1996). But there is something missing. As one critic puts it:

> Cars have not only become as mechanically predictable as a washing machine, design seems to have gone the same way. In an increasingly globalised and homogeneous industry it is barely possible to find a pure original … Even the greatest marques seem now to come out of a well-thumbed recipe book passed around designers. The new Jaguar XK8 looks like the Aston Martin DB7 and the Porsche Boxster like the Mercedes SLK (Moore, 1996).

By contrast, the typical British sports car company utilised a minimum amount of machinery, was not heavily capitalised and tended to prefer hand assembly methods which demanded the employment of skilled craftsmen. In exceptional cases, individual components were the product of advanced research and development, but by and large marques bought basic parts, such as chassis and engines, from volume producers. Morgan, for example, turned to Coventry Climax and then Standard, for its early engines. The survival of craft techniques in the specialist firms was promoted by the exclusive nature of the products, which allowed high prices to be charged, and provides a link with traditional methods for which Britain became renowned in the nineteenth century but which the arrival of mass production methods rendered uneconomic in most industries by the following century (Whistler, 1995, 12). For the best of the breed of British sports cars, desirability remained at a premium.

The emergence of the British sports car

The British motor industry emerged, uncertainly, in the twilight of the nineteenth century and by the eve of the First World War had grown to around 140 marques, with Coventry their epicentre. Few, however, could claim originality of design, the trend being to copy foreign practice. In 1896, the Red Flag Act, which restricted the speed of motor cars to a mere 4-mph (2-mph in towns) was repealed and a new limit of 14 mph was imposed. This reflected both a desire for safety and the speed limitations of the pre-1914 motor car. Indeed, the world land speed record, set in 1898 by Count Chasseloup-Laubat, was just 39 mph! In Britain, speedometers did not in fact become compulsory until 1937, two years after a compulsory driving test was introduced for public safety.

The quest for greater speed propelled the evolution of faster vehicles. The Automobile Association boosted its early membership by flagging down members who were inadvertently straying into a police speed trap. The present speed limit of 30 mph in built-up areas was introduced in 1935, but for a time there remained no restrictions outside towns and cities, prompting sports car owners to utilise country roads to test the capabilities of their vehicles. In 1967 came the 70 mph speed limit on motorways (Eason, 1996). Part of the sports car's desirability arose from its ability easily to break the speed limit. At the same time, as roads became more congested and speeding more dangerous, the racing track and owners clubs, that the most demanding questions of their sports cars on private roads, became more asked and more popular.

Before 1914 20 mph was considered 'fast' and any makes which could exceed this were exceptional. Such was the case with British sports cars, which began to emerge from models built for competition trials, with Napier, Wolseley and Vauxhall in the vanguard. When Selwyn Edge carried off the Gordon Bennett Trophy in 1902 the victory gave Napier claim to having the first successful competition model (Whyte, 1985, 123). The first British sports car proper is however usually considered to be the 4-litre Vauxhall 'Prince Henry' named after the Prinz Heinrich (of Prussia) trials in which it excelled. It was designed by engineer Laurence Pomeroy who first made his mark with a high-revving, 3-litre 20 hp Vauxhall. This was driven successfully in the 1908 Royal Automobile Club and Royal Scottish Automobile Club 2000-mile trial by the company's managing director, Percy Kidner, who wanted to project a sporting image through participation in races and trials. Vauxhall remained in the luxury car market until 1925 when they were taken over by General Motors (Whyte, 1985, 123).

In the 1920s two-seater sports cars with open cockpits came into vogue, gaining in popularity throughout the interwar period. The typical model of the early 1920s was substantial, with a price to match. One of the most remarkable of the post-war breed was the Bentley 3-litre, named after its cylinder capacity rather than horsepower (15.9 hp) to avoid confusion with the average tourer. It was the creation of Walter Owen Bentley ('W.O.') whose work with aero-engines and locomotives and selling of French DFP cars somehow inspired him, with the *Autocar's* artist putting his dream on paper. The pointed radiator and winged B emblem were W.O.O.'s idea; the radiator grill followed the DFP design, except that it was more rounded. Bentley drew inspiration from the Continent: the 1912 Peugeot and 1914 Grand Prix Mercedes were his role models. Most British designs, he lamented, were good only for short trips: 'I wanted a car that could be driven hard without minding' (Adeney, 1988, 130).

First announced in May 1919, the Bentley 3-litre did not exist in prototype form until Christmas of that year when its noisy launch in London's sedate Baker Street earned the wrath of the matron of a local nursing home! The first deliveries were promised for June 1920, but did not materialise until more than a year later, by which time the chassis price had risen from £750 to £1,150. This proved no deterrent, sales rising steadily to reach 404 by 1924. A classic had been born.

Critics were struck by the solidity of the Bentley 3-litre and could not let W.O forget his past as an apprentice in the Great Northern Railway's Doncaster workshops. One, Ettore Bugatti, an Italian car-maker, cruelly suggested that 'Monsieur Bentley makes the fastest lorries in the world'. There was nevertheless no shortage of buyers for this eminent sports car. Among the purchasers were royalty (Prince George, fourth son of King George V), leading actresses (Gertrude Lawrence and Bea Lillie) and a millionaire (Woolf Barnato) who gave prominence to the model by driving it at Brooklands. In all 1,613 Bentley 3-litres were produced before the model was wound up in 1929. With its demise the fortunes of the Bentley marque plummeted, and two years later it was taken over by Rolls Royce, ending its sports car connections (Montagu, 1995b).

Some classic marques – the MG and the Morgan

Small sports cars were in vogue in France throughout the 1920s. In Britain it was Morris Motors, which was the unlikely progenitor of the breed. Cecil Kimber managed Morris Garages, a dealership in Longwall Street, Oxford, distinguished by the modified Morris Cowleys and Oxfords, which were sold under the grand-sounding name of 'The MG Super Sports Morris'. The process evolved to a point where outside components were bought in, rendering the cars more individual. Legend has it that the renowned Octagon MG badge was based on the shape of Kimber's dining table.

1928, the year in which the MG Car Company was established, witnessed the launch of the MG Midget, made possible through William Morris introducing the small Morris Minor as a rival to the Austin Seven. The exceptional overhead camshaft engine was a Wolseley design, inherited when Morris took over the marque in 1927. To the basic engine and chassis Kimber mounted a cheap two-seater body made up of fabric-covered plywood within an ash frame. MG's telephone number in Oxford was 251, a number that was retained when MG relocated to a new factory in nearby Abingdon, with 251 also forming the debut chassis number of any new model. Acquiring the bodies for just £6.50 a time, Kimber managed to keep the selling price down to a very affordable £175. The result was to introduce the British sports car to a mass audience – orders in the first year alone produced more Midget sales than all the previous MG variants combined. When British Leyland took over MG, its failings were exemplified by losses of £1,000 per model on transatlantic sales, leading to the closure of the marque half a century after its illustrious birth. Thankfully, Rover decided to revive the famous name, bringing out the stunning MGF in 1995, a high-tech successor to classic MGs (Eason, 1995).

The Morgan marque was started by H.F.S. Morgan, a former draughtsman with Great Western Railways, who established his own company at Malvern, Worcestershire in 1911. For a time, he concentrated on three-wheelers, which, in 1935, finally gave way to four-wheelers. In 1954 came the company's crowning glory, the Plus Four, which became very popular at home and overseas. The Morgan company was unusual in refusing to move with the times, continuing to use traditional craft methods of construction. Indeed, the basic Morgan designs of today derive from the mid-1930s, but they are highly coveted precisely because of the mystique surrounding the name and the individualistic methods of construction to the extent that the present day owners cannot keep up with demand (Willson, 1995, 176–7).

Jaguar

Sir William Lyons went through a series of experiments before finding all the right ingredients to create the specialist car of his dreams: stylish, swift, competitively priced and instantly recognisable as one of the Jaguar line. Starting out in partnership in Blackpool in 1922 designing, producing and marketing streamlined motor-bike sidecars, Lyons soon branched out into motor car bodies, with his first attempt at a sports car being a two seater body on a Wolseley Hornet chassis. His first genuine sports car came in 1935, when the SS90 was launched – so-called because of its alleged top speed of 90 mph. The SS100 quickly followed, but critics were quick to point out that the 2.5 litre version, powered by a Standard engine, could not attain its maximum speed, falling short by around 5 mph.

What distinguished Lyons' sports cars in the beginning were design and price more than speed. Lyons established a distinctive low rakish look, which made his models instantly recognisable. Later on, Lyons relinquished responsibility for the basic design, but he remained responsible for the fine detail – the 'light line'. If the light was unbroken on the side or the wings of a prototype then the line was good. Unbelievable selling price was a key ingredient for Lyons. An astute salesman, he recognized that the public wanted value for money. The SS100 retailed at only half the price of the BMW 328 while even the much more sophisticated and powerful XK120 sports car required just a third of the asking price of the Mercedes 300SL.

SS Cars could not survive after the horrors of the Second World War and Lyons elected to rename his company Jaguar Cars Limited. The name 'Jaguar' was no accident: it was carefully selected by Lyons because it had 'an exciting sound' and the feline creature was renowned for its agility and speed. This could not be said of Lyons' pre-war models, which relied on souped-up Standard engines, and he was only too aware that his company's Achilles' heel was its lack of an in-house production engine. When war interrupted production and personnel were required to undertake nighttime fire-watching in case of *Luftwaffe* incendiary bombs, Lyons astutely gathered key design personnel for his observation team. Lyons outlined his plan for a high-performance engine, which was also appealing to the eye.

By 1948 the XK engine had emerged (X standing for experimental, K for the last in the line of prototypes). Featuring twin overhead camshafts (normally only available on the most expensive models), it boasted six cylinders and a capacity of 3.4 litres. The remarkable new engine formed the power base for a new sports car, the XK120, which caused a sensation when it was launched at the 1948 Earls Court Motor Show. The press were invited to a test track where an XK120 far exceeded its advertised top speed, achieving 133 mph, making it the fastest production car in the world. The XK engine was continuously developed and refined in the 1950s over which period its capacity increased from 3.4 to 3.8 litres. The first E-Type

Jaguars were equipped with the 3.8 litre version. In the early 1960s the XK engine block was redesigned, thereby increasing capacity to 4.2 litres.

The E-Type was Lyons' crowning glory before his retirement in 1972. Evolved from the D-Type, it was ahead of its time in so many ways when it was launched in 1961, heralding the new swinging decade. Its high-performance characteristics were unusual for its day: 'WHAM – and you are doing 150 mph!' proclaimed one headline. It was promoted as the most advanced sports car in the world and with good reason, innovations including independent rear suspension and disc brakes. The E-Type's success was sustained by continuous improvements. In 1966, for instance, legroom (always at a premium in sports cars) was improved and a four-seater version became available. Some of the modifications were driven by increasingly tough American regulations. The 1969 Series 2 E-Type was encumbered with a host of requirements, from stronger bumpers to a detuned engine to meet emission regulations, which made for a safer vehicle out of kilter with the free spirit of the original E-Types (Discovery Channel, 1994b).

The Austin Healey

Austin Healey lasted for just 17 years and today surviving models are among the most coveted. Donald Healey was a Cornishman who developed an obsession with mechanics, especially the aeroplane and motor car. His mother once complained that he was worse than a farmer talking constantly about livestock. Healey's fascination with aircraft led him to an apprenticeship with the Sopwith Aviation Company. Then, with the outbreak of the Great War, he lied about his age to join the RFC, only to be invalided out of the service when his fighter aircraft was hit by anti-aircraft fire. From now on Healey would concentrate exclusively on motor cars.

Building a garage next to his parents' home, Donald slowly but surely built a reputation as a rally driver, graduating from local events to national rallies and trials until finally he hit the international stage in 1929 at the Monte Carlo Rally. Although he managed seventh place in his 833 cc Triumph Super Seven the following year, Healey recognised he needed a more powerful vehicle to win and elected for the 4.5 litre Invicta, triumphing in the 1931 event despite some hair-raising experiences.

Experience with Riley, Triumph and Humber followed, which served to further Healey's ambition to produce his own sports car. His dream machine was a scaled down Invicta devoid of the handling problems, which his rallying experiences had made him so keenly aware of. Basing his operations in Warwick after the Second World War, Healey aimed to produce a small car capable of over 100 mph. His connections placed him in good stead: the production site was owned by Wally Allen, a former Triumph director, while the power unit was a Riley engine. In 1948 a body blow was suffered when the government imposed a 66.6 per cent purchase tax on motor cars costing over £1,000 which put Healey's existing models, a saloon and roadster, beyond the reach of their target audience and by 1950 production had ceased.

The immediate result was the Healey Silverstone, a two-seater introduced in 1949 which came in just below the tax threshold at £975. But its design harked back to the 1930s while it was powered by a modified Riley engine, which first appeared in 1926! Healey recognized he needed a new engine. Having first thought of General Motors, a chance meeting with the head of Nash Kelvinator on board the North America-bound *Queen Elizabeth* persuaded him to opt for their engines after a Nash-powered Silverstone came fourth at Le Mans. And so the Nash Healey was born with Nash Kelvinator providing the engines and gearboxes while Farina of Turin produced the bodies. The Warwick factory fitted the American components after which the chassis went to Turin and thence to the United States, the key market. The arrangement was far from ideal and contributed to Jaguar's cost advantage in the United States.

Healey was only too well aware of the significance of the American market where consumers expected cheap motor cars. A frequent transatlantic traveller, Healey recognised that there was a gap in the market between the large Jaguar XK120 and the small MG TD. He leapt at the opportunity, stealthily approaching Len Lord, Austin's supremo, to seek access to the Austin A90 Atlantic overhead valve engine, which began life in wartime as the intended power unit for a British jeep. Lord was receptive to the idea, not least because the A90 Atlantic had flopped in the American market. For his part, Healey was enthralled because the engines were offered at around half the price he was paying Nuffield for Riley engines.

A new sports car had to be designed around the engine. Gerry Coker, a young stylist from Humber, was heavily influenced by Italian designs and produced as low a profile as possible consistent with the engine's requirements which dictated the height of the bonnet. Healey, never easily satisfied, was not happy with the grill to the extent that he parked the model against a pillar at the 1952 Earls Court motor show to show off what he considered to be its best feature – its rear profile. The unveiling caused a sensation at the show. A journalist asked Healey who was the Italian designer, to which he responded: 'Oh no, just a country boy who works for me.' The new sports car's biggest admirer was Lord, now head of BMC, who approached Healey with a proposition. He might be able to turn out a few hundred cars a year for a small profit where BMC could mass-produce them at a rate of 700 a week. Healey had intended to hand produce the model but was taken with Lord's offer and a deal was made on the spot. Part of the deal was that the model's name was changed to the Austin Healey 100 4 (100 standing for its speed, 4 its engine's cylinder capacity).

The Austin Healey continued under a series of variants with BMC, but it can be argued that the purity of the sports car had been compromised with ultimately fatal consequences. The most desirable models were the few which Healey still produced themselves, such as for racing. The Austin Healey 100 6, produced by BMC, was intended to be more consumer friendly than the typical sports car, with a smoother engine to allow a non-expert to drive it with ease. If purists were offended by this aberration, their eyebrows rose even higher in 1962 when the Austin Healey 3000 received wind-up windows. Ultimately, the marriage between a mass manufacturer and a specialist producer was doomed to failure. BMC's attentions switched to the hugely popular Mini from 1962 and Austin Healey production was moved from Longbridge to MG's base at Abingdon. It was the beginning of the end. By the 1960s the Austin Healey had lost its lustre, was over-produced and became distinctly old-fashioned in a fast moving decade labelled 'swinging'. In 1968, British Leyland's supremo, Donald Stokes, decided there was not room for two sports car lines in the new organization. The Triumph line (TR6 and 7) was favoured to the Austin Healey which went out of existence (Wood, 1984, 54–71; Discovery Channel, 1994a).

British sports cars and the racing track

Sports cars were built for speed and quickly established an affinity with the racing track. There is nothing quite like the winning of a race for boosting sports car sales. An early example was Frank Clement who won the Junior Sprint at Brooklands in May 1921 in the recently launched Bentley 3-litre. In 1949, William Lyons, seeking favourable publicity for the new XK120 sports car, lent three to racing drivers for a prestigious sports car race at Silverstone. Two of the entries claimed first and second places, with Jaguar only denied a clean sweep by a puncture to the third model. By the summer of 1950 Jaguar was struggling to produce enough XK120s to meet demand (Discovery Channel, 1994b).

Most of this demand derived from the United States, where Phil Hill made his racing reputation in an XK120. To secure one, he needed to come to England and take one back with him on the *Queen Mary* as 'personal baggage'! In November 1950 Hill came first in a sports car race at Pebble Beach, California, the first in a series of victories for the XK120 on American soil (Discovery Channel, 1994b). As well as speed, endurance also became a selling point for British sports cars. Ian Appleyard, a Jaguar dealer and Lyon's son-in-law, achieved a series of Alpine successes in the XK120. When he learnt of the new 24-hour race at Le Mans, W.O. Bentley remarked: 'I think the whole thing's crazy; nobody will finish. Cars are not meant to stand that sort of strain for 24 hours.' The opening race confounded such scepticism, with 30 of 33 starters managing to complete the event. Bentleys went on to notch up four straight victories between 1927 and 1930 (Montagu, 1995b).

Jaguar managed five victories in seven years, a record matched only by Bentley. The XK120C was a special competition version of the road car, originally entered for the 1951 Le Mans and featuring a modified rear suspension and aerodynamic body. Three were entered, with one romping home by a winning margin of 60 mph. Two years later, disc brakes were added, giving Jaguar superior stopping power to Ferrari. On this occasion, first, second and fourth spots were achieved, sending Jaguar's publicity department into overdrive. In 1954 came the new D-Type with a superior aerodynamic shape modelled on an aircraft. The following year witnessed Jaguar's most dramatic victory at Le Mans when Mike Hawthorn fought off the challenge of Ferranti and Mercedes, in the process establishing a new lap record of over 122 mph. As so often, Jaguar introduced another innovation, on this occasion low profile radial ply racing tyres.

In October 1956 Jaguar officially withdrew from racing – though they continued to support racing drivers who entered events individually, which provided an opportunity to test and advertise the performance of new models. For instance, the first few E-Types were earmarked for customers known for their racing predilections. Jaguar benefitted from racing in two main ways: first, the publicity generated from success; second, technological innovation driven by the need for success which could be introduced into production models. The public was given access to racing car speeds and handling for a reasonable price. Jaguar clubs were established across the world with members anxious to see what models could do on private tracks (Discovery Channel, 1994b).

Colin Chapman has been called 'the most able, most dynamic, most buccaneering character to grace the British motoring scene' (Montagu, 1996). The badge on his classic Lotus sports cars reads 'ACBC', standing for Anthony Colin Bruce Chapman. He established Lotus Engineering Company in the early 1950s, locating its operations in the stable block of the Railways Hotel, Hornsey, which his father managed.

Lotus became renowned for small, lightweight high performance sports cars, which could take corners at speed and handled well, ideal racing characteristics. It was Chapman who pioneered the all-in-one car body and chassis – today a standard production practice. Starting out by dealing in 'five quid bangers' after the war, in 1947 Chapman converted an Austin Seven into a competition car, christening it his 'little Lotus blossom' after his girlfriend, Hazel Williams. Lotus Engineering sprang up from an order for a 'Lotus special' which was inspired by success in competition. Chapman's background as a structural engineer at British Aluminium served him in good stead, enabling him to design 'spaceframe' chassis. His designs were assisted by the Costin brothers, Frank and Mike, from the De Havilland Aircraft Company, who added an aerodynamic quality to Lotus sports cars which, in the mid-1950s, reigned supreme in small-capacity sports car racing.

Fame came when Tony Vandervell, a millionaire bearings manufacturer, gave Chapman a commission to redesign his Formula One Vanwall car, which won the F1 Constructors' World Championship. The first rear-engined Lotus, the Type 18 of 1960, provided Sterling Moss with victories in the Monaco and American grand prix. Even greater kudos followed when Scottish racing ace Jim Clark won two F1 world championships in 1963 and 1965, only missing out on a hat-trick on the last lap of the final race in the intervening year. Racing success naturally increased demand for Lotus road models, with the Lotus Seven kitcar selling by the thousand. Things were never the same after Clark was killed in 1968. Although Mario Andretti added another F1 world driving crown to Lotus's list of honours in 1977–78, giving Chapman his sixth F1 constructor's title (placing Team Lotus second only to Ferranti in the history books), financial troubles were mounting. Chapman himself suffered a fatal heart attack on 16 December 1982, aged only 54 (Montagu, 1996). Already involved in the DeLorean project, Lotus did not survive the twin blows of association with this white elephant and the loss of its entrepreneurial driving spirit and was taken over by General Motors in 1986, who in turn sold Lotus on to Bugatti in 1993. But though independence had gone, the legendary Lotus name lives on in spirit.

The American connection

The 'Special Relationship' was never so special as when it came to British sports cars. It began when American GIs, stationed in Britain, took to the MG TC, and continued through a succession of classic British sports cars, including the Jaguar XK120, Austin Healeys and TR Triumphs. The British sports car played its part in aiding the balance of payments during the 'export or die' era of the Attlee years (1945–51). 10,000 MG TCs were manufactured during the period 1945 through to 1949: of these two out of every three produced went abroad. The appearance of 'the most feline of all Jaguars', the XK120, in 1949 added further impetus to the export drive with no less than 85 per cent of the 12,000 manufactured until 1954 being shipped abroad, most of them across the Atlantic. Moreover, while British volume producers, such as Rootes and Standard, were unable to maintain their impressive export performance once the sellers' market of the early post-1945 period had evaporated, this was not true of the specialist producers. Take the case of the TR6. Of the 95,000 produced between 1969 and 1975, the proportion that found an overseas market was ten times as great as that for the domestic market. Nor was this an exception. 387,000 MGB roadsters were produced of which all but 49,000 found an overseas buyer; 81, 000 of the 101,000 MGAs manufactured were for the US market; and two-thirds of the Jaguar E-types produced between 1961 and 1974 went abroad, primarily to American states (Selby, 1996c).

The late 1940s and 1950s turned out to be the golden years of the British sports car in the American market. Over the next two decades there was a relative decline in their popularity as they were generally overtaken in quality and reliability – the most important selling features – by home made models like the Ford Mustang and foreign rivals. MG and Triumph scored particularly badly, with older models still being built with components harking back to the 1950s. The new TR7 epitomized all that was wrong with British Leyland, with motoring tests exposing a number of deficiencies. The arrival of the super efficient Japanese Datsun on the scene only served to accentuate British Leyland's reputation for poor quality and safety-averse products in the United States (Whistler, 1995, 244–9).

A notable exception to this trend was Jaguar. The American market became crucial to the Coventry-based specialist producer. 'Jaguar is a special breed of car', proclaimed a US advert. Another suggested that 'there's no such thing as a typical Jaguar owner. What there is are people looking for the untypical in life' (Discovery Channel, 1994b). Of 7,500 XK120s produced between 1949 and 1954, almost 6,500 were built with left-hand drive, with most destined for American highways and freeways. What distinguished Jaguar was its willingness to assess the competition in the American market and react accordingly. By the late 1950s the XK120 could not compete with faster and more sophisticated American sports cars. The E-Type rekindled the American appetite for Jaguars, which American owners dubbed the 'XKE'. Some 80 per cent of E-Type production had left-hand drive and changes for the American market were incorporated on all models (Discovery Channel, 1994b).

The cultural impact of the British sports car

After the Second World War, a wider range of sports cars became available that were aimed at a wider public. Among them were the Austin Healey Sprite, MG Midget and Triumph Spitfire. The Triumph Sports range, for example, launched by Standard, a volume producer, represented an attempt to open up a mass market through a relatively inexpensive product. The success of the range peaked with the TR6, launched just after Standard-Triumph was subsumed into British Leyland, despite whose inefficiencies it survived in production until 1976. But purist critics never took to such models, with the more severe seeing them as a bastardisation of the sports car genre. Big Healeys were loathed as cumbersome while Triumph's evident cost-cutting (for instance, no external door handles were fitted until 1957) drew ripples of displeasure (Willson, 1995, 208–13). Such variants were distinguished from their purer (and costlier) relatives by terms such as 'neo-sports' or 'fun' cars.

Such developments notwithstanding, there remained an aura of exclusivity to the best of the breed. The image of British sports cars was enhanced by their status as playthings of the rich and famous. Princess Elizabeth, the future queen, was courted in her future husband's MG (*Daily Express* 1996). The TC MG was in fact Naval-Lieutenant Phillip Mountbatten's first new car. It evidently served its purpose well, notwithstanding speculation that the king and queen frowned on the notion of their daughter, the monarch-in-waiting, travelling in a blaring and tiny sports car. That was in the 'Age of Austerity'. Today's royals would frown upon any sustained association with cheaper models. The royal connection with fast cars was continued two decades on when Prince Phillip's eldest son, the Prince of Wales, selected the MGC coupe as his first car (Montagu, 1995c). Today, the more prestigious and expensive Aston Martin range provides his choice of driving vehicle for his much-publicised private life.

The Aston Martin DB5 first appeared in the third 007 vehicle, *Goldfinger* (1964). 'Now pay attention Bond', enjoins Q as he demonstrates the capabilities of the wonder car. To say it was not a normal production model would be an understatement. Machine guns hiding behind the front side lamps, a bullet-proof shield, smoke effects, an ejector seat for unwelcome passengers, tyre-shredding wheel hubs and rotating licence plates were just some of its extraordinary features (English, 1995). It even had a radio telephone, a futuristic device then which is now commonplace in the age of the mobile 'phone.

Film producer Harry Saltzman had first approached Aston Martin about the possibilities of employing a film version of the DB5. Sensing a unique market opportunity, the firm decided that although the vehicle would feature a host of special features unique to the movie, in essence it would not depart from a production car to enhance its selling potential. The one-off vehicle cost around £15,000 to produce, some three times the price of a normal production model.

The Aston Martin's transformation into a multi-gadgeted vehicle for James Bond did wonders for sales. Such was the demand to see the special DB5 that Aston Martin constructed two more duplicates for promotion purposes (Wood, 1992, 117–22). Dudley Gershon, the service manager, recounted:

> As soon as the film was shown, a massive wave of publicity hit us, the like of which no other car firm in history has ever experienced. All of a sudden every ten year old boy knew the name Aston Martin, and this, or else James Bond, was shouted or chalked on every DB4 or DB5 ... It ran in an amused way through every strata of society, and if we had been able to produce 50 DB4s per week then we could have sold them (Wood, 1992, 122).

I still vividly recall being taken by a favourite uncle to see the film *Thunderball* (1965), in which the DB5 made its second appearance, at a time when Bond movies

148

were all the rage. Although Sean Connery could never conceal his Scottish accent, he was superb in the role of the all-action British agent who always contrived to save the West in the end, despite numerous hazards en route and distractions in the form of alluring ladies who inevitably succumbed to his charm and masculinity, often accompanying 007 in spectacular drive chases.

Audiences were enthralled. One of the purchasers was one of the leading lights of the Fab Four, Paul McCartney. A toy model came out from Dinky, though it never successfully replicated the original except for the rotating number plates. The desirability of the DB5 was enhanced by the fact that there was only a limited production run of around 900 between 1963 and 1965. The production model of the four-litre, six-cylinder car gave owners a top speed of 141 mph, with the ability to accelerate to 60 mph from a standing start in eight seconds. Like Bond, the DB5s have proved remarkably resilient, not least because of the durable steel platform chassis (Selby, 1996b).

The sports car has always been renowned as a magnet for beautiful women. In the classic comedy series, 'Steptoe and Son', the episode 'Top Gear' sees Harold acquire a second hand sports car, conjuring visions of instantaneously improving his status with the local 'crumpet'. Thereupon Harold invites Maureen to Brighton for the weekend, eliciting an immediate acceptance as she drools over the rag-and-bone man's new toy. When Maureen has departed, Harold leaps onto the car body in mock worship. Unfortunately, Harold's purchase conflicts with his meddling father Albert's desire for a colour television, for which pleasure he is childishly prepared to leave home and stay out all night in the bitter cold. Albert's stubbornness sees him hospitalised with Harold shamed by police and doctors into selling his sports car and using the proceeds to meet his grumpy father's wish. As he ruefully sells his pride and joy, he spots Maureen waving goodbye as she is driven away at speed by another suitor in a sports car.

For a motoring élite of daredevil drivers who live life in the fast lane, the sports car represents the ultimate dream vehicle. British sports cars, by and large, have been classic and desirable, retaining their appeal even beyond their commercial shelf life. Much of this can be attributed to the individuality of the models which, in turn, may be traced to the peculiar characteristics and idiosyncrasies of the motor car magnates and designers who created them in the first place. They pursued their own dreams and in seeking to market the perfect sports car they knew they had a ready audience willing to be persuaded. Of course, there is no such thing as perfection: tastes and technologies never stand still, meaning there is always room for improvement. Today's models set new standards, but they are also measured against the standards of the past. The fastest sports car of today will inevitably become second best in time. What can be said is that the classic British sports cars were among the best of their day. As such they will always retain a premium on their market value for they remain potent symbols of their time, representing past eras in a vibrant and living way. They are the ultimate icons of motoring nostalgia.

Bibliography

Adeney, M. (1988) *The Motor Makers: The Turbulent History of Britain's Car Industry*, Collins, London

Chapman, G. (1996) 'True to Type?', *Daily Telegraph*, 9 March.

Copps, A. (1996) 'Obsessed with Britain's Classic System', *The Times*, 23 March.

Daily Express (1996) 'Courting Queen's Letters up for Sale', 1 April.

Discovery Channel (1994a) 'Classic Wheels: Austin Healey'.

Discovery Channel (1994b) 'Classic Wheels: Jaguar'.

Eason, K. (1995) 'The Octagon Returns in Perfect Shape', *The Times*, 23 October.

Eason, K. (1996) 'The Gun Doesn't Kill: Speed Does', *The Times*, 18 May

English, A. (1995) 'Bond's in a BMW – But His Other Car's Still a DB5', *Daily Telegraph*, 28 January.

Hutton, R. (1996), 'One for the Spartans', *Sunday Times*, 14 July

King, P. (1989) *The Motor Men*, Quiller Press, London.

Langley, J. (1996) 'The E-Type is Still My Type', *Daily Telegraph*, 5 October.

Montagu, Lord (1995a) 'Twelve Cars that Made Britain Great', *The Times*, 25 March.

Montagu, Lord (1995b) 'Bentley's Tour de Triomphe', *The Times*, 25 March.

Montagu, Lord (1995c) 'The Midget that Grew into a Giant', *The Times*, 22 April

Montagu, Lord (1996) 'He Made Lotus Blossom', *The Times*, 6 January.

Moore, T. (1996) 'Epitaph for a Wild and Glorious Age', *Daily Express*, 2 November.

Nye, D. (1980) *Sports Cars*, Ward Lock, London.

Selby, D. (1996a) 'Flying Frump of the 1950s', *Sunday Times*, 18 February.

Selby, D. (1996b) 'Lots of Opportunities in Old Metal', *The Times*, 25 May.

Selby, D. (1996c) 'Left Hand Down a Bit, Old Bean', *Sunday Times*, 31 March.

Whistler, T.R. (1995) *At the End of the Road: The Rise and Fall of Austin-Healey, MG and Triumph Sports Cars*, JAI Press, London.

Williams, D. (1996) 'Drive a Classic Bargain', *Daily Express*, 18 May.

Whyte, A. (1985) *101 Great Marques*, Octopus, London.

Willson, Q. (1995) *The Ultimate Classic Car Book*, Dorling Kindersley, London.

Wood, J. (1984) *Classic Sports Cars: The History of the Legendary Car Companies*, Octopus Books, London.

Wood, J. (1992) *Aston Martin DB4, DB5 & DB6: The Complete Story*, Crowood Press, Ramsbury.

11

Four Wheels Good; Two Wheels Bad: The Motor Cycle versus the Light Motor Car – 1919–39 [1]

Steve Koerner

Writing in a 1926 issue of the *New Statesman*, R.E. Davidson reflected on the importance of the motor cycle as a means of providing cheap personal transport for the working classes. To Davidson, its implications for British society went far beyond a matter of simply conveying people from one point to another:

> There will be no need to prate of a new spirit in industry when wages permit the workers to escape from an industrial environment for a few hours every weekend [and] a week or more every summer.

Moreover, this most democratic form of personal transport, 'the poor man's car' in the words of Leo Amery, had an important role for improving social relations. As Davidson concluded: 'The motor cycle is no ally of the acrid bitterness of the class war.'[2]

At around the same time, Sir Harold Bowden, chairman of the Raleigh Bicycle Company, which was then still manufacturing motor cycles, praised what he termed 'the hobby of the ordinary wages earner'. He too saw it as a useful lubricant for easing abrasive social relations. In Bowden's words:

> Give a man a motor cycle to ride and to tend and mend in his spare time and you take from him one of the chief causes of disgruntlement.[3]

These words are remarkable because, although nearly always cheaper than motor cars, the number of motor cycles on British roads had actually been exceeded by motor cars a short time before (see Tables 1 and 2).[4] The motor cycle could no longer, in a numerical sense at least, be considered the most popular form of personal road transport in Britain, a situation which has persisted until the present.

So what had happened to cause the eclipse of what had purported to be the most accessible form of motor transport for British wage earners? This chapter will examine the competition between the motor cycle and the motor car for an expanding market of personal motor transport in Britain during the interwar period. It will describe how the motor cycle industry tried to regain market share from its four wheeled competitors by developing innovative motor cycle models and also by seeking out new consumers, especially among women. It will conclude that, although the industry was affected by factors outside its control, it was frustrated mainly by its own self-imposed constraints. The focus will be far more on motor cycles than motor cars[5] if only because so little is available about the former, especially during the period in question.[6]

The motor cycle and car industries had emerged from the bicycle trade roughly around the turn of the century and, for a while, several companies such as Rover, Triumph and Sunbeam produced motor cars and motor cycles simultaneously. Despite their common origins, the two industries had diverged early on, ownership between them becoming mostly separate by the 1920s (Koerner, 1995, 58, 59). However, in contrast to the motor car industry, the motor cycle industry, which was composed in large part of dedicated producers, remained entirely British owned and operated right up until it crashed into bankruptcy during the early 1970s (Smith, 1983, 3, 4). Indeed, what little motor cycle manufacturing that remains continues to be so right to the present (Goodwin, 1993, 10).

In other respects, the motor cycle industry shared some common characteristics with its motor car counterpart, having started out with a vast number of firms of varying sizes then slimming down during the late 1920s and 1930s. For example, in 1925 there were approximately 120 firms in Britain manufacturing motor cycles; by 1939 this total had been reduced to 32. As with the motor car industry, several of the larger motor cycle companies, a so-called 'Big Six', dominated, followed by a number of medium sized firms.[7] There were as well specialised firms that built expensive sports and touring machines along with those that built proprietary engines for the use of smaller manufacturers. The two industries also shared a number of general supply and accessory firms such as Dunlop tyres and Joseph Lucas electrics.

Nearly always cheaper than a motor car, the average British motor cycle was not necessarily small. Although the various firms manufactured a wide variety of machines, ranging from lightweights (with engines up to 150 cc capacity) to giant 1000 cc twin cylinder behemoths, the most popular models were in the 350 cc to 500 cc engine capacity classes. This inclination towards larger displacement motor cycles had been established right from the beginnings of the industry. In 1913, for example, models available to British consumers were powered by engines of between 170 cc to 600 cc displacements, with the majority in the 350 cc to 500 cc classes. Eight years on, the smallest engine displacement size on the market was still only 211cc and even as late as 1925, only one firm offered a machine under 100 cc.[8]

Thus, in terms of speed and general performance, the average British motor cycle could reasonably be expected to hold its own, if not exceed, the average motor car. The predilection for larger-sized motor cycles is suggestive of the fact that, especially when attached to sidecar combinations, they provided a cheaper substitute for the far more expensive motor cars, as well as being used solo for sports and touring purposes.

The British motor cycle evolved during its formative years as transport for the use of wage earners, although the more stylish and sporting segments of the wealthier classes were also enthusiasts.[9] The sporting element was especially important and present from virtually the beginning. However, because there were no professional consumer surveys conducted until the 1950s, it is difficult to determine exactly what kind of people bought motor cycles. One insight into the market can be found among those who were attracted to sporting events. Published accounts describe these enthusiasts as representing a wide spectrum of British society.

For example, the annual Isle of Man TT (Tourist Trophy) races were the premier motor cycle sporting event. One journal noted that among those present 'universities and public schools vie with the garage hands and Birmingham stockbrokers in their interest'. The crowds on the Island were reportedly teeming with 'thousands of youngsters in Harris tweeds with club ties; as many north-country artisans with their sweethearts; and the greedy efficient people who sell cycles in every city and town from Land's End to John O'Groats'.[10]

The interest in sport extended into company boardrooms as well. Harry Collier, son of Matchless founder Henry Collier, who would become one of the company's joint managing directors, raced semi-professionally and had a distinguished career at the TT. At Ariel, owner Jack Sangster was a trials rider before the First World War and James Norton, founder of Norton, was also no stranger to the race track. In fact, industry managers often made a point of letting their customers know that they too shared an equal interest in motor cycle sports activities. In 1939, for example, a number of managing directors rode their motor cycles in a procession to the Donington racetrack at the season's opening. Attending such events undoubtedly gave them an opportunity to mix with many of the people who either already owned their motor cycles or might soon be buying a new model and so gain a better appreciation of changes in the market.[11]

Indeed, the sports and competitions ethos permeated the motor cycle industry at all levels, from the manufacturers' board rooms right through to the retailers. The close relationship between the industry and sport was widely recognised. One technical journal noted that there were 'undoubted commercial advantages that follow upon success in this [the TT] and other trials of a sports character.' It was also observed that placing such emphasis on sporting events was 'a useful device in breaking down sales resistance.' Thus a firm whose motor cycles did well at the TT was almost certain to enjoy improved sales shortly afterwards.[12]

Motor cycle racing was seen not only as the ultimate criteria for the soundness of particular models but also as a 'proving ground' for design generally. It was often maintained that the stringent demands of the race track had beneficial results in terms of development in brakes, suspension and engines which were subsequently applied to less sporting models. As one press report noted, such was the significance of the Isle of Man TT races that: 'many firms devote the greater part of their energies to the attempts to win in one or more of the classes, while scarcely a firm in the trade can plead complete indifference to the commercial value of a good performance.'[13]

Two important reasons why two-wheeled motor transport had been more popular than its physically larger four-wheeled competitors were cheaper running costs and general convenience, especially with respect to storage. Writing in 1924, one motor cycle advocate claimed that the would-be motor cyclist need only pay an annual road tax of £4 (compared to £6 for a motor car) along with the additional advantage of cheaper petrol consumption. Although he conceded that other costs were roughly about the same, the motor cycle, with or without a sidecar, was a far easier vehicle to garage than a motor car, an important factor for inhabitants of Britain's crowded urban districts.[14]

Even the fact that a motor cycle often demanded more mechanical maintenance than a motor car was not necessarily considered a drawback. As another proponent of two wheeled motor transport noted: 'the motorist is content with a much lower standard of performance than the great majority of motor cyclists. The car, to its owner, is simply a means to an end, an invention for comparatively rapid movement, expected to function with as little attention as the train receives from its passengers.'[15]

Ultimately the issue came down to a question of purchase price. For many years there was a considerable gap between the prices of the two vehicle types which favoured the motor cycle. Until the early 1920s even a smaller new motor car cost between £250 and £500, a cyclecar (a three wheeled automobile-like vehicle) approximately £220, while a good quality 500cc motor cycle sidecar combination cost around £150 (Worthington-Williams, 1981, 15, 101). Little wonder, shortly after the First World War, that a visiting American automotive engineer observed motor cycles 'held the same position in England as Ford in America' and 'that the class of people who possessed Fords in America have motor cycles in England' (Heather, 1918/1919, 56)

Then in 1922 motor car manufacturer Herbert Austin gave the first indication that the nature of the equation was going to change. Significantly, and with more than a little audacity, he announced his plans for a light motor car at the annual dinner of the Birmingham motor cycle club. Austin Motors was, he declared, in the process of designing a small-sized, low-powered automobile which would later become known as the Austin Seven and scheduled to soon go into production. Austin was supremely confident of its future and predicted his new motor car would 'knock the sidecar combination into a cocked hat' (Wyatt, 1982, 20).

Indeed, in his private instructions to design assistant Stanley Edge, Austin was explicit about the dimensions of this vehicle, which were not to exceed those of a sidecar combination and thus fit easily into the same garage space. In this way some of the inherent advantages of the motor cycle combination would be undercut. When the Seven was launched in July 1922, Austin announced that the potential buyer was 'the man who, at present, can only afford a motor cycle and side car, and yet has the ambition to become a motorist' (Church, 1979, 77).

Initial sales of the Austin Seven certainly justified its creator's hopes, insofar as within a few years it became the company's best seller. Some 14,000 of them were built in 1926 with 22,500 in the following year; in fact, over the period 1927 to 1937, annual production of this model averaged between 20,000 to 27,000 units, amounting to a total of nearly 300,000 vehicles (Wyatt, 1982, 62, 66, 162). Priced at £225 in 1923, the Austin Seven may have cost at least £70 more than a typical 500 cc motor cycle sidecar combination but it was still only £25 more than a 770 cc combination unit (Church, 1979, 84).

Higher volume production was followed by still lower costs and throughout the late 1920s and on into the end of the following decade, prices of the light or so-called 'Baby' models like the Austin Seven, steadily fell (see Table 3). Other motor car manufacturers followed Austin's lead. By 1931 Morris Motors announced its £100 'Minor' and similar types such as the Standard 8 and 10, the Hillman 'Minx' and Ford's own 8-hp model were soon available in showrooms around Britain. In fact, there was a sharp increase in the sales of motor cars with ratings of less than 10-hp and between 1929 and 1936 the numbers of these machines registered for road use increased by 236,353 to 842,514 vehicles, or 256 per cent.[16]

Shortly afterwards, there emerged a concurrent development which was probably even more damaging to motor cycle sales. This was the growth of the used motor car market, which seriously eroded the economy appeal of the motorised two wheeler. This was especially acute in the competition between motor cycle sidecar combinations and light motor cars (users of solo motor cycles would not necessarily be as tempted to switch their machines for a four-wheeled vehicle). In the late 1920s there was still a distinct price advantage

155

between a 350 cc or 500 cc motor cycle combination and a used 8-hp motor car (see Table 4). By 1936 this difference had nearly vanished (Miller, undated, 6). Indeed, registration figures of motor cycle combinations show a consistent deterioration, far more acute than those of solo motor cycles (see Table 6)[17]

In large part these lower motor car prices and greater registrations were a reflection of the manufacturers' willingness to adapt American style production techniques. Herbert Austin, for one, was keenly interested in modern American practices, especially those of Ford, and visited the USA at least twice during the 1920s where he undertook detailed examinations of certain American auto factories. Austin Motors Works Director, C.F. Engelbach, was so enthusiastic about American manufacturing techniques he recommended that, in the future, Board members and company officials 'should go over at least every other year' to see what the Americans were getting up to.[18] For manufacturers like Austin, larger-scale production was the obvious solution to the adage 'small cars equal small profits'. Indeed, by the mid-1920s, his was the first British automobile company to use a moving assembly line and, within another several years, large parts of the motor car industry had adapted flow production techniques (Church & Miller, 1977, 163).

Furthermore, the average motor car was marked by steady technical improvements such as electric starters, enclosed all-metal bodies (providing far better weather protection) and vastly improved suspension systems which made it more and more appealing to the general buying public (Newcombe & Spurr, 1979, 42–3, 48). By contrast, motor cycles had remained comparatively technologically stagnant and continued to demand more of their operators: they had to be kick started, there was no effective protection against inclement weather, suspension systems were questionable, and the motor cycle remained by nature inherently unstable. Carrying capacity, even with a sidecar, was still less than that offered by even the smallest standard motor car. Despite the best efforts of designers, motor cycle riders and their pillion passengers remained far more vulnerable to injury than if they were in a motor car.[19]

Notwithstanding the steady encroachment into its markets by motor cars, motor cycle production and road registrations did not actually drop, at least for a few years. Between 1925 and 1929, production rose from 120,000 to 147,000 units and road registrations jumped from 558,911 to a pre-war high of 731,298 machines (see Table 1). Average prices only gradually increased and in some instances even slightly declined. For example, a typical 250cc machine cost £36 in 1925, £37 in 1929 and £40 in 1934. A 500 cc model went from £50 to £45 to £54 and a 1000 cc model from £75 to £66 to £72 over the same period of time while side cars cost, on average, between £15 to £30 extra, depending on the type.[20]

There was, however, another serious problem affecting sales, which had nothing to do with price. Throughout this period motor cycles had begun to suffer in terms of social acceptability and prestige. Ownership of a two-wheeled vehicle simply did not have the same cachet that increasingly came with ownership of four-wheeled motor transport (Brunner, 1928, 33, 34). One motor cyclist was forced to admit that his chosen mode of travel put him at a disadvantage with his peers. 'I must agree,' he noted, 'that occasionally people in business are rather inclined to look down their noses at a fellow who turns up on a motor cycle.' Such attitudes persisted throughout the interwar period. At the end of the 1930s, a trade journalist deplored what he described as 'the suburbanite, not too sure of his own social standing, who is a bit doubtful about what the neighbours are thinking if he is seen going about by motor cycle instead of a small car.'[21]

In 1926 the extent of the shift away from two and three wheeled towards four wheeled motor transport was demonstrated during a debate about the relative merits of the light motor car and the motor cycle sidecar combination held between Coventry graduates of the Institution of Automobile Engineers and their Birmingham counterparts. Proponents of the latter vehicle found themselves defending a losing cause. The participants generally agreed that the motor cycle continued to enjoy the merits of cheaper cost and performance, but was suffering from its lack of comfort, especially protection against inclement weather. If the aim of personal motor transport was 'to cover the maximum distance with the minimum of fatigue' the motor car now had a substantial advantage with the general buying public. The motor cycle, by contrast, was now mostly relegated to enthusiasts.[22]

Much the same phenomenon was observed in key overseas markets as well. In Australia and New Zealand, for example, motor cycle dealers informed British manufacturers that sales had been hurt by four-wheeled competition. One Australian retailer described how increasing numbers of second hand Austin Sevens were threatening the motor cycle trade. However, he warned, it was the '2nd hand American car market' that most impeded motor cycle sales. Formerly, 'it was the custom of many motor cyclists to buy first a solo machine, then a side-car outfit, and eventually a motor car. A large percentage of them now begin by purchasing solo machines, and sooner or later acquire cars without becoming buyers of sidecars.'[23] Nor was this process exclusive to the so-called 'White Dominions'. A report received from East Africa at around the same time reached much the same conclusions: 'In the old days most chieftains rode Sunbeam bicycles and the sons rode Raleigh bicycles. Nowadays, the Raleigh is common amongst the natives and the chieftains use American cars, whilst the sons ride motor cycles.'[24]

Was the motor cycle industry indifferent to these threats or did it try to respond to the erosion of its position as provider of cheap personal transportation? In fact, during the opening phase of this period a number of new models of motorised two wheelers were introduced in a bid to maintain competitiveness. However, the initial response to the challenge posed by the light motor car did not come from the more established motor cycle manufacturers but rather from a group of newcomers to the industry.

The response was manifested during the early 1920s by a collection of unusual machines, which found their way onto display stands at the annual Motor Cycle Shows. These were noticeable for their unorthodox designs, quite unlike anything else emerging from the factories of more established motor cycle firms. One of these, the 'Ner-a-Car', incorporated many features which were thought to be missing from standard motor cycle design and explicitly tried to appeal to would-be motor car buyers. This two-wheeled vehicle had a small engine (211 cc at first, later increased to 350 cc), an automobile-like chassis along with some body work that kept the operator from being soiled by road dirt and which afforded at least a degree of weather protection. Indeed, the 'Ner-a-Car' was advertised as a motorised two wheeler that looked like an automobile (it was popularly called the 'Motor assisted mudguard') and cost £65 in 1923, fully equipped with electric lighting. Moreover, publicity for the 'Ner-a-Car' was specifically directed at non-motor cyclists. Unlike the traditional motor cycle firms who nearly always appealed to readers of journals such as *The Motor Cycle* and *Motor Cycling*, advertisements for the 'Ner-a-Car' were placed in publications like *Church Times* and even appeared on the front page of a May 1922 issue of *The Daily Mail*.[25]

Other machines of a similar type also attempted to exploit a perceived gap in the market for personal motor transport. The 'Unibus', for example, was marketed under the banner 'The Car on Two Wheels' and was manufactured by the Gloucestershire Aircraft Company. Another aviation firm, A.V. Roe, produced the 'Monocar' which was said to have been 'designed to combine the simplicity of the motor cycle with a car's comfort'.[26]

Then there were scooters, which had been designed, in large part with non-traditional consumers such as women in mind.[27] Advertising for these machines portrayed women using them not only for leisure purposes, like tours through the countryside, but also to help out in activities such as shopping expeditions. Scooters came in many forms and were also manufactured by firms outside the established motor cycle industry. The ABC 'Skootamota', hailed as the so-called 'Wonder Machine' (and built by the Sopwith Aviation and Engineering Co.) along with the Kenilworth scooter are examples of the type.[28]

Yet neither the car-like vehicles nor the scooters lived up to the expectations of their originators. Sales were inhibited by the sheer novelty of their designs, especially those like the 'Ner-a-Car'. Not only did they fail to locate a new strata of consumers, but, since dyed-in-the-wool motor cyclists looked down upon anything which deviated from the orthodox as 'sissy machines', they failed to find many adherents among established consumers as well.[29] Sales were hurt, moreover, by a number of technical flaws. The scooters, in particular, suffered from lower specifications than conventional motor cycles, some, for example, did not even have seats (Hough and Setright, 1973, 84). Consequently, this first initiative fizzled out after only a few years (Ayton et al, 1979, 86, 87).

The next attempt to broaden the market and stimulate flagging sales occurred when dedicated motor cycle manufacturers tried to develop a market among women, who, as a group, had hitherto ridden motor cycles in far fewer numbers than men.[30] In fact, efforts to sell motor cycles to women had begun as early as 1913, when a number of manufacturers introduced so-called 'womens' models'. These had open, bicycle type frames and generally carried smaller capacity engines than those found on regular machines.[31]

After the war, the campaign intensified. Popular motor cycle magazines, such as *The Motor Cycle* and the *Motor Cyclist Review*, had regular female contributors. Mabel Lockwood-Tatham, for example, wrote a column in the former publication entitled 'Through Feminine Goggles' and the latter carried 'Entirely for Eve' authored by 'Cylinda'. Their articles contained practical advice about motor cycling apparel and suggestions about the best type of motor cycles for the aspiring female motor cyclist. Other columns and features contained information about motor cycle maintenance along with information about touring and holiday destinations.[32] The industry also promoted publications such as *Motor Cycling for Women*, a book written by Betty and Nancy Debenham, which contained a foreword prepared by Manufacturers' Union Director H.R. Watling, that praised the role of women in the motor cycle world.[33]

The manufacturers used a variety of other methods to try and drum up greater sales of their products among women. In 1923, for example, manufacturers planned a 'rally for lady motor cyclists' and at least two companies pointedly used women instead of men to publicise their machines. In one instance, Dunelt, a smaller Midlands-based firm, arranged for a German woman, Suzanne Koerner, to ride one of their machines during mid-winter from Berlin to its Birmingham factory.[34] On another occasion, the Raleigh company provided a lightweight model to Marjorie Cottle, a well-known competitions rider, to use on a well publicized 1,400 mile journey around Britain.[35]

The manufacturers also encouraged women to participate in motor cycle sports. This had been a successful way of promoting sales among men and no doubt they thought it could work with women as well. In 1926, for example, the Manufacturers' Union decided to honour a number of popular female motor cycle competition riders at a banquet held during the annual motor cycle show.[36] Press releases announcing the event were sent to a number of magazines such as *Nursing Times*, *Home Notes*, *Home Chat* and *Womens*

Weekly, which were invited to send reporters in order to give the event the fullest possible public exposure to a female audience.[37] Nevertheless, despite the amount of publicity this and other such events received the campaign to increase sales of motor cycles to women also ended in failure.[38]

In part, this was a result of a general prejudice against women riding motor cycles as being somehow unfeminine. This prejudice created a defensive attitude among even some of the most dedicated enthusiasts. As one female motor cyclist explained: 'It seems that the fact of a girl being the rider of a motor cycle immediately labels her as being 'mannish' – admittedly an unpleasant characteristic – uninterested in frocks and frills, careless of home life, and devoid of any desire for women friends.'[39]

There were others who simply disapproved of women who associated with motor cycles and motor cyclists. Again this reflected an opinion that motor cycle riding conflicted with what was considered socially acceptable female behaviour. One newspaper, for example, ran a feature on the subject, which referred to the 'flapper with the dentifrice smile, errant pigtail ... who perches precariously sideways on a jazz cushion [pillion seat]'.[40] The real cause for the manufacturers' inability to convince more women to buy motor cycles, however, was that they were unable to resolve their own contradictory attitudes towards a market containing more women. Because of the industry's emphasis on racing and the glorification of power and speed, it had created an aura of masculinity around the motor cycle which was acknowledged, if not always admired, by enthusiasts and non-enthusiasts alike. The problem was that the campaign promoting the greater use of motor cycles among women also acted to undercut that same aura which was such an important factor in maintaining existing sales. This made one part of the industry work at cross-purposes with another.

For example, only a few months before being honoured for her competition victories, Marjorie Cottle had been banned from a racing event on no other grounds than her gender.[41] Indeed, this does not seem to have been an isolated instance and, judging from coverage in the motor cycle press, women had largely dropped out of competition events by the early 1930s.[42] In fact, women had already been barred from membership in the Motor Cycle Club (MCC) as early as 1910 and would not be readmitted until 1946.[43]

However, the mere presence of the potential for increasing the size of the market through attracting more female motor cyclists and other non-traditional consumers led to further debate within the industry. This debate revolved around what other measures should be taken in order to revitalise sales. This controversy was also fuelled by a rising level of public concern about motor cycles or more particularly the manner in which their riders operated them. These sentiments found a voice in a section of the popular press. The 1926 the *Evening Standard* pondered this matter and fingered the culprit:

He was a disagreeable young man who wore his cap the wrong way round, and he transported himself by means of his horrible machine from the place where he belonged to places which did not want him, where he generally left empty bottles and paper bags. It did not diminish his unpopularity that he was much subject to ridiculous mishaps. He sometimes broke his neck or that of his (generally feminine) companion, and he was hated for this too.[44]

Increasing numbers of road accidents and the noise emitted by speeding motor cycles had become an especially widespread irritant. The Home Office received a number of complaints about the racket caused by motor cycles allegedly racing along public roads throughout the country at all hours. In response to public pressure, the police began to crack down on motor cyclists, frequently bringing them to court on charges of speeding or lack of effective silencing equipment.[45]

The latter point was a sensitive one for the manufacturers, who claimed that the increased number of violations were the result of 'vague and uncertain' regulations administered in an arbitrary fashion by police and the courts.[46] These were not the only public officials who were considered biased against motor cyclists. Coroners were thought to be especially hostile and the manufacturers were often deeply offended by their findings, which were considered to be full of harsh condemnations against the reckless behaviour of young motor cyclists. In 1934, Manufacturers' Union Director H.R. Watling had actually petitioned the Lord Chancellor, urging him to prevent coroners from including such gratuitous criticism in their reports.[47]

By the late 1920s, such was the state of public sentiment that many motor cyclists, as well as senior representatives of the industry, were convinced that they had become virtual social pariahs. A confidential internal report summed up the situation:

> In practically every part of the country the general public is definitely antagonistic to motor cyclists; the Press is prejudiced against them; the police harry them; the authorities regard them with disfavour. Outside their ranks, motor cyclists can barely muster a friend.[48]

However, not everyone drew the same conclusions about how to deal with this uproar against motor cyclists. Some critics, both within and outside the industry, pointed out that the manufacturers' preoccupation with the large and powerful sports oriented machines was the root of the current difficulties. Instead of servicing a growing market, the industry was instead catering 'largely for young, and active, riders of sport machines, whose first demand is

161

for speed, pure and simple'. This, by implication, 'narrows down exceedingly the market for motor cycles'.[49]

Such controversy stimulated discussion about the need to develop a so-called 'Economy' or, as it came to be more widely known, 'Everyman' motor cycle, which was defined as a machine that was 'a light, silent, low-powered machine capable of a speed not greater than 30 mph, clean and reliable'. Its proponents argued that not only would such a machine defuse much of the criticism about noise and speed but it would also attract many non-motor cyclists into the market. In the words of Manufacturers' Union Director H.R. Watling, these were people like 'the parson, retired civil servant, the business man and the clerk'.[50] The problem was that there was no clear consensus within the industry of what exactly constituted an 'Everyman' machine. Was it to be an entirely new design, a light weight motor cycle or simply a motorised bicycle?

There may not have been consensus about its specifics but there was certainly great interest in the concept of a new type of motor cycle. In 1929, for example, one motor cycle journal offered to sponsor a special motor cycle trial in order to encourage the manufacture of 'a type of motor cycle which is not actually in production at present'. The winner of the trial was promised a prize of £500. Response to this offer, from readers at least, was considerable. The letters to the editor pages were full for several issues afterwards with opinions, for and against, on this question.[51] However, the manufacturers proved reluctant to rise to the challenge and the 'Everyman' trial was never even held through lack of entries.[52]

Another way the industry tried to counter antipathy against the motor cycle was to try and influence their press coverage. To that end, in 1929 the Manufacturers' Union hired Sir Basil Clarke of Editorial Services Ltd for the purpose of conducting what was described as 'motor cycle propaganda.'[53] This 'propaganda' took several forms and, by its own account, Clarke's company churned out a torrent of press releases and feature stories for Britain's newspapers. In its first report to the Manufacturers' Union, the company proudly boasted of its success in the nation's newsrooms: 'Not once, but many times, sub-editors have either used our own tendentious headlines, or have actually strengthened them by the additions of words of pro-motor cycling tendency.' It even prepared letters to the editor for the signature of people believed sympathetic to the industry. However effective the services of Clarke's organisation may have been is hard to measure and, in any case, its services were terminated in 1931 for reasons of economy.[54]

Moreover, the industry had become convinced that the root cause of its inability to expand the motor cycle market was due to what it thought to be excessive government taxation, which had dampened consumer demand. As a result, far more energy seemed to be been expended in trying to convince the

Minister of Transport and the Chancellor of the Exchequer to lower the tax on machines under 250 cc engine capacity than in actually designing and manufacturing a more popular lightweight motor cycle type.[55]

BSA, for example, the largest firm with the best engineering resources to develop such a machine, took hardly any action at all. On the contrary, by 1939 the company had actually dropped its only small displacement model (in the 150 cc engine class) from its sales catalogue. (see Table 5). The fact was that throughout the late 1920s and into the 1930s the few moderately successful lightweight or 'Everyman' type motor cycles, such as the 250 cc Francis-Barnett 'Cruiser' model, that did appear came mainly from the small to medium sized firms.[56] Overall, the majority of motor cycles registered for road use continued to be in the 350 cc to 500 cc categories (see Table 6).

Nonetheless, proponents of the 'Everyman' motor cycle had uncovered a serious weakness in the motor cycle industry, one that in the end it was either unable or unwilling to try and resolve. If, as some thought, the solution was to copy the burgeoning success of the motor car industry and manufacture cheaper, lightweight machines, British motor cycle companies were curiously reluctant to introduce American style production techniques. In particular, they displayed a marked abhorrence to the concept of a moving assembly line.

This attitude was in part a reflection of deeply held beliefs in the concept of 'craftsmanship' and the labour intensive factory methods which the British motor cycle industry was convinced gave it an edge over international competitors. Manufacturers made no secret of their contempt of 'mass production' an idea which they believed was 'foreign to British instincts.' [57] When he delivered his evidence to the Committee on Industry and Trade in March 1925, Manufacturers' Union Director H.R. Watling claimed that, because the industry was so 'fiercely competitive,' it had been segmented into 'groups which concentrate on special designs for special classes of users, for the user seems to be as individualistic as the manufacturer.' Under those circumstances, he continued, 'it is useless to think of "mass" production for the industry in general' (Committee on Industry and Trade, 1924–27, 451, 452)

This attitude remained entrenched nearly to the end of the interwar period. One trade journal stated outright that mass production methods would, by definition, depreciate the industry's high manufacturing standards. The Norton company quite openly proclaimed that it was proud of the fact that it did not have a moving assembly track at its Birmingham factory. To convert to that type of production was, in its mind, a highly undesirable development. In fact, it only added an assembly line in the months preceding the outbreak of war in 1939 and only then because of pressure to meet military contracts.[58]

Ironically, despite all the rhetoric about 'craftsmanship', British motor cycles were notorious for their mechanical unreliability. For example, in 1936 the editor of *The Motor Cycle* informed the Manufacturers' Union that he was

163

afraid to publish all the 10,000 letters he had received from irate customers, since 'publication would have a damping effect upon other readers' enthusiasm'. This type of criticism was not at all exceptional and was never really answered. In 1939 consumer discontent had reached the point where the Manufacturers' Union actually created a special committee to investigate a range of problems ranging from persistent oil leaks to faulty electric equipment.[59]

The competition between the motor cycle and light motor car was decisively resolved during the period in question. For motor cars in general, this was an era of almost continual expansion. Between 1925 and 1938, road registrations jumped from 590,156 vehicles to 1,984,430 and production output (although more erratic during the early 1930s) increased from 132,000 to 342,390 units. It has been suggested that there was room for yet more growth but nonetheless, by most standards, these were still years of success (Bowden, 1991).

In contrast, the motor cycle industry presents an entirely different picture. After 1925 growth was sluggish and, after a peak year in 1929, both production and road registrations went into long term decline, the latter reaching a nadir of 499,265 machines in 1938 (see Table 1). In the face of the motor cycle's various shortcomings relative to its four wheeled competitor, it is probable that there was little prospect the manufacturers could have maintained the position they had enjoyed before 1925.

Yet, there was some realistic hope that the motor cycle industry may have again become more competitive with the light motor car through creation of an expanding market for the cheaper 'Everyman' machines. It is true some manufacturers did demonstrate initiative in their efforts to develop machines like the 'Ner-a-Car' and the scooters, however, these efforts came from outside the industry. Later on, the larger firms, those with the greater resources to enable them to experiment, showed the least inclination to do so. The unwillingness of the manufacturers, excepting several smaller firms, to seriously try and produce an 'Everyman' machine, is indicative of the prevailing attitudes in the industry.

Perhaps they believed there was no potential for such a motor cycle. Nonetheless, the failure to cultivate a market among women, surely the key to any plan to expand the number of motor cycles and motor cyclists, foundered on the industry's inability to reach consensus on the issue. This made efforts at constructing a coherent strategy based on an 'Everyman' machine a near impossibility. Moreover, even if the opposing viewpoints on the question had been resolved, it is doubtful, in light of the manufacturers' reluctance to introduce larger scale production techniques and to solve the persistent quality control problems, whether they had the required engineering and managerial skills, never mind the aptitude, to service an expanded market.

The motor cycle continues to be seen, albeit more rarely than before, on British roads. Although the number of machines in use grew again after 1945, reaching an all-time peak of 1,795,555 during 1960, long term decline commenced once more thereafter (Ministry of Transport, various years). In 1992 only 582,000 machines were in use, fewer than the 655,200 that had been on the road in 1949! (Motor Cycle Industry Association, 1993). In vivid contrast, the number of motor cars have continued to grow throughout the post-war era, reaching a total over 22 million in 1992 with few prospects of any substantial reduction (Automobile and Truck International, 1994).

It was the combination of these factors, particularly the industry's self-imposed constraints, that ensured the dreams of those who promoted the concept of the two wheeled 'poor man's car' remained just that. Instead of becoming the workhorse of Britain's personal motor transport system or an instrument for greater social harmony, the motor cycle has found a secure if limited place as a vehicle associated with leisure and recreational activities.

Table Section

Table 1

British Motor Cycle Registrations, Production, Imports and Exports, 1919–38

	Registrations	Production	Imports	Exports
1919	114,722	65,000	1,481	8,330
1920	287,739	100,000	4,277	21,304
1921	373,200	80,000	2,130	8,104
1922	377,943	60,000	965	7,280
1923	430,138	80,000	1,011	16,156
1924	495,579	110,000	402	37,911
1925	558,911	120,000	867	47,114
1926	628,955	120,000	75	48,121
1927	681,410	160,000	149	53,000
1928	712,583	145,000	76	59,906
1929	731,298	147,000	103	62,377
1930	724,319	126500	236	42,689
1931	626,649	74,700	108	23,247
1932	599,904	70,400	16	19,537
1933	562,656	52,200	16	17,731
1934	548,461	58,500	20	16,807
1935	521,128	64,700	0	18,000
1936	510,242	55,200	0	20,500
1937	491,718	82,014	200	25,400
1938	499,265	65,100	200	19,800

Source:
Review of the British Cycle and Motor Cycle Industry 1935, BCMCMTU; Michael Miller
(n.d), *The British Motor-Cycle Industry before 1939* (unpublished) and, *The Motor Industry of Great Britain*, SMMT 1939.

Note:
The figures for motor cycle registrations in this table are not, because of different methods of calculation, always consistent with those contained in Table VI. In instances of inconsistency, those from this Table will prevail.

Table 2

British Motor Car Production, Registrations, Exports and Imports, 1919–1938

	Registrations	Production	Exports	Imports
1919	109,715	n/a	n/a	n/a
1920	186,801	n/a	4,294	n/a
1921	245,882	n/a	1,966	n/a
1922	319,311	n/a	1,338	12,992
1923	389,767	71,396	3,256	14,429
1924	482,356	116,600	11,007	10,800
1925	590,156	132,000	17,771	31,781
1926	695,634	153,500	14,858	10,923
1927	800,112	164,553	16,139	18,194
1928	900,557	165,352	18,192	22,582
1929	998,489	182,347	23,891	21,520
1930	1,075,081	169,669	19,226	9,751
1931	1,103,715	158,997	17,104	2,118
1932	1,149,231	171,244	26,942	2,762
1933	1,226,541	220,779	33,802	3,619
1934	1,333,590	256,866	34,877	10,851
1935	1,505,019	311,544	44,193	13,563
1936	1,675,104	353,838	51,173	12,323
1937	1,834,248	389,633	53,655	18,609
1938	1,984,430	342,390	44,130	n/a

Source: *The Motor Industry of Great Britain*, SMMT, 1939.

Table 3

Comparison of Prices for an Austin Seven Motor Car and Three Models of Motor Cycle Sidecar Combinations

	Austin Seven £	BSA 550cc £	Triumph 550cc £	Ariel 500cc £
1922	225	142	155	125
1923	165	100	115 17s	107
1924	155	85 10s	107	90
1925	141	87	88 5s	77 10s
1926	145	74	82 17s	71 10s
1927	145	n/a	67 17s	71 10s
1928	125	66 10s	–	66 10s

Source: Roy Church (1979) Herbert Austin. *The British Motor Car Industry to 1941,* Europa Publications, London.

168

Table 4

Comparisons of Prices of New Motor Cycle Side Car Combinations with Second Hand Cars: Selected Years

Sales Season	1929/30	1932/33	1934/35	1935/36
Comparison I.				
1. Price of a New 350 cc Combination.	£63.3	£64.7	£66	£68.1
2. Price of a 2 year old 8 hp motor car.	£81.2	£73.1	£66.1	£66.6
Comparison II.				
1. Price of a new 500cc Combination.	–	£72.9	£74.7	£79.3
2. Price of 3 year old car not exceeding 10 hp.	–	£72.2	£65.4	£68.5
Ratio: 2:1	n/a	.99	.88	.86.

Source: M. Miller (n.d.), *The British Motor Cycle Industry before 1939*, unpublished.

Table 5

Type of BSA Motor Cycle Sold, by Engine Displacement Size, 1926 to 1938

	Up to 150 cc	150 to 250 cc	Over250 cc	Total
1926	nil	11,057	1,042	29,099
1927	nil	8,878	19,125	28,003
1928	nil	4,851	14,927	19,778
1929*	nil	4,884	18,871	23,755
1930	nil	6,320	18,713	25,033
1931	nil	1,880	10,514	12,394
1932	nil	357	12,216	12,573
1933	nil	3,455	7,524	15,028
1934	1,501	5,995	7,532	15,028
1935	776	5,118	7,836	13,730
1936	650	6,593	8,848	16,091
1937	9	6,679	11,875	18,563
1938	2	4,759	8,824	13,585

First nine months of 1929 only.
Source: Modern Records Centre, University of Warwick, MSS 19A/2/37.

Table 6

Motor Cycles, by Engine Displacement Class, on the Road 1933–38, Motor Cycles Registered in Great Britain during the year ending 30 September

	1933	1934	1935	1936	1937
Solo motor cycles:					
Up to 150 cc	21,068	25,703	27,124	30,703	31,809
150cc–250 cc	131,706	137,193	134,904	136,500	135,46
Over 250 cc	244,554	220,608	197,319	188,913	182,87
Subtotal	397,328	383,504	359,374	356,116	350,15
Motor cycle Sidecar Combinations:					
UP to 150 cc	24	13	27	45	58
150cc–250 cc	1,315	1,634	1,241	1,295	996
Over 250 cc	144,636	140,589	131,041	124,159	114,99
Tricycles	19,353	22,716	24,911	24,165	21,374
Total:	562,656	548,461	516,567	505,779	487,57

Source: Ministry of Transport Return showing the number of mechanically-propelled vehicles registered for the first time under the Road Act, 1926.

Endnotes

[1] The material contained in this chapter is drawn from a PhD dissertation, entitled 'The British Motor Cycle Industry 1935–35', completed in 1995 at the University of Warwick.

[2] See 'A "highbrow"of motor cycling', *New Statesman* 17 April 1926 and 'A Flourishing Industry', *Daily Telegraph*, 6 October 1926, both contained in the papers of the industry's trade group during this period, the British Cycle and Motor Cycle Manufacturers' and Traders' Union (the 'Manufacturers' Union'), news clipping collection, MSS 204/4/2/3, on deposit at the Modern Records Centre (MRC), University of Warwick.

[3] See 'A Word for the Motor Cycle', *Daily Mail* 28 August 1926.

[4] In 1912 there were 69,501 motor cycles and 57,000 motor cars registered on British roads, totals which in 1920 had grown to 287,739 of the former and 122,000 of the latter vehicle type. Figures are derived from the Society of Motor Manufacturers' and Traders (1928) *The Motor Industry in Great Britain*, and the BCMCMTU (British Cycle and Motor Cycle Manufacturers and Traders' Union) (1935), *Review of the British Cycle and Motor Cycle Industry*, BCMCMTU, Coventry.

[5] There are no comparable accounts of the British motor cycle industry as there have been of its motor car counterparts, such as George Maxcy and Aubrey Silberston (1959), *The Motor Industry*, George Allen & Unwin Ltd., London, or more recently, Roy Church (1994), *The Rise and Decline of the British Motor Industry*, Macmillan, London.

[6] See Michael Miller, 'The British Motor Cycle Industry before 1939', (unpublished paper, University of East Anglia) and Steve Koerner (1995), 'The British Motor Cycle Industry during the 1930s', *Journal of Transport History*, Third Series, Number 1, March.

[7] The 'Big Six' comprised, in alphabetical order, Ariel, BSA, Matchless (previously H. Collier and Sons and later AMC), Norton, Royal Enfield and Triumph.

[8] See the 'Buyers Guide' contained in *The Motor Cycle*, issues dated 20 November 1913, 17 March 1921, and 27 November 1924.

[9] Motor cycles, for example, were very popular with public school boys and Oxbridge students. See 'Schools in Competition' and 'Cambridge varsity MCC in the Chilterns', both in *The Motor Cycle*, 11 January and 8 February 1923 respectively.

[10] See 'About Motoring', *New Statesman*, 12 June 1926.

[11] The Donington event was described in an untitled feature contained in *The Export Trader*, June 1939, 250.

[12] See 'Motor Cycles' *The Automobile Engineer*, August 1928, 273, and 'Motor Cycle Sport', *The Export Trader*, July 1937, 231.

[13] See 'Record Buying in the Home Market', *The Times* 25 June 1925, and 'Cycle and Motor Cycles. Prospects in Empire Markets', *The Times Trade Supplement*, 9 August 1924, both contained in news clipping volume MRC MSS 204/10/1/1. See also 'Motor Cycle Design – a Brief Resume of Twenty Five Years Development', *Automobile Engineer*, August 1935, 285–89.

[14] See 'The Passenger Motor Cycle', *The Motor Cycle*, 23 October 1924, 578–83. The issue of garaging was especially important. At a meeting of the Institution of Automobile Engineers, one participant noted that the majority of the working classes will for the sheer joy of using the open road, purchase something. The motor cycle with the detachable sidecar is the only machine they can possibly have for convenient garaging, so that I think this type of machine will always retain its popularity as long as mankind is forced to live in houses with restricted accommodation. See the remarks of L.J. Shorter as reported in the discussion which followed the delivery of W. Halcot Hingston's paper (1921/22), 'The Light Car and Motor Cycle and Sidecar' contained in the *Proceedings of the Institution of Automobile Engineers*, xvii, ii, 25.

[15] See 'Sympathetic Tinkering: Motorist and Motor Cyclists Compared', *The Motor Cycle*, 6 March 1924, 308.

[16] See (1937) *Road Traffic Census, 1936 Report*, HMSO, London, 10. Over the same period of time, the number of motor cycles registered for road use dropped from 731,298 to 505,779, or a decrease of 31 per cent.

[17] The continuing slippage of the price differential between the two vehicle types was well understood in the motor cycle industry. As one trade journal commented, 'Why should a man be expected to pay £60 for a motor cycle when he can get a really first class used car for even less?' See 'Making Motor Cycle Sales' by 'A Well-Known Dealer', *Motor Cycle and Cycle Trader*, 29 January 1937, 80–81.

[18] See Austin Motor Company *Minute Books*, 752, entry for 25 September 1927, contained in MRC MSS 226/AU/1/1/1.i and notes from 'The Visit of the Chairman and Mr. E.L. Payton to the USA' (no date but circa 1922/1923), contained in the Austin Motor Company Directors' Minute Books, MRC MSS 226/AU/1/1/1ii.

[19] This was a point sometimes discussed in popular journals during this time, see for example, 'Finality of Design. Has the Motor Cycle Field Stagnated?' *The Motor Cyclist Review*, November 1929, 229.

[20] See British Cycle and Motor Cycle Manufacturers and Traders' Union (1935), *Review of the British Motor Cycle Industry*, Coventry, BCMCMTU and *Buyers Guide* for 1925, op. cit.

[21] See Richard Twelvetrees (1929) 'Motorcycle or Car?', *The Motor Cycle*, 203–4 and Frances Jones (1939) 'Attack the Market from the Top', *The Motor Cycle and Cycle Trader*, 18.

[22] The debate was reported in the popular motor cycle press, see 'Sidecar v. Cheap Car', *The Motor Cycle*, 30 December 1926, 154.

[23] See memo entitled 'Trade in Australia', dated 5 November 1925, and contained in GUARDBOOK MRC MSS 204/3/1/12.

[24] See memo entitled 'Trade in East Africa', dated February 1927, contained in Guardbook MRC MSS 204/3/1/15.

[25] The 'Ner-a-Car' was the brainchild of American automobile engineer C.A. Neracher who received financing from the Gillette safety razor company. It was built in Britain by the Sheffield Simplex Company at a former Sopwith aircraft factory at Kingston-upon-Thames, Surrey. See 'The Lightweights', *The Times*, 31 November 1921, contained in the Manufacturers' Union newsclipping volume MRC MSS 204/10/1/1; Peter Watson (1990) 'Look, no hands!, *Classic Bike*, 34–8 and Bart H. Vanderveen, (1975), *Motor Cycles to 1945*, Frederick Warne and Co., London, 33.

[26] Ads for these machines can be found in the catalogues of the annual Cycle, Motor Cycle, Cyclecar and Accessories Exhibition, contained in volume MRC MSS 204/4/1–20. See also 'The Single Track Carette', *The Motor Cycle*, 19 January 1922, 71–2 and E.C MacIntosh (1924), 'My Car on Two Wheels', ibid, 876.

[27] The scooter is distinguished from the orthodox motor cycle by, among other things, its open frame, the rearward position of the engine, smaller wheels, the seating arrangement and bodywork. See C.F. Caunter, (1982) *Motor Cycles, A Technical History*, HMSO, London, 81–2.

[28] Scooter ads can be seen in the catalogues of the annual Cycle, Motor Cycle, Cycle car and Accessories Exhibition, contained in op. cit.

[29] One popular motor cycle journal admitted that the average British motor cyclist was apt to look with some disdain on anything which savours of the motorised bicycle or out of the ordinary. See 'First Steps in Motor Cycling', *The Motor Cycle*, 2 August 1923, 160.

[30] In 1925, Manufacturers' Union Director H.R. Watling estimated that there were only about 25,000 female motor cyclists in Britain at a time when there were more than half a million registered motor cycles. See "The 'Utility' Motor Cycle', *The Motor Cyclist Review*, September 1929, 129–30.

[31] See 'Buyers Guide' contained in op. cit. One reporter at the 1921 Motor Cycle Show was impressed with the range of lightweight machines specifically designed for women. These are the daintiest and prettiest little vehicles imaginable ... perfectly adopted for shopping excursions as for long runs in the country. See Capt. P.A. Barron (1921) 'Women and the Motor Cycle Show', *Daily Mirror*, 1 December, contained in news clipping volume, MRC MSS 204/10/1/1.

[32] See 'Through Feminine Goggles' *The Motor Cycle*, 15 December 1921, 816–17 and 5 February 1923, 212–14. For 'Cylinda', see 'Entirely for Eve', *The Motor Cyclist Review*, January 1929, 348.

[33] The book contained chapters with titles such as 'Our First Side Car Tour' and 'The Road Girl's Complexion'. See Betty and Nancy Debenham (1928), *Motor Cycling for Women*, Pitman and Sons, London.

[34] See 'Notes of Conference between London Representatives of Manufacturers and London Agents', dated 16 May 1923, contained in Minute Book MRC MSS 204/1/1/4 and Suzanne Koerner (1927) 'From Berlin to Birmingham', *The Motor Cycle*, 19 May, 810–12.

[35] One reporter observed that not only had she demonstrated that physical strength was not required to successfully operate a motor cycle but the fact that Miss Cottle always manages to look nice when engaged in her exploits, and not the least like a professional motor cyclist, produces the best possible impression on the public. See L.F. Jones (1926), 'The Appeal to the Feminine', *Garage and Motor Agent*, 17 July, 532. Thanks to Sean O'Connell for drawing this article to my attention.

[36] See untitled memo dated 21 September 1926, contained in Guardbook MRC MSS 204/3/1/16.

[37] See untitled memo dated 26 October 1926, contained in ibid.

[38] See 'My Lady comes to Town' by 'Hildegarde', *The Motor Cycle*, 14 October 1926, 694–97.

[39] See Mabel Lockwood-Tatham (1922) 'The Modern Girl and the Motor Cycle. A Defence of the Motor Cycling Sporting Girl', *The Motor Cycle*, 5 October, 472–93.

[40] See Rex Brittain (1921) 'The Pillion Girl', *Evening News*, 27 August, contained in clipping volume op. cit.

[41] The Manufacturers' Union, together with the Royal Automobile Club, controlled sporting events through an affiliated organisation, the Auto Cycle Union.

[42] Cottle was certainly not banned from these events through any lack of talent or physical endurance on her part. During the Scott Trial, for example, she had reportedly finished the course while burly men had given up from sheer exhaustion. See 'My Lady Comes to Town', op cit. Nor was Cottle exceptional; female riders had been successful elsewhere as well. See 'Women Motor cyclists', *Daily Telegraph*, 16 October 1926, contained in clipping volume, op. cit.

[43] The reasons for their original expulsion remain obscure. See 'The MCC Decides', *The Motor Cycle*, 31 January 1946, 87.

[44] See leading article entitled 'The Chariot of Youth', *Evening Standard*, 5 October 1926, contained in newspaper clipping volume, op. cit.

[45] See PRO (Public Record Office) HO45/23019 which contains a number of these complaints, especially file 659888/16, entitled 'Noise of motor vehicles'. See also PRO HO45/11100 which covers public concerns about motor cycle races on beaches and PRO HO45/456309/2, file entitled 'Motor cycle speed trials'.

[46] See copy of a brief from the Manufacturers' Union to the Ministry of Transport, dated 15 March 1926, contained in Guardbook MRC MSS 204/3/1/13 as well as a memo dated 12 August 1926 entitled, '87/26. Silencing of Motor Cycles', contained in Guardbook MRC MSS 204/3/1/14.

[47] Mention of Watling's approach to the Lord Chancellor about British coroners is contained in the Manufacturers' Union *Annual Report* for 1934, 3, MRC MSS 204/4/3/2.

[48] See 'Memorandum on the effect of noisy motor cycles on public opinion' presented by the RAC Motor Cycle Committee, dated October 1926, contained in Guardbook MRC MSS 204/3/1/14.

[49] See T. Gardener (1930) 'Motor Cycles for the Masses', *The Motor Cyclist Review*, January, 314.

[50] See H.R. Watling (1927) leading article, entitled 'An Untapped Market', ibid, July, 15 and "The Utility" motor cycle', op. cit.

[51] See 'A Plea for 'Everyman' motor cycle', *The Motor Cycle*, 3 January 1929, 30. Letters in response to the editorial were printed in the 17 and 24 January, 7 February and 21 March 1929 issues of the journal.

[52] See memos, both entitled 'Proposed "Everyman" utility motor cycle trial', dated 12 January 1928 and 2 September 1930 respectively, contained in Guardbooks MRC MSS 204/3/1/9 and 204/3/1/24.

[53] Clarke was paid 2,000 Guineas along with £500 expenses during the course of his first contract. See minutes of the Manufacturers' Union Management Committee meeting of 4 June 1929, contained in Minute Book MRC MSS 204/1/1/8.

[54] See Clarke's undated report, which is attached to a memo entitled 'Propaganda for motor cycling', dated 20 November 1929 and contained in Guardbook MRC MSS 204/3/1/20. In a report dated June 1930, Clarke stated that he had drafted letters for the Presidents of the Amalgamated Engineering Union and the Transport and General Workers' Union. The report is contained in Guardbook MRC MSS 204/3/1/24. For the reasons for ending Clarke's contract, see minutes of the Manufacturers' Union Management Committee meeting of 14 July 1931, contained in Minute Book MRC MSS 204/1/1/10A.

[55] A copy of the Manufacturers' Union brief to the government on the subject of motor cycle taxation is contained in PRO BT 59/24/589. The question of what position to take with respect to taxation was thoroughly canvassed in the pages of the Manufacturers' Union *Quarterly Journal*, especially in the February, August and June 1930 issues. Copies of the *Quarterly Journal* are on deposit in MRC MSS 204/4/2/5.

[56] See Peter Watson (1985) 'Bridging a Gap', *Classic Bike*, February and Jonathon Jones (1991) 'Comfort with Cleanliness', *The Classic Motor Cycle*, July.

[57] See 'Motor Cycling Achievement of 1924', *Daily Telegraph*, 31 December 1924, contained in newspaper clipping volume MSS 204/10/1/1/.

[58] See 'The Final Inspection', *The Motor Cycle and Cycle Trader*, 7 February 1936, 84 and 'Performance in the Making', *The Export Trader*, May 1938, 192–93. The Norton company also tried to keep numbers of female workers in its factory 'to a minimum', on the grounds that they compromised quality control.

[59] See memo entitled 46/36 Motor Cycles: Criticisms by Users, dated 18 March 1936 and contained in Guardbook MRC MSS 204/3/1/39 and memo entitled 99/39. Motor Cycle Sales Investigation Committee', dated 16 June 1939, contained in Guardbook MRC MSS 204/3/1/47.

Bibliography

Automobile and Truck International (1994), *World Automotive Market Report*, Hunter Publications, Elk Grove Village, Illinois, USA.

Ayton, Cyril et al (1979) *A History of Motor Cycling*, Orbis Publishing Ltd, Norwich.

Bowden, S.M. (1991) 'Demand and Supply Constraints in the Inter-war UK Car Industry: Did the Manufacturers get it Right?', *Business History*, 33, 2, April.

British Cycle and Motor Cycle Manufacturers and Traders' Union (1935) *Review of the British Cycle and Motor Cycle Industry*, BCMCMTU, Coventry.

Brunner, Christopher T. (1928) *The Problem of Motor Transport*, Ernest Benn Ltd, London.

Caunter, C.F. (1982) *Motor Cycles, A Technical History*, HMSO, London.

Church, Roy and Miller, Michael, (1977) 'The Big Three: Competition, Management, and Marketing in the British Motor Industry, 1922-30', in *Essays in British Business History*, (ed.) Barry Supple, Clarenden Press, Oxford.

Church, Roy, (1979) *Herbert Austin. The British Motor Car Industry to 1941*, Europa Publications, London and (1994) *The Rise and Fall of the British Motor Industry*, Macmillan, London.

Committee on Industry and Trade (1924–27) *Minutes of Evidence*, HMSO, London.

Debenham, Betty and Nancy (1928) *Motor Cycling for Women*, Pitman and Sons, London.

Goodwin, Bill (1993) 'Making a Success out of Triumph', *The Engineer*, 14 October.

Heather, D.S. (1918/1919) 'A Survey of Current Motor Cycle Design', *Proceedings of the Institution f Automobile Engineers*, XII.

Hingston, Halcot (1921/1922) 'The Light Car and Motor Cycle and Sidecar', *Proceedings of the Institution of Automobile Engineers*, XVII, ii.

Hough, Richard and Setright, L.J.K. (1973) *A History of the World's Motor Cycles*, George Allen and Unwin Ltd, London.

Koerner, Steve (1995) 'The British Motor Cycle Industry during the 1930s', *Journal of Transport History*, vol 16, no 1, March.

Miller, Michael (nd) 'The British Motor Cycle Industry before 1939', unpublished, University of East Anglia.

Ministry of Transport (1937) *Road Traffic Census, 1936 Report*, HMSO, London; (various years) *Highway Statistics*, London, HMSO.

Motor Cycle Industry Association (1993) *The UK Motorcycle Industry in a Nutshell*, Coventry, MCIA.

Newcombe, T.P. and Spurr, R.T. (1979) *A Technical History of the Motor Car*, Adam Hilger, Bristol.

Smith, Barbara (1983) *The British Motor Cycle Industry, 1945–75*, Birmingham, University of Birmingham.

Society of Motor Manufacturers and Traders (SMMT) (various years), *The Motor Industry of Great Britain*. SMMT, London.

Turner, Edward (1942–43) 'Post-war Motor Cycle Development', *Proceedings of the Institition of Automobile Engineers*, XXXVII.

Worthington-Williams, Michael (1981) *From Cyclecar to Microcar. The Story of the Cyclecar Movement*, Dalton Watson Ltd, London.

Vanderveen, Bart H. (1975) *Motor Cycles to 1945*, Frederick Warne and Co, London.

Wyatt, R.J. (1982) *The Austin Seven. The Motor for the Million, 1922–29*, David and Charles, London.

12

Taste, Status and Middle Class Motoring in Interwar Britain

Sean O'Connell

This chapter will analyse the ways in which considerations of taste and social status defined the choices available to interwar car buyers, manufacturers and dealers. Previous work has acknowledged the effect of middle-class taste on car design and the proliferation of models. Here, significant new evidence will be unveiled indicating that similar notions also affected the ways in which the car was sold. In particular it will be shown that despite the apparent success of hire purchase, it was a form of payment which was looked upon with a great deal of ambivalence. As a result manufacturers and dealers soft-pedalled their use of this method of payment. It was rarely featured in advertising, for example, and strict limitations were placed on its use by finance companies. The extent to which this previously unacknowledged factor may have limited market growth will be assessed.

Acknowledging and employing the insights of business and economic historians, this study also utilises the methodology and theory of social-historical analysis in order to present an interdisciplinary explanation of the diffusion of car ownership in interwar Britain. As part of this approach the first systematic oral history of interwar motorists has been undertaken as part of the research for this project. In designing the research methodology for this study I owe an intellectual debt to a growing band of scholars who recommend that explanations of consumption move away from the study of one element of the consumption process, towards a more integrated approach that takes account of production, distribution, advertising, marketing, uses of the product and so on (McCracken, 1988; Fine & Leopold, 1993; Mort, 1996).

Supply versus demand: competing interpretations of the diffusion of car ownership 1918–1939

The interwar years saw the arrival of Britain's first era of mass motoring. The number of private cars rose from just over 100,000 in 1918 to slightly over two million in 1939 (Mitchell, 1988). Historians have offered a variety of explanations for this growth, not least of which was the very appreciable decline in prices. For example, employing 1924 prices as an index of 100, prices in 1928 had fallen to 80 per cent of their 1924 level and by 1936 stood at 49.8 per cent of that level (Society of Motor Manufacturers and Traders, annual). These reductions were due largely to the production of smaller cars together with the increased rationalisation and efficiency of production. The rising levels of real income amongst the middle classes were also instrumental in extending the market, particularly following the recovery from slump in the early 1930s. Hire purchase is also widely believed to have had a significant impact on the market, with an estimated 60 per cent of all sales involving some form of deferred payment in 1927 (Bowden, 1991, 254).

Despite the impressive rise in ownership, criticism has been offered of the industry's failure to adopt Fordist policies and thereby attain a truly mass market. Adopting a supply-side perspective, Wayne Lewchuk has accused the largest motor manufacturers of conservatism in two respects. Firstly, he alleges short-termism in respect of an apparent preference to meet shareholders' demands for dividends rather than in the investment necessary to develop a mass market (Lewchuk, 1986, 147). Thus between 1924 and 1929 Morris Motors retained only 50 per cent of net earnings within the company, a figure that dropped to 25 per cent in the period 1934–38. Secondly, he believes motor manufacturers failed to take full control of the production process, instead following a 'British system of production' allowing trade unions to set production targets through the operation of piece-work (Lewchuk, 1987).

However, Lewchuk's arguments have been repudiated for a number of reasons. Firstly, doubt has been cast on Lewchuk's assessment of union influence (Tolliday, 1987). But, most tellingly, analyses of demand-side constraints have cast serious doubt on the advisability of any policy of Fordism (Bowden, 1991; Bowden & Turner 1993a; 1993b). Adopting an econometric approach centred on consumer demand theory, their work points to the skewed distribution of income in interwar Britain as a stumbling block preventing an adoption of fordist mass production policies. Put simply, it is maintained that the manufacturers developed a system of production, which met the conditions of the British market. The market was limited to the wealthiest amongst the professional and commercial classes because of skewed income distribution and the high costs of running a car.

Whilst these interpretations are extremely informative they pay only limited attention to the role that taste and status had in the development of the market. In this chapter this omission will be rectified. Two arguments will be central to the analysis offered. Firstly, that every aspect of the consumption process must be included in the equation. Secondly, each of these aspects should be studied using the insights of business, economic, and social history.

Designing cars for the interwar middle-class market

The role of taste and status in the developing market for cars has not been entirely ignored by economic and business historians. They have acknowledged their impact upon the design and production strategies of manufacturers in the 1930s (Church & Miller, 1977; Tolliday, 1987; Bowden, 1991). In particular, the shift by the major motor manufacturers from a policy of price competition in the 1920s towards one of model/price competition and product differentiation in the 1930s has been widely noted. Manufacturers followed this route for two reasons. First, throughout the interwar years, market saturation was felt to be imminent given the skewed distribution of income in the British economy. Any policy of Fordist mass production was therefore dismissed as impractical. Second, manufacturers were responding to growing signs amongst their existing market of an increased desire to express status and individuality through the choice of motor car. This trend was demonstrated both by the poor sales of cheap economy cars, such as the 1931 Morris Minor S.V., and the increased employment, by individual buyers, of coach builders who created special bodies for less expensive cars such as the Austin Seven and Wolseley Hornet.

The Morris Minor S.V. was introduced in 1931 at a cost price of £100 and appeared to represent one of the last attempts by a British manufacturer to place cost price entirely ahead of aesthetic considerations. It was a spartan car, modelled on the successful Ford Eight, pared down to the absolute minimum with only a three-speed gearbox and a windscreen wiper with only one blade. It did not sell well at all, as Miles Thomas, sales manager at Morris Motors at the time, recalled in his autobiography. He claimed that orders, in fact poured in for the more expensive and better-equipped Morris Minor.

> It was an interesting exercise in consumer preference that although attention was undoubtedly attracted to the Morris Minor by the fact that one *could* be purchased for as little as £100, the actual buyers wanted something that showed that they had *not* bought the cheapest product. And so everybody was happy. No one wants to keep down with the Joneses! (Thomas, 1964, 168)

A decade earlier, with cars in short supply following the war, a cheap Ford was often the only car available to buyers. With no other purchase in prospect many bit the bullet and bought one and then engaged in efforts to camouflage the true identity of their car. The pages of the *Autocar*, for example, regularly featured photographs of Fords with new bodies placed on their chassis.

By the late 1920s companies such as Thrupp and Maberley and designers like William Lyons were busily catering to desires for individuality in the motoring community, providing special bodies to glamorize cheap models such as the Austin

Seven and Wolseley Hornet. By 1932, Wolseley were producing a Hornet chassis with no body to allow customers to have their own special bodies built to their own taste without the need to pay for two sets of bonnets, wings and running boards (*Autocar*, 22 April 1932). In 1933 *Autocar* reported on this phenomenon, expressing surprise at the number of expensive bodies being built at Thrupp and Maberley despite the recession.

> Of course, you have to pay for it in the same way a woman has to pay for a dress from one of the great *couturieres*. But, like her, you get something different, and you won't take someone else's car from a park by mistake. All of which is very nice to us English, a distinction loving people if ever there was one. (*Autocar*, 16 December 1933)

This tendency indicated that middle-class motorists were establishing the same patterns of differentiation and status seen in housing, dress, and many other areas of consumption. Cars came second to the family home in price, but the mobility they offered ensured that they acquired, what Roy Church has called, 'a special dysfunctional utility, as objects of status' (Church, 1981). The horsepower rating of a motorist's car indicated something about the owner's status, as well as the tax rating it fell into. Manufacturers built a model in each category so as not to miss out on a particular market niche. A statement from the Vauxhall company, issued in the 1930s indicated that the manufacturers were aware of what were described as 'psychological rather than economic' factors.

> This tax business has become an obsession in the mind of the motorist. An 'eight', he realises, costs less in tax and insurance than a 'ten' or a 'twelve' and so on: and other factors have largely to be ignored. There is a class-consciousness in horsepowers, and the manufacturer has to build a model for every class, and to suit every purse. (*Political and Economic Planning*, 1950, 65)

So, as *Political and Economic Planning* observed, manufacturers produced a cheap, small model of seven or eight horsepower, hoping it would capture a large market whilst also offering a number of other models, designed to appeal to the better off. Such a policy avoided the risk inherent in single model production whilst enabling manufacturers 'to cultivate technical, aesthetic or snobbish appeal'.

Certain marques also came to be identified with different social groups – as Graham Robson has noted: 'It would never have done, for instance, for a respectable bank manager to be seen in a sports car and certainly he would never have considered any type of imported car' (Robson, 1979, 35). 'Appropriate' cars for the gentry were Armstrong-Siddleys, Bentleys, Lanchesters and Rolls-Royces but they studiously avoided Humbers – which were seen as the cars of the staid middle-aged middle classes. As a conventional car, Humbers proved a safer choice than the SS.1, and its immediate successors, which had an unfortunate reputation that was very widespread. A string of negative appellations were applied to this car by oral interviewees and in motoring literature. The SS.1 was often referred to as 'a cad's car', or 'a Promenade Percy's car': it also had a reputation as a flashy car favoured by 'spivs' and 'shady traders'. It is in this context that it gathered the unfortunate sobriquet of the 'Jew's Bentley'. The SS car was probably the first to have its chassis designed by body-builders, giving it an attractive and expensive appearance. The *Autocar* review on its unveiling said that it was a £310 model that looked like a £1000 car (*Autocar*, 9 October 1931). This discrepancy between looks and cost may explain some of the animosity towards the car. Pierre Bourdieu argues that taste functions as a marker of class: 'taste classifies and it classifies the classifier' (Bourdieu, 1986, 1–2). Thus, the hierarchical consumption of goods provides an insight into social relations: in the case of the SS car its comparatively low cost allowed new social groups to enter the sports car niche. Hence its buyers came to be viewed as intruders in a sphere of motoring they had previously been unable to join, with the result that they were classified – by the 'Bentley Boys' and others amongst motoring's cognoscenti – as a motoring nouveau riche whose sense of good taste had not caught up with their purchasing power. If the car were judged on looks alone today's visitor to transport museums might well decide that the SS was more attractive than the Bentley.

Thus annual model changes, increased accent on styling, and accessories on even the cheapest cars, together with production of models in all price and horsepower categories, kept unit costs high, inevitably hindering the industry's ability to reduce retail prices. (Bowden, 1991, 263). By 1938, the six largest producing groups were turning out forty different types of engines and in the case of twenty-six of these engines fewer than a thousand units were being manufactured annually (Bagwell, 1974, 212). By 1939 the Nuffield Organisation, the largest manufacturing group, was producing eighteen basic car types. Although their size made it possible to go further in terms of large-scale production techniques than others, the number of designs of each component resulted in the employment of many general purpose tools, thereby increasing production costs. So, in catering to middle-class concerns about social status, manufacturers helped to create a self-fulfilling prophecy, whereby their actions reinforced the belief that the market for cars would remain stubbornly within the higher income brackets. This much has been recognised before, but did the middle classes and their caste-like desire for stratification affect other aspects of the diffusion of car ownership?

The role of hire purchase re-assessed

It will now be argued that similar patterns of middle-class taste and status shaped the marketing, selling and uses to which cars were put in the interwar years. The remainder of this chapter will focus upon attitudes towards hire purchase, which has been widely credited with extending car ownership in this period. British buyers were offered hire purchase terms from 1912 (Crowther, 1971, 185), and by 1927 it was estimated that 60 per cent of all sales in Britain involved deferred payment (Bowden, 1991, 254). However, the expansion of instalment selling in Britain was not as great, proportionately, as in some countries. By 1927 the German figure was 75 per cent, the Italian 75 per cent and in the affluent USA the number making use of such facilities was 64 per cent (Bowden, 1991, 254). In France, where, rural buyers were notoriously suspicious of hire purchase, the figure was lower, at 50 per cent (Fridenson, 1981, 127–54). Why, with the exception of France, were the British figures the lowest amongst the major car-buying nations? A trawl through the pages of the trade press, the *Motor Trader* and *Garage and Motor Agent*, reveals a series of ambivalent attitudes towards hire purchase on the part of dealers and car buyers. These reflect not only business concerns, but also tension between social sensibilities and the possible symbolic implications of hire purchase.

In 1936 the chairman of the Motor Finance Corporation declared in the *Motor Trader*: 'So far as I am aware, no manufacturer and no dealer has, as yet, attempted to use hire purchase facilities as an advertising stunt to sell his vehicles to the public' (*Motor Trader*, 26 February 1936). Sampling of advertising placed in the *Autocar* and the *Motor* reveals that deferred payment plans were mentioned, but only on an irregular basis, with such schemes being mentioned in only 3.59 per cent of advertisements surveyed for the period 1919 to 1938. On occasions when they were mentioned they were often placed, discreetly, in the small-print of the advertisement's text. This would suggest that manufacturers found hire purchase a somewhat delicate subject to broach with their middle-class public. That public shared the same reticent outlook. Although more and more car-buyers made use of what were dubbed 'out of income systems' it was done with great discretion, as was recalled by Graham Robson.

> Although there was a good deal of hire purchase activity, even at the beginning of the 1930s, it was always a rather hole-in-the-corner and furtive way of raising the money. Somehow (and such were the fiscal standards of the day) hire purchase was always considered to be a 'not quite nice' way of financing one's purchase and it was never talked about. (Robson, 1979, 35)

The motoring press also exhibited something of a guarded attitude towards this aspect of the industry. The leading motoring journal, the *Autocar*, ran regular articles on the practicalities of car ownership, with coverage of such subjects as buying new or second-hand cars and motor insurance. However, in the interwar years, they produced only one small article directly referring to hire purchase. Even this brief piece, written in 1937, was tucked away inside the back cover, and described hire purchase as a 'little known side of the automobile industry' (*Autocar*, 10 September 1937). The *Autocar* itself had certainly done little to make it better known. This circumspection would seem to have been derived from attitudes towards hire purchase demonstrated by middle-class motorists. Reports from the trade press revealed that many buyers were prepared to go to great lengths to conceal their use of instalment payments. In 1924 the *Garage and Motor Agent* reported that motorists using instalment plans were 'shy of putting their orders in the hands of local agents'. London car showrooms were popular for this reason, offering 'the privacy the provincial purchasers feel is their's when far from their homes'. The article concluded by conjecturing that the 'shame' attached to the use of deferred payments would pass in time. In the mean time, dealers were advised to cultivate the 'utmost security and secrecy', in order to secure this type of business. At the same time, details of hire purchase schemes should be placed in the footnotes of trader's advertising, so as not to risk the loss of cash customers. (*Garage and Motor Agent*, 26 January 1924) The inference was clearly that such clients liked it to be very apparent that they were indeed cash buyers.

The experiences of a sample of interwar motorists, currently totalling thirty-eight and rising, have also been drawn upon during this research. They provide further evidence to indicate that hire purchase was frowned upon by many middle-class consumers. Several mentioned that buying on the 'never-never' was just not done. One man told me 'Every car I paid cash. I was brought up by a very strict Scots father who taught me the only thing you bought on tick was a house' (Interviewee Four, born London 1901). In total, only 16.66 per cent of respondents who offered information on methods of payment recalled the use of hire purchase. Obviously, this evidence is at odds with what is known about the widespread use of hire purchase. As has been seen, its estimated use by the late 1920s stood at around 60 per cent of all sales. Perhaps the samples drawn upon here are simply unrepresentative. It is also conceivable that some respondents are still unwilling to reveal their use of hire purchase. It might also be possible, particularly in the case of female correspondents that they were actually uninvolved in the financial side of the purchase and remained unaware of how the deal was transacted.

It must also be borne in mind that the utility value of car ownership involved more than simply being able to travel from A to B. Ownership conferred social prestige, offering the means for a display of success and financial stability in the owner's chosen field. In 1920, *Motor Trader* argued that potential owners could be hooked by the argument that 'a car is taken by a number of people as an outward and visible sign of prosperity, (and will) help his credit, and his status in the town'

(*Motor Trader*, 3 November 1920). Any suggestion that a car had been bought on the 'never-never' would tarnish this image of sound social and financial standing.

If the 'shame' of buying via hire purchase died down, as *Garage and Motor Agent* suggested it would, it was still strong enough in 1935 for that journal to describe the continuing 'old-fashioned but powerful prejudice against hire purchase on the part of the very class of people who are most justified in employing it'. Again the popularity of London motor marts was mentioned, as were those of provincial centres which could also offer the 'hire-purchaser the impersonality and privacy that belong to crowds (*Garage And Motor Agent*, 2 March 1935). Once again dealers were advised to be discreet when using hire purchase. The suggestion offered on this occasion was that traders use advertising to stress that deferred payment schemes were carried out in the strictest confidence. The Society of Motor Manufacturers and Traders also noticed the phenomenon of the attraction of London for hire purchase buyers. They reported, that in 1938, 34 per cent of new cars sold within the London region were purchased by customers whose homes were outside the area (Society of Motor Manufacturers and Traders, 1940, 85). It is possible that London was popular amongst car buyers because it offered a wider choice of models. But, if that was so, trade insiders did not make reference to it, focusing instead on the anonymity offered to hire purchase buyers by the capital's car showrooms.

The evidence provided by Robson's motoring memoirs, interwar motorists, the motoring and trade press and the figures for London sales indicate that, despite its wide use, hire purchase remained a subject requiring delicate handling by all concerned. Our story so far must also give rise to a number of new questions about the diffusion of car ownership in interwar Britain. Two will be addressed in the remainder of this chapter. How many sales were lost through this ambivalence? Did many potential buyers postpone their entry into the car market due to uneasiness about hire purchase? To seek possible solutions to these questions it is necessary to probe the attitudes of motor traders, manufacturers and the financial establishment towards deferred payment schemes.

The motor industry, finance houses and hire purchase

Motor dealers greatly preferred cash paying customers, there being several reasons for this. Obviously cash in the bank was preferable to awaiting outstanding payments. There was also much confusion, particularly in the 1920s, about the legal situation with regard to hire purchase. Many dealers feared fraud by unscrupulous buyers, who might be tempted to resell a car just acquired under the hire purchase system. When this did occur, it was very often the trader who was left with the financial consequences. The United Dominions Trust (UDT), the largest finance house involved in motor-related hire purchasing, ensured that all agreements were drawn up between the customer and the trader (Bowden & Collins, 1992, 124). These business concerns created a degree of insecurity around instalment payments and contributed to an atmosphere of ambivalence towards hire purchase, which paralleled that demonstrated by car-buyers. Doubts also emanated from the same concerns that determined the behaviour of middle-class consumers. Most obviously, as has already been intimated, fears of offending the economic and social sensibilities of potential customers led dealers to soft-pedal on the issue of hire purchase. So, although dealers appreciated that the future of their business involved embracing hire purchase, that embrace was at times a little tentative.

They were particularly suspicious of schemes suggested as a means of expanding the market beyond those with high incomes. On occasions when such initiatives were submitted they were met with criticisms which carried more than a hint of class prejudice. In 1924 Ford's 'Weekly Purchase Plan' was greeted with hostility by 'Ford Dealer', in an article in the *Motor Trader*. For a minimum weekly payment of £1 over two and a quarter years, the plan enabled customers to take delivery of a Ford car. 'Ford Dealer' believed it was 'really very difficult to examine the scheme seriously as it appears to be so obviously unsound and impossible'. However, it was admitted that dealers had earlier considered hire purchase itself to be unworkable. The language of the article then becomes very revealing:

> To turn down the scheme because it is *undignified* is also unwise because we do many things in everyday life that our grandfathers would not have touched for this reason ... The understanding of the scheme – that it enables a man of small means (say from £250–600 per annum) to purchase a car – might have a grain of substance in it if it were not for the fact that *any man who is so financially weak in this way has no business to buy a car at all* ... a man who cannot pay ... this small sum (the £25 deposit on a Ford hire purchase deal) must be in a very bad way and *an undesirable customer*. (*Motor Trader*, 26 March 1924, italics added)

The language used here is very interesting because it illustrates a distrust, not only of the Ford scheme, but also of those who might have used it. The whole concept was viewed as the type of new American business methods which past generations of British businessmen would not have sullied their ledgers with. Such schemes did carry an increased element of risk for traders, but arguments opposing the extension of hire purchase frequently articulated fears about greater risk in terms of the potential dishonesty of customers attracted by innovations in instalment buying. An argument grounded entirely on economic rationale might have been expected to raise, instead, the subject of high running costs and the ability of less wealthy motorists to meet them. This would have been particularly relevant in the case of the Model T, which attracted the very high horsepower tax rating of £23 per annum. Ironically, in the United States of America, the Ford Weekly Plan had been established because Henry Ford disapproved of the concept of hire purchase (Olney, 1989, 389). By June 1924, 80,000 Americans had received delivery of their car by this means, and a further 170,000 were in the process of paying for one.

In 1929 *Garage and Motor Agent* argued against the extension of hire purchase payment plans. It urged that eighteen months be the maximum time allowed for the completion of payment. Such a scheme would attract 'those who *can* afford to run a car, although they have little capital' whilst repulsing 'the undesirable element which has little hope and less intention of ratifying the agreements into which it enters' (*Garage and Motor Agent*, 17 August 1929).

In a well known comment on British carbuyers of this era, cited earlier, Miles Thomas suggested that their motto was: 'No one wants to keep down with the Joneses!' It would seem that many dealers were reluctant to do business with the Joneses in the first place. A solidly upper-middle-class market provided motor dealers with a lucrative trade in accessories, repairs and fuel. For this reason dealers were content with the policy of price/model competition which developed in the 1930s. Indeed the *Motor Trader* advocated formal price fixing in 1934, arguing that the vast majority of dealers were 'not anxious to see any reductions in prices, especially in the case of small and inexpensive cars'. Indeed, they would have welcomed 'an informal agreement' amongst the leading manufacturers that raised prices by '5 or 10 per cent' (*Motor Trader*, 11 July 1934).

As Martha L. Olney has pointed out, manufacturers initially viewed hire purchase as a means of ensuring a smoother cash flow (Olney, 1989, note 38). This was particularly the case in Britain, where throughout the interwar period large numbers of cars were bought in late spring, or following the Motor Show in October and November. Dealers were also forced into dealing with finance companies in order to pay in advance for the stock they were to receive from the manufacturers. Hire purchase was not, therefore, simply introduced as an aid to extending the market, but also as a means of regulating cash flow. There is no doubt that the extension of hire purchase facilities was extremely important in the growth of the motor vehicle market, but the ambivalent attitude of consumers towards its use does seem to have reinforced both dealers' resistance to projected extensions of the instalment principle and manufacturers' reluctance to trumpet hire purchase in advertising campaigns. One 1934 article in *Motor Trader* made this point explicitly, citing trader reluctance for the absence of a campaign to push this form of sale (*Motor Trader*, 10 October 1934). It remains questionable whether or not a campaign to publicise and de-stigmatise hire purchase might have increased sales of new cars in the 1920s and 1930s, or whether the social sensibilities of middle-class consumers were simply too resistant to such a ploy. Many buyers were clearly prepared, out of necessity, to make use of hire purchase when purchasing a family car, but they were extremely reluctant to acknowledge it. If a manufacturer had broken ranks and trumpeted their

186

hire purchase facilities, or offered lengthier instalments, would they have found their cars stigmatised in a middle-class market where both business and social sensibilities were so important?

There is little evidence to suggest that manufacturers considered extending the length of hire purchase payment plans. If they did, the fact that so many companies dealt with the UDT would have been an important factor. By 1929 they ran hire purchase schemes for Austin, Chrysler, Crossley, Darracq, Dodge Bros, Essex, Fiat, Hudson, Lea Francis, Morris, Renault, Rhose, Singer, Sunbeam, Talbot, and Wolseley (Bowden & Collins, 1992, 25). Their managing director, J. Gibson Jarvie, was a familiar figure to readers of the trade press where he campaigned on behalf of his company and hire purchase. Innovative as the company was, they were careful to appeal to traditional banking virtues, as the bulk of their financial backing emanated from City institutions. When they received further backing from the Bank of England, in January 1930, they felt that they had achieved full respectability within the City. Montagu Norman, the governor of the Bank of England, had been under pressure from the Labour government to set a lead for the financial sector in the reorganization of British industry. He chose to back the UDT because of its combination of innovation and traditional virtues and, importantly, because of their insistence that they did not finance luxuries.

This last point sat uneasily with the fact that cars were very much seen as leisure items in this period. For example, Winston Churchill's raid on the Road Fund in his 1926 budget was justified as the taxation of a luxury hobby in a time of national need. However, the UDT's repudiation of the financing of luxury goods suggests that it had more than just bad debtors to consider when setting the payment plan for instalment purchases. As early as 1927 Jarvie had urged traders to dismiss notions of no deposit hire purchase sales, arguing that if people couldn't raise the necessary 25 per cent they could not 'by any stretch of the imagination be considered desirable hire purchasers' (*Garage and Motor Agent*, June 1927). Furthermore, the UDT and other finance houses imposed a system of qualitative and quantitative credit rationing. The preferred hire purchaser was a householder who owned a business and was married with children. Such types were seen as having the greatest incentive to complete payments (Bowden, 1994, 254). Jarvie also believed in 'cooperation' – the stifling of domestic competition behind existing tariff walls (Bowden & Collins, 1992, 132). He must have felt comfortable, therefore, dealing with a motor industry which competed on model differentiation as much as price and relied heavily on the heavy duties imposed on motor vehicle imports to limit the impact of foreign competitors. Such shared attitudes were hardly conducive to experimentation with more innovative selling techniques than those employed by competitors. The UDT had the funds to invest in an extension of the time scale on hire purchase agreements but this was not the inclination of themselves, the Bank of England, motor manufacturers or dealers. In mid-1933, for example, the UDT was using only 15–20 per cent of the credit facilities available to it from financial institutions. (Bowden & Collins, 1992, 132). In the same period motor manufacturers were diverting large percentages of their profits towards shareholders' dividends rather than reinvesting them in mass production techniques (Lewchuck, 1986, 147). Theoretically, at least, the manufacturers could have attempted market extension by extending hire purchase payments to ease the burden on buyers.

Conclusion

If hire purchase terms had been eased would there have been enough new customers to make the move worthwhile? In the late 1930s the SMMT had decided, as they had always done, that potential car-buyers would come from the wealthiest sections of the middle classes. They assumed that anyone earning less than £250, to take 1938 as an example, would be unable to afford the purchase and running costs of a car (Society of Motor Manufacturers and Traders, 1938). Such assumptions ignored the possibility that consumers are capable of restructuring finances and spending when a prized commodity comes within reach.

The preliminary data provided from the on-going oral history of interwar motorists suggests that by the late 1930s ownership was a reality for a small, but significant, section of the wealthiest amongst the working classes as well as many within the lower middle classes. Many working-class consumers, in particular, were willing to share the purchase or running costs of a car within the extended family, or amongst friends. For example, the Watkin brothers, both employed in the Coventry motor industry, shared the cost of a second-hand Standard Big Nine, bought for £47 from a workmate in 1936 (Interviewee One: born Nottingham 1907). In other cases friends or associates offered financial help in meeting the prohibitive running costs of a car in return for its use on occasional weekends or family holidays. In all 11 per cent of informants have provided examples of car-ownership being facilitated by some form of car-sharing between friends or brothers. Another possible path to car ownership involved husband and wife both being employed in relatively well-paid jobs, or one or the other securing employment in a second job. The sample includes a number of examples in which a wife's wage contributed to the finances of a car-owning family, as well as several cases where the wages of a working daughter or son provided a family with extra capital. All these possible paths to ownership are missed by a simple analysis of head of household income statistics – the statistics relied upon by the SMMT at the time and recent econometric analyses of the market. Of course, such buyers usually acquired second hand cars rather than new models. However, if manufacturers and dealers had aggressively promoted sales to the better off amongst the working-classes the resulting income might well have facilitated greater liberalisation of instalment sales of new cars amongst the lower-middle classes.

However, the manufacturers and dealers did not respond to such developments in the market. Beneath the discussions about its utility value the car was firmly entangled in a web of middle-class mores and meanings. Perhaps greatest amongst these was that the car was an expression of its owner's individuality and position in society. So any campaign to sell cars, even used cars, on a cooperative basis with several friends, workmates, or members of an extended family sharing the expensive running costs was out of the question. Dealers and manufacturers were involved in the sale of a prestige, luxury item and continuously sought to portray their cars as such. Any radical plan to sell cars on a joint ownership basis would have tarnished their product in the status-conscious world of middle-class motoring.

However, a liberalisation of hire purchase terms, allied to a publicity campaign to de-stigmatise its use in both new and second hand car sales could have attracted more lower-middle-class buyers, in particular. Econometric analysis of the 1930s market suggests that car ownership amongst the lower middle classes was lower than might have been expected (Bowden & Turner, 1993, 66). By extending hire purchase payment plans manufacturers and dealers would have provided themselves with an outlet for cars which otherwise sat in showrooms for long periods awaiting the attentions of a more socially acceptable buyer. But, as has been seen, there were a number of cultural and business factors that made such a policy unlikely.

The quantitative and qualitative credit rationing employed by finance houses, such as the UDT, must also have served to restrict sales. It would be interesting to learn what proportion of applicants for hire purchase were turned down through one of the more subjective elements of this rationing. Jarvie's stipulations about solid, respectable hire purchasers were intended to establish his company's form of instalment paying as 'quite distinct from the working-class 'tick' system of accounts' (Bowden & Turner, 1993, 253). But it also ensured that even some professional groups, who were not recipients of a regular income, were deemed a credit risk. Equally significant were the parallel anxieties amongst traders, manufacturers, and consumers about the use of hire purchase.

Economic and business historians have supplied extremely valuable perspectives on the diffusion of the motor car in interwar Britain. This chapter has attempted to fuse these perspectives with a more social-historical analysis in order to initiate a new interdisciplinarity to the question at hand. In the process, it has become clear that cultural norms, class perceptions, and taste were all factors in the spread of such a significant consumer item as the car. Just as middle-class culture and taste fashioned the way a car looked, it also defined the ways in which it could be sold. In the process, areas where growth in ownership could have occurred were limited.

Acknowledgements

I would like to thank Jill Greenfield and Chris Reid for reading several drafts of this work and providing excellent suggestions for its improvement. As always any remaining weaknesses in the argument are my own.

Bibliography

Primary Sources

Oral interviews, questionnaires and correspondence with 38 interwar motorists.
Autocar
Garage and Motor Agent
Motor
Motor Trader
Society of Motor Manufacturers and Traders, The Motor Industry of Great Britain, (annual)

Secondary Sources

Bagwell, P. (1974) *The Transport Revolution From 1770*, Batsford, London.

Bourdieu, P. (1992) *The Logic of Practice*, Polity Press, Padstow.

Bourdieu, P. (1986) *Distinction a Social Critique of the Judgement of Taste*, Routledge, Padstow.

Bowden, S. (1991) Demand And Supply Constraints the Inter-War UK Car Industry: Did The Manufacturers Get It Right?, *Business History*, 33.

Bowden, S. and Collins M. (1992) 'The Bank Of England, Industrial Regeneration, and Hire Purchase Between The Wars', *Economic History Review*, 35.

Bowden, S. and Turner, P. (1993a) Some Cross-Section Evidence on the Determinants of the Diffusion of Car Ownership in the Inter-War UK Economy, *Business History*, 35.

Bowden, S. and Turner, P. (1993b) Demand for Consumer Durables in the Interwar Period, *Journal of Economic History*, 53.

Bowden, S. (1994) 'The New Consumerism', in P. Johnson (ed.), *Twentieth Century Britain: Economic, Social and Cultural Change*, Longman, Singapore.

Church, R .and Miller, M. (1977), The Big Three: Competition, Management, and Marketing in the British Motor History, 1922–39 in B. Supple (ed.), *Essays in British Business History*, Oxford.

Church, R. (1979) *Herbert Austin*, Europa, London.

Church, R. (1981) 'The Marketing of Automobiles in Britain and the United States before 1939', in A. Okochi and K. Shimokawa (eds), *The International Conference on Business History 7: The Development of Mass Marketing*, Tokyo.

Church, R. (1994) *The Rise and Decline of the British Motor Industry*, MacMillan, Basingstoke.

Crowther, Lord, (1971), *Report on Consumer Credit*, HMSO, London.

Fine, B. and Leopold, E. (1993) *The World of Consumption*, Routledge, London.

Foreman-Peck, J. Bowden, S. and McKinlay, A. (1995), *The British Motor Industry*, Manchester University Press, Manchester.

Fridenson, P. (1981) French Automobile Marketing 1890-1979, A. Okochi and K. Shimokawa (eds), *The International Conference on Business History 7: The Development of Mass Marketing*, Tokyo.

Jackson, A.A. (1991) *The Middle Classes 1900–1950*, David St John Thomas, Nairn.

Lewchuk, W. (1986) The Motor Vehicle Industry, in B. Elbaum and W. Lazonick (eds), *The Decline of the British Economy*, Clarendon Press, Oxford.

Lewchuk, W. (1987) *American Technology And The British Vehicle Industry*, Cambridge.

Lewchuk, W. (1985) 'The origins of Fordism and alternative strategies: Britain and the United States, 1880-1930', in S. Tolliday and J. Zeitlin (1987), *Between Fordism and Flexibility, the International Motor Industry and its Workers*, St Mary's Press, New York.

Maxcy, G. and Silbertson, A. (1959) *The Motor Industry*,

McCracken, G. (1988) *Culture and Consumption: New Approaches to the Symbolic Character of Consumer Goods and Activities*, Indiana University Press.

Miller, M. and Church, R. (1979) 'Motor Manufacturing', in N.K. Buxton and D. Aldcroft (eds), *British Industry Between the Wars*, Scolar Press, Menston.

Mitchell, B.R. (1988) *British Historical Statistics*, Cambridge University Press, Cambridge.

Mort, F. (1996) *Cultures of Consumption: Masculinities and Social Space in Late Twentieth-Century Britain*, Routledge, London.

Olney, M.L. (1989)'Credit as a Production-Smoothing Device: The Case of Automobiles, 1913–38', *Journal of Economic History*, 49.

Political and Economic Planning, (1950) *Motor Vehicles*, London.

Robson, G. (1979) *Motoring in the 1930s*, Cambridge.

Thomas, M.W. (1964) *Out on a Wing*, Michael Joseph, London.

Tolliday, S. (1987) 'The Failure of Mass Production Unionism in the Motor Industry, 1914–39', in C. Wrigley, (ed.) *A History of British Industrial Relations Volume II*, Harvester, Brighton.

191

Part Three

PRODUCING AND SELLING CARS

13

Shop Floor Culture in the Coventry Motor Industry, *c.* 1896–1920

Brad Beaven

In Coventry now they are celebrating the centenary of the motor car. But it is in the nature of people to recall the makes of yesterday's vehicles while forgetting the painful history of the community which produced them. (*Observer*, 28 April 1996).

Traditionally, car workers have been portrayed as one of the first groups of operatives to exchange craft benefits for economic reward. Indeed, the piece work system, so prevalent in the motor industry until the 1960s, symbolised the birth of this 'new' worker since it appeared to give operatives the motivation to work harder and discourage solidarity amongst colleagues. In arguing this view, historians have drawn evidence from the activities of the trade unions which were sectional in their outlook, continually focused on piece rates, job classifications and relations with rival unions. However, since there has been a lack of serious research on the shop-floor experience of workers in the motor industry prior to 1939, our image of the typical car worker is largely derived from postwar sociological studies (Zweig, 1961; Beynon, 1973). Indeed, although historians have by no means neglected the motor industry, analysis of car workers has largely been institutional in approach. For some historians, the car worker represents an ideal case study of the development of trade unionism in the 'new' industries (Zeitlin, 1980); for others the structure of industrial relations within the motor industry have been incorporated into models explaining Britain's economic decline (Lewchuk, 1986). However, the institutional perspective has a tendency to impose the economistic and sectional demands of trade unions onto the car workers themselves. Furthermore, with fewer than 25 per cent of car workers unionised at any one time prior to the Second World War, it is clear that an analysis of institutional structures neglects the vast majority of the workforce (Claydon, 1987, 304). These approaches are unsatisfactory if we are to determine the workers' *experience* of production rather than the trade unions' or employers' interpretation of the work place.

Indeed, it has been noted on a number of occasions elsewhere that at present 'no serious historical study of British car workers has ever been written' (Thompson, 1988, 49).

Traditional interpretations of Britain's industrial development have suggested that important changes occurred in people's experience of work during the late nineteenth and early twentieth centuries. In place of the declining artisan trades, with their blurred distinctions between work and leisure, came the emergence of the 'new' industries which were associated with rigid and regular working hours and the close supervision of workers. Within this context, the motor industry would appear to be a prime example of a 'new' industry. Consequently, Carr has claimed that:

> the workers became the instruments of the machine. It is hard to imagine a description of a work place that could be more at odds with the traditional craft union view of the skilled worker in his autonomy in the workplace. (Carr, 1979, 256)

In another important study, Haydu has argued that the attempt by workers in the engineering industries between 1890–1922 to control the work process was not reflected in Coventry. Haydu maintains that: 'Coventry workers stand out among British engineers – before and after the [first world] war – in their weak unofficial organisation and their pre-occupation with economic rewards rather than workshop control' (Haydu, 1988, 163). Haydu's thesis rests upon the assumption that a strong craft presence in the workplace was a prerequisite for radical factory politics, a vital ingredient that Coventry appeared to lack. Significantly Carr and Haydu reach conclusions on the nature of the Coventry worker that are based, almost exclusively, on the analysis of extant official trade union documentation. As a result, both Carr and Haydu reflect contemporary trade union concerns that the motor industry, particularly in Coventry, produced a 'new' type of worker, ready to reject trade union participation and accept his or her loss of autonomy in the workplace in favour of financial gain.

The article will argue that the car worker was not merely motivated by economic reward but was, in fact, also concerned with gaining a degree of autonomy within the work-process. Evidence will be drawn from Coventry which has been strongly associated with the 'typical' car worker since the industry was founded in the city in 1896. The article is divided into three. First, the paper will identify the age, gender, place of origin and skill level of the workforce that were attracted to the industry. Indeed, an analysis of the social background of early car workers will help determine whether workshop culture was shaped by traditional craft practices or migrant workers conversant with trade union militancy (Zeitlin, 1980). Second, the nature and function of shopfloor culture will be investigated through to the early 1920s. Shop-floor culture will be taken to mean a culture which was established through informal practices and customs familiar to workers on the shop floor (Willis, 1983). Finally, the article will argue that the impact of the First World War and the arrival of scientific management placed increasing pressure on informal workplace practices.

The origins of the workforce involved in Coventry's motor industry can be traced back to the establishment of the cycle trade in the city. The production practices prevalent in the cycle industry demanded a pool of workers that were usually young and semi-skilled (Beaven, 1994, 37–41). Thus by 1906 it was reported that: 'the use of automatic machines in the production of cycles becomes greater every year and this has had not a little to do with the reduction in the price of the finished article' (*Midland Daily Telegraph*, 15 March 1906). Indeed, Coventry's staple industries prior to the establishment of the cycle trade, weaving and watchmaking, had both adopted similar work processes by the end of the nineteenth century. For example, the watch industry, which has traditionally been perceived as clinging to its craft heritage, had by the late nineteenth century transformed its production methods and recruited semi-skilled operatives (Davies, 1992). In 1907, a journalist who visited Rotherham, Coventry's leading watchmakers, commented that:

> a visit to Messrs Rotherhams' great watchmaking factory reveals the plan on which the division of labour is now carried into effect ... the subdivision of labour is even more complete in this plan than the older one, and machinery can be employed for making large quantities of each part also in a way that was not possible working on a more restricted scale in the former method. (Woodward, 1975, 65)

Consequently, by 1896, when Britain's motor industry was established in the city, Coventry had become a magnet for the young semi-skilled worker. Indeed, the census reflects the growing importance of this sector of the population. In 1901, there were 6,001 cycle and motor workers in Coventry, rising to 13,000 in 1911. Of these 13,000 workers, 10,188 were under 35 whilst over 5,000 were under 25. The vast majority of workers in the motor industry were male. In 1911, there were only 1,116 women operatives from a total of just under 13,000 motor and cycle workers.

However, the influx of women workers was increasing and matched, in percentage terms, the rise in male employment in the cycle and motor industries between 1901–11 (Lancaster, 1986, 64). As early as the 1890s, newly formed car component firms were employing large numbers of female operatives. In 1899 White and Poppe, an engine supplier, employed over 130 women on fuse work. A former manager recalled that the women 'worked the capstans ... attended to the autos, milling machines and did inspections'. The women had previously worked in Coventry 'weaving, cleaning cycle parts and that sort of thing' and were 'good pals with the men in the shops' (*The Limit*, 1 July 1918). As a result, the Amalgamated Society of Engineers appears to have viewed the motor industry as essentially assembly work and instead focused attention on preserving the work practices in the machine tool sector which had a long tradition of employing apprenticed engineers (Coventry Record Office, Acc 1243/1/1–14, ASE Coventry District, 21 April 1899). Significantly, then, there was little resistance to female employment from male workers, a feature which characterised Coventry's industrial development during this period (Hinton, 1973, 221). However, concerns at the number of women entering the motor industry were raised in other quarters. Ten years after the establishment of the industry, one correspondent to a local newspaper complained that:

> girls and lads went straight from school to a fiery furnace of temptation, where purity was practically certain to be destroyed. The struggle to produce cheap machines had resulted in a traffic in the souls of women.

Indeed, one Coventry engineering firm estimated that up to 60 per cent of its workforce was female, a figure not regarded as unusual at the time (*Midland Daily Telegraph*, 9 May, 1906).

Clearly, Coventry could not entirely meet such a specific demand for labour and, as a result, migration to the city became an important factor. In just a twenty-year period, Coventry's population grew from 52,742 in 1891 to 106,349 in 1911. According to one historian, the most notable feature of the period to 1911 was the diversity of source areas. Bill Lancaster has shown that there were no distinct north or south movements or rural-urban patterns, whilst there is little evidence to suggest there was movement from mining areas. However, two significant source areas were London and the west midlands (including Coventry) which accounted for the birth place of 2,846 and 81,097 Coventry citizens respectively in 1911 (Lancaster, 1986, 61–3). London and the West Midlands were important, not only as sources of migration, but also as urban areas conversant with the work practices of the new light engineering trades. Thus, during this embryonic stage of the motor industry, when work practices and customs would have become established on the shopfloor, the majority of workers comprised young male workers from areas that did not have traditions associated with trade unionism and industrial militancy (Zeitlin, 1980, 127).

The high levels of young male workers and the increased importance of women operatives to 1914 would suggest that the Coventry motor industry did not possess an influential body of skilled craftsmen. Coventry apprentices were entered into the 'Coventry Freeman Admissions Journals' after completing a seven year apprenticeship and, consequently, the first motor car apprentices would have emerged during the early years of the twentieth century. The journals reveal that very few apprentices completed their indentures at motor car firms during a period traditionally characterised as the 'craft production' era. On average, less than three apprentices qualified from motor car firms each year between 1905–21. Moreover, once the individual firms are considered, there appears little in the way of a consistent and coordinated apprenticeship strategy. Daimler, often perceived as embracing craft-centred production techniques, only produced six apprentices during this period, a figure which represented the highest number of apprentices from a single firm. Indeed, significant car firms based in Coventry, such as Standard Motor Company, Singer and Rover, do not appear to have produced any apprentices during this period (Coventry Record Office Acc BA/C/Q/20/12, Freemen's Admissions, 1905–39). The car firms' neglect of the apprenticeship system is also confirmed through workers' own experience of training. C.A. Callaway was a car body builder who trained during the 1920s at Armstrong-Siddeley the luxury car maker. However, although the production of luxury car bodies was often associated with the skilled apprenticed engineer, Callaway underwent no such training. He recalled that 'you were given a job, given a detail then you'd pick it up ... watch someone else do it ... you done it [training] on your own [sic]' (Interview, Callaway, 1987). A similar informal training experience was encountered by E. Parry, a body builder with Universal Panels, a firm which produced luxury bodies by hand. Parry described the conditions and training in the factory as 'very poor' as the 'apprenticeship' consisted of 'making tea' and 'watching others at work' (Interview, Parry, 1987). Significantly, both workers were members of the skilled body builders union, the National Union of Vehicle Builders (NUVB) without completing a formal seven-year apprenticeship. Likewise D.G. Bain, a body builder with SS Swallow (later to become Jaguar), explained that:

> there was no training given whatsoever. You went there and you're was a wing fitter. You seen how the other people did it and then you went away and did it the same [sic]. (Interview, Bails, 1987)

It is clear that many firms throughout the interwar period lacked a co-ordinated apprenticeship scheme, a factor recognised by E.W. Hancock the works manager of Humber during the 1930s. In 1935, Hancock demanded from the board of directors 'a first class pupils and apprentice association', the provision of lecture rooms at the works and permission for part-time day classes at the local technical college, a system that Humber finally established in the same year (Interview, Hancock, n.d). If the small number of apprentices are considered against the fact that there were just under 13,000 people working in the motor and allied industries in 1911, it becomes clear that the actual skilled apprenticed workman, with his associated status and traditions, could not have significantly shaped shopfloor culture during the formative years of the motor industry.

However, despite the lack of apprenticeships in the Coventry motor industry, a number of historians have claimed that Coventry's nineteenth-century craft-based trades of watch making and weaving which had placed the skilled worker at the centre of the productive process, ensured that skill was later 'socially constructed' in the emerging motor industry. Thus, Thompson has maintained that 'the deskilling of car making, which began as a luxury craft trade of skilled engineers and coach builders, and was transformed into the classic industry of repetitive semi-skilled assembly line production, is a story well known.' (Thompson, 1988, 49). However, by the 1890s, the weaving industry was a semi-skilled industry, which had lost its seven year apprenticeship system in the 1830s and had been exposed to factory discipline since the 1850s (Beaven, 1990, 86). The watch industry, which began to supply components to car manufacturers at the turn of the century, had long since discarded its seven year apprenticeship system (Beaven, 1993, 111). In 1906, it was reported that traditional methods of production had become practically extinct:

> men were kept 7 years to learn a branch of the watch trade that really any skilled man could pick up in a week or two. Nowadays in the factory system that sort of work was performed by women. The men ... become foremen or leading hands. (*Midland Daily Telegraph*, 1 January, 1906)

In line with the changes in the watch trades, Donnelly, Batcheler and Morris have recently argued that at the very beginning of Coventry's motor industry a 'significant proportion of the work in the machine shops was of a repetitive nature, incorporating the use of jigs, fixtures and dedicated machine tools' (Donnelly et al, 1995, 138). For example in the 1920s, within four hours of starting work at Standard, A. Abbott was training young girls to work milling machines. Abbot explained later that he had 'never even seen a milling machine before that day' (Interview, Abbott, 1985). Indeed, employers introduced automatic machinery into the shop and recruited semi-skilled labour with considerable ease during a period supposedly dominated by craft principles and practices (Donnelly et al, 1995, 138).

Since the craft practices of weaving and watchmaking had died out during the nineteenth century, the new industries in Coventry faced little or no protest from workers or unions in employing young semi-skilled labour from outside the region (Hinton, 1973, 221). As a result, it would be unlikely that the concept of skill, socially constructed or otherwise, could have somehow survived to shape the work practices in the motor industry. The belief that 'skill' was the all important factor shaping shopfloor culture in the motor industry was largely derived from trade unions during the period, especially when negotiating pay with employers. Moreover, the vast majority of car workers were not officially organized and the few that were in trade unions appear not to have been committed to their 'skilled' status. There is strong evidence to suggest that when the opportunity arose, many workers in jobs defined as skilled opted to join semi-skilled unions with their cheaper rates. Carr's analysis of the membership of skilled unions to 1939 led him to conclude that:

> it is quite possible that skilled workers voluntarily opted for the semi-skilled sections, as they cost less. If this was the case, it would show an attitude to trade unions quite different from the traditional pride of holding a skilled man's card (Carr, 1979, 464).

Pride in the 'skilled' craftsmen, then, did not have the exclusive and elitist connotations that have traditionally been associated with skilled labour.

If the experience of shopfloor work did not stem from a 'craft tradition', what was the nature of shopfloor culture? The analysis of shopfloor culture between 1896–1920 presents methodological problems. Whilst there is a wealth of information relating to production techniques in motor and science journals, there are few available sources that shed light on shopfloor culture. Alongside the local press, the most obvious access to the workers' experience of factory life is through oral history. Furthermore, the First World War Munition Tribunals, established to adjudicate on disputes between masters and workers, also provide a unique insight into workplace practices since evidence from operatives was often published verbatim. These sources reveal a set of common experiences which go some way in uncovering the nature and function of shopfloor culture in the motor industry.

In assessing the nature of shopfloor culture in the motor industry, evidence suggests that most workers ranked car firms according to three criteria; pay, job security, and the system of supervision imposed. There can be little doubt that for car workers based in rural areas, such as Oxford, pay was the most important factor (Pagnamenta and Overy, 1984, 225). However, in Coventry, certain employers gained good reputations amongst the workforce through the system of supervision they implemented rather than rates of pay. Given that pay was generally high in Coventry and the fact that the seasonal nature of the car trade affected the whole industry, the most significant differences between motor firms was the system of supervision employed by management (Haydu, 1988, 5). For example, during a twelve-year period, Chris Beaven was employed in nine different jobs, seven of which were in car firms. Although he was employed as a polisher in Humber, Rover, Standard and Armstrong-Siddeley, Beaven experienced very different forms of supervision. The supervision ranged from 'tough supervision' in which 'you had to work hard' at Humber to Rover which was 'a good job' since:

> there wasn't a moving track ... at the Rover you could push them along, it was slower and it was more money, you could do what you wanted at Rover.

Likewise at Armstrong-Siddeley, 'they didn't bother you a bit, you weren't rushed'. Consequently, there was a hierarchy of good employers since Beaven explained that 'Swallow in those days were very poor ... you could always get a job at Swallow, but you couldn't always get a job say at Standard or Rolls Royce ... Rover was also well thought of' (Interview, C. Beaven, 1995). Other workers at Triumph reported a 'complete absence of bullying by the foremen and the shop was much more go as you please', whilst Maudslay was described as 'fairly comfortable' (Carr, 1979, 249). Similarly E. Parry, who worked for Universal Panels, recalled that 'the conditions were very easy. I never used to clock in, I never lost quarters because sometimes if I was late he would just shout at me but that was it' (Interview, Parry, 1987). Significantly, then, it was the nature of the management's supervision rather than rates of pay which determined, for many workers, whether a firm was a good or bad employer.

Given that some motor firms did not implement harsh supervisory measures, a shopfloor culture emerged which reflected the work experience of the semi-skilled. Despite, the harsh conditions and monotonous nature of some jobs, many of the semi-skilled attempted to look for meaning in their work and impose frameworks that went far beyond the financial incentive. Added to the fact that for most of the period to 1939, the trade unions within the motor industry were extremely weak and that artisanal 'craft practices' had not been introduced into the industry, workers constructed their own informal methods of defence that revolved around collectively creating their own work schedules. Thus, even when under strict supervision, workers attempted to exercise their abilities and gain some enjoyment from and autonomy within their work, a factor which was reflected in the culture of the shopfloor. Indeed, the most striking feature of the shopfloor culture was the attempt to gain some autonomy within the work process. As a result, firms which were more tolerant of this shopfloor culture gained good reputations amongst workers.

Prior to 1918, it was a commonly held assumption amongst car workers that once they had completed a 'fair' day's work they were entitled to go home. Indeed, the Munition Tribunals during the First World War confirmed that false time-keeping was widespread amongst workers in motor factories. For example in 1917, a woman working in a large engineering factory in Coventry was found to have clocked-in her sister who was not in the factory at the time. In her defence she argued that 'I am only one of thousands' who clock-in friends and relatives in their absence (*Midland Daily Telegraph*, 24 July 1917). Indeed, commenting on another case during the same period, R. A. Rotherham, a director of a large car component firm, noted that false time-clocking had become 'unfortunately too frequent' (*Midland Daily Telegraph*, 9 August 1917). Significantly, operatives who left the works early did not usually do so unilaterally. Instead the decision to leave the factory was often discussed and taken by a group of workers. In one Munition Tribunal it was reported that a motor firm had instructed its staff to work Saturday afternoons, a demand which prompted the workers to hold an informal workshop ballot:

> as a result of a ballot it was agreed not to work on Saturday afternoon, [the] men having 'played off' owing to shortage of materials. This evidence was supported by other workmen, and it was stated that it was not fair to make the men work on Saturday afternoon when others had been sent home through shortages of materials. (*Midland Daily Telegraph*, 13 March 1918)

Against the backdrop of weak unionisation, this form of workshop democracy and collective decision making not only ensured that workers earned similar piece work wages, but also sanctioned and legitimised their actions. Thus in another case, one Munition Tribunal was surprised to learn that in the motor industry 'it was the custom for moulders to go home when they had finished their work, without receiving a pass-out'. One moulder, Ernest Bott, complained that the decision of whether his work was finished and when he should go home rested with the workforce not the superintendent (*Midland Daily Telegraph*, 13 March 1918). Indeed, even during the First World War, workers considered that they possessed the right to select their own work routine. In 1918, a group of semi-skilled workers at an erecting shop, whose job was described as 'monotonous', were reported to a Tribunal. It was alleged that:

> the men stayed out purposely that afternoon because they did not want to do the job ready for them to do and which would have been given

them by the foreman had they stayed in.

According to the foreman of the shop, 'he thought the men refused to do the work offered them because they wanted a holiday' (*Midland Daily Telegraph*, 6 February 1918).

Despite the lack of a strong trade union presence, informal collective action by workers was sometimes successful in shaping employers' decisions on conditions and working hours. In 1917, workers involved in the stamping industry, which supplied components to the motor trade, convinced a government commission on the necessity of drinking in the workplace. A Commission of Enquiry on the light metal working industry in the west midlands reported that restrictions on drinking beer during the First World War had initiated industrial unrest:

> The commission was frankly amazed at the strength of the objections to the liquor restrictions. These come not only from men in the habit of drinking beer, but from those who were life-long teetotallers and yet recognised the need of beer to those working in certain occupations ... it must be remembered that we are dealing with men who all their lives have been accustomed to drink beer as and when they want it ... it must be recognised it is more than a drink ... it is certainly a social habit or a custom of life, as two witnesses expressed it.

The commission's investigation of the shopfloor workers reveals an interesting solidarity between drinkers and teetotallers on the importance of drinking in the workplace. The fact that teetotallers endorsed the view that beer was 'more than a drink', demonstrates that workers linked restrictions on drinking in the workplace with a loss of control of the work process. Indeed, faced with the overwhelming hostility of workers to alcohol restrictions, the report recommended that the drink 'supply should be largely increased' (Modern Record Centre, MSS 36/19, Industrial Unrest, 9). The workers' desire to organise their own drinking breaks was not restricted to male employees. With more women being brought into the new industries during the First World War, Munition Tribunals dealt with a number of cases relating to women drinking in the workplace. However, the authorities tended to impose harsher punishments on women workers than their male counterparts, since the authorities could not accept that drinking was an accepted custom among women. In one such case in 1917 a Munition Tribunal heard that an engineering firm dismissed three women after being caught drinking in the workplace and presenting themselves 'in an intoxicated condition'. On top of their dismissal, the women were fined 10s each (*Midland Daily Telegraph*, 12 April 1917).

Another important area of work which workers succeeded in maintaining was the 'unofficial holiday'. Evidence suggests that the tradition amongst engineering workers of failing to work immediately after a holiday continued into the First World War (Wright, 1867, 109–30). One worker was said to have:

> lost the day after the holiday and sent a letter explaining how the clock was slow and that was how he came to lose the time. The firm's representative said there were summonses that day against 40 men for losing the day after Whitsuntide. They did not prosecute anyone after Easter.

Other excuses ranged from 'a particularly bad thunderstorm' to there being 'too many on the platform to buy a ticket' (presumably because most people were taking a day trip), though significantly the vast majority could not offer an excuse. The poor attendance at this firm was not an isolated incident. Such was the widespread failure of Coventry operatives to return to work after a holiday, the employers decided, for the first time, to close all factories for a week for the next holiday in a bid to stamp out workers unilaterally determining their holiday entitlement (*Midland Daily Telegraph*, 6 July 1917).

Clearly, the degree of success that informal action by workers achieved depended very much on the role of the foreman. Until the post-war period, it was common for foremen to turn a blind eye to the actives within the workshop. According to one engineer, foremen were 'more or less in with it' because 'if the output was there next morning, that's all that mattered' (Interview, Spicer, 1987). Prior to the First World War, it was common for car workers, particularly in the coach building sector, to receive little attention from supervisors as 'the men would collect the wood from the stores on a Monday morning' and then it had to be 'cut, shaped and assembled into the frame of the car by the following Saturday morning'(*Coventry Evening Telegraph*, 29 May, 1985). Indeed, sometimes it took police intervention to bring a stop to workers organising their own work schedules. In one engineering firm five men were summoned to a Coventry Munitions Tribunal for 'neglect of work and card playing'. It was reported that:

> A night policeman said that at 5:05 am in one of the corners of the heavy shop of a local factory he found five men in front of whom were cards and 6d of money ... the firm's representative urged the necessity of card playing in factories being suppressed and put in the shop rules, which were framed and exhibited in all parts of the works.

Card playing and gambling within the factory was an extremely common activity in which youths and senior workers participated. In one incident a factory representative lamented that 'it was a painful thing to see boys of fourteen found gambling with men of thirty in the works and in working hours' (*Midland Daily Telegraph*, 5 March 1918). Indeed in many cases, the large number of prosecutions for card playing was the result of reports by diligent policemen rather than works foremen (*Midland Daily Telegraph*, 5 April, 17, 20 July, 16 August 1917).

However, there can be little doubt that the First World War proved an important turning point for the role of the foreman in the motor firm. For the first time, the activities within the workplace became scrutinised by Munition Tribunals. In short, the foreman had to be seen to be doing his job, particularly in ensuring workers remained within the factory during specified hours. Thus it is no coincidence that it was during this period that foremen from the motor firms in Coventry complained that the life of a shop foreman 'has been past bearing, he is repeatedly insulted' (*Midland Daily Telegraph*, 30 November 1917). Indeed, in the summer of 1917 they formed the 'Coventry Engineering Foremen', so that supervisors were not left to 'struggle alone' (*Midland Daily Telegraph*, 16 August 1917). Despite the postwar growth of 'scientific management' and the push towards volume production, workers, albeit a little more covertly, continued to impose collectively their autonomy within the work process (*Machinery*, 1 November 1928). A case in point were the activities of workers in ML Magneto, an electrical component supplier to car firms. The nature of the electrical components trade firmly placed it in the 'new industry' sector with few skilled engineers and large numbers of young semi-skilled male and female workers. However, the work routine of the operatives continued to revolve around collective decisions made by the work group even after the war. S. Spicer, who worked in the Magneto shop, soldering battery lead terminals, recalled that:

> we had a holiday. We used to have to work all Friday night ... half of us would clear out and go to the first house Hippodrome ... then if you'd got the money, they'd come back and the rest of you would go to the second hours Hippodrome ... we used to go over the wall in the Burges into the Hippodrome.

Although the firm set overall production targets, operatives tended to work to their own schedules, often blurring the distinction between work and leisure. Thus, in order to ensure production had an appearance of continuity, Spicer maintained that if they knew they would be working nights:

> we'd do a lot of small magnetos and hide them everywhere ... then we used to sit up all night playing cards because we'd fetch these magnetos out from where we'd hid them (Interview, Spicer, 1987).

The interwar period continued to witness operatives attempting to manipulate the work process to their own ends, particularly through the gang system which increased in importance during the 1920s and 1930s. Thus, although the supervision of the work place became more stringent, some characteristics of the pre-war shopfloor culture continued to persist.

This article has argued that studies which have adopted an institutional perspective have presented a misleading profile of the car worker. The stereotypical car worker, with his pre-occupation with economic gain over job control, sits uneasily alongside the evidence presented here. Through diverting analysis away from official trade union structures towards the dynamics of the workplace, this paper has provided an insight into the experience of work in the motor trades to 1920. Indeed, in focusing upon the workplace two important features emerge. First, that the shopfloor culture which emerged during the formation of the motor industry, was derived from the conditions and experiences of semi-skilled workers rather than an inherited or diffused craft culture. Second, that far from possessing a conservative and passive shopfloor culture, workers adopted strategies which gave themselves some autonomy within the work process. Moreover, it has become clear that the manipulation of the work process was a collective activity, an action legitimized and sanctioned by the work group. In other words, attempts at 'job control' were not simply the actions of the skilled, but a process in which the rest of the work group recognized and participated. Historians who have focused on the economistic and sectional nature of the engineering trade unions have overlooked the informal workplace organization that endeavoured to control their own work patterns. Despite, the growth of scientific management after 1918, there can be little doubt that important strands of the pre-war workshop culture continued to survive and shape the workers' experience of factory life during the interwar period.

Acknowledgements

My thanks to Dr Ken Lunn and Dr Dave Andress for commenting on earlier drafts of this chapter.

Bibliography

Interviews

Abbott, J. 'Oral History of Coventry Motor Industry', 26 November 1985, Acc 1662/2/22, Coventry Record Office.

Bails, D.G. 'Oral History of Coventry Motor Industry', 24 August 1987, Acc 1662/2/102, Coventry Record Office.

Beaven, C. Author's collection, 12 July 1995.

Calloway, C. 'Oral History of Coventry Motor Industry', June 1987, Acc 1662/2/145, Coventry Record Office.

Hancock, E.W. 'Oral History of Coventry Motor Industry', n.d. Acc 1662/13/1–7, Coventry Record Office.

Parry, E. 'Oral History of Coventry Motor Industry', 29 September 1987, Acc 1662/2/169, Coventry Record Office.

Spicer, S. 'Oral History of Coventry Motor Industry', 11 June 1987, Acc 1602/2/153, Coventry Record Office.

Secondary Sources

Beaven, B. (1990) 'Custom Culture and Conflict. A Study of the Coventry Ribbon Trade during the First Half of the Nineteenth Century', *Midland History*, 15.

Beaven, B. (1993) 'The Growth and Significance of the Coventry Car Component Industry', 1895–1914, *Midland History*, 18.

Beaven, B. (1994) 'The Growth and Significance of the Coventry Car Component Industry, 1895–1939', unpublished PhD thesis, De Montfort University.

Beynon, H. (1973) *Working for Ford*, Penguin, London.

Carr, F. (1979) 'Engineering Workers and the Rise of Labour in Coventry, 1914–39', unpublished PhD thesis, University of Warwick.

Claydon, T. (1987) 'Trade Unions, Employers and Industrial Relations in the British Motor Industry, 1918–45', *Business History*, 29, 3, July.

Davies, A.C. (1992) 'Time for a Change? Technological Persistence in the British Watchmaking Industry' , *Material History Review*, 36, Autumn.

Donnelly, T. Batcheler, J. and Morris, D. (1995) 'The Limitations of Trade Union Power in the Coventry Motor Industry', *Midland History*, 20.

Haydu, J. (1988) *Between Craft and Class. Skilled Workers and Factory Politics in the United Sates and Britain, 1890–1922*, University of California Press, California.

Hinton, J. (1973) *The First Shop Steward s Movement*, Allen and Unwin, London.

Lancaster, B. (1986) 'Who's a Real Coventry Kid? Migration into Twentieth Century Coventry' in T. Mason and B. Lancaster (eds), *Life and Labour in a Twentieth Century City. The Experience of Coventry*, University of Warwick, Coventry.

Lewchuk, W. (1986) 'The Motor Vehicle Industry' in B. Elbaum and W. Lazonick (eds), *The Decline of the British Economy*, Oxford University Press, Oxford.

Pagnamenta, P. and Overy R. (1984), 'All Our Working Lives', BBC, London.

Thompson, P. (1988) 'Playing at being Skilled Men: Factory Culture and Pride in Work Skills among Coventry Car Workers', *Social History*, vol. 13, January.

Willis, P. (1983) 'The Class Significance of School Counter Culture', in J. Purvis and M.

Hales (eds), *Achievements and Inequality in Education*, Routledge, London.

Woodward, J. (1975) 'Rotherhams: Watchmakers' , unpublished report, Coventry Record Office.

Wright, T. (1867) *Some Habits and Customs of the Working Classes*, Tinsley Brothers, London.

Zeitlin, J. (1980) 'The Emergence of Shop Steward Organization and Job Control in the British Car Industry', *History Workshop Journal*, 10, Autumn.

Zweig, F. (1961) *The Worker in an Affluent Society*, Heinemann, London.

Contemporary Sources

Coventry Evening Telegraph.

Machinery.

Midland Daily Telegraph.

ASE, Coventry District Journal, Acc 1243/1/1-14, Coventry Record Office.

Freemen's Admissions Journal 1905–39, Acc BA/C/Q/20/12, Coventry Record Office.

'Industrial Unrest, Commission of Enquiry into Industrial Unrest. Report of the Commissioners for the West Midlands area, 1917', MSS36/19 Modern Record Centre, University of Warwick.

14

Cars, Culture and War

Tom Donnelly

Since its earliest days the role of the automobile in Britain's economy has been well documented. Yet the car industry remains a source of considerable controversy on topics as diverse as strategy, structure, exports, trade unions and entrepreneurship. Few hard and fast conclusions on any of the aforementioned topics have been arrived at and so the industry remains and will remain for a long time a fruitful field of research. General surveys of the industry (Wood, 1988; Adeney, 1988; Church, 1994) pay very little attention to the impact of World War II on the industry while more specifically oriented works (Thoms & Donnelly, 1985; Whiting, 1983; Hayton & Harvey, 1993) focus very specifically on the experience of firms in the Coventry and Oxford areas. Finally, although Corelli Barnett discusses the role of the industry during hostilities (Barnett, 1986) the approach is rather generalist and is primarily a study in political economy.

The industrial cultural effects of World War II have though, by and large, been ignored by writers and this is a significant gap in our knowledge of what was a period of considerable upheaval and change throughout British industry. As with so many things in business it is often difficult to define culture in both specific and general terms, especially when it is bound up with the management of change and such an invigorating challenge is well beyond the scope of this particular exercise. Kilmann et al define culture as an underlying theme that gives meaning and direction within an organization, while for Deal and Kennedy culture is a company's way of doing things, a life of shared understandings and power balances within organisations. (Gore, Murray, Richardson, 1992) Culture is complex and exists at different levels in organisations and involves a whole range of factors that interact with each other; such as assumptions, rituals, leadership and heroes, rewards, norms and communications. At its most dynamic, culture can be a strong asset, particularly when bound up inextricably with change, which in itself acts as a dynamic. The subject of industrial or business change, too, has evoked considerable discussion, ranging from Kurt

Lewin's original concept of force field analysis to more recent corporate studies by Moss Kanter and Mintzberg (Moss Kanter, 1989; Mintzberg, 1995). Change itself is a process, sometimes quick, but more often than not incremental (Quinn, 1988) and many of its component parts are common to those of culture in that existing behaviour, patterns and values of work, structures and work processes, power and influence may all be affected by the aims, objectives and processes of change. Depending upon circumstances change may be welcomed, embraced willingly with both emotion and logic or it may be emotionally resisted out of fear and uncertainty. Regardless of these two outcomes change has to be managed and used to strengthen or weaken existing cultures or help create something more creative and dynamic (Thompson, 1993).

Before entering into a discussion on culture and change in the car industry during the Second World War, it would be useful to provide a contextual background. The interwar years were an extremely mixed period for the auto industry as a whole. The cessation of hostilities in 1918 opened a short-lived boom in the industry which died in the early 1920s with no lasting upswing in sight until the following decade. The period also witnessed the weeding out of a number of smaller concerns either through failure or absorption through merger. By 1930 the whole of the British automobile industry was dominated by what was known as the Big Six consisting of Morris and Austin who by 1938 controlled 44 per cent of the market, Ford had 18 per cent with by far the greater part of the remainder shared between Vauxhall, Rootes and Standard (Church, 1994, 37). The increasing market control of the major producers was matched by their power in the labour market. Following the defeat of the Engineering Unions in the 1922 Engineering Employers Lock Out and the demise of the Workers Union, with the exception of the National Union of Vehicle Builders, labour was almost cowed into submission and it was the employers who held sway throughout the 1920s exercising almost a hire and fire culture. It must be emphasised though, as has been argued elsewhere, that the Unions, especially the Amalgamated Engineering Union and the NUVB, were their own worst enemies and hindered the growth of unionism by retreating into craft exclusiveness by refusing to admit the semi-skilled and the unskilled. It was only when the Transport and General Workers Union appeared on the scene in the 1930s that unionism began to flicker. Until then the British car industrial culture was employer driven and led by powerful men such as Morris, Austin, Lyons, Siddeley, Black and the Rootes Brothers who imposed their stamp or trade marks on the culture of their individual concerns (Donnelly, Morris, Batchelor, 1995).

The coming of the Second World War and the war itself brought in considerable changes that were to affect the British car industry's cultural behaviour right down to its near disintegration in the early 1970s when British

Leyland all but collapsed. These changes affected power relationships, the role of subgroups, unions, women, employers, government and the work processes themselves. The main harbinger or signal of change was the government. From the end of the First World War until the mid-1930s the government had left the industry to its own devices. The rising threat posed by Nazi Germany and the lessons learned from the early stages of the war in 1914–15 convinced the government of the need to be much better prepared in the event of renewed fighting with Germany, and in this the motor industry was too important to be left out and ignored (Thoms, 1989). The government under Lord Swinton invited leading Midlands car manufacturers to participate in what was to become the Shadow Factory Scheme. This is not the place to discuss the overall merits of this approach to war preparation, but what is of immediate importance is to realise the importance of an external influence that was to change the industry's energies away from the vagaries of the market place and force it into cooperation within its own structures, but also with concerns from outside the industry. Prominent among those involved with the scheme were Herbert Austin, the Rootes Brothers, Spencer Willis of Rover, Geoffrey Burton of Daimler and John Black of Standard. William Morris refused initially to participate. What was unique about this scheme was that a group of men who usually competed against each other and who were ever mindful of commercial secrecy found themselves forced into cooperation not only by the threat of war, but by a powerful external agency, namely the British government, that was to force them to change and to embark on a steep learning curve as well as to expand their operations geographically as the Shadow Factory Disposal Scheme got under way.

It must not be thought though that all was sweetness and light among the manufacturers and that all differences were buried in a 'great war effort'. Conflict existed on the nature of economic cooperation, especially with Colonel H.A.P. Disney, the Air Ministry's head of production, over the precise form that production would take between the car firms and the British Aeroplane Company. This was not a minor dispute, but one which centred on issue of control of production as well as the educative process concerned. Disney argued that the best three of the participating firms should erect factories for producing and testing engines with the others being confined to supplying components. Obviously the larger and more efficient firms would have benefitted from this, but as with many cultural/political debates, a less than optimum solution was adopted partly because of the Air Ministry's own poor planning and by the inflexible approach of the car manufacturers led by Austin, who favoured the manufacture by individual concerns of specific parts with Bristol and Austin being responsible for assembly (Thoms, 1989, 3). Difficulties with the motor manufacturers were not confined to Austin. Morris, too, represented a source of disquiet and conflict and can be said to have resisted the tide of necessity and change. After joining in initially with the Shadow Factory Scheme Morris withdrew his Wolseley Shadow factory arguing that it was not needed and that as Wolseley already made aero engines sufficient capacity existed. In this Morris tried to play the powerful potentate who would not be dictated to by civil servants and closed down the Wolseley factory. Eventually Morris rejoined the scheme and was persuaded to make Spitfire fighter aircraft. Again the politics at work reflected the delicate situation that existed between the 'Car Barons' and the government and a face saving formula was found. Morris was technically allowed to build aircraft at Castle Bromwich with the minimum of interference from the government. Morris's active participation was short lived as there soon followed clashes on production methods between Morris and Vickers, the Spitfire's parent company. Morris had planned operations on a mass production basis which delayed the achievement of output targets whereas the RAF was demanding immediate output. Adding to the clash were debates on modifications to the aircraft with the obvious impact on long production runs. In the end during a monumental clash with Lord Beaverbrook the Air Minister, Morris offered his resignation over the issue and his bluff was called. This incident is symbolic for it shows that the government was in charge and that it would not be dictated to by the potentates of industry and even in the immediate postwar years, government was to continue to hold the industry in thrall (Adeney, 1988).

The need for cooperation from the automobile manufacturers was complemented by the necessity of ensuring that there was an adequate labour force with sufficient skill to meet the requirements of the war effort. In the 1920s the labour market in the car industry had been slack with employers encountering little difficulty in recruiting or getting rid of whom they wanted. The environment changed markedly in the middle of the following decade and gradually the market tightened with skilled labour becoming scarce in the middle 1930s as demand for cars rose. Certainly by the time of the onset of discussions on the Shadow Factory, labour shortages were being encountered in the Midlands, especially in the Coventry area (Donnelly, Morris, Batchelor, 1995, 148). So intense did the pressure become that labour poaching became a way of life in the industry as employers embarked on a policy of labour enticement through offers of enhanced wages which employees were only too willing to accept as they hopped from firm to firm. By 1940 shortages of apprenticed trained toolmakers and fitters had become so serious in the Midlands that John Black of Standard wrote to the Air Chief Marshal, Sir Wilfred Freeman, expressing his grave concern at the situation, pointing out that in his opinion Standard would be unable to meet its output targets. What made matters worse was that highly skilled men actually volunteered for the forces out of patriotism and there was nothing that the firms could do about it. This type of cultural conflict on where duty actually lay manifested itsFloreelf a year earlier when, much to the consternation of the employers, the navy launched a heavy recruiting campaign in the Coventry area which proved particularly successful at Morris engines. In the middle of this exercise the Coventry and District Engineering Employees Association issued an instruction to its members saying that while workers should not be discouraged from volunteering for the colours neither should they be given any encouragement to do so (Thoms & Donnelly, 1985).

Competition for labour caused problems for the employers and while they struggled to maintain a public face of solidarity with strong aversion and opposition to labour poaching, their behaviour belied this. Prior to upwards pressure on the labour market the employers, whether in Coventry, Birmingham or Oxford, had been able to recruit mainly from their travel to work areas, but by 1939 they found it necessary to advertise nationally as well as indulging in poaching. In 1939 there was a predicted shortfall of 7,000 operatives in Coventry and Major Smith Clark of Alvis, which had suffered badly from poaching, pleaded for 'solidarity and a uniform approach' to try to achieve some stability in the market place. Despite assurances from his fellow employers his pleas fell on deaf ears and within four weeks he too was offering golden handcuffs in the form of special bonuses to retain labour. Smith Clark ingeniously argued that his action was purely defensive and should not be construed as a recruiting ploy. How many of his colleagues believed him is a moot point. The self confident Sir John Black was much more open in policy and behaviour when he informed the CDEEA that Standard would determine its own labour policy and that if the association objected then the connection between it and Standard would be severed.

There were a number of potential solutions to the manpower problems, all of which involved change. These included attracting labour from other areas, using short training programmes to upgrade the unskilled and the semi-skilled, deskilling specific jobs, increasing mechanisation and lastly using women and youths on jobs traditionally reserved for men. All of this had serious implications for work practices, wage rates, labour relations and unions, to say nothing of the demands made by the increased use of new technologies.

Beginning with patterns of labour recruitment, the Oxford car complexes had traditionally recruited from the immediate rural hinterland as well as from declining trades within the immediate vicinity of the city, whereas Ford's Dagenham plant drew extensively on Essex and East London (Whiting, 1983). In the case of the Central Midlands matters were much more complex. Birmingham's factories were able to source themselves from the city and the Black Country and from as far afield as Kidderminster and Worcester. Coventry perhaps shows the most complicated labour recruitment pattern of all and our knowledge of these patterns is heavily dependent upon the work of Shenfield and Florence on the 1941 Labour Exchange Registration Books for the city (Shenfield & Florence, 1943–45). These books contain the name of the exchange where the insured was first registered and so it was possible to construct a limited picture for the year 1941 on the movement into Coventry's car and other war industries. The classification in the books was divided into 'Coventry' and 'foreign', the latter including Birmingham, but not the rest of Warwickshire since it was assumed that these registrations concerned daily commuters. The findings demonstrate that before the war the proportion of 'foreigners' was high with approximately 25 per cent of the city's migrant workers present in 1939 having arrived in the twelve months prior to July of the same year. Surprisingly the following year, 1940–41, witnessed a decline in male arrivals, but was compensated by an increase in females and boys drawn from the surrounding area including villages and towns in Warwickshire, Leicestershire and Northamptonshire. It is suggested that many of the newcomers were secondary wage earners in the family and, living in fairly rural districts and villages, had little alternative but to travel and seek work wherever it could be found, and Coventry beckoned willingly. In addition to the changes in local recruitment, change, too, occurred in attracting labour from further afield. In the 1930s, apart from Greater London, the major suppliers of inward migration to Coventry were the depressed areas of Lancashire, Tyneside, Clydeside, Cardiff and Newport. Over the three years 1939–41, however, there was a distinct change in the pattern with the geographical shift tilting in favour of Greater London, East Anglia, Leicestershire and Northamptonshire, even though in absolute terms Lancashire, Clydeside and the Cardiff and Newport axis continued to predominate numerically. By 1941 migration from the Hinckley area of Leicestershire accounted for 4.2 per cent of all 'foreign' registered males and for 16 per cent of similar females, while those from Greater London accounted for 10.7 and 14.4 per cent respectively. What is more important than a mere shift in geographical recruitment is that the migrant intake in this period more than likely included a large proportion of workers without experience in either factory, mine or workshop and were woefully short of essential engineering skills. Such a change in labour sourcing though was only to be expected once employment picked up again in the depressed areas as their own indigenous industries were drawn increasingly into the war effort. Thus the factories received labour, but of a kind that required swift training in a period of change and quick integration into the work process to maximise its utility (Thoms & Donnelly, 1985).

A major task for any firm whether in peace or in war is to ensure that its employees are trained and integrated sufficiently to accept or even own the firm's mission, vision and objectives, which in this case was meeting the production targets to achieve the overall essential goal of a necessitated satisfactory conclusion to hostilities. Wartime production the maintenance of very high output targets which involved considerable change in both the processes and patterns of work. This the manufacturers attempted to realise through capital investment and the efficient use of labour and materials. Rootes Securities, the separate body that governed all of the company's Shadow Factories, attempted to ensure that every operation that could feasibly be automated in their No 2 aero engine factory was done so by 1940 to achieve mass production, a move which paralleled Morris's approach to the Spitfire factory at Castle Bromwich. Similarly, new machine tools were installed at Rootes No 1 aero engine factory and heavy capital investment took place at Standard, Jaguar, Alvis, Daimler and Austin. Indeed one could argue that such a change in an industry that was so dependent on craftsmen might not have taken place so quickly had it not been for the exigencies of war (Croucher, 1982). Despite the increase of mechanisation, a considerable volume of work still had to be effected by hand, especially in airplane and engine factories. Early production of aircraft was carried out in traditional factories with craftsmen working on individual parts at their benches. Though often highly skilled and precise, such methods could not deliver the quantity and quality demanded and so production by jig and tool increasingly became the norm. This was especially true in the Shadow Factories which had been designed to achieve the highest possible standards and where no developmental work was to be allowed to hinder production schedules.

With the swift trend towards mechanisation and jig and tool amid shortages of skilled labour, there arose, though muted at first, a call for dilution that became more and more vocal. Though the principle of dilution was acceptable to both management and unions, the issue had to be carefully managed. The stumbling block was primarily fear on the part of the unions, who concerned about the possible adverse impact of dilution on their wages and employment practice. It could be argued that this was an emotional and even natural response, but resulted from experience born out of the interwar years and even the late 1930s when, during rearmament skilled men, even in Coventry, had occasionally found difficulty in finding employment (Thoms & Donnelly, 1985). Going beyond the car industry there was a fear that government would use dilution as a means of repressing wages, while for their part management feared that it was a possible cause of disputes at a time when peaceful industrial relations were of paramount importance. Concern was also expressed that the price demanded by the unions for their co-operation would be excessive wages increases for the remaining craftsmen at a time when employers were becoming aware of the need to restrain costs. Moreover some employers still hoped that a combination of technical advance and a higher intake of youths would lessen the demand for skilled labour. In the end the unions accepted dilution provided there were guarantees of a return to established practices once the emergency was over.

The process of dilution however was not easy. It was not simply a matter of recruiting labour and throwing it onto a production line or a workshop and expecting it to perform. Almost emergency measures were called for involving both in-house and external training. In Coventry unskilled and semi-skilled workers were retrained or upgraded by being sent on courses at the local technical college, but even then there was the familiar complaint that the courses were too theoretically biased with insufficient practical elements. Once begun, dilution progressed relatively quickly and in 1940 Humber began to use semi-skilled men to strip aero engines and immediately the AEU protested that this overstepped the agreed levels of dilution. A compromise was reached that the operation could be carried out by the unskilled, provided they worked under the supervision of a skilled man. In other words the fear factor did not go away and the union members were ever watchful of not only what was happening in their own factories, but elsewhere as well. Management, too, was able to manipulate the position to its advantage, as happened at Armstrong Whitworth in 1943. The coppersmiths complained that they should have full control over the installation of all pipework in Lancaster bombers. The debate centred on whether the pipes were 'fixed' or merely 'assembled'. The firm was able to demonstrate that at A.V. Roe's Manchester plant, although the coppersmiths made the pipes, their installation was carried out by the semi-skilled as was also the case at Vickers Armstrong's Weybridge plant. Though of little real importance in themselves, these examples demonstrate how each side jockeyed for position, sometimes losing, sometimes gaining, a situation far removed from the 1920s, as we shall see later.

The impact of war had tremendous consequences for two particular groups of stakeholders: women and trade unions, both of whom had been virtually marginalised for most of the interwar period. During the First World War women made considerable inroads into the car and aeronautical factory labour forces and this effort was well noted by the employers, but less so by the unions who saw their performance as a threat to male jobs and a means of depressing wage rates. With the onset of peace and subsequent demobilisation male cultural dominance re-established itself quickly and women were pushed back into minor work such as sewing squabs. Throughout the next two decades women's position throughout the car industry was weak and neither of the two main unions, the NUVB and AEU, would have anything to do with them. Indeed when a group of women at Rover in 1930 appealed to the AEU for help in refusing the imposition of the Bedaux system of payment upon them, their request was refused, but the fledgling T & G came to their rescue. Indeed, it was the latter union that took the initiative in organising women rather than the two more powerful bodies who were more content to defend their male presence and craft exclusiveness (Donnelly & Durham, 1989).

Though few figures exist for individual firms, the inflow of women into the car and aircraft factories was swift despite employer reluctance (Thoms, 1989, 42). In 1939 women represented roughly 10 per cent out of a total engineering work force of 1.4 million, but within three years this figure had swollen to well over a third of a labour force of 3 million in the engineering industry (Adeney, 1988, 186). Sadly no overall data exists to indicate the varying degrees of skill which women had on joining or leaving employment. However in 1940 75 per cent of them were employed either in semi- or fully skilled occupations and by 1944 this figure had risen by a further 10 per cent. Perhaps only a tiny proportion of these could be loosely described as 'apprentice trained', but equally a large number necessarily acquired a certain degree of skill, especially in the Central Midlands, for local classifications of skill to apply. Finally, as Inman argues, only a few women engineering workers would have acquired sufficient expertise to deserve the title highly skilled status, (Thoms & Donnelly, 1988; Inman, 1957, 59). Whatever standard of skill achieved required training. Rootes and Standard, for example, were two of the first firms to take on women and put them through formal schemes of training. By May Standard employed over 700 females in its No 2 aero engine factory and at the same time was processing them through its training school at a rate of 75 per week. Similarly between June and December 1941 Rootes trained 102 machine operators, 61 inspectors and 15 fitters.

It must not be thought that women were overly anxious to rush into factories and in some areas female recruitment proved difficult. In Coventry, for instance, the demographic structure of a disproportionately high number of young families led to a considerable reluctance to go into the factories. Similarly in both Coventry and Birmingham middle-class women often considered factory work beneath their status and preferred to follow other pursuits. Moreover, despite Ministry exhortations and recruitment drives women's household duties and family commitments were time consuming in themselves and, in the case of Coventry, city centre bombing during the blitz had made shopping very difficult. In other words, as throughout the period a combination of factory and domestic work was tiring and arduous many firms such as Humber had to compromise on hiring many women on a part-time basis (Thoms, 1989). Despite wartime propaganda women's work was every bit as arduous as that of the men they replaced. For instance, at Rootes' physical laboratory comparatively young girls toiled amid such noxious and dangerous chemicals that a rota system had to be devised for their own safety and comfort (Thoms & Donnelly, 1985). Similarly

Anne Marie Sweeney has shown the dangers involved in working on the pressings at Cowley as well as the discomfort caused by oil seeping through clothing and onto legs causing a condition known as oil rash (Sweeney, 1993). The reality was far removed from the wartime films of Mrs Miniver.

Much of the debate on the women's wages and conditions of work centred on interpretations of the Relaxation Agreements under which they were allowed to perform traditional male jobs, and this led to casuistry and cynicism of an extremely high order as work rates and processes were viewed from different angles and not always to women's benefit. Thus when female inspectors at Standard complained in 1941 that they were not being paid the full rate for the job they were informed that since their task involved merely a visual inspection of the job, their task therefore differed significantly from that of their male colleagues who were expected to conduct a more thorough examination. Indeed, this example is fairly typical of widespread attempts to devalue the status of women's work throughout Coventry's engineering industry. So blatant was the discrimination at Rootes that Jack Jones, the T & G District Officer, warned the company that unless it adopted a more enlightened policy towards its female employees it would have difficulty in recruiting labour of the calibre required. Yet by contrast when Lyons at Jaguar discovered that two women packers were being underpaid he responded positively. Culture is often described as the way things are done and this in itself was used to justify paying women less. The usual trick was to break down specialist jobs into their constituent elements and then arguing that things were now done differently so less pay was justified. Overall, women never achieved wage parity with men and as Sweeney again has shown even when women sought support from the unions for equality they were told 'there's a war on' (Thoms & Donnelly, 1985, 133; Sweeney, 1993, 123).

Despite unequal treatment women gained considerably from the war. Apart from rising self-confidence, they learned how to use industrial muscle at Cowley, for instance, by banding together to resist speed-up and by striking with or without union backing, eventually being elected as shop stewards and learning to negotiate with management rather than leave it all to men. As Sweeney claims 'a whole generation of women in Oxfordshire experienced not only factory life but trade unionism' (Sweeney, 1993, 122).

If any group found its cultural environment changed and its power increased during World War II it was the trade unions. Following the successful employers' Lock Out in 1922, the unions were effectively driven out of the car industry, especially the AEU, although the NUVB fared somewhat better. To be a union member in some firms let alone a shop steward was to put oneself in danger of the sack. Clearly for most of the interwar period the employers were in the ascendancy and it was only the tightening of the labour market on the advent of war that caused the balance to shift (Donnelly, Morris, Batchelor, 1995). It must not be thought though that the onset of war was like a magic wand that caused cultural change. Indeed it took more than an event. Normally, as Whiting has shown unions tried traditionally to organise from below and gain influence through rank and file membership. This changed and agitation from below was replaced by organisation from above thanks to government (Whiting, 1983).

Crucial to the enhanced role of trades unions was the enactment of legislation. Ernest Bevin realised that union co-operation was essential to the war effort and under the Essential Works Order of 1941, which was aimed at bringing a degree of order to the market for skilled labour, both unions and employers were drawn together in that firms' ability to hire and fire was restricted with all hiring being done through union offices. This and other wartime legislation provided a degree of employment protection almost unheard of in the 1920s and early 1930s, especially for the unskilled (Whiting, 1983). The importance of this legislation should not be underestimated because apart from pulling unions back into the mainstream of employer–labour relations, it provided an orderly framework in which negotiations could be conducted sensibly. It also elevated the status of shop stewards by lessening their vulnerability to dismissal and enabled union activists to be placed carefully in particular factories through labour exchanges. Indeed a feature of this period was the dramatic increase in the number of stewards in Coventry which peaked at 441 in 1943 to the extent that the stewards could actually threaten the status and role of the union bureaucracy. It must be stressed though that by far the great majority of stewards and rank and file trade unionists supported the war effort while at the same time trying to improve the welfare of workers. Even the Communists threw their weight behind the war effort once the Red Army became involved, though this did not reduce their opposition to capitalism (Thoms, 1989; Adeney, 1988).

Legislation on its own could not create a co-operative and trusting culture and many employers, mindful of the changed environment remained suspicious of unions, seeing certain officials, often without justification, as 'Reds under the bed'. A hilarious example of this occurred when on being asked about wage levels by Jack Jones, Harry Harley of Coventry Gauge and Tool pulled a revolver on Jones claiming that he was asking for sensitive information, was therefore a spy, and promptly summoned the local constabulary to arrest him (Donnelly & Thoms, 1989). On a more serious note the issue of co-operation crystallised when Bevin set up Joint Production Committees. Initially employers were sceptical of the contribution that unions could make to any debate on production, but after union criticism of management, often very public, JPCs began to appear. How effective they were is uncertain. Lewchuk claims that at

Longbridge the JPC represented an advance in a search for improved efficiency, but considering the continued absolutist rule of management that continued there and subsequent strikes the case remains unproven (Lewchuk, 1987). In contrast the reports of JPC meetings that filtered back to the CDEEA indicated that often such meetings had proved helpful and constructive and that gradually employers' opposition to them was waning (Thoms & Donnelly, 1985). Basically the jury is still out on this issue.

As has been noted earlier the upwards movement in trade union fortunes were top down inspired rather than bottom up; in other words it was institutionally driven by government in the person of Bevin, and perhaps the best example of this is how Ford was almost dragged into co-operating with its workforce. Ford had a well established and documented history of being anti-union and, given what was happening in other parts of the country, it was inevitable that an attempt would be made to draw it somewhat into line with other firms. Yet controversy remains about how Ford was eventually brought to heel. Friedman and Meredeen have argued that once Bevin became Minister of Labour it was only a matter of time, whereas the more sceptical Tolliday claims that the government's role was ambiguous. There is no doubt that Ford was in breach of the Essential Works Order when an activist was sacked at Trafford Park but the issue came to a head when union activists occupied the managerial suite at Dagenham. Ford proved willing to negotiate, but not with activists or stewards, only with the TUC in the person of Walter Citrine, its leader, and with Vic Feather, destined later in life to lead the TUC in equally troubled times. The outcome of the negotiations, conducted mainly by Feather on the union side, was that though unions were recognised, stewards were specifically excluded from negotiations with bargaining being placed in the hands of full-time officials. With Ford coming on board, the government had achieved overall a degree of union recognition, welfarism and social peace. Unions, albeit somewhat temporarily, had taken a delicate step towards the corridors of power (Friedman and Meredeen, 1980; Tolliday, 1985).

The question remains as to what the impact of the changes, wrought by the pressures of war, had on the industry in both the short and the long term. Current thinking on culture and change advocates that when enacted under positive conditions change should promote superior management, worker commitment and rewards (Gore, Murray and Richardson, 1992). Space precludes a full discussion of that issue in depth, but a summary attempt at least is necessary.

Adeney claims a considerable amount of pride could be taken in war production, that this was justifiable and that the industry had undergone changes that were to have long term consequences in relation to the economy as a whole, (Adeney, 1988). Barnett on the other hand is much more sanguine and argues that despite the pressures of war there were considerable shortcomings to be found in the factories. For example, he points to the findings of the Production Efficiency Board which found repeated instances of poor management, poor labour relations and low productivity, and yet he concedes that not all of these could be laid at the door of management. Frequently the situation was compounded by wildcat strikes since official stoppages were banned by the Essential Works Order (Barnett, 1986). Other commentators have found similar evidence, but it is fair to say that despite the presence of towering giants in the industry like Lyons and Black the quality of management appears to have been mixed. At Herberts, for instance, as elsewhere in Coventry, there was a reluctance to use stop watches to establish the characteristics of jobs but to reserve their use to calculate piece rates because of union opposition. The impression arises of the beginnings of a quasi-managerialist role by shop stewards which was to become a long term feature of the Midlands industry right down to the 1960s. Indeed frequently it was the stewards who ended wildcat strikes rather than management, while John Black at Standard was only too willing to call upon the services of Jack Jones to deal with problems that ought to have been the prerogative of management (Thoms, 1989; Jones, 1989). The importance of this lies in the fact that, while there was a wariness on each side, compromise had to be reached and this was achieved through Works Conferences, in which, although failure to agree was often an initial outcome, the issue was frequently pursued until a decision was achieved. In previous decades managerial power would have prevailed through the right to manage.

During the interwar years the car industry was characterised by seasonal activity in which work alternated between frenzied activity and lay-offs with absenteeism being frequent. It was hoped this would change during the war and that a work culture would be established. Sadly it was not. One major reason for this was that wages in the car factories were high (as they had always been) and with higher still wages, and often encouraged by overtime, a day's wages could be easily foregone and borne with relative ease. Similarly, it was found very difficult in Coventry to break the habit of 'knocking off' early to catch a particular bus. Equally, management found it difficult to end the tradition of long breaks prior to and after lunch and before finishing time, both well-established traditions. Equally women frequently tried to get away early to do shopping much to the chagrin of management and government officials, both of whom felt powerless to do anything about it (Thoms, 1989; Barnett, 1986). Finally, high wages in the automobile industry became even more established as a long run culture with the coming of the Coventry Tool Room Agreement which guaranteed that skilled men in the city, especially fitters and turners in the tool room, should be paid at a calculated monthly rate which should not be less than the average hourly rate paid to production workers in the selected factory. There is little doubt that in the short run this mechanism substantially benefited apprenticed trained men, but more importantly it became a benchmark that in the post war years was used throughout the car industry until its abolition with the coming of Measured Day Work in the Midlands (abolished in the late 1960s), (Thoms & Donnelly, 1989).

In contrast to high wages the Second World War did not lead to sky high profits for the manufacturers as it did in the First World War even though initially the potential was there. At first government contracts were awarded on a cost plus basis, which in itself was lax and which probably encouraged wage drift, and with frequent modification to jobs this certainly was the case. Inevitably though the government in the face of rising costs changed to fixed price contracts in which the price per batch of aircraft or whatever war material was ordered was reduced as the production time lengthened. For instance, in 1940 Standard received £7,413 for each of the first forty Oxford Trainers made, but thereafter the price was reduced so that for units 351–508 the company was paid £4,425 per aircraft. Indeed Adeney has shown that overall profits were nowhere near as high in real terms as they were in the 1914–18 conflict, with Ford averaging £400,000 per annum during the war years and Vauxhall amassing similar sum (Thoms & Donnelly, 1985, 139; Adeny, 1988, 184).

The final topic discussed is whether the experience of war changed the culture of fear that had hung over the industry since the Engineering Lock-Out of 1922. The answer is both yes and no. Victimisation was still apparent in the early years of war. Indeed in 1940 the AEU spent much of its time dealing with such cases. By 1944 both employers and unions were beginning to consider the implications of a return to peace. Many managers were unsure of their ability to convert their premises back to peacetime production while maintaining high levels of output and pay during a period when the market was expected to be tough once government contracts ceased to flow. Similarly, workers had no wish to return to the seasonal employment as before 1939 and were anxious to retain what gains they had made since war broke out. With those issues in mind both sides became increasingly unsure and there is clear evidence of a tendency to revert to a more authoritarian style of management with attempts to deflate wages and talk of redundancies. In Coventry, for example, uncertainty was increased by the closure of the Nuffield Mechanisation plant with management announcing that it was no longer central to their plans. Equally symptomatic of uncertainty and fear was a widespread attempt by unions to ensure that in the event of redundancies dilutees, women and youths, should be dismissed first so that scarce jobs should be reserved for 'skilled men'. Union fear can be easily understood when in 1945 Rootes shrunk its total work force at its Ryton plant from 3,123 to 98.

The trend towards a more awkward and anachronistic managerial approach which provoked fears of a return to earlier decades crystallised in events at Humber in 1945 when for several months the works manager adopted an extremely abrasive attitude towards the labour force. Complaints against him at a works conference ranged from his refusal to allow payment of a subsistence allowance to transferred workers to padlocking tea urns. Labour relations eventually deteriorated so badly that nearly 5,000 workers came out on strike for nine days, refusing to go back despite the efforts of union officials and the CDEEA. When work eventually resumed the atmosphere was more one of a truce than of peace. Mistrust and friction continued into the following year and was exacerbated by management attempts to enforce wage cuts in breach of locally agreed wage rates and when coupled with the installation of new machinery, the workers feared the spectre of redundancy. The workers' response was a go-slow which led to the dismissal of 500 men. Perhaps more importantly there was a widespread fear that this dispute would spread to other firms in the industry and yet neither side wanted a return to old style confrontation and eventually a compromise was achieved through the recognition that cooperation between both sides of industry was essential if there was to be an orderly return to peacetime production.

Overall the cultural changes of the Second World War on the car industry were important both in the short and long term. Perhaps the most important factor to emerge was that government realised the importance of the industry to economic growth, the balance of payments and regional economic policy and from 1945 right down to the crisis of British Leyland and Chrysler and the advent of Japanese firms the government has tried to exert an influence over the industry's development, though as Wilks has shown, not always successfully (Wilks, 1988). With the exception of William Lyons at Jaguar the war saw the final demise of many of the old style entrepreneurs and the establishment of a newer managerial group which was to guide the industry. It was the new breed of John Blacks that was to be instrumental in the long run.

Of equal importance was the increasing status and security of trade unions even though for a period in the 1950s the fortunes of unions varied between firms. Ford kept shop stewards at a distance and even today prefers to negotiate directly with senior union officials rather than shop stewards. In contrast Sir John Black, as he was to become, worked willingly with both district officials and plant stewards, while Rootes, according to Richardson, became a self-governing republic with the unions, despite internal squabbling, virtually running the Ryton plant (Richardson, 1972). The enhanced status of unions though during the war did not automatically ensure industrial peace. Victimisation continued into the 1950s, wildcat strikes continued, but more importantly both sides realised the need to negotiate and cut a deal was paramount and this certainly was a legacy from the war as government tried to influence both sides because of the industry's importance to the economy in an increasingly competitive environment.

The position of women though must be seen in a broader perspective than simply the auto industry. Though women worked hard, often in difficult conditions, and had to combine both factory and domestic roles, their position in the industry always remained subordinate and they were treated as such by employers and unions. Indeed after the war by far the majority of women were replaced by men, but what is far more significant is that a very large group of women were exposed to factory work of a particular type and as, noted earlier, this went a considerable way in the long run in establishing confidence among women to stand up for themselves, not just in industry, but in society in general. The war then overall must been seen as a positive force for change even if its impact was not fully felt or understood properly until much later.

Bibliography

Adeney, M. (1988) *The Motor Makers: The Turbulent History of Britain's Car Industry*, Collins, London.

Barnet, C. (1986) *The Audit of War*, Macmillan, London.

Church, R. (1994) *The Rise and Decline of the British Motor Industry*, Macmillan, London.

Croucher R. (1982) *Engineers at War*, Merlin, London.

Davey, J. (1967) *The Standard Card 1903–63*, Sherbourne Press, Coventry.

Donnelly, T., and Durham, M. (1989) *Labour Relations in the Coventry Motor Industry 1896–1939*, Centre for Business History, Coventry University, Coventry.

Donnelly T. Morris, D. and Batchelor, J. (1995) 'The Limitations of Trade Union Power in the Coventry Motor Industries 1896–1939', *Midland History*, XX, 137–150.

Donnelly, T. and Thoms, D. (1989) 'Trade Unions, Management and the Search for Production in the Coventry Motor Car Industry 1939–75' in C. Harvey and J. Turner (eds) *Labour and Business in Modern Britain*, Cass, London.

Donnelly, T. and Thoms, D. (1989) Interview with Jack Jones.

Flink, J. (1988) *The Automobile Age*, MIT Press, Cambridge, Mass.

Friedman H. and Meredeen S. (1980) *The Dynamics of Industrial Conflict; Lessons form Ford*, Macmillan, London.

Gore, C., Murray, K. and Richardson, B. (1992) *Strategic Decision Making*, Cassell, London.

Inman P. (1957) *Labour in the Munitions Industries*, HMSO, London.

Lanning, C. et al (1985) *Making Cars*, Routledge & Kogan Paul, London.

Mintzberg, H. et al (1995) *The Strategy Process*, Prentice Hall, London.

Moss Kanter R. (1989) *When Giants Learn to Dance*, Simon and Schuster, London.

Quinn, J.B. (1980) Strategies for Change: Logical Incrementalism, Gower, London.

Richardson, K. (1972) *Twentieth Century Coventry*, Macmillan, London.

Shenfield, A. and Florence, P.S., (1943–45) *Labour for the War Industries: the Experience of Coventry*, Review of Economic Studies.

Sweeney, A.M. (1993), 'Women Making Cars, Making Trouble, Making History' in T.

Hayton D. and Harvey (eds), *The Factory and the City: The Story of the Cowley Automobile Workers in Oxford*, Mansell, London.

Thompson, J.L. (1993) *Strategic Management: Awareness and Change*, Chapman & Hall, London.

Thoms, D. (1989) War, Industry and Society, Routledge, London.

Thoms, D. and Donnelly, T. (1995) *The Motor Car Industry in Coventry since the 1890s*, Croom Helm, London.

Whiting, N.C. (1983) *The View from Cowley*, Clarendon Press, Oxford.

Wilks, S. (1988) *Industrial Policy and the Motor Industry*, Manchester University Press, Manchester.

Wood, J. (1988) *Wheels of Misfortune: The Rise and Fall of the British Motor Industry*, Sedgwick and Jackson, London.

15

Images of Disorder: Car Workers' Militancy and the Representation of Industrial Relations in Britain, 1950–79

Tim Claydon

In November, 1979 Derek Robinson, a leading shop steward in the Amalgamated Union of Engineering Workers at British Leyland's Longbridge factory in Birmingham, was dismissed. Sir Michael Edwardes, the company's Chief Executive, authorised the sacking on the grounds that Robinson had attempted to organize opposition to Edwardes' 'recovery plan' for BL and because he had kept Longbridge in ferment and upheaval for 30 months. In a television interview, Edwardes stated that under Robinson's stewardship there had been 523 industrial disputes at Longbridge involving 'the loss of 62,000 cars and 113,000 engines, worth £200 million' (Edwardes, 1983, 109). A further important factor in the dismissal was Edwardes' perception of the motives behind Robinson's actions. Robinson was known to be a member of the Communist Party and his attempt to organise opposition to the programme of change at BL was seen by Edwardes as reflecting what he described as the Communist Party's aim 'to replace the existing structure of society by every means at its disposal and with a number of our shop stewards as their willing instruments' (ibid).

Derek Robinson had gained a formidable reputation during the late 1970s. Known as 'Red Robbo' in the media, he was described as the 'most powerful single trade union figure in BL' and for this reason his dismissal came as a shock to many. One Midlands trade union official said that he could not believe his ears when he first heard the news (Webb, 1979). Confrontation with the workforce and trade unions seemed to be assured. Robinson's supporters organised a strike to secure his reinstatement and it appeared likely that the trade unions would give the strike their official support. Robinson's reputation, however, also encouraged press comment in favour of his dismissal. Thus *The Times* demanded of Robinson' union:

> Will they opt to save one job – or 100,000? And do the trade unionists of the West Midlands want to lose their jobs – for good – in order to defend the militant who has done more than anyone else to destroy their company? (*The Times*, 27 December 1979)

Robinson and his supporters in fact failed to receive the backing of their own union and Longbridge workers, faced with the threat of dismissal and the closure of the plant, voted overwhelmingly against strike action to secure his reinstatement. Robinson remained dismissed and Edwardes set about reducing shop stewards' influence in the plant and undertaking major reforms of working practices.

This outcome came to be seen as one of the key events in the reshaping of industrial relations, not just in BL but in Britain as a whole. Many within the labour movement were shocked by the AUEW Executive Committee's decision not to give official backing to the initial protest over Robinson's dismissal, since it was seen as exposing shop stewards to 'a new era of uncertainty and weakness' and opening up a 'challenge to the whole basis of trade unionism'. Thus the Labour Editor of *The Times* wrote, 'If Sir Michael Edwardes can get away with sacking a shopfloor representative as apparently invulnerable as Mr Derek Robinson, then no shop steward is safe' (Routledge, 1979).

At the same time, the predominant opinion of outside commentators was that British Leyland, and therefore the British motor industry, was in danger of being destroyed by the actions of a minority of workers and their shop stewards. Industrial relations problems at British Leyland had for some time been seen as exemplifying in acute form wider problems in British industrial relations. Headlines and leading articles in the national press spoke of 'anarchy' threatening wages and jobs, and of BL being 'endangered by a minority' (*The Times*, 21 June 1978, 17; 29 August 1978, 13). Right-wing commentators in particular were quick to use BL to build a case against what they represented as overprivileged and irresponsible trade unions. Thus Paul Johnson, writing in *The Times* eighteen months before the Robinson episode, inveighed against trade unions' legal 'privileges' which allowed them 'the fun of bullying cabinet ministers, of scoring victories over parliament and the judiciary, of gathering the quangoes and peerages, of strutting self-importantly on the creaking and increasingly unimportant stage of British public life.' He went on to argue the need for British workers 'to be rescued from the incompetence of their leaders' as 'mounting evidence' showed that 'union power not only kept real wages low but, by starving industry of investment, actually creates structural unemployment on a vast scale'. Referring to British Leyland, Johnson commented on the need to remove barriers to investment in order to raise real wages and create jobs, and argued that this would necessitate 'dismantling much of the legal privileges and political-economic power of the union élites' (Johnson, 1978)

The dismissal of Robinson and the aggressive implementation of changes in working practices and shopfloor industrial relations at BL, coupled with the closure of BL plants at Speke on Merseyside and Abingdon, Oxfordshire, were seen by many as marking the onset of a new phase of 'macho management' in British industry under the recently elected Thatcher government. Robinson himself became the latest figure in public demonology, embodying much of what was seen to be wrong with Britain in the 1970s; destructive industrial militancy, left-wing subversion and the overweening power of organised labour. His was the name recalled in saloon-bar discussions of industrial relations before a new bogeyman was created in the form of Arthur Scargill.

My reason for dwelling on this episode is that it seems to me to illustrate how central a position in political and economic discourse industrial relations had come to occupy by the late 1970s. In this essay I hope to show that by the time of the Robinson affair industrial relations had come to be seen as the key issue in British politics. Growing concern with Britain's declining economic performance and disenchantment with the role of the state in economic and social life during the 1960s and 1970s were closely bound up with, and increasingly analysed in terms of, industrial relations problems and the issue of trade union power. It is not my purpose here to provide an actual account of industrial relations in the motor industry during the post-war period. Rather, it is to try to show how industrial relations in the motor industry dominated public perceptions of British industrial relations as a whole and therefore shaped the way in which the growing sense of crisis in British political and economic life came to be articulated. Increasingly, images of industrial relations were seen as reflecting British society as a whole. And if industrial relations were one of the defining images of British society, the motor industry was the lens through which this image was projected and, arguably, distorted.

Much of the research for this essay took the form of an examination of industrial relations reporting in *The Times, Daily Telegraph* and *Daily Mirror*.[1] Use of press reports raises the question of how to analyse and assess their influence. While this is not the main purpose of this essay, it is necessary to pay some attention to the question. It is clearly too naive to regard mass media as simply 'reflecting' something called 'public opinion' (Hyman, 1989, 151). Neither, however, can the media be regarded as simply manufacturing public opinion, since people engage actively and selectively with media representations of events. The position taken here is that of Colin Hay who has argued that 'media influence does not reside in the power of direct ideological indoctrination, but in the ability to frame the discursive context within which political subjectivities are constituted, reinforced and reconstituted' (Hay, 1996, 261). It is argued here that press reports of specific events constituted a series of narratives which in turn became subjects of a further process of what Hay refers to as meta-narration. In this process, specific events reported from the motor industry were presented as defining a more general malaise within British industrial relations, the British economy and the state. The meta-narrative so constructed presented an account of Britain's problems which, while not closing off alternative narratives completely, generated a set of discursive parameters within which 'mainstream' debate was conducted. However, this process itself reflected underlying assumptions and priorities in British politics. Some brief consideration of these is therefore necessary in order to establish a framework of analysis.

British political culture and the shaping of industrial relations

Alan Fox (1985) has shown how liberal individualism had emerged as the key concept in British politics by the nineteenth century and how it shaped the way in which organised labour came to be integrated into the political structure. Trade unions emerged as a defensive working class response to economic liberalism. They asserted their legitimacy in terms of pre-industrial 'liberties' – the freedom of corporate groups to claim status, rights and protections which had been embodied in earlier organisational forms such as the craft guilds. The influence of this concept of liberties was seen in the gradual, albeit hesitant, acceptance of the right of workers to organise collectively in order to regulate relations with employers. Concomitantly, more employers came to see practical advantages in dealing with trade unions (Fraser, 1974). At the same time, economic conflicts and the bias in English common law towards the individual and against the collective continued to threaten trade unions' ability to act on behalf of their members. Consequently they committed themselves to principles of political liberalism in order to secure a recognized place within the British polity. This, together with the need of the ruling classes in Britain to maintain social and political stability and preserve the privileges of property in the face of a growing and increasingly organised working class, led to modifications of liberal individualism in favour of liberal collectivism from the late nineteenth century onwards. This took the form of legal protections for trade unions and extensions of state responsibility in areas of social and economic policy. However, as Fox notes, the price the unions paid for this was to become bound by the constitutional principles to which they had appealed for their own protection. Specifically, this meant the separation of economic and political activities and strict limits on the use of industrial strength for political ends. It also meant the acceptance of constitutionalism in their internal systems of government and their dealings with employers. This was to be expressed in terms of a basic acceptance of the managerial prerogative in industry and the principle of union members honouring voluntary collective agreements negotiated on their behalf by their representative officials.

In order to survive and grow trade unions had therefore adapted to Britain's economic and political structure and in doing so had become part of it. However, it is important to note the ambiguous role of trade unions within British society and the tensions present in the accommodation that was effected between liberal individualism and liberal collectivism. In their espousal of constitutionalism trade unions have laid claim to be managers of discontent, bringing order to industrial relations and acting as agents of 'system integration', claims which gained growing recognition and acceptance from the mid-nineteenth century onwards (Fraser, 1974). At the same time, as collective organisations of workers they pursue aims and employ methods which bring them into conflict with employers, the state and sections of the public. While trade unions have not usually sought to challenge the fundamental basis of British capitalism, they retain significant oppositional characteristics within it. This has given rise to perceptions of a 'crisis of system integration' at times when trade union leaderships appear to have refused to be bound by constitutionality or to have been unable to ensure that their members act constitutionally.

Moreover, the continuing tensions between liberal collectivism and liberal individualism in British political discourse have been fundamental to the way in which public attitudes and policy on industrial relations have developed. In the following sections of this chapter I shall try to show how, durng the post-war period, a growing sense of political and economic crisis was articulated largely in terms of a crisis of system integration in industrial relations with the motor industry as the main focus of public attention. I shall also argue that as efforts to resolve this crisis appeared to fail more fundamental criticisms of Britain's socio-economic and political structures were mounted on the basis of a reassertion of liberal individualism against the predominance of liberal collectivism.

The motor industry and the meta-narrative of 'disorder'

Disorder and the potential for disorder in industrial relations were matters of public concern and comment throughout the 1950–80 period. As far as the motor industry was concerned the main focus of attention was the apparent growth in the incidence of 'unofficial' industrial action, that is, action initiated at the workplace without the prior sanction of the officers of the union and usually in breach of agreed procedures for dealing with disputes. This was seen to reflect a decline in the authority of trade union leaderships over their members which was associated with the growth in the number of shop stewards at workplace level, an increase in their independence from full-time union officials and in their growing influence over rank-and-file members. Concern over the role of shop stewards was further fuelled by a preoccupation with communist and other far-left infiltration of trade unions, mainly through shop stewards and their organisations. These developments were represented as weakening the capacity and the commitment of unions to operate constitutionally, thereby calling into question their ability to fulfil their role as agents of system maintenance.

This is not to say that the motor industry was always seen as the major source of threat to stability and order in industrial relations. The dock strike of 1966 and the coal strikes of 1972 and 1974, for example, had more obvious impacts upon peoples' lives and probably generated a more widespread and immediate sense of crisis in the economy than did disputes in the car industry. The climactic events of the so-called 'winter of discontent' were located mainly in the public sector, although it should be remembered that they commenced with a strike at Ford. The significance of industrial relations and in particular, industrial conflict in motor manufacture lay in the ongoing nature of its discussion in the media and the way in which images from the motor industry came to be the common currency of industrial relations discussion and debate. It might almost be said that, by the late 1960s, in their almost daily representation in press, TV and radio reports, motor industry industrial relations came to be a lurid form of soap opera, albeit usually without the sex.

Unofficial strikes and workplace 'militancy'

An examination of the index to *The Times* covering the years from 1960–80 reveals that there were more reports of and commentary on labour issues in the motor industry than in all other industries or sectors together except during the few years when there were national stoppages in key areas such as the docks, coal, transport and power. The frequency of references rose sharply after 1968. During 1964–68 there were between 234 and 282 references each year. During 1970–78 there were between 291 and 629 references each year with more than 365 references in all but two years. The majority of these concerned disputes and industrial action. Moreover, the pattern of strikes that had developed in the motor industry from the 1930s onwards was one of 'unofficial' stoppages. The rising incidence of unofficial strikes from the 1950s onwards, together with the rapid growth in the industry's importance to the economy, resulted in considerable media interest. The concentration of media reporting on strikes in the motor industry thus focused attention and discussion of industrial relations matters on this particular form of industrial action. From this there developed what we might call a meta-narrative of militancy and disorder in British industrial relations.

Unofficial strikes were viewed as a threat to system maintenance because they were taken to indicate declining authority of union leaderships over their members and a growing readiness of members, led by 'militant' shop stewards, to take unconstitutional action in breach of agreed disputes procedures. Moreover, given the highly integrated nature of motor manufacture it was possible for a relatively small group of workers to halt production in a plant and, should the stoppage be of significant duration, to disrupt or even halt production in other plants and firms. Turner, Clack and Roberts, in their major study of industrial relations in the motor industry, estimated that from the mid-1950s to the mid-1960s, layoffs of workers not directly involved in strikes added between 50 and 60 per cent to the number of 'lost' working days which could be attributed to the strikers themselves. (Turner, Clack & Roberts, 1967, 55–6)

Industrial relations in the motor industry therefore came to be represented in terms of sectionally militant shop steward organisation in the workplace and unofficial strikes beyond the control of full-time union officials. There was, of course, a genuine basis for this. The early establishment of trade union organisation in motor plants, often in the face of considerable management hostility, had owed much to the efforts of industrially militant and sometimes politically radical workers who built workshop organisation during the 1930s and 1940s. Their politics and tactics sometimes brought them into conflict with more conservative full-time officers, but the main reason for the independence of shop steward organisation was that no single union had a sufficient proportion of its membership employed in the motor industry before 1950 to stimulate them into paying much attention to the specific needs of car workers (Turner, Clack & Roberts, 1967). By the 1950s shop stewards in most motor plants had developed experience and self-reliance in their dealings with management. Moreover, the continued reliance on piecework in the car industry provided much scope for shopfloor bargaining over rates and times allowed for jobs and also for conflict.

These real features of the industry received considerable emphasis and were represented as indicative of 'disorder' in relations between management and workers in the car assembly and components factories. Major disputes over redundancies in the motor industry in 1956 and a general increase in strike incidence during 1957–62 led to expressions of opinion that industrial relations had deteriorated to the extent that unofficial disputes were having an adverse effect on Britain's export performance. In response, in 1960 the Trades Union Congress set up an inquiry into unofficial strikes, concentrating on the motor industry and shipbuilding, which were 'major industries ... notorious for strikes' (*The Times*, 20 May 1960, 14). Its report concluded that industrial relations had not worsened sharply as was being reported and that disputes did not threaten British prosperity. This was however, unacceptable to *The Times*. It accused the TUC of 'minimising' the costs of unofficial strikes and of having 'little to offer on what is perhaps the central problem, the usurpation of unions' authority by joint committees of shop stewards...' (*The Times*, 22 August 1960, 9).

Reports of the activities of shop stewards in the motor industry became increasingly frequent during the 1960s and 1970s. Much of this reporting was concerned with the role of stewards in the conduct of industrial disputes. While there was an acknowledgement that most stewards played a useful and constructive role, the most detailed reporting tended to focus on caucuses of stewards who were claimed to be in control of car plants, tip-offs concerning the existence of shadowy groups rejoicing in names such as the 'M6 Cabinet' and elections for senior shop steward posts where 'extremists' were competing for positions with 'moderates' (see for example, *The Times*, 12 March 1966, 8; 6 June 1974, 2; 4 July 1975, 4). The need for unions to control workshop representatives in order to prevent 'extremist' influence from taking hold was a recurrent theme during the 1960s and 1970s and the unofficial strike was taken to be an expression of this influence.

Academic research was critical of this depiction of workplace industrial relations. The popular distinction between 'official' and 'unofficial' strikes had little meaning in practice. Up to the late 1960s at least, it was rare for trade unions to declare their opposition to a stoppage of work by their members (Turner, Clack & Roberts, 1967, 55–6). Moreover, as Paul Edwards found:

> in one plant with a strong shop steward organization and with a relatively high level of strike, (sic) strikes could not be seen as a breakdown of order. They were one means whereby the 'relative power of management and workers over the work situation' was altered or maintained. In other words, strikes were part of the 'constant negotiation of order' in the factory and not something divorced from that process. (Edwards, 1982, 18)

Nevertheless, a more traditional and less sophisticated concept of order which was rooted in the exercise of managerial prerogative within the terms of formal collective agreements was repeatedly insisted upon by politicians, employers and management representatives, journalists and commentators and at times by some prominent national trade union officials. By the mid-1960s there were strong signs that popular conceptions of the nature of industrial relations in the motor industry were being used to define industrial relations as a whole. In 1965 unions and management agreed to set up a Motor Industry Joint Labour Council under an independent chairman, Jack Scamp, to investigate disputes. At the end of 1966 the Council reported on its activities, recording nearly 600 unofficial stoppages in eight firms during the first half of 1966. According to the editor of *The Times* this was 'not far from anarchy'. He also went on to assert that:

> The motor industry presents the most extreme example of chaos in the workplace, but it is not alone. The infection is spreading ... Basically it is the result of the failure of managements and unions to come to terms with full employment. Many managements have lost control and many unions are helpless. (*The Times*, 22 December 1966, 11)

The generalisation of concern about unofficial strikes from the motor industry to other sectors led to growing consideration being given to legislation to curb unofficial action. This was supported by some employers, although the Confederation of British Industry remained opposed to any major extension of legal intervention such as making collective agreements legally binding. In 1964 the Prime Minister referred to the possibility of legislation if the motor industry did not provide a means of reducing the number of strikes (*The Times*, 4 September 1966, 6). It was this consideration of the possible need for closer legal regulation of trade union activities that led in 1965 to the Wilson government appointing a Royal Commission chaired by Lord Donovan.

The issue of what role legislation should play in industrial relations was the main item in the initial terms of reference of the Royal Commission on Trade Unions and Employers' Associations set up under the chairmanship of Lord Donovan in 1965. Ironically, the commission concluded that legislation would do little to improve industrial relations and that the answer lay in developing formal collective bargaining arrangements at company and plant level in recognition of the shift of power within trade unions to the shop floor. In coming to this recommendation the commission had relied heavily on evidence from employers, union officials and shop stewards in engineering, and some of the most influential witnesses were from the motor industry.

The influence of the commission's report was considerable. Its findings were generally seen to provide an authoritative analysis of Britain's industrial relations problems and its recommendations showed a clear path to reform which retained the commitment to minimal legal regulation which had characterised the British approach to industrial relations. In brief summary, it argued that there had been a shift of power within trade unions to the workplace, which was now the principal locus of bargaining over pay. Disorder stemmed from the lack of formal procedures to regulate workplace bargaining. Therefore what was needed was to put them in place.

The close resemblance between the commission's analysis and the features of the motor industry did not go unnoticed. In fact a criticism of the Report by one academic was that it had drawn generalised conclusions on the basis of the problems of a few important industries in which relatively high levels of conflict had always been present (*The Times*, 28 August 1968, 24). The relevance of this for this essay is its demonstration of the strong influence that the motor industry had in the development of an authoritative narrative of British industrial relations as a whole.

It is arguable that the public obsession with car industry disputes was a major factor giving rise to the enduring belief that Britain was unusually strike-prone. Despite academic analysis (Turner, 1969) and official surveys which showed that the vast majority of workplaces, even in manufacturing, were strike free in any single year and that an almost equally large majority had not experienced a strike in four years, references to the 'British disease' kept appearing in newspaper articles and other media. On 2 December 1976 *The Times* printed two articles. The first reported on Department of Employment findings that during 1971–73 98 per cent of manufacturing plants had been strike free and that strike activity was 'not an epidemic' in Britain (Jones, 1976). The second was a leading article which also discussed the Department of Employment's findings. Determined to manufacture some grounds for concern at Britain's strike record, it argued that while the 'myth' of strikes as the British disease could be scotched by 'literalist methods' it was harder to demolish it as a 'symbolic truth'. It went on to ask whether strikes in Britain might not be more damaging than they were elsewhere, asserting that although there was no method of showing this, 'the impression is irresistible' because of the high incidence of unofficial strikes and their knock-on effects on other groups of workers, a clear implicit reference to the motor industry. Eighteen months later another leading article appeared headlined 'Anarchy threatens wages and jobs' and continued:

> Over the past two decades there has been a steady and serious erosion of the central authority of most of our major unions. Nowhere has this been more apparent than in the motor industry. (*The Times*, 2 June 1978, 17)

The article then went on to discuss specific developments at British Leyland. Once again we can see evidence of elision of the specific and the general, the primary narrative being transformed into the meta-narrative.

Shop stewards and 'political extremism'

The 1950s saw several well-publicised instances of conflict between organised shop stewards and management which were embarrassing for national union officials and early on encouraged a portrayal of uncontrolled and undisciplined stewards and members impeding the orderly operation of collective agreements. This concern over unofficial strikes and unions' lack of control over their members was fuelled by periodic reports of Communist and Trotskyist infiltration and control of shop steward organization in the motor industry. Allegations of such activities came from politicians, employers, trade union officials, shop stewards and rank-and-file workers themselves. Trade unions officials imbued with the principle of constitutionality in union affairs tended to be at least as exercised over 'extremism' as employers. In March 1953 the Transport and General Workers Union withdrew from the Austin Joint Shop Stewards Committee on the grounds that it contained communists and the union's General Secretary, Arthur Deakin, spoke of communists who aimed 'to cause industrial disruption, regardless of the real interests of the workers' (*The Times*, 2 March 1953, 4–5). The TGWU set up a new shop stewards committee which claimed to be 'wholly concerned with wages, hours of work and conditions of employment' and determined to 'break with a policy which has led to a number of disputes and has been inspired, so it is said, by sectional interests on political rather than industrial grounds' (*The Times*, 9 March 1953, 4).

The greatest *cause célèbre* of the 1950s however, was the 'bellringer' dispute at Briggs Bodies, Ford's bodymaking plant at Dagenham. Conflict had been endemic in the plant ever since Ford took it over in 1953. Over 600 unofficial stoppages were recorded during 1953–57. In 1957 a strike occurred over the dismissal of John McLoughlin, the chairman of one of the shop committees. A Court of Inquiry led by Lord Cameron was appointed to investigate the circumstances of the strike. Cameron found a highly developed shop steward organisation, with its own substantial funds, operating largely independently of the unions; as Cameron put it 'a private union within a union' (Beynon, 1973, 48). Cameron was also concerned at communist influence among the stewards and argued that the Briggs shop stewards committee should be brought under the control of the union. This theme was taken up by William Carron, President of the Amalgamated Engineering Union:

> For a long time now the subversives have been at work at Briggs. Last

year alone, there were 200 stoppages in the plant. In my view those subversive types were responsible for most, if not all of them. (Beynon, 1973, 53)

Carron's views were echoed in a House of Commons debate following the Cameron Report. One Tory MP asserted that shop stewards were frequently a Communist Party 'fifth column' in British industry. Another said that many people who supported free collective bargaining were 'worried by the activities of a small number of wreckers who had disproportionate influence' (*The Times*, 20 April 1957, 4). *The Times* itself intoned that the Briggs shop stewards' committee was 'a cancer on the body of trade unionism' and that 'through its agency, communist influence had penetrated far ... It is up to the unions to find an effective counter if they are to protect their members and preserve democracy' (*The Times*, 12 April 1957, 4).

Carron repeated his attacks on 'wreckers' who, he said, made it impossible for union officials to carry out negotiated settlements, at a meeting of the National Committee of the AEU. His speech was the subject of leading articles in *The Times* and the *Daily Mirror* which claimed that as communist influence over national officials had waned it had targeted shop steward organisation (*The Times*, 26 April 1960, 13; *Daily Mirror*, 26 April 1960, 2).

It is unclear how widely held the agitator theory came to be during the 1960s and 1970s. Its use by trade union leaders perhaps needs to be examined in the light of internal political rivalries and tensions within the unions themselves. There were politicians, such as Lord Chalfont, who clearly believed in the reality of a revolutionary take-over of trade unions which he saw as part of a wider pattern of social and moral disintegration. In February 1975 he introduced a debate on 'subversive and extremist elements in our society' arguing that they had infiltrated the AUEW and the TGWU and that there were people 'who virtually controlled' the labour force at Chrysler's Ryton plant and at Leyland's Longbridge factory (*The Times*, 26 February 1975, 4). In October 1978, inspired by a forthcoming book by the *Daily Express* journalist Chapman Pincher, he wrote:

When it was announced last week that the motor industry now has a worse strike record than any other industry in the country I was able, without undue strain, to contain my astonishment. Anyone who really believes that the Ford crisis is all to do with the government's pay policy is likely to believe anything. It is part of something much more profound and much more significant which is happening to this country... Chapman Pincher's book represents ... incontrovertible evidence of the kind of industrial and political sabotage which is now bringing the British car industry and the whole British economy to its knees. (Lord Chalfont, 1978, 12)

Most of those who were closely involved in industrial relations had little time for such visions since they were clearly out of line with expert opinion given to the Donovan Commission, whose best-known comment was that shop stewards were 'more of a lubricant than an irritant' in industrial relations (Donovan, 1969). A number of reports from those who regularly reported on the industry in the press discounted most of the allegations concerning extremist influence (Webb, 1976, 2; Hodgkinson, 1976, 4) and argued that talk of 'Trots, plots and conspiracies' had diverted attention from serious issues (Corinna & Townsend, 1976, 19). Nevertheless, allegations of extremist conspiracies kept on surfacing. In a leading article entitled 'The British Leyland Millstone', the editor of *The Times* asserted that

> There is evidence, for example, that the immediate cause of much of the current trouble is a well-orchestrated and vocal campaign of opposition to an extension of the social contract ... At individual plants more direct revolutionary elements may well be at work. (*The Times*, 22 February 1977)

As can be seen these allegations tended to be based on speculation or hearsay or often unsubstantiated allegations by individuals with personal or political grievances. Workers themselves freely admitted the presence of Communist and Trotskyist members among their shop stewards, but they equally insisted that they were not 'controlled' by them. Influential stewards were so by virtue of their ability to represent the interests of the membership rather than their ability to manipulate members for political purposes (Turner, Clack & Roberts, 1967; Hodgkinson, 1976a).

The primary significance of the allegations of extremist influence is that they reinforced the argument that unofficial strikes were illegitimate and represented a loss of union authority, control and representativeness. In doing so they provided a further basis for a populist electoral appeal to curb 'militant' power through the legal regulation of union activities. Both of the main political parties retained an interest in legal reform. Barbara Castle's attempt, on behalf of the Labour government, failed in the face of trade union opposition. However, with the election of the Conservatives to power in 1970 the move for legal reform gained fresh impetus.

Allegations of political extremist influence were clearly a factor in this development. Thus in 1971 Robert Carr argued that legislation in the form of the Heath government's Industrial Relations Bill had become necessary to ensure that 'small, tightly-knit groups of militants' using the 'phoney' democracy of the mass meeting could not continue to use workers as 'pawns' in a power game in which 'The militants hold the balance of power between peace and war ... regardless of the true wishes of the majority of their fellow workers' (*The Times*, 27 March 1971, 2). In these respects developments during the 1980s had in some ways been prefigured a decade earlier.

The failure of the Industrial Relations Act in the face of union opposition and employers' indifference seemed at first to confirm the need to work within the framework of liberal collectivism. However, as Britain's economic condition worsened during the 1970s and government attempts to combat inflation and rising unemployment were seen to founder on the rock of trade union and, in particular, rank-and-file opposition, faith in liberal collectivism weakened and a mounting challenge came from those who wished to restore liberal individualist principles in the form of a free market economy and a minimal state. Here we return to Derek Robinson. Within the constructed narrative of post-war British industrial relations he was represented the central problem of the period – workplace disorder and a test of liberal collectivism in industrial relations. As this narrative came to be reconstructed by the political Right in the late 1970s and 1980s, he became the 'enemy within' who could not be safely integrated into the British polity and who therefore invalidated the liberal collectivist project.

The evidence presented here together with a host of other press reports and articles suggests that by the 1970s a series of narratives concerning industrial conflict in the motor industry had been woven into a much larger one which represented British industrial relations as endemically disorderly and strike-prone. The factual basis for such a judgement was weak. The average annual incidence of stoppages rose during the late 1940s and throughout the 1950s but then remained at a plateau throughout the 1960s before falling during the 1970s. The average annual number of working days 'lost' through stoppages did rise, more than doubling between 1951–55 and 1966–70 from 2.38 million to 5.53 million before rising very rapidly to over 13 million during 1971–75. However, throughout the 1960s working days lost through strikes per thousand employees in Britain were fewer than in Australia, Canada, Finland, Iceland, Ireland, Italy and the United States. The increase during the 1970s, which had very little impact on Britain's position in the international 'league table', was largely explained by unprecedented strikes of public sector workers over the effects of incomes policy on absolute and relative real wages rather than a general breakdown of order in industrial relations (Jackson, 1987). The role of extremists was certainly exaggerated if not wilfully misrepresented by those who pushed that line in the face of evidence from the workers themselves. This is not to say that industrial conflict during the 1970s was in any way insignificant but to point out once more that specific problems were transformed into a wider narrative of crisis in industrial relations as a whole, a breakdown of relations between capital and labour (Hay, 1996). This undermined and challenged unions' claims to constitutionalism and effective system integration by representing the unions as having lost control of their members.

In developing this meta-narrative, responsibility for Britain's industrial malaise was laid at organised labour's door. The key image was one of trade unions unable to control their more militant members and this was portrayed as a major factor in Britain's industrial decline. Small matter that industry had a long history of weak management and underinvestment. It was the activities of workers that were visible and they could readily be represented as being misguided in the light of the need for 'common-sense' and co-operation to overcome industry's problems. Moreover the apparent lack of common-sense was used in support of the argument that the dark forces of extremism must be at work.

In this the media did play a role. It was in the media that the narrative construction of industrial relations took place. The specific events in the motor industry were represented in terms of their threat to the general conditions which had been established for the integration of organised labour into the British polity. As the situation of the economy worsened during the 1970s and industrial conflict became more widespread, the notion of disorder came to be applied more generally in the construction of a further meta-narrative of disorder and crisis in British industrial relations as a whole. This increasingly involved a critique of the liberal-collectivist state. The main elements of this critique were as follows. The necessary legal protections which allowed unions to act on behalf of their members in disputes with employers were increasingly represented as 'privileges' which put trade unions above the law. In this situation, it was argued, policies of full employment had put trade unions in a position of unassailable power which they abused in two ways. In the political arena, it was argued, the leaders of the large trade unions made their co-operation with government conditional on the provision of further legal 'privileges' and protections. However, in the industrial sphere power within the trade unions lay, not with elected full-time officials, but with groups of organised workers and their increasingly militant shop stewards. Not only did this encourage the undisciplined pursuit of competing sectional interests without regard for their wider, cumulative effects on the economy; it also meant that any commitment entered into by union leaders with government or employers could never be honoured.

This notion of the abuse of power was deployed to call into question the relationship between trade unions and government. The alleged ability of trade unions to influence and frequently frustrate government policy was seen as a challenge to the democratic process and a breach of the conditions of constitutionality under which unions had been integrated into British society (see for example, *The Times*, 12 July 1977, 15). During the late 1970s many of those who presented this account of crisis still believed that some form of accommodation between unions and the rest of society was possible through reforms to liberal collectivism. However, the ground had been prepared for a reassertion of liberal individualism which gathered pace during the early 1980s and marked its new ascendancy with the passage of increasingly restrictive trade union legislation and the disavowal of any notion of 'social partnership' between the state, capital and organised labour.

Acknowledgements

I would like to thank my colleague Professor Ian Beardwell for his helpful comments on an earlier version of this paper.

Endnotes

[1] These newspapers were chosen to compare how two 'newspapers of record' and a popular newspaper with a broadly pro-labour stance approached industrial relations issues. It was quickly apparent that although there were differences in tone, the way on which industrial relations issues were represented were very similar across all three newspapers.

Bibliography

Beynon, Huw (1973) *Working for Ford* Allen Lane, London.

Chalfont, Lord (1978) 'The Secret Saboteurs Bringing Britain to her Knees', *The Times*, 2 October.

Corinna, M. and Townsend, E. (1976) 'Still a Long Road to Peace at Leyland', *The Times*, 9 September.

Donovan, Lord (1969) *Report of the Royal Commission on Trade Unions and Employers' Associations 1965–68*, HMSO, London.

Edwardes, M. (1983) *Back from the Brink*, Collins, London.

Edwards, Paul, (1982) 'Britain's Changing Strike Problem?', *Industrial Relations Journal* 13, 2.

Fox, A. (1985) *History and Heritage. The Social Origins of the British Industrial Relations System*, Allen & Unwin, London.

Fraser, W. Hamish (1974) *Trade Unions and Society 1820–80. The Struggle for Acceptance*, Croom Helm, London.

Hartmann, P. (1976) *The Media and Industrial Relations*, Centre for Mass Communication Research, University of Leicester.

Hay, Colin (1996) 'Narrating Crisis: the Discursive Construction of the Winter of

Discontent', *Sociology*, 30, no 2, May.

Hodgkinson, N. (1976) 'Workers Say Grievances Are Real, Not Agitators' Invention', *The Times*, 16 September.

Hodgkinson, N. (1976a) 'Car Worker Defends 'One Out All Out' Policy', *The Times*, 18 September.

Hyman, R. (1989) *Strikes,* 4th ed., Macmillan, London.

Jackson, M. P. (1987) *Strikes, Industrial Conflict in Britain, USA and Australia*, Wheatsheaf, Brighton.

Johnson, Paul (1978) 'How Long Before the Unions are Saved from their Leaders?', *The Times,* 23 March, 16.

Jones, Tim (1976) 'Theory of Strikes as English Sickness Challenged by Survey', *The Times*, 2 December, 4.

Nichols, T. (1986) *The British Worker Question* 'Routledge and Kegan Paul', London.

Routledge, Paul (1979) 'The Challenge to Labour Over the Robinson Affair', *The Times*, 1 December, p.12.

Turner, H.A. (1969) *Is Britain Really Strike-Prone?*, Cambridge University Press, Cambridge.

Turner, H.A., Clack, G. and Roberts, G. (1967) *Labour Relations in the Motor Industry*, George Allen & Unwin, London.

Webb, Clifford (1976) 'Leyland Sees No Evidence of Plot by Militants to Force Strikes', *The Times,* 1 September.

Webb, Clifford (1979) 'Why Sir Michael Had to Bite the Bullet', *The Times,* 28 November.

16

Imagination and Passivity in Leisure: Coventry Car Workers and their Families from the 1920s to the 1970s

Paul Thompson

The rise of car factories in the twentieth century took place within a context in which the spheres of work and leisure were already clearly demarcated. It is important not to exaggerate this separation, particularly in the case of car workers. Indeed, as I have described elsewhere, one of the most remarkable developments of the mass assembly phase in car factories was of unofficial leisure activities on the shopfloor in defiance of management and as a celebration of lost work skills: 'playing at being skilled men' (Thompson, 1988). Nevertheless it is clear that a distinct sphere of leisure activities outside work had emerged, and the processes of its demarcation and the development of forms of 'rational recreation' from the late eighteenth to the late nineteenth centuries have been the subject of some particularly notable studies by social historians (Thompson, 1967; Malcomson, 1973; Lowerson & Myerscough, 1978). One of the key issues debated has been how far the more 'respectable' working-class culture which emerged was shaped by middle-class influences and desires for 'social control' remoulding popular leisure culture, or by an autonomous dynamic for self-improvement within the skilled working class (Crossick, 1978; Gray, 1976, 1981; More, 1980; Yeo, 1981).

The subsequent developments of leisure in the twentieth century are clearly equally important, for its sphere grew dramatically during the period. Average factory working hours fell from 55 in the first decade of the century to 40 or less, giving effectively an extra day and a half a week for potential leisure activity. At the same time real wages rose dramatically, opening up the possibility of new forms of leisure activity: car workers' wages in particular trebled between the 1930s and 1980s. This was the context of the rise of the mass media, mass tourism, and the booming of multiple aspects of the leisure industry. Indeed, by the late 1980s even Coventry itself was attempting to convert its image from a proud manufacturing city to a honey-pot for tourists. Moreover a very similar debate has emerged, at least politically, as on the question of nineteenth century leisure: how far has mass culture imposed itself on a passive working class, or is it a response to working-class values?

This question was especially a matter of debate in the New Left movement in the late 1950s, and subsequently among researchers at the Centre for Contemporary Cultural Studies at Birmingham. Surprisingly, they never used the ethnographic or life history interviews through which they could have observed and asked directly what leisure activities meant to ordinary men and women. Ruth Finnegan's notable recent study of Milton Keynes shows impressively how for example in music – although perhaps the most commercialised of all aspects of leisure – there is today an astonishing degree of popular participation and creativity (Finnegan, 1989).

Nor have social historians made a significant contribution to this debate. Indeed, they have left the whole topic of recent leisure astonishingly neglected. There are no satisfactory interpretative overviews at all; and most of what has been published focuses simply on sport.[1] The only study particularly concerned with Coventry, by Hideo Ichihashi, focusses overwhelmingly on the municipal and commercial provision for leisure, rather than what ordinary men and women made of their chances for leisure. The most illuminating new development has been the examination of gender differences in leisure, most notably in Andrew Davies' local portrait of Manchester and Salford working-class culture before 1939, which is also exceptional in that it does make good use of oral history interviews (Ichihashi, 1994; Davies, 1992; Abendstern, 1986; Stanley, 1987). In short, the historical study of twentieth-century leisure has scarcely begun.

My contribution here is based on an oral history study of car workers and their families in Coventry and Turin carried out in the 1980s. I want to start by giving some indication of the variety of leisure patterns that this evidence reveals, between different groups and over time. But the principal questions which I want to explore concern the meanings of leisure and the space it gave for imagination. And in doing so, I want to keep in mind two possible shaping forces. On the one hand, increasingly national, was the growth of the mass media and leisure industries; on the other, local and directly experienced, was the changing character of work in the factory. Twentieth-century car workers had not only more free time, but they and their families had more resources which could be given to it. If opportunities within the factory seemed to be narrowing, could compensation now be more readily found in leisure? How far did car workers seek in their free time to exercise neglected skills, to express their creativity?

A simple answer is of course impossible. Just because free time allows of more choice than work time, it is much harder to characterise. The variety of ways of spending time off is indeed, in itself, quite striking. The range and experience of leisure activities differs, moreover, in a number of crucial ways: by age, by gender, by temperament – individual and family; and over time.

Of all these divisions, perhaps the most resilient of all has been age. There are marked and persistent differences between the leisure activities of children, young adults, older adults and the elderly. I shall not comment on the largely hidden leisure world of the elderly (Thompson, Itzen & Abendstern, 1990). Children also had a play world of their own: traditional street games, exploring and camping in the countryside, collecting stamps or cigarette cards of footballers or motor cars. Most parents took very little interest in children's play, but there were a few striking exceptions, to which we shall return later.

Leisure patterns from the late teenage years until marriage were equally distinct, but by now much more sharply divided by gender too. Young men and women were likely to be more eager for company and also more physically active. Although no activities were exclusively theirs, it was above all they who filled the cinemas and dance halls. Much of their leisure, however, was already separate. Thus sport was overwhelmingly a male activity; although it was the younger men who tended to play and the older men to watch. And it was only teenage boys and young men who could be found 'always messing about with cars ... engines or anything else like that', or building a motor cycle for track riding in the garden shed: playing at their future world of work.[2]

Unmarried girls, by contrast, were more focused on social activities which could lead to courtship and marriage. At the same time most of them were much more strictly controlled by their parents than boys. Even a relatively free girl, who every Wednesday night 'used to have a bath and do me face and maybe go out with the girls ... hen party or something', had to be in on time.[3] And girls were expressly excluded from activities such as football, boxing and fighting, and like older women, were unable to drink in the pubs and clubs as freely as men.

After marriage, these differences became still sharper. Apart from family tennis, sport became exclusively an interest of their husbands; and so, almost always, was the garden or the allotment. Women scarcely figure in the more remarkably inventive activities we shall be describing, although it should be added that this must in part be a reflection of how they and others viewed their own leisure. Cooking was seen as housework, and dishes were made to be consumed, not kept for subsequent admiration. And their own exclusive minority pursuits – the church, or knitting and sewing – gave markedly less scope for individuals to shine. As June Freeman remarks of knitting, it is 'a common art', yet 'few art forms have as bad an image. At one time to knit was synonymous, for many, with being dull and dreary' (Freeman, 1986, 7; Parker, 1984).

The reason for this divergence in practice and attitude is simple: while for mothers, parenthood was seen as a primary social obligation, for men it was simply an option. For men a clear distinction remained between work and leisure, so that they still had time for enjoyment after work; for women, motherhood had no time limits. In addition women were likely to have less energy to spare on recreation because they were less well nourished than men, and less well provided with health care.

Certainly attitudes varied between families. There were always some couples who focussed their leisure time jointly on activities as a family. As a car worker married in 1933 put it, 'we've always wrapped ourselves round the family'. And another, married in 1972, said: 'I am a father and she is a mother: and our job is to bring up the kids, because we brought them into the world, and we want to be with them, and that's our greatest pleasure in life.'[4] But at the other end of the spectrum were many husbands who scarcely participated in family life, such as – to take an extreme case – the Standard track worker who was also a club drummer, so that he was out every night: 'I never see him,' his wife lamented, 'He used to come home for his meal and out playing at night ... I was always in bed fast asleep when he came home.'[5]

For married men, in short, family-centred leisure remained a choice. But for a mother it was a matter of duty, of social destiny. It was a destiny, however, which could be accepted in more than one spirit. One woman, who had been a pupil teacher before marriage, had five children to bring up with little help from her self-educating Standard engineer husband, and so only rarely was able to slip out from home to church. Yet as her daughter remembers, she looked for fulfilment precisely in motherhood: 'She was all for the home and the kids. Heart and soul in it.'[6] There were also a few wives who were lucky enough to have husbands who believed that women needed regular time off from domestic work, just as they did themselves from the factory. Thus one toolmaker and his wife went out on shifts: on Thursdays she went to the pictures or a show or a dance, after 'my two children was in bed, and he'd look after them. That was my night out because he had Saturday night and Sunday night and the rest of the nights'. They only went out together on Sundays.[7]

Couples who always went out together were exceptionally rare. Among the older men, one husband stands out as an exception: a Daimler foreman toolmaker who married in 1917 and, his wife recalled, 'never mixed', but instead, 'was my friend and he – wherever he went, I went. And wherever I went, he went'.[8] Rather more commonly, other men went out with their wives from time to time in a group of couples: 'we've always tried to go out, have a night out, always gone dancing, things like that'.[9] One car wirer married in

1966 was a part-time fireman and went out monthly by coach to a show or dance with the firemen: 'they organised the whole thing. And your wife would be given an orchid and a box of chocolates on the way in.' [10] This was, however, an exceptional thoughtfulness.

More often men took their own comparative freedom for granted. And especially among the youngest generation, there were at least some wives who became overtly discontented with their lot. One young wife of the 1970s told her rugger-playing, Sunday – fishing and club-man husband: 'You've gotta take me out … Even if you just take me to the pub and I had one drink, you've gotta get me out of this flat, it's driving me crackers.' [11]

These differences in attitudes to leisure, and also the extent, to which patterns were changing over time, can be well seen in the development of the annual family holiday from the 1920s onwards. The growing popularity of a stay away from home, in the country or more commonly at the sea, in itself reflected rising living standards. It did not become a majority pattern before the 1930s. Earlier on, 'holidays for some people round our way were absolutely unheard of; we never went, I never saw the sea: never saw the sea till I was 21.' [12] Even as late as the 1950s, if a semi-skilled car worker had several young children they might take no holidays away from home: 'we couldn't afford it.' [13] Similarly, it was the low wages paid to young workers, as well as the social taboo against courting couples sharing a room together, which explain why the seaside holiday – in contrast to the day outing – only became a typical leisure pattern of the young unmarried in the 1960s. Meanwhile rising family incomes had extended the pre-war week's holiday to the post-war fortnight. It became much rarer for the breadwinning father to be left behind at work, or for a cheap holiday in the country to be secured by staying free with rural relatives; the train journey to a seaside boarding house gave way to travel by family car to a camp or caravan site; and finally families began to buy their own caravans, and to lend them to their own kin.

Within these changing patterns, however, families could choose to spend their holidays in very different ways. In terms of arrangements, these ranged from the individual to the group package. Some went away on their own, some stayed with other relatives, and some went with groups of friends. Others by contrast went to organised holiday camps such as those run by the Standard for its workforce or the Coventry Co-operative Society, or to straightforward commercial camps like Holimarine. [14] Similarly, there was a great variety in how time was spent. Some remember holidays as active times of walking or swimming; while for others, relaxation itself, the joy of time off, was the greatest pleasure in getting away from the factory. Thus a Standard bodyshop worker described his typical day by the sea in Cornwall:

I'd go down the seafront, two deck chairs, morning paper, and I'd sit there, and after a bit I'd go and have a dip, come out, pick me pen up and a list of paper and pick me horses what I'm going to back. Then when it'd get a bit hotter I used to go and have another dip, back, have a dry off, slip me trousers on, go down the town, the centre, put me bet on, come back, and get in the deck chair, all morning and all afternoon. And I used to play games on the sand or just sit in the deck chair. And then at night, we'd go for a good walk.[15]

Yet again, choice turns out to have been much more of a man's privilege. This man was not childless; but he could safely leave that responsibility, as normally, to his wife in the other deck chair. In this sense holidays meant little change for most women; and in addition, very many wives continued also to be responsible for feeding their families.

Even on boarding house holidays the wife might supply the ingredients for the landlady: 'you took your own food in and they cooked it for you.' [16] Once families began to rent their own accommodation or go camping, the tasks became increasingly demanding: 'women were still doing the housework and cooking ... It was just a different environment, that was all.' [17] A Standard engineer's daughter remembers her mother would: 'take a beach hut and cook the meals, cook, feed us at the beach hut and we used to go back to the rooms and sleep at night. But it was all planned like an African expedition.' [18] Thus the rise of the family holiday, while offering extra freedom to men and to children could be for some women more like overtime work. One can well understand the car factory driver's wife whose boy remembers their camping holidays as: 'quite enjoyable for me, but me mother used to suffer in silence.' [19]

If we shift the focus for a moment to changes over time, the family seaside holiday was clearly one of the most notable reflections of the rising resources in working-class households which provided one of the principal dynamics of change. The differences between the oldest generation and those who followed are equally striking in terms of leisure at home. Andrew Davies has shown how in the poorer districts of Manchester and Salford older forms of outdoor leisure – such as walking in the park, the monkey parade' of eyeing teenage girls and boys, or street football and gambling – survived as the typical activities partly because poverty restricted participation in the new commercialised leisure: 'you has to pay to go to the cinema, or to watch professional football.'[20] And no doubt the continuing high use of city parks even today is encouraged by free entry.[21] But in more prosperous Coventry such older forms of leisure would only seem typical for some of the older generation, for whom as late as the 1920s free time might remain quite elementary. A turner's son remembers how: 'in the summer you could see them all sitting out in the street, the families, on the steps, and the kids used to play tip-tap in the street ... The women used to be sitting out on the steps, they'd have a chat with one another – course they was all close together.'[22] For this generation, even a day excursion by rail was a luxury: 'very few out of any street saw the sea', as a Daimler foreman's son put it.[23] Some of the most common free time activities were to help meet basic family needs: men grew vegetables in the garden or allotment, women sewed and knitted. Both pursuits have become much less widespread as families have gained more ready money.

Nevertheless, the transformation of this earlier world is only partly due to rising incomes; equally important has been the impact of technological innovation. Appropriately, one primary force has been the spread of motor transport. Up until the 1950s most families walked, and some cycled; only a very few had cars, and a number of young men were buying motor bikes. But within a decade the family car was becoming a normal expectation. Nationally, as late as 1945 fewer than 3 per cent of people owned a car, but within twenty years half of all households had them, and Coventry itself was noted for its 'very high' car ownership. (Bédarida, 1990, 256; Ichihashi, 1994, 439) It ousted the children's games from their space in the street, and it made walking or cycling for adults a deliberate leisure choice rather than a necessity.

The second transforming influence has come with the rise of the mass media. Theatre and music hall were already rapidly giving way in the 1920s to the cinema, which was in its heyday from the 1930s until the 1950s, with nationally half the adult population attending weekly: appealing to both men and women, and far more than mass spectator sport ever attracted.[24] Within some homes the radio or gramophone record player had already arrived to provide a more professional entertainment than the weekend family sing-song around the piano. But again, the crucial change came only in the 1950s, with the advent of television. Under a thousand Coventry working-class homes had television sets in 1950; by the 1960s they were almost everywhere, more essential furniture to the living room than the piano had ever been to the parlour.[25]

The impact of television was undoubtedly dramatic. 'Course I mean most people used to go out six and seven nights a week,' one club treasurer recalled, 'now only go out two nights at the most. And the rest of the nights – first thing in the morning, "Where's the paper?" or "What's on? Is Dallas on? Is Coronation Street on?" That's the only thing they can talk about nowadays.'[26] Inevitably some older forms of leisure were squeezed aside: particularly family parlour games, cards and music making. 'We had used to have a piano, and the children they've all learned to play it, but then with all the radio and television, that dies off. We did get rid of it eventually.'[27] For a time, indeed, even the pubs seemed to be emptying. The mass audience of the cinema crumbled the palatial Odeons and Plazas closing for conversion into warehouses or, sometimes, bingo halls continuing to provide an outing for some older women. Inside many homes television became the focus of sociability: one family lived mostly in the room 'there the television was'; while in another home, 'it was always on at mealtimes, and still is'. [28] In another instance where, 'most of their spare time was spent watching television, to be honest,' as a Humber driver's son recalled, 'my dad used to sit with his feet up on the mantelpiece, literally, watching the television. Actually managed to wear through it.' [29]

It would nevertheless be misleading to see television as a simple determining force. It did not come free, so that for a long time some did not have it at all, while for many getting television meant not only a deliberate choice, but also sacrifice. A gearcutter's children had their first family holiday in 1951, so it was a hard decision when a year later: 'we were given the choice of a television or a holiday and we chose a television, as a family.' [30] It is also important that once bought, in some families television was switched on only selectively, or in others, although used more automatically, 'not always watched when it's on'. [31] As one Standard trackworker's wife put it: 'I've never been one to sit and solidly watch, I keep jumping up and moving around and fidgeting and doing things.' [32] To a greater or lesser extent both the ownership and use of television thus remained a matter of choice.

The exercise of this choice can also be seen as partly reflecting individual differences in temperament and personality. Some liked to use their free time actively, others to relax passively. There were men, as we shall see, who sought to exercise in leisure the same kind of skills as they had learnt for working in the car factory. At the other extreme, others wanted the very reverse of their factory experience: the open air, quiet, and nature. They found it most often in their allotments and gardens, or on summer walks. One Standard engineer would sit for hours, 'fishing, angling, canal fishing'. [33] A Courtauld spinner found:

> his relaxation was going out in the country. He was a man who used to love to cycle out in the country ... In his early working life when he came off the six o'clock shift in the summer, instead of cycling home he used to cycle out into the countryside to get some fresh air ... Six o'clock in the morning, there's a special time of the day. [34]

Similar contrasts also influenced patterns of sociability, although in this respect they are better understood in terms of contrasting styles of family households and networks. Although Davies has also referred to this, the importance of family cultures in leisure, and also the intergenerational transmission of such patterns, have not been explored and would provide a rewarding field for research. [35] Here we can only hint at this possibility through the instance of one Coventry family which combined and recognised two highly contrasted family traditions. On one side the father was an extremely hardworking self-employed electrician, whose 'only hobby' was to dress up in a smart uniform and play the cornet or flute in the Coventry Silver Band. He had no wish for either leisure or visitors at home: 'my dad would never have company'. So his son gravitated to the house of his father's younger brothers and sisters, where the atmosphere was entirely different: 'I almost lived over Craven Street ... There was more life over there.' Apart from the two young aunts, company was drawn by a billiard table and the playing skills of one uncle – later a successful publican – who was 'a champion, he'd got no end of cups': so 'there was always a lot going on'. The Craven Street home and his parental household were in social contact: but only just. Once a year, at Christmas, the pattern was reversed, and the uncles and aunts were invited back to his father's house. It was the only day of the year in which the parlour fire was lit. The visiting relatives would sit there playing cards. But as the clock struck ten at night, his father would disappear upstairs, and come down laden with coats. 'That was the signal for them to go home. And they obediently used to get up, put a coat on and vanish. That's how it was. Once a year we had company.'[36]

Over time, some things remain strikingly persistent; and again, we can sometimes see deliberate choice as a part of this. Some leisure activities were extensively practised in everyday working-class culture throughout the century. Among every generation, the most frequently mentioned of all leisure activities is going out for a drink to a club or a city or country pub; and after that, football, dancing and visiting relations. But there are also continuing small minorities who chose to be different, such as the 'great readers', and self-educators like the Standard engineer who learnt Esperanto and: 'used to correspond with people all over the world about stamp-collecting – regrettably, leaving the burden of the house to his better-educated wife.'[37] Such self-education was an old Coventry tradition, going back to Victorian artisans like the weaver, geologist and autobiographer Joseph Gutteridge who would discuss natural science with fellow free thinkers at the Coventry Mutual Improvement Class (Gutteridge, 1893). And it is a tradition which remains much the same today, with the one important difference that it has broadened to include as many women as men.[38]

Rather than looking a leisure principally in terms of change over time, or gender, or differences between age groups, however, our focus here will be on the meanings in different types of activity and the kinds of pleasure and self-expressiveness which car workers and their families could find in each of them. We shall look at them in four main groups. The first is forms of leisure closely related to the body; the second, to the natural world; the third, to human sociability; and the last, to personal creative skills.

First there are those activities which relate, more or less directly, to men and women's own bodies: most notably, sport, fighting, sexuality and dancing. These are in no way special to car workers and their families: on the contrary, they are to be found in almost every known human culture. In twentieth-century Coventry they were above all young people's activities, and at least in the case of sport and fighting, young men's.

Young men played especially football, but also cricket and tennis, and they swam and boxed. Young women could also play tennis or swim, but otherwise were only accepted as spectators. As one Standard car worker's daughter put it, 'We took a certain interest in sport, you know at one time we used to support the works football team.'[39] Young husbands might play on at first, but for most sport became sooner or later a passive social occasion, as for the toolmaker, a cricket umpire and football fan, who to watch a match: 'always put on his Sunday best: he always changed into his Sunday shirt on a Saturday afternoon.'[40] The two sports followed by older rather than younger men, bowls and watching horse races, demanded notably less physical energy. Fighting was still more markedly restricted to younger men: and so much so that in retrospect it is only rarely mentioned spontaneously,[41] although rough, if not dangerous encounters were undoubtedly a longstanding aspect of the city's youth gang culture.

The memories we have are also reticent in pointing to the kinds of fulfilment found in these activities; although one can assume that not only the physical bodily exercise, but also the dance-like expressiveness in moving through space, and the rough physical contact between men and men, were fundamentally important. Less surprisingly, reticence also deeply obscures memories of sexuality.

Here, however, the pattern of memory itself changes over time, pointing to some of the meanings behind these silences. In the earlier interviews, sexual expressiveness is explicitly mentioned only in denial. Courting, dancing and promenading began only in late teenage years. A car worker's daughter who – in the late 1940s – had her first boyfriend at 18 thought of herself as typical: 'we went out in perhaps a group of girls, but we all went out and came home together – there was no question of anybody picking anybody up and going off with them – and we went out, perhaps four of us ... in groups then.'[42] Another woman met her future husband dancing, but she says that 'my friend and I were just going to the dances, and we weren't bothering with fellas at all.'[43] Men too can remember being equally inhibited. A car fitter's son, who felt himself 'tongue-tied as far as girls were concerned – I was absolutely tongue-tied', hid himself away: 'I did quite a lot down at the chapel, and the Young Men's Bible Class as we got older ... That's why the first girl I fell in love with, I was too shy, and didn't have a chance. I write to her even now...'[44]

253

There are some others among the older generation who do recall the pleasures of sexual attraction at dances, or of promenading up and down the street on the monkey parade or, as it was more often called in Coventry, the 'unny run': as one woman put it: 'If you fancied them you'd turn round and look, and if you didn't, just walked past with your nose in the air.'[45] But she had to be back home by ten: and such memories invariably touched on social constraints too. The control of teenage daughters by fathers could be not only severe, but directly intrusive too. A Daimler assembly worker's daughter who was a keen dancer remembers how her parents – at a time when contraception was hard to ensure – were always 'frightened you'd bring trouble home', insisting she was home by ten and not allowing her to bring a boy home until she was over twenty. More than this: 'my dad often used to come looking for me ... As I say, my friend, when her dad used to whistle, we'd all run – half past nine.'[46] But this was only an extreme aspect of a much more generalised self-restraint. As one Standard apprentice put it: 'Let's be fair, if you could get a girl – to take her home – and you were doing well, you spent a month dancing with her and you were allowed to take her home. And you spent another month and you might kiss 'em goodnight. I mean there was none of this ...'[47]

With the youngest generation, however, there are clear signs of a major shift in attitudes to sexuality. A very different kind of memory begins to appear among some at least of those who were young adults from the 1960s onwards. It is of pleasure in physical sexuality for its own sake. A Jaguar trimmer recalls holidaying with his fiancée as centred on bed: 'a really good night, get up about dinner time to go down to the beach, get ready for the night. What more do you do on holiday when you're single?'[48] An apprentice electrician was predatory, and proud of it: 'I love girls ... that was one of my main interests in life ... I can't think when I had my first piece of tail but – well I can, but I'm not telling you. When I first started taking a positive interest as a hobby, I suppose, I'd be 16.'[49]

Not surprisingly, this explicit sexuality is more often a male form of memory. But it is also found among women. A bricklayer's daughter who 'ran away to get married' at 17, described how for the two years before: 'I was having regular sex with him then, and I'd probably been having sex since I was 14.' She had met her future husband at a church youth club and 'fell in love with him at first sight':

> He never looked at me, and I was really upset; and he was different, he was from Scotland, so I quite fancied him, he'd got a lovely body; so the next week, I decided 'I'm gonna get this man' ... And I got on the shortest skirt I could find, and it had a really low neckline, and it was

short anyway, but I chopped it even shorter: and anyway, he noticed me that week. So – so we started going out together.

She had to explain away to her mother the grass on her coat from the railway embankment.[50]

Dressing up was an expressive skill closely linked to courting. Sally Alexander has remarked on how for a young London woman between the wars dressing up was a key step in becoming an independent adult, and the excitement, even 'bliss', that it brought in itself (Alexander, 1989). One young woman described the pleasure of coming home from town on a Saturday afternoon: 'go in home and have a bit of tea, and then put a few rollers in your hair, curlers in your hair – those dinky curlers in those days – put your dinkies in your hair – wash your hair, put a few dinkies in it, tie a scarf on it, walk all the way to the GEC to the dance, and dance all night...'[51] In a more ironical fashion, a group of young married couples who went to escape family life in Blackpool: 'took some wigs and funny hats, and called ourselves the Mad Hatters ... We were running riot at that hotel and it was the best weekend we'd had for ages.'[52]

Traditionally, dressing was linked to the exercise of female craft skills, but surprisingly, apart from one or two women who became hairdressers, these are rarely mentioned. This is particularly striking since contemporary evidence shows that knitting and sewing were widespread activities among Coventry's women factory workers.[53] Remarkably few seem to have practised dressmaking or altering clothes for themselves. It appears that already both young women and men preferred to buy ready-made clothes. It is also noticeable that it is the men rather than the women, even in the older generations, who especially recall dressing in original and imaginative ways. 'I started clothing myself, I went in for plus fours, and Oxford bags and blazer', a rugger-playing Standard bodymaker of the 1920s remembered, 'because I'd got to keep up with the lads in the team.'[54] Again the pace quickened in the 1960s: 'I was a teddy boy,' recalled a Rootes track worker, 'velvet collars and cuffs'; an apprentice 'had my woollen mohair suit and dark blue and everything and starched collar and gold cuff links,' and so on.[55] Clothes undoubtedly provided, at least for these brief years of young adulthood, an important form of creative self-expression.

Dancing was another: for the interwar generation especially, it was almost unique as a socially accepted form of sexual play, moving to music in close physical contact, men and women, but also women and women. Women especially remember dancing. Some were so enthusiastic that they were out 'dancing every night, six nights a week'.[56] Others went on marathon dancing outings to Blackpool: 'you would leave home at four o'clock by train and for 3/9d you'd go on the train, you'd see the illuminations and you'd go in the

255

dance hall at eight o'clock till twelve, then you'd travel back, get back about five o'clock in the morning and go to work at eight o'clock'.[57] The setting was undoubtedly part of the fun. The popular GEC dances, for instance, were held in a: 'beautiful ball room, all red plush chairs all around, red velvet chairs all round the outside, and gilt pillars in between, a fountain in the centre, and spring boards, a beautiful place.'[58]

A few keen couples went on dancing after marriage, in some cases semi-professionally. One car worker's daughter remembers how her mother made dancing dresses while her father organised dances: 'used to have bills what he's put in shop windows ... We were in the dancing world, he was a dancer, and taught dancing.'[59] Others danced just for fun, into old age: so much so that a Coventry Museum tea dance revival in 1984 proved immensely popular, drawing coachloads to the special silver, pale green and pink ballroom crowded with white-haired couples, moving gracefully to the elderly jazz trio.

The music was of course equally essential: 'a good band' made the night out.[60] Typically the bands were local and their players almost all men. They grew out of a much more diffused enjoyment of music in working class family homes. By the 1930s some young people were using records for entertainment, like the Morris machinist who would: 'buy a record out of Woolworth's 6d each, go home to my mates, put it on his record player – and I had a record player; we used to have a real good time.'[61] But the piano remained an important piece of furniture for most families. In some it was purely decorative: 'Nobody played it, no, no. It was an ornament and it was polished every week ... It used to have brass candlestick holders on the side, yes.'[62] But much more typically, the piano was regularly used for sing-songs at family occasions, and in many homes, every weekend. Some families had several musicians, like the coachbuilder and his son who played violins with a cousin at the piano: 'that was your Sunday, listening to their violins, and singing'. (Interestingly they had acquired a radio set, 'but it didn't rule the family'.)[63] Bands too were part of a long tradition. Joseph Gutteridge remembered in the Coventry of the 1830s not only family music as 'among the happiest experiences of my youth', but also strolling street bands, glee parties and regimental bands (Gutteridge, 1893, 88)'. By the interwar years there were also works bands. Cornet-playing in the Coventry Silver Band was the sole recreation of one father of the 1920s; while a Ferguson setter of the 1950s was so addicted to pipe bands that he and his whole family 'used to follow them in a works coach'.[64]

The dance bands which flourished in Coventry from the 1920s until the 1950s were thus simply the liveliest manifestation of a much wider working-class musical culture which in this period provided important opportunities for creative self-expression. We hear in our own interviews of band-playing enthusiasts 'mad keen on jazz', and percussionist husbands and pianist brothers who played nightly in regular dance bands, some, it should be added, to the dismay of their abandoned wives.[65] But the seething enthusiasm of these Coventry musicians is still more vividly recalled in *Dance Band Days*, a collection of memories specially published for the museum's revival exhibition. Syd Howe, for instance, as an 18-year-old in the mid-1920s was working at Morris Motors:

> It was all shift work there, and after finishing night shift at 6 a.m. would make my way to the Cafe just above the factory where there was a very nice piano and my workmates often got me playing. One Saturday one of them asked if I played anywhere. When I said 'No' he became very interested and asked me if we could get together as his uncle was to open a new hotel in Coventry.

This was the beginning of 'Reg Adams and his Band'. Syd's 14-year-old brother became its drummer with 'expert tuition from my father who played Cornet, Tenor Horn and later the Drums. Dad played in several brass bands' – both works bands and military bands. Les Thompson explains how his grandfather played the cornet for the Coventry Silver Band and both of his parents were cathedral choristers, 'so it was only natural that music and singing was a feature in our home.' He himself combined car factory work and band playing for more than twenty years.

> About 1932, when I was about 17 and working at the Daimler, I was persuaded by my friends (who played instruments) to buy an alto-saxophone from Harry Cranes in Gosford Street for £5. This was quite extraordinary as I always thought I would play drums or trumpet. Anyway for 7/6d a month I had this instrument so I set about teaching myself to play and read music. After a few months my friends, who played together in a small band, asked me if I would do a gig for them

They formed the Hollywood Band together. 'Most small bands organised their own dances by hiring the Assembly Room of a club or pub, putting an ad in the "Telegraph" and charging 6d for admission.' The more successful would progress to private functions in the bigger halls like the Corn Exchange or the Drill Hall, and half-a-dozen became permanent at regular dance halls like the Gaiety or the Coliseum. Some, like the Synco-Scamps of the 1920s, had started as jazz groups, but typically soon moved towards mainstream dance 'sweet music'. Les played for the Standard Dance Orchestra during the war, when American forces, dance bands were an important new influence *(Dance Band Days*, 1984).

257

By the 1950s jazz was again back in fashion, but the older large bands found themselves outmoded. They petered out quickly: by the 1960s only one big band still had its own hall. Certainly dancing remained as popular as ever among Coventry youth. But the old bands were much less often replaced by new local groups. The music scene had become much more national, professional and competitive. Enthusiasts probably continued to be as active as ever, not only continuing to play jazz, but responding to new musical fashions such as folk, country, rock and pop; but amateur bands less often held the stage at the big venues and main occasions.[66] Still more important, at the same time – and equally a reflection of the new power of the mass media and the entertainments industry – weekend family music around the piano had been supplanted by the television. Coventry's long-flourishing working class musical culture was thus undoubtedly shrinking at its base; and with it, one of the most expressive of all the forms of car workers' leisure. A second major group of leisure activities relate to the natural world: gardening, allotments, walks and outings to the countryside. Unlike the first group, these are not culturally universal, but characteristic of urban populations: but again, in no general way specific to car workers.

Up until the 1950s gardening and allotments were for married men second in popularity only to the pub or club.[67] Wives scarcely ever participated;[68] indeed one may suspect that for many men the attractions of the garden, the garden shed, or the more distant allotment, included not only the intrinsic pleasures of working the soil and growing plants, but also a refuge from the family home. A refuge with a perfect moral justification: for men mostly grew vegetables rather than flowers, and were therefore, as good husbands, providing for their families in leisure as in work.

For some car workers too, the spirit in which they gardened could be close to that of worktime, like the coachbuilder whose daughter recalls: 'You never saw any dirt on my dad's tools. They were always clean ...even to his lawnmower, his spade and fork ... He'd always wipe them down with an oily rag when he'd finished with them.'[69] And for most men gardening, especially on the allotment, was part of a male culture of gifts, discussion and competition. Some growers were keen competitors in vegetable and also flower shows. One Standard bodymaker, a keen clubman, did 'a lot of horticultural judging', and was an officer of the Coventry Chrysanthemum Society. He himself was another fanatical enthusiast somewhat at his family's expense, growing chrysanthemums in a garden greenhouse. 'Growing would take every spare minute you had and couldn't go on holidays.' His wife had to come back from her work to water the plants during the day and he would: 'put muslin over the top to stop any condensation, the water, instead of dropping on the flower would drop onto the muslin.' As the great nine-inch blooms matured in the autumn, the whole household would succumb to stage nerves, above all from fear of fog: 'I've said to the wife, "Well I'm frightened tonight, I'm going to have to fetch them in." So we've rolled the carpet up in the house here and I've had a hundred pots and I've had the flowers touching the ceiling. And kept ready for doing the show.' [70]

Gardening still remains – in a more modest way – a minority enthusiasm. It is now less widespread among men, partly because rising incomes have made vegetable-growing seem much less useful. But on the other hand, as the vegetable plot has given way to the flower garden, their wives more often play an active part.

Outings into the surrounding countryside had long been popular among Coventry families and also youth. Joseph Gutteridge wrote of his delight in the Lammas lands and commons which still encircled Coventry in the 1830s and: 'prior to their enclosure, were to me in my youth a veritable paradise. I would roam over them without let or hindrance, and my earliest feelings of pleasure in wild flowers, insects, and birds were acquired upon these wastes' (Gutteridge, 1893, 84). A hundred years on, although most of the commons had disappeared under housing, walking remained as popular a family pastime as music: typically Sunday afternoon walks 'by the canal or through the fields'. [71] A ribbon-weaver's daughter remembers how 'if he took us for a walk he used to be able to point out all the different wild flowers, and he made things with the grasses, so I've got happy memories of him.' [72]

For older boys and girls the relatively open access to the countryside (as compared with the present) provided an important safety valve for expressing teenage independence from their parents. They would often go off on their own, exploring the woods, swimming in the streams: 'we walked for miles and miles and miles; 'everywhere it was lovely countryside.' [73] One remembers holidays when a boy for the:

> long walks in the woods surrounding Coventry. We'd probably go out in the morning, perhaps four or five of us, and spend the entire day walking and roaming as we lived off the countryside. We ate, whether they were the blackberries or whether they were the hedgenuts, all the herbs of the hedgerows – we knew which we could eat and which we couldn't eat. [74]

And although walking became a less common pastime from the 1950s, there were still married couples who 'used to go for country walks, used to push the pram for miles on Sunday', and parties of teenagers who went to the woods at Coombe Abbey in the 1970s, swimming, cooking baked beans and potatoes and camping out: 'we stopped that night in the woods.' [75]

Nationally, popular access to the countryside has been transformed in the last hundred years by the advent of first the bicycle from the 1890s and then the cheap motor car from the 1930s. Coventry was a principal manufacturing for both of these successive innovations, so that it might be expected that its prosperous working class would be notably early in exploiting these new means for leisure transport. This does not appear to have been so. At least until the 1950s, the majority of car workers' families explored the countryside on foot. A much smaller number also ventured out of the city by bicycle: families, informal groups of young people, and also a very few in clubs, sometimes attached to the factory: 'he was a big cyclist, and he'd got his cycling club going for the Morris.'[76] Nobody, however, mentioned that in Coventry 'getting a "big" bike' was 'a rite of passage, ... a sign of arrival at real adolescence', as Richard Hoggart recalls it in his own inner city Leeds neighbourhood in the 1930s (Hoggart, 1957). Some others bought motorbikes: 'we used to go all over on that.'[77] It is worth noting too, since the city also manufactured aeroplanes, that one husband belonged to the Coventry Gliding Club, and would spend the weekend camping in an old caravan with his menfriends: 'they were out on the field all day, for one short trip on the glider they all had to work and pull their weight with the winch launch and fetching the gliders in and keeping the time sheets. It was a day in the fresh air.'[78]

The crucial change, however, came only with the family car: and it came surprisingly late, in most families only from the 1950s onwards. There were a minority of families who bought cars in the 1930s, 'a first little Morris', usually specifically with family holidays and outings in mind: 'for the lad mostly.'[79] In this spirit a printer's family bought a car, but 'the only time it was ever used was when we went out on a Sunday. He didn't use it to go to work or anything like that, he used to use a pushbike' (and his son in turn became a keen cyclist too).[80] But such car-owning families seem to have been less than one in five at this time.[81] One car worker's son remembers how even in the 1950s, when his father bought an antiquated Minx: 'I think we were about the only family with a car in the actual road.'[82]

Once adopted, however, the car greatly increased the range of choice for family outings, in parallel with the typical post-war works outing. As the *Coventry Evening Telegraph* commented in 1950, 'the older generation whose idea of a works outing was a trip by wagonette to some rural venue a few miles outside the city, may well regard with incredulity the notion of a works outing by plane to the Continent.'[83] But in practice the objective to the day outing remained little changed, retaining its rural image: to a Cotswold village, 'parks, historic houses ... fruitpicking on the farms', for a picnic in the open air, or to a country pub with a garden – sometimes a group of neighbouring families going out 'boozing' together in a fleet of half a dozen cars.[84] But if the objective remained the same, the new means transformed the experience. The outing was no longer a day out wandering in the open air, but a passive pleasure wrapped in a metal box. As a Jaguar rectifier's wife put it, 'I like driving, just looking at the countryside, but the kids get bored with that, so they don't always like to come'; while a Talbot inspector had given up in despair: 'when we go out for the day there's such a lot of tension before we go, the wife gets uptight and I feel absolutely exhausted before we even leave the house – and I don't enjoy it that much.'[85] The car brought the countryside closer, but proved a barrier to it too.

The third form of leisure activity was sociability: visiting kin, or relaxing with mates and neighbours. Again, there is little, which can be specifically linked to work in car factories, although the forms which it took were influenced both by the city's rapid growth through immigration and the high wages its workers enjoyed. Because so many Coventry families had migrated into the city, a high proportion only saw kin at Christmas or holidays. Even some of those who had kin in the city were not in regular contact.[86] For others, however, the typical family Sunday walk might be to see a grandparent in another part of the city; and there were a small minority of old Coventry families with so many relatives living close by that they formed a social world in themselves. One engineer's wife had her mother-in-law, grandfather, mother and two aunts 'all within three streets; ... we were always visiting our family'; and a Rootes machinist and his family regularly went on holiday camping or caravanning with his two brothers and their children, while during the year: 'every afternoon, there's four of us play cards ... We're a close-knit family, still.'[87]

These were exceptions. Coventry working-class sociability centred above all on the pub and the club rather than the home. There were certainly some memories of notably welcoming homes and also, much more rarely, a group of young couples with children who helped each other with childcare might also, in the evenings: 'be in each other's houses, listening to music and drinking coffee.'[88] But these were unusual: in general, as indeed also among the 'affluent workers' of Luton, visiting friends at home was not common (Goldthorpe et al, 1969).

The rarity of home-based sociability created more of a difficulty for women than for men. Some women went with friends to places where married women could meet: especially church societies, or to the cinema with a friend, and also to the Co-operative Women's Guild, or to whist drives – 'they had one at the GEC social club and it'll be perhaps a hundred tables, well that's 400 people' – and the bingo which succeeded them.[89] In its heyday the cinema became particularly important: Leo Kuper found that in Canley in the early 1950s half the women went weekly. 'Going to a show is an occasion for active neighbouring; it expresses an established relationship, and also provides the opportunity for greater intimacy' (Kuper, 1953, 153). But its heyday lasted little more than twenty years, and its passing left a gap.

Both pub and club were dominated by men, who used them more regularly, and often just with men. A young man would typically go drinking with 'two or three lads from Morris' and this pattern might continue after marriage: 'he'd get blind drunk'; 'he was a man's man'. [90] Nevertheless, going out for a drink was also the most remembered leisure activity of Coventry wives. Some again went alone: a lathe turner's son recalled that: 'you'd always know when me mother was in [the pub] because the cat and dog would be outside. They'd follow her up and they'd sit there till she came out'. [91] Some pubs had special sections for women, like the Ring of Bells: 'the passage, long passage, probably be a dozen old women in there, no men, and the men used to sit in the smoke room ... Oh yes, yes, she knew everybody up there ... – did like half a pint.' [92] More typically, a wife would come down later to join a husband who had gone out earlier in the evening to the pub, to enjoy a 'game of dominoes and old-time chat.. In those days their enjoyment was around the pub with a good sing-song.' [93] The Daimler foreman toolmaker whose wife maintained, 'wherever he went, I went; and whenever I went, he went,' so that they were always at the pub together, was altogether unusual. [94]

For married couples the pattern of using the working men's clubs was similar. A Triumph fitter's son recalled how 'e was a member of the Radford Social Club, and they would go and he liked to drink, my father would like to drink his couple of pints, two or three pints, and I think my mother liked the Guinness, and they would go down join in and meet their friends, down at the Radford club.' [95] An Alvis millwright would :

> get washed, shaved, Sunday morning, go up to the Club, have a couple of drinks, come back, have a sleep in the afternoon, get up and have tea, and then they'd both go out ... They would sit in a group of people, the wives would sit together, and the husbands would sit round the table, and each one would shove off wherever he wanted to go – the darts, cards, dominoes, snooker[96]

The Coventry clubs did, however, directly reflect the financial resources of the car-working families which supported them, and hence undoubtedly had advantages over the city's pubs. They offered a wider range of activities, and, as Leo Kuper was told in the 1950s:

> the atmosphere is jollier; you pass the time of day, even if you don't know the people. The sociability is different. Even if you go into a strange club people will speak to you: it's not like that in a pub ... You're assured of decent company, no rowdiness ... You've got a

committee and you can demand things; at a pub, all depends on the manager. (Kuper 1953, 123)

And already by this stage, in contrast to the pubs from which children were strictly excluded by law, clubs provided for children as well as for wives, organising concerts and outings and setting aside at least some rooms where they could play, providing that they did not disturb the adult members. Ruth Cherrington, daughter of a Canley carworker, has written of her childhood in the 1960s that she: 'can always remember the Club, just as easily as I can remember my own home, because it has been such a close part of the lives of my family ... The Canley Club has been a family institution right from the start.' And it remains so today (Cherrington, nd, 2, 5).

The final group of leisure activities is much more unusual. Even with them, only a few are specifically connected with car factory work. Nevertheless, in relation to the imaginative and creative potential of leisure they are especially significant. These are a group of home-based activities, in which men – and only men feature in these memories – developed special craft skills in their free time. Sometimes they directly reflected work skills and attitudes. More generally, it seems likely that they were providing outlets for skills and creativity in making and producing things, which for most could no longer be fulfilled in mass production factory work.

Some of these activities overlap with those connected with the natural world. Our chrysanthemum-grower belongs here too, along with dog and pigeon-breeders. One market stallholder and his son were keen pigeon racers. 'As soon as me dad got the ring off the pigeon's foot me brother would go like the clappers down the post office, open the door and shout, "Time please," and he'd give her the ring and she'd stamp it with the official stamp, and he'd take it back to me dad.'[97] A hard-drinking Daimler tinsmith's family were dog racing enthusiasts: 'all gamblers, the lot of us ... We even bred our own greyhounds, had them racing twice a week ... We used to dye them, oh we was up to all tricks ... They know a good dog, you see, so you had to try to disguise them. We used to have tins of blacking and black, brown ... Oh, they were all at it.'[98] Animal sports of this kind – including earlier, cock-baiting – were a long-standing Midland's popular tradition.

Another group of men turned their hands to home improvement. Certainly for some this was a very direct reflection of work skills. A toolmaker, 'one of the finest toolmakers in the Midlands', his wife recalled, made candlesticks and picture frames for the parlour: 'he made all these.'[99] Another toolmaker 'put all the radiators in, put the central heating in, put a new bathroom suite, made those gates and those railings, built that veranda, built the garage.'[100] One mechanic took up repairing radios as a hobby, another clock-repairing. In the same spirit an Armstrong–Siddeley coachbuilder was a cabinet-maker at home, making furniture in his shed – bookcases, a table, a coal scuttle – 'and it was a super coal scuttle ... it was bent like that, it's shaped and he put chrome handles on and – it lifted up, ever so nice – a lovely piece of furniture.' He also built a garage, and 'the veranda at the back, I built all that'. [101] A bodyshop man 'put all new windows in this house, and you can clean them from inside or out, without going outside, they're all pivoted.' [102] And another coachbuilder 'came out with his woodcrafts again' in transforming a bought billiard table with extra mahogany pieces, 'he covered the table and polished it all, so it was like a great big table, and we used to have visitors and all his mates used to come.' [103]

Some men of this disposition, especially after 1945, as indeed increasingly nationally, renovated and improved entire houses: 'I did all that myself,' a gearcutter married in 1976 explained, 'we lived in one room for over 18 months.' [104] For women this could be an uncomfortable experience: 'one of the complaints that my first wife had was that it was like living on a building site, because nothing was ever finished.' [105] But for men, as their lasting pride in their work makes clear, it could be a deeply satisfying exercise of their skills – and even exhilarating. One Daimler engineer, married in 1922, obtained the upper floor of a house for his wife and child, until then living with her parents. 'It'd been knocked about as well inside and wanted a lot of work doing, but I wasn't worried about that. And I took it straight away ... With a mate we must've put a hundred hours in on this house, putting it straight.' They rebuilt the fireplace, scraped the walls, and distempered right through:

> Well the mate I'd got working with me, we used to go at night, and weekends ... My mate was really chuffed – he wanted to have a go at this stippling. Well your base'd be cream as a rule ... and you'd get a little try of paint of different colour and you'd dip the sponge in and you'd dab it round and you'd get a nice design. Well over the mantelpiece that's there, he used to put his practice designs on there – it was Joseph's coat over the bloody mantelpiece, there were all the colours of the rainbow. [106]

Far fewer, but from our point of view of special significance, are those men who used their free time to realise the dream of the factory itself in the transport machine. One paint sprayer bought his first car in 1936: 'It was red, two shades of bright red, and it would do 70 mph and I used to see to it that it did. It was great. I loved it and I had a little terrier and he used to live in that car, he used to sleep in it, and I had that little sports car for about three years.' [107] Speed – and above all, the colour: as at work. Yet it is a considerable surprise to find how rarely building cars or motorbikes, or even tinkering with them, is prominent in these memories of leisure.

Certainly there was a flourishing world of motorcycle clubs and magazines, and the family car became a must: but it seems as if for most, the essential pleasure was in the joy of movement itself, rather than in its mechanics. Thus a spinner's son remembers how his father bought his first car in 1951, and kept it looking beautiful: 'he treated 'em, he used to polish, he polished them until they shone, and even round the engines everything was spick and span'. But he never mended it himself: 'at that time it was always taken to the garage to be done.'[108] And mending cars, like making them, remained essentially a job, even when later on, as engine design was simplified, it became a regular domestic task for husbands.

Undoubtedly car-mending became and remains a widespread activity outside factory hours. George Whitlam remembers how his Uncle Wal in the 1930s was:

> my favourite uncle as he was a motorbike and motor car fanatic. He had his small engineering factory, complete with lathes and capstans and he could turn a piece of steel into almost any part which might be needed in a motorbike or car. Speedway riders regularly used to call upon him to help them out (Whitlam, 1984, 5).

Car workers themselves, as I have described elsewhere, were constantly smuggling out of the factory small metal parts which they had made for their own purposes (Thompson, 1988). It has been suggested that during these decades, as the demand for traditional skills in the factory declined: 'technology became a hobby, old artisan skills found new outlets as men did their own servicing ... Male conversation increasingly turned to "decarbonising", "adjusting tappets", "feeler gauges" and gaps for plugs along with the ritual moans about punctures' (Holt, 1989, 199). But the evidence from Coventry car workers' families contradicts any suggestion that mending bikes or cars had become a valued hobby for them. It is very striking to find in all these memories, so deeply concerned with the skills of car-making within the factory, how few spoke of this as a pleasure activity of their own free time. Only one, a bodymaker who belonged to a Vintage Car Club in the 1930s, recalled his pride in rebuilding a car for his own use:

> I did over 3,000 miles in my old Riley, and when I bought it I stripped it all down, body off and everything, and I did the engine, the gearbox, and everything in it, axle, all the lot, I rebuilt it and did it up, and then I did the body, and did that up. And it lasted me for 300,000 miles.[109]

There were also two others who valued their own car-making skills equally highly, but very significantly, they not only used them to work for money in their spare time, but also, in both cases, through so doing opened a path for upward social movement. One became a manager, the other the owner of a small paint spraying business. The first, an enthusiastic reader of car magazines, built rally cars as an evening job. He commented misleadingly: 'I think everybody in every trade, you know, carries out their trade on the side.'[110] The second is Henry Hopkins, lifelong enthusiast for paintspraying, inside and outside the factory, still at work in his seventies. He speaks for a lost world:

> I got one next door I just done. Fellow that moved into our bungalow, he's rebuilding a vintage Riley. Well I was a Riley man out and out. I worked at the Riley for a good many years. And when he told me he was rebuilding it, I said, 'When you get it up to the painting stage, I'll give you a hand with it' ... He said, 'It's a black Riley and it's just taking shape now'. I did it, ah. During the last month I done it. I've not completely finished it off.
>
> But – there's a young lady friend of mine rung me up just before Christmas. She's bought an Allegro that wanted some touching up. 'Would I do it?' ... And I did this job for her, with this bloke – it cost £90 by the time I'd done it. And I delivered it for her to run me back – I took it to show her, so that she could see that I'd done it, and she paid me the £90 and then her mother called me back. She said, 'Here you are, have another tenner', she said, 'because we were thinking it would cost £200' ...
>
> And that's how I've been all my life. Everybody that I've ever worked for have always come back, when they've wanted something done ... I used to have them queuing up.[111]

It is interesting that the pattern is very similar when we consider the role of fathers in passing on work and leisure skills to their children. In general, while most mothers handed down domestic skills to girls and to a lesser extent to boys, the learning of male skills of any kind in or around the house from fathers was rarely remembered. One boy who was always 'fiddling with something ... taking things to pieces' remembers how he: 'used to help me dad do the car ... I used to watch him and help him do that – and passing him spanner and things like that. Even when I was at school I used to be the local mechanic, and do all the teachers' cars. I've always been interested in cars.'[112] But a direct involvement of this kind was very rare. Most men were left to pick up gardening, or decorating, or car maintenance, for themselves. Nor did car worker fathers normally transmit their work skills to their sons. Fathers would typically speak for their sons, to get them into the factory; but once there, they were apprenticed to another older skilled man, or, from the 1940s, taught through formal training schemes. Few car workers talked about work at home, either to their wives or to their children. As regards both work and domestic skills, therefore, the typical Coventry father served only as a mute model.

It was also notably unusual for fathers to have any active involvement in their children's play. Only a minority – roughly one in ten – did so. In these instances, however, the transmission was strikingly often creative. We have already noted musical families. Others were painters. One bike turner: 'was artistic, my father was, and I feel I follow him ... – an idealist. I can remember him teaching me drawing and painting, and taking me out to look at the stars, and telling me about the stars.'[113]

Two fathers, however, stand out especially for the ambitiousness of their involvement with their children: each sons, and both subsequently socially mobile as a direct result. One car worker altered his 14-year-old son's bedroom:

> so that he could carry out his chemistry experiments, even put a sink in and work bench. We split the room in half and put up a partition so that his bed was one side and ... the other side was a laboratory. He'd got running water and everything, bunsen burners – I bought all these sorts of things and he and another lad from down the road who went to the same school, they used to carry out experiments.[114]

His son became a graduate electronics engineer. Still more remarkable, and closer to realising the dream of the ultimate transport machine with the help of their fathers, were two other boys:

> They always used to be making rockets ... They saved the fireworks when it came to Bonfire Night, and then they made these rockets, they made them from cardboard tubes, with nose cones on ...

> They used to set 'em off at the back there. One of the neighbours would be at the bottom with a pull rope and a pole hinged in the centre, and we let it off at the top of the garden...

> Every little while they used to make these nose cones for these rockets and they'd have one of these tiny little glass phials and they'd put a spider in it and put a parachute on the end. It was a standing joke round here, see this little parachute coming down...

> He made a rocket and he says to me one day, he says, 'We're going to fire this with remote control' ... They'd opened one of the squits and put the gunpowder in the pan, and they got an electric bulb, flashlight

bulb, broke it and got in a piece of tin and wired it up to the battery, so that when they switched it on the element lit and ignited the gunpowder and sent it off ... Yes, they were brilliant.[115]

Of these two boys, still friends, one went into aeronautics in Britain, while the other became a postgraduate space researcher in the United States.

Paradoxically, therefore, those who took the most passionate leisure interest in the kinds of skills needed to construct transport machines were not only exceptional, but highly unlikely to become or remain ordinary car workers. And conversely, for the majority it is remarkable how few men, outside their regular working hours, found important fulfilment in the crafts skills of car making. Was it that their very struggle to sustain the meaning of skill within the factory, their sustained defensiveness, had proved too painful for most of them to still find their own free joy in the same skills at leisure? Over decades, indeed over generations, factory work had step by step narrowed the idea of skill until it had for most car workers lost all its original broad meaning. But it had also built deep into their minds a wall between work and pleasure.

This therefore encouraged a strong tendency for men to use their manual skills in quite different ways. As Richard Holt puts it:

> although the equation between the declining demand for skill at work and its displacement into the world of play is a risky business, those who used their tools – the prized symbol of the skilled man – to build kennels and coops in their backyards or near the allotments where they grew their prize leeks and 'crysanths' were surely cultivating a kind of craftsmanship ... [and finding in it] the enjoyment of making and digging, of working a piece of wood, or raising a plant from seed. (Holt, 1989, 193)

But an inevitable consequence of such a transmission was that the skills used were not particular to those required for work. We may see this, as partly explaining why there seems to have been little very specific about the leisure patterns of car workers within the wider urban working-class culture. They did not even take noticeably early to the leisure use of the motor car. Certainly the concentration of skilled, migrant, high-earning families in Coventry had its impact on the city's sociability, with the notable importance of clubs as against neighbourhood and kin contact. But the typical features of its leisure culture, from pubs and football and dancing to autodidacts and musicians, had developed well before the invention of the motor car, and could be found in most other urban manufacturing cities.

These leisure patterns, as we have seen, varied between different age groups, by gender, and over time. Throughout, women had much less chance for expressiveness and creativity than men. There were also some developments, such as the advent of television and of the motor car, which had a general tendency to make leisure more passive by undercutting once widespread activities such as music-making and walking. These changes had a national rather than a local dynamic. But it is important to recognise that, especially when they were innovations, decisions to buy cars or television, and also how to use them, were made by the families: so that choice remained important. The majority of families, moreover combined television with three or more other leisure activities. And most crucially, invariably, whether in dance or dress, in music or painting, in growing or making things, in invention, or in looking at the night sky, the leisure activities available provided openings for imagination and creativity: which in each generation were seized by a few. While changes certainly destroyed some types of creativity in working class leisure, its vitality ensured that new paths were always developed. The expressiveness of car workers and their families was far from smothered.

Acknowledgements

This chapter derives from 'A Comparative Study of Car Workers in Britain and Italy', a joint international project carried out with Luisa Passerini. The British project was funded by the Leverhulme Trust and I am particularly grateful for their support. I also wish to thank the Nuffield Foundation through whose Fellowship I was able to write for three months in Turin, during which I wrote the first drafts of this paper, and also of 'Playing at Being Skilled Men' (Thompson, 1988). I am also grateful for comments on earlier versions of this chapter from Natasha Burchardt, Simon Clarke, Leonore Davidoff, and Andrew Davies.

Most of the one hundred British interviews were recorded by Linda Grant as Senior Research Officer on the project and by Peter Lynam. These interviews and transcripts are deposited in the Coventry City Record Office. All the interviewees were either carworkers themselves, or the children or spouses of car workers, or both. They were born between 1892 and 1955.

The parallel set of a hundred Turin interviews are held at the palazzo of the Provincial Government. The Italian side of the project ended unexpectedly due to a political change in the provincial government which then withdrew its support, but a report was written on the leisure aspect of the research by Marcella Filippa, 'Working-class leisure and culture in Turin, 1920–50'.

Endnotes

[1] Perhaps the nearest to an overview is provided through some of the brief sections in a book with wider aims, (Bourke, 1994). Helpful interpretative perspectives are suggested by some sociological studies of contemporary leisure (Bramham, Critcher & Tomlinson, 1995).

On sport, descriptive recent overviews are offered by Holt, 1989, and Jones, 1989; essays on individual sports by Mason, 1989. Journal articles on the theme have been very rare.

[2] Interviews 57 (b. 1955); and 8 (b. 1947).

[3] Interview 19 (b. 1947).

[4] Interviews 14 and 31.

[5] Interview 71 (b. 1945).

[6] Interview 45 (b. 1917).

[7] Interview 21 (married 1920).

[8] Interview 39.

[9] Interview 35 (married 1938).

[10] Interview 38.

[11] Interview 19.

[12] Interviews 36, (b. 1913); and 62 (b. 1916).

[13] Interview 31 (b. 1944, one of six children).

[14] The Coventry Co-operative Society's camp near Rhyl on the North Welsh coast was the most durable of all such co-operative ventures, launched in 1930 and still immensely popular until the late 1960s (Ward & Hardy, 1986, 17–19).

[15] Interview 28 (married 1933).

[16] Interview 6 (b. 1912).

[17] Interview 42 (b. 1922).

[18] Interview 45 (b. 1917).

[19] Interview 66 (b. 1942).

[20] Davies, p. 1 and chapters three and four.

[21] According to recent estimates, over 40 per cent of the British population use city parks, over eight million daily (*Guardian*, 30 January 1996).

[22] Interview 26 (b. 1910).

[23] Interview 29 (b. 1908).

[24] The cinema audience peaked at around 30 million *c.* 1945; its audience and turnover were around thirty times as great as that of its nearest rival, football. There were calculated to be 10 million bicycles in use in the 1930s, and over 800,000 allotments, both much higher figures than later (Jones, 1989, 44, 51; Mason, 1989, 165; Bourke, 1994, 83).

[25] *Coventry Evening Telegraph*, 27 January 1950. By 1960 there were 82,000 TV licenseholders in the city (Ichihashi, 1994, 437). Nationally, in 1950 there were 300,000 TV and 11,800,000 radio licence holders; within seven years their numbers were equal; while by 1965 there were 13,200,000 TV as against only 2,700,000 radio licencees.

[26] Interview 50 (married 1935).

[27] Interview 3 (married 1938).

[28] Interviews 46 (b. 1948); and 23 (married 1952, bought TV 1959).

[29] Interview 66 (married 1938).

[30] Interview 18 (daughter).

[31] Interview 30 (married 1948); for selective use, e.g. interviews 12 and 57.

[32] Interview 23 (married 1952).

[33] Interview 45 (daughter, b. 1917).

[34] Interview 41 (son, b. 1929).

[35] Davies, 1992, 37, refers to the importance of family networks in shaping leisure patterns, for example when a man drank with his brothers. I have myself studied intergenerational family transmission in terms of work models, family relationships, and attitudes to housing, but not in terms of leisure, although this would be readily possible from the three-generational interviews of

the 'Families and Social Mobility' project (Bertaux & Thompson, 1993; Bertaux & Thompson 1997).

[36] Interview 71 (b. 1914).

[37] Interview 45 (son, b. 1917; his mother had been trained as a teacher before marriage, but had to give up her own career).

[38] A classic instance was Dictionary Bill' Smith of Red Lane, 1909–81: to whom is dedicated *Red Lane Reminiscences*, Red Lane Old Residents Association, Coventry, 1983.

[39] Interview 9 (b. 1927).

[40] Interview 33 (son, b. 1907).

[41] Exceptions include interviews 29 (b. 1908) and 43 (b. 1940).

[42] Interview 9 (b. 1927).

[43] Interview 15 (b. 1913).

[44] Interview 12 (b. 1905).

[45] Interview 14 (b. 1914).

[46] Interview 6 (b. 1912).

[47] Interview 10 (b. 1928).

[48] Interview 3 (b. 1942).

[49] Interview 31 (b. 1944).

[50] Interview 68 (b. 1955).

[51] Interview 6 (b. 1912).

[52] Interview 19 (married *c*. 1970).

[53] A series of interviews in the GEC works magazine show that among women workers, knitting and sewing, and dancing, were the two leading leisure activities, practised by a third each: Ichihashi, 1994, 283–4.

[54] Interview 28 (b. 1908).

[55] Interviews 43 (b. 1940); and 31 (b. 1944); c.f. 46 (b. 1948), 'used to think of myself as a mod'.

[56] Interview 35 (b. 1914); see 34 (b. 1916), who went 'almost every night', unknown to her parents, with her dance band pianist brother.

[57] Interview 62 (b. 1916).

[58] Interview 35.

[59] Interview 36 (b. 1913).

[60] Interview 62 (b. 1916).

[61] Interview 20 (b. 1918).

[62] Interview 41 (b. 1929).

[63] Interview 22 (b. 1920); c.f. 37 (b. 1915), two pianists and a banjo.

[64] Interviews 71 (b. 1914); and 9 (married 1950).

[65] Interviews 63 (b. 1935); 34 (married 1939); and 71 (married 1945).

[66] This certainly has been shown to be true in nearby Milton Keynes (Finnegan, 1989).

[67] A series of interviews in the GEC Works Magazine in the late 1940s found that among mengardening was the most popular leisure activity, practised by one third of them, more than sport: Ichihashi, 1994, 283–4.

[68] One exception is interview 6 (b. 1912).

[69] Interview 22 (b. 1920).

[70] Interview 62 (married 1938).

[71] Interview 2 (b. 1914).

[72] Interview 5 (b. 1906).

[73] Interviews 34 (girl, b. 1916); and 35 (girls, b. 1914); see interviews 16, 25, 31, 47.

[74] Interview 54 (b. 1916).

[75] Interviews 41 (married 1954); and 68 (girl, b. 1955).

[76] Interview 15 (born 1913).

[77] Interview 32 (b. 1909); c.f. interview 29 (b. 1908).

[78] Interview 23 (married 1952, came to Coventry 1957).

[79] Interviews 39 (married 1917; they had a motorbike first); and 14 (married 1933).

[80] Interview 48 (b. 1924).

[81] In the city as a whole approximately a fifth of all households owned a car, twice the national average (Richardson, 1972, 278). The interviews also suggest that less than a fifth of working-class households were carowners. Nevertheless, the proportion was clearly much above that typical for working class communities in the 1930s.

[82] Interview 43 (b. 1940).

[83] 14 January 1950.

[84] Interviews 62 (married 1938); and 32 (married 1934).

[85] Interviews 68 (married 1972); and 63 (married 1961).

[86] for example interview 63 (married 1961).

[87] Interviews 57 (married 1953); and 47 (married 1943). see Goldthorpe, Lockwood, Bechofer & Platt (1969), 150ff; 38: of Luton factory workers *c.* 1960, only 30 per cent men and 44 per cent wives were born in Luton, and of those with living parents, 56 per cent men and 48 per cent women had neither in town, and only 13 per cent men and 18 per cent wives had parents within ten minutes walking distance.

[88] Interview 74 (married 1971); for hospitable families, for example. interviews 22 (b. 1920) and 71 (b. 1914).

[89] Interview 37 (b. 1915).

[90] Interviews 3 (b. 1942); 15 (born 1913); and 44 (married 1951).

[91] Interview 8 (b. 1911).

[92] Interview 36 (b. 1913). For other memories of women using Coventry city pubs, see *Red Lane Reminiscences* 1983, 95.

[93] Interview 24 (b. 1924).

[94] Interview 39 (1892).

[95] Interview 11 (b. 1922).

[96] Interview 25 (b. 1936).

[97] Interview 28 (b. 1908).

[98] Interview 29 (b. 1908).

[99] Interview 21 (married 1920).

[100] Interview 54 (married 1942).

[101] Interview 40 (married 1936).

[102] Interview 56 (married 1935).

[103] Interview 22 (b. 1920).

[104] Interview 55; see interviews 48 (married 1948) and 57 (married 1955). Peter Wilmott has described how from the 1930s onwards in Dagenham many husbands installed new heating systems, tiled fireplaces, collapsible tables, etc, in their rented council houses (Willmott, 1983, 86).

[105] Interview 41 (married 1954).

[106] Interview 1.

[107] Interview 32 (b. 1909).

[108] Interview 41 (b. 1929).

[109] Interview 56 (married 1935).

[110] Interview 43 (married 1960).

[111] Interview 32 (b. 1909).
[112] Interview 43 (b. 1940).
[113] Interview 5 (b. 1906); see interview 72 (married 1935).
[114] Interview 41 (married 1954).
[115] Interview 40 (married 1936).

Bibliography

Abendstern, Michele (1986) 'Expression and Control: a Study of Working Class Leisure and Gender, 1918–39' PhD dissertation, University of Essex.

Alexander, Sally, 'Becoming a Woman in London in the 1920s and 1930s', in David Feldman and Gareth Stedman Jones, (eds). (1989) *Metropolis: Histories and Representations since 1800*, Routledge, London.

Bédarida, François (1990) *A Social History of England 1851-1990*, Routledge, London.

Bertaux, Daniel, and Thompson, Paul, (eds). (1993) *Between Generations: Family Myths, Models, and Memories, International Yearbook of Oral History and Life Stories*, 1, Oxford University Press, Oxford.

Bertaux, Daniel, and Thompson, Paul (eds) (1997) *Pathways to Social Class: a Qualitative Approach to Social Mobility*, Oxford University Press, Oxford.

Bourke, Joanna (1994) *Working Class Cultures in Britain, 1890–1960: Gender, Class and Ethnicity*, Routledge, London.

Bramham, Peter, Critcher, Charles, and Tomlinson, Alan (eds). (1995) *The Sociology of Leisure*, Spon, London

Crossick, Geoffrey (1978) *An Artisan Elite in Victorian England*, Croom Helm, London.

Dance Bond Days (1984).

Davies, Andrew (1992) *Leisure, Gender and Poverty: Working-class Culture in Salford and Manchester, 1900–39*, Open University Press, Milton Keynes.

Finnegan, Ruth (1989) *The Hidden Musicians: Music-making in an English Town*, Cambridge University Press, Cambridge.

Freeman, June (1986) *Knitting: a Common Art*, Minories, Colchester.

Goldthorpe, John, Lockwood, David, Bechhofer, Frank, and Platt, Jennifer (1968–69) *The Affluent Worker*, Cambridge University Press, Cambridge.

Gray, Robert (1976) *The Labour Aristocracy in Victorian Edinburgh*, Clarendon Press, Oxford.

Gray, Robert (1981) *The Aristocracy of Labour in 19th Century Britain*, Clarendon Press, Oxford.

Gutteridge, Joseph (1893) *Lights and Shadows in the Life of an Artisan*, Curtis and Beamish, Coventry.

Hoggart, Richard (1957) *The Uses of Literacy*, Chatto and Windus, London.

Holt, Richard (1989) *Sport and the British: a Modern History*, Clarendon Press, Oxford.

Ichihashi, Hideo (1994), 'Working Class Leisure in English Towns, 1945 to 1960, with special reference to Coventry and Bolton', University of Warwick PhD dissertation.

Kuper, Leo (1953) *Living in Towns,* Cresset Press, London

Jones, Stephen G. (1989) *Sport, Politics and the Working Class: Organised Labour and Sport in Inter-war Britain*, Manchester University Pess, Manchester.

Lowerson, John, and Myerscough, John (1978) *Time to Spare in Victorian Britain*, Harvester Press, Hassocks.

Malcolmson, Robert (1973) *Popular Recreations in English Society, 1700–1850*, Cambridge University Press, Cambridge.

Mason, Tony (ed.), (1989) *Sport in Britain: a Social History*, Cambridge University Press, Cambridge.

More, Charles (1980) *Skill and the English Working Class, 1870-1914*, Croom Helm, London.

Parker, Rozsika (1984) *The Subversive Stitch: Embroidery and the Making of the Feminine*, Women's Press.

Red Lane Old Residents Association (1983) *Red Lane Reminiscences*, Coventry.

Richardson, Kenneth (1972) *Twentieth Century Coventry*, Macmillan, London.

Stanley, Liz (1987) 'Essays on Women's Work and Leisure and Hidden Work', Sociology Department, University of Manchester, Manchester.

Thompson, Edward P. (1967) 'Time, Work Discipline and Industrial Capitalism', *Past and Present*, 38.

Thompson, Paul, (1988) 'Playing at Being Skilled Men: Factory Culture and Pride in Work Skills Among Coventry Car Workers', *Social History*, 13, 1.

Thompson, Paul, Itzin, Catherine and Abendstern, Michele (1990) *I Don't Feel Old: the Experience of Ageing*, Oxford University Press, Oxford.

Ward, Colin, and Hardy, Dennis (1986) *Goodnight Campers! The History of the British Holiday Camp*, Mansell, London.

Willmott, Peter *The Evolution of a Community: a Study of Dagenham after Forty Years*, Routledge, London.

Whitlam, George (1984) *My Family*, Hillfields Community Education Project, Coventry.

Yeo, Eileen and Stephen (eds). (1981) *Popular Culture and Class Conflict*, Harvester, Brighton.

17

'Mini Loves Dressing Up':[1] Selling Cars to Women

Jenny Rice and Carol Saunders

This essay will use the experience of selling cars to women to illustrate the tensions between the reality and the rhetoric of women's lives. It argues that in reality women's lives have changed; their increasing economic and social independence have been accompanied by greater car ownership but the rhetoric is to confine them to the small car market. This is significant because of the symbolic power with which cars are imbued and which is differentially distributed by gendered advertising discourse. Contemporary advertising, like many cultural forms today, draws upon post-modernist practices of decentring and fragmenting positions of authority and power and thus could offer female car consumers, a marginalised group, access to more positive images. However, although campaigns appear to be adjusting their strategies to incorporate new dynamic images for women, to suggest that this represents a shift in recognising real power is an illusion as they continue to incorporate stereotypical female views when marketing small cars.

The acquisition of cars by women during the twentieth century can be seen as paralleling their increased participation in the work force where male employment is projected to fall while 'for women it has been rising'.[2] Their participation was initially primarily to support the demands for labour in the two world wars but more recently in response to changes in family size and structure, growth in educational parity and the benefits of financial independence. They have permeated employment sectors which were previously male preserves and helped to accelerate changes in the social, economic and cultural relationships this century. Employment outside the home has resulted in greater financial independence and the evidence indicates a narrowing of the gap between male and female earnings.[3] This has been accompanied by a growth in the proportion of women entering the higher paid professional and managerial sectors.[4]

Such economic and career developments have had an effect on their lifestyles. Not only does increased income encourage consumer spending on such items as cars, but also lifestyle changes for women have required more mobility. This is borne out by the increase in driving test successes, 'Each year since 1983 women have taken more tests then men' (*Social Trends*, 1992, 226). Women drivers are a steadily increasing group; between 1988/91 and 1992/94 male driving licence holders increased by only 1 per cent while females increased by 5 per cent (SMMTL, 1996, 314). Women have become drivers and car owners at a faster rate than men, female car ownership has risen by more than 20 per cent in the last five years, compared with 8 per cent in the male ownership[5] and women now make up over 50 per cent in the purchasers of the new car market.[6] Given their lifestyle changes it is perhaps surprising that they continue to be targeted as potential purchasers of small cars.

This dissidence is borne out in the recent Condé Nast's reader survey of their female drivers which found that their interests were not catered for. Women, in reality, are a major buying sector: 84 per cent of women bought their own cars; and their preferences in a new car include aspects more commonly associated with the middle or executive range of cars such as safety (93 per cent),[7] design (92 per cent) and power (82 per cent) (Condé Nast, 1996). Although Condé Nast's survey cannot be seen as a representative survey of the entire female market for new car sales (it publishes *Vogue*, *Tatler*, *Vanity Fair*, *Home and Gardens* and *World of Interiors*), it is likely to reflect the views of women most able to afford to buy new, as opposed to second-hand cars. Therefore their interests, while possibly marginal, must be viewed as relevant. The most interesting conclusion of the Condé Nast survey was that a considerable percentage of respondents, 58 per cent, 'believe that car advertisements don't recognise their changing role in the process of buying a car' (Condé Nast, 1996, 3). Is this the case? To examine this accusation, this article will explore the discourses of advertising and marketing strategies that target female car buyers.

Advertising seeks to promote and sell products. However, to achieve these aims, key objectives must be to attract the current market and the possible future market. Much of advertising in the field of cars seems to emphasis the first and neglect the second. Though the sales of small Rover models compared to their middle sized and larger ones show more women buyers in the small car market (55 per cent) and less in the lower and upper medium and executive class (29 per cent, 14 per cent and 6 per cent) (NCBS, 1997), Paul Flatter of the Henley Research Centre believes that the number of women drivers will exceed men and that the growth in younger women drivers (53 per cent in the 25–35 age bracket) will result in a dominance of the buying market by women in 20 years time (the average age of Rover buyers in all categories is in mid-1940s (NCBS, 1997). This potential future market is unlikely to be satisfied by just the small car sector and thus advertising should be creating aspirational images targeting these possible future buyers.

However, the apparent lack of aspirational images for women in car advertisements becomes even more of a concern if it is assumed that, as Baudrillard suggests, advertising is part of the ongoing stages of a commodity's development of symbolic meanings (Baudrillard, 1988). If, as Leiss indicates, advertisements have a 'place of special prominence in our lives' (Leiss, Kline & Jhally, 1986), it is possible to read car advertisements in ways which look at the gendered distribution and confirmation of symbolic power. It is contended that whilst advertisements have changed over time, women continue to be marginalised by symbolic rhetoric which has implications for their image, self-image and reality of their lives. Even where strong female role models are chosen, for example Ruby Wax's link with the Vauxhall Corsa, her preoccupations are feminine. Her car is used for shopping and for making a hasty retreat from a health club where she has been undergoing beauty treatments. Whilst women appear to be the target for the small car market, research, such as Condé Nast's, suggests that there is a disjuncture between their own expectations as drivers and those of the advertisers. Whilst the small car sector has grown steadily, advertisements rarely focus on power (a preference of 82 per cent of Condé Nast respondents) as their primary selling point. How is this discontinuity between buyer and market being perpetuated and what are the implications for women and their lifestyles? An investigation of the small car market, in particular Rover as one of the key manufacturers of popular small cars, provides a certain amount of evidence which emphasises this discontinuity.

Rover manufactures cars across a wide range of small, medium and executive models. Its segment of the market is 9.8 per cent.[8] In particular, they sell two of the popular small car models, the Mini and the Metro. In terms of targeting potential buyers for this category, two areas will be examined here: the construction of customer profiles for sales staff which highlight key characteristics they should expect in their customers; and advertising of the product which is crucially informed by the customer profile.

The marketing of a product depends on a clear vision of the image of the product and its buyer. The product information circulated to retailers reflects this, particularly in its profiles of prospective buyers. These present a clear picture of potential customers in relation to each model on sale and hence, provide a blueprint for their sales strategy. During the 1980s, Rover launched a range of new and remodelled cars, which are still sold today. Top of the range is the Rover 800 Series, introduced in the late 1980s, through to the Metro and Mini at the lower end. The 'Driver Image' for the 800 Series, distributed to sales staff, is male.[9] Whilst the potential driver of the Fastback model is, 'Lively,

Younger, Ambitious, Up and Coming', the 'Driver Image' of the Saloon model is, 'Conservative, Mature, Successful, Established'. The Fastback driver, the texts suggests, 'could be managing directors of small companies, or professionals, such as architects, chartered accountants or solicitors' (*Rover Fastback Product Information*, 11). All these descriptions are placed alongside male silhouettes. The medium-sector models, the Rover 200 and 400 Series[10] are aimed at families and yet the sales brochure suggests that 400 buyers are those 'who know and value engineering excellence.' (*Today's Cars*, 24). As this is seen as conventionally a male discourse it might be the husband who is viewed as the customer to target. The Metro's customer profile of the 1980s is the only one to mention a 'housewife' as a potential customer:

> So, the new Metro range aims for blanket penetration of the small car sector, from the young housewife's second-car runabout to the young executive's high-performance sports car (*Metro's Wider Appeal*).

Finally the Mini as the smallest of the small car range is seen as used by 'one or two people for short journeys' (*Metro's Wider Appeal*). In 1996 the product information confirms that its buyers are not 'families seeking a second or third car', but 'increasingly tend to be single, well-educated professional and managerial people desiring a fashion statement' (*Rover Production Information*). Though there appears to be no direct reference to gender in the product information it is geared to a young market, and the discourses make use of language more commonly associated with young women than young men. In the 1990s promotional brochure, *Today's Cars*, the Mini is described as 'always been the chic and cheeky small car'. In the Mini range the Mayfair is described as 'classier ... (and) elegant with its attractive wheel trims'. Furthermore the car is clearly personified in many of the descriptions as a woman (even the name may be female). Examples include the City model's 'flaunting Mini's exciting new body colours' and phrases such as, 'Trust Mini to keep it cleaner' (a reference to its exhaust catalyst) and provocatively, 'Minis always get away with it!' Does Mini encourage the female consumer to identify with not only the small car but also to connect women with smallness and therefore marginality capacity? It is significant that the more powerful Mini Cooper has always been associated with men, from the racing car style of the film *The Italian Job* to real race car drivers such as Enzo Ferrari and John Rhodes who drove them.

The customer profile must also be a key determinant of advertising images. It is pointed out in the profile information that:

> The IMAGE of a driver is not always the same as the customer who buys the car. People ASPIRE to this image. They want to be

associated, for example, with youthfulness or ambition - but that doesn't necessarily mean that they themselves are either youthful or ambitious! (*Rover Fastback Product Information*, 12).

Creating the 'Image' is the focus of advertising. Leiss et al describe advertising as a 'privileged form of discourse', ' one which 'we accord what it says a place of special prominence in our lives'. This importance of advertising is crucial in the relationship between the consumer and the commodity's product promotion is most obviously displayed in the form of advertising. In this article the focus will be on two examples of advertisements for the Mini. These were chosen to represent a significant historical period of change for women. The first advert from 1976 follows the important legislation covering sex discrimination and equal pay in 1975; the second, from 1996, provides a contrast with a contemporary image. Likewise this period has also seen a significant change in advertising discourse which reflects the upsurge of post-modernism. Whilst signalling a change in the form and style of advertisements, it may not be reflected in a substantial change in the production–consumption relationship.

Sex has never been a problem for us

Mini Equinox

The 1976 advertisement clearly targets female readers as its first sentence draws attention to the number of women Mini drivers:

> Six out of every ten British Minis on the road are probably being driven by women.

This advertisement, though playing at both a denotative and connotative level, is easily accessible. Its signifiers of the couple, environment and caption relate to obvious signifiers of youth, boldness, fashionability and these have recognisable significance in their own systems and therefore easily create a new signifying system for the Mini car. So its meaning is closed to a variety of interpretation. However, as the Rover profile material on addressing customer's image aspirations highlights, there is also the important element of identification, both between the customer and the product: the red car shows a boldness that matches the obvious boldness of their sexual and social relationship and that of this new era of emancipation and the customer and the image to which they aspire. Although the reader may not be able to afford the Mini, there are certain signifiers that aspiring car owners could interpret, such as identifying with the fashion statements, the sexual relationship, female drivers, female emancipation interests (and also correspondingly, the double standard that still existed in social practice).

The wording of the text beneath the picture, though clearly making reference to the Sex Discrimination Act, adopts a patronising manner. Phrases such as, 'Supercover after-sales protection takes a load off a woman's mind' and '... the new comfort and luxury of the Mini pampers the gentle sex' illustrate this. The by-line pun, 'Sex has never been a problem for us' plays with levels of meaning, both in terms of the legislation or the 'Act', and the act of sex at a time when sexual behaviour was less restrained by fear of AIDS. In many ways this is accessible advert emphasising up-market ordinariness. The picture encourages the reader to interpret it as reality. It presents an idealised picture of youthful sexuality that flaunts their physical relationship both through the language of the advertisement and the cosiness of the internal gaze. It also appeals to lifestyle aspirations via the context of the cobblestone mews.

As has been suggested, this advert is accessible. This is a feature of first-wave advertising which drew attention primarily to functional features of the product. Lee suggests that such instant accessibility to a large market was the motivating factor in designing adverts (Lee, 1993). Therefore the level of signification had to be uncomplicated. The message of this advertisement is similarly uncomplicated; it might address aspritational desires but it nevertheless confirms women's lack of symbolic power.

The 1996 Mini Equinox advertisement shown here is one of a series of three similar poses of women. It represents the present wave of advertising in the more radical advertising agencies; a phase which emphasises style rather than product. As Lee suggests there is 'The concentration upon style, form and image, rather than use-value, content and substance' (Lee, 1993, 154). Advertising since the 1980s has become seen as an art form more concerned with its own internal creativity than with actually selling a product. This can lead to inaccessibility if readers lack the knowledge to know 'how to engage with the dominant codes in literature, art or philosophy' (Rice & Saunders, 1996, 92). The danger is that customers are excluded if advertising copywriters attempt to use exclusive codes of advertising discourse.

The Equinox advert displays this exclusiveness. It shows an image of a young women presented as a 'super model'. She is wearing four items of clothing, a shiny blue and pink tight-fitting jacket, silver gloves, glossy tights and shiny blue high heels. Her clothes sport 'Equinox' symbols. Her extended left hand holds a fake dog on a lead and to complement its dog collar she wears a similar 'dog collar' made of a blue choker with an 'Equinox' symbol at its centre. In place of a skirt there is an Equinox Mini. These elements work as signifiers creating meanings which only become accessible by drawing on cultural capital of style. Whereas in the first advert the consumer is drawn into the product through identification with the image of the customer; in the second, an example of objectification, the consumer is not encouraged to enter *into* the cosy world of the advert but is forced, by the gaze of the model, to remain outside, and view the model as an object not connected to the viewer in any way. The disdainful image reinforces this by distancing the audience through gaze, body posture – right hand on hip, and lack of environmental or written context. The androgynous, almost drag queen, dandyish pose further emphasises this by the exclusion of the viewer from a shared lifestyle. One key feature of post-modernism, dedifferentiation, a blurring of the relationship between the image and the spectator, is problematic here. At one level the relationship between the image and spectator is polarised, yet her knowing look could be seen to be inclusive.

The product is in the frame but it is incorporated into the single image of the woman as her skirt. The product operates at the level of metaphor, playing with the relationship between the mini skirt and the car. If the car *is* the skirt, what does this signify? Rover's internal product information suggests that this interplay is a pastiche, playing on the Mini car as a mini skirt. A link made in their most recent advertising material where Peter Sellers is quoted from June 1979 as saying:

> For anyone between 25 and 45, the Mini was part of growing up. it gave mobility to millions and bankrupted textile mills by leading the way to mini-skirts (sigh).

The popular impression of the mini skirt is that it represented the new freedom that women had in the 1960s and this can be translated to the freedom of the Equinox Mini car. Yet this nostalgia, an element of pastiche itself, is problematic. The Mini skirt signified sexual freedom yet wearing one was fraught with problems of revealing too much! Furthermore the signals it gave off in terms of sexual availability at a time when female contraception was only just becoming commonly available to most young women was not without its worrying monthly moments! Yet nostalgic perceptions continue in the post-modern period. Even the image of the economically unproductive woman being created by the super model image is nostalgic; the image recalls the up market New Look poses of the 1940s which continued to dominate until the early

1960s when it was common for 'unemployed' society women to show off designer clothes. It could be seen that this advertisement with its playful nostalgia is displaying the tendency of advertisements to be subject to 'postmodernist cultural de-differentiation of representations and commodities' (Lash, 1990, 197) by bringing together images of high and low culture (society woman and drag queen) and mixing historical moments; and in 'the colonisation of the commodity by culture' (Lash, 197) as the significance of the Mini is tied to the nostalgic cultural references.

Cultural capital, pastiche and nostalgia have all been identified as elements of postmodernism. Jameson refers to pastiche as:

> ...one of the most significant features or practices in postmodernism today' and as 'like parody, the imitation of a peculiar or unique style, the wearing of a stylistic mask, ... without parody's ulterior motive, without the satirical impulse, without laughter, without that still latent feeling that there exists something normal compared to which what is being imitated is rather comic . Pastiche is ... parody that has lost its sense of humor. (Foster, 1983, 113)

And goes on to suggest that pastiche 'satisfies a deep (might I even say repressed?) longing to experience ... again' (Foster, 1983, 116).

Although the Equinox Mini advert utilises post-modern pastiche (and interestingly the use of the word by Rover copywriters shows how much it is a feature of current discourse), how far can we say that such an advertisement is post-modern and is so, what are its implications? It certainly displays the crucial post-modern elements of cultural capital, pastiche and nostalgia. It uses, as Harvey suggests, in relation to adverts, the post-modern technique of superimposition of ontologically different worlds that bear no necessary relation to each other (Harvey, 1989, 64) and a concern for signifier rather than signified (Harvey, 1989, 102). However because of its overriding economic purpose Lee suggests that adverting can be said to 'reproduce social meaning' (Lee, 153) in fact it must in order to fulfil its economic purpose. Though certainly many adverts offer what Lee describes as a:

> 'decentred reading position'; a plurality of reading positions based upon an unstructured combination of signifiers and a narrative form that does not invite ideological recognition, identification or closure. (156)

And if it denies an authoritative position and emphasises difference it might seem to support a feminist interpretation. Certainly it has been argued that postmodernism with its decentred positions offers opportunities for women to be less marginalised:

> feminist theorists enter into and echo postmodernist discourse as we have begun to deconstruct notions of reason, knowledge, or the self'. (Connor, 230)

If post-modernist practices, as evident in the Equinox, advert are liberating, the advertisements should reflect the shift in the changing role of women. Does this advert do this? We would argue that it does not. The image is not empowering. Though there has been a narrowing of the gap in wages between man and women, more women are in employment, a high proportion of women are professionals, yet, at the same time women are not being encouraged to see themselves in aspirant terms. It is not merely in advertisements such as the Equinox which offers a less than positive image of women. Advertisements featuring Rover cars still portray men as drivers of the more powerful models. In a recent *Cosmopolitan* magazine an advertisement showed the larger Rover 200 being driven by a man yet a female driver of a Mini in an advertisement for insurance (*Cosmopolitan*, September 1996, 82). Post-modern advertising has not been the saviour of the feminist struggle to recognise women's economic and social progress. Connor would not be surprised. He is pessimistic of post-modernism's freedoms:

> feminism may find itself, not as the vibrant voice of postmodernism, but, as the repressed, managed rupture of postmodernism, merely a part of speech within it'. (1994, 231)

If the car industry is to gear itself up for the future market dominated by women buying new cars, it needs to urgently address its marketing strategies and in particular start presenting advertisements that recognise the changed economic and social positions of women in the late twentieth century.

Endnotes

[1] *It's the image of you* (1996), publicity material for the Mini, Rover Group Ltd, Birmingham.

[2] *Social Trends*, 1996, no.26, Central Statistical Office, HMSO, London, p.84. 'In Britain the net expansion of 2.5 million workers achieved between 1951 and 1971 was made up almost entirely (2.2 million) of women coming into wage labour.' Whitelegg, E. et al, (eds) (1982), *The Changing Experience of Women*, Martin Robertson & Open University, Oxford,

106. In 1951 women were 30.8 per cent of the economically active labour force which rose in 1966 to 35.7 per cent, *Social Trends*, 1974, no. 5, Government Statistical   Service, HMSO, London, 99; and in 1994 53 per cent of women were eonomically active, *Social Trends*, 1996, no. 26, Central Statistical Office, HMSO, London; 'the economic activity   rate   of   married women has increased steadily from 59 per cent in 1975 to 73 per cent in 1992' *General Household Survey*, 1992, OPCS, p.7.

[3] Between 1975 and 1995 female earnings as a percentage of male earnings rose from 71 per cent to 80 per cent, Equal Opportunities Commission published statistics, as at January 1997, source: *New Earnings Surveys*, 1975, 1985, 1995. The Equal Pay Act became law in 1975.

[4] In 1995 33 per cent of all employees were female managers and administrators, 40 per cent were professionals and 48 per cent were associate professional or technical, Equal Opportunities Commission, details of Employment by Occupation, 1995, source: *Labour Force Survey*, Spring 1995.

[5] Reference to Cowie research, Paul Flatter, *The Times*, September 1996, 7.

[6] *The Lex Report on Motoring* states that more women than men bought new cars in 1995. Paul Flatter, *The Times*, September 1996, 7.

[7] *Which* in conjunction with The Department of Transport, Euro NCAP, FIA,   the   RAC and AA's safety tests on cars reported in its February 1997 edition   that the Rover 100 was 'The worst model, ... offered very little protection for the occupants' 9. As Gavin Green of the *Independent* commented, the Rover 100 was 'castigated' and: 'Although it was not tested, it is a fair bet that the Mini, which is even older than the Metro, would have done even worse.' He further reported that in conversation with a safety chief of a large car manufacturer he was told that the safest model was 'The biggest. You can't overcome the laws of physics. A two-ton car will always do better in a crash than a one-ton car.' 8.2.97, p.21.

[8] Statistics provided by the Society of Motor Manufacturers and Traders Ltd, January 1997.

[9] Interestingly, the Mercedes Benz W124-120 SL 3 litre class had, until 1989, sold 50 per cent of its cars to women, possibly due to what John Evans, Head of Corporate Communications described as softer, gentler lines. The falling sales to men were seen as linked to so many being driven by women. There was then a philosophy change resulting in the present 5-litre design which he described as having more austere lines and as being more aggressive looking. Overall the sales of the car are now rising, i.e. more men buying them and this has resulted in women's sales down to 13.5 per cent.

[10] The Rover 400 was launched in 1990.

Bibliography

Baudrillard, J. (1988) *Selected Writing*, Polity, Cambridge.
Condé Nast (1996) *Women's Motoring Survey*, The Condé Nast Publications Ltd, London.
Connor, S. (1989) *Postmodern Culture*, Basil Blackwell, Oxford.
Foster, H. (1983) *Postmodern Culture*, Pluto Press, London.
General Household Survey (1992).
Harvey, D. (1989) *The Condition of Postmodernity*, Basil Blackwell, Oxford.
Labour Force Survey (1995).
Lash, S. (1989) *Sociology of Postmodernism*, Routledge, London.
Lee, M. (1993) *Consumer Culture Reborn*, Routledge, London.

Leiss, W., Kline, S. and Jhally, S. (1986) *Social Communication in Advertising*, Methuen, London.

NCBS (1997) *Pan European Statistics*, Rover Group Ltd, Warwick.

New Earnings Survey (1975, 1985, 1995).

Rice, J. and Saunders, C. (1996) 'Consuming Middlemarch: the Construction and Consumption of Nostalgia in Stamford', *Pulping Fictions*, Pluto Press, London.

Robertson, M. (1982) *The Changing Experience of Women*, Open University, Oxford.

Social Trends, (1974, 1992, 1996), Central Statisical Office HMSO, London.

Society of Motor Manufacturers and Traders Ltd (1996) *Motor Industry of Great Britain 1996*, London.

18

Transports of Difference and Delight: Advertising and the Motor Car in Twentieth-Century Britain

Tim O'Sullivan

'Get into ... the Ka ...', 'Its a drivers car ... so drive it', 'When you're flying, its good to know that your luggage isn't', 'You've got to search for the hero inside yourself ', 'For a quiet car, its making a lot of noise', 'It'll drive you sane', 'Ask before you borrow it', 'In Italy, no one grows up wanting to be a train driver', 'Leave it all behind'...

These are just a few of the slogans which advertisers have used in recent campaigns to promote particular brands of car in Britain. Echoes of slogans and catchphrases such as these, with their accompanying images, personalities, music, appeals and promises, are omnipresent in modern popular culture. Whether for cars, or for the seemingly endless array of other goods and services which flow through daily life in modern consumer societies, advertisements are often thought to be more or less exclusively about these images and slogans and their persuasive impact upon consumer consciousness. Behind the seductive surface of the often spectacular imagery of modern advertising culture however is a large and powerful industry which mediates between producers and consumers and has considerable consequences for the overall shape and commercial viability of media sectors.

For instance, total expenditure on advertising in the UK in 1994 amounted to some £10.17 billion (BRAD Digest, 1996, 99). Advertising cars and motoring was one of the top three major product categories of this total, following closely behind retail and financial services. 1995 saw record expenditure by UK car manufacturers on advertising their products and brands, resulting in 15 entries in the year's top 100 advertisers league (*Marketing Week*, 1996, 45). In that year in the UK, 46 car manufacturers spent some £500 million on 487 campaigns. Their expenditure on advertising across the combined press and magazine sectors and on commercial radio was extensive but in commercial television, which saw significant expansion in that year, it has been estimated that on average, the UK television viewer watched in excess of seven hundred car commercials, almost two per day (Dwek, 1996, 34). In the month of January 1996 for example, television advertisements were regularly broadcast promoting 36 models of car, produced by 15 different car manufacturers. Subsequent research which aimed to find out which adverts in general were most liked by viewers, indicated that the television campaigns for the Peugeot 406 and for the Volvo 850 scored highly, with those for the Citroën AX and the Vauxhall Corsa also attracting support from viewers (Mills, 1996, 56).

By any standards, advertising cars is a big and competitive business in the 1990s, amounting to a large slice of the total advertising spend of modern times. For instance, the tenth biggest car advertising account in the UK in 1995, was that of the Ford Fiesta at £11.4 million. This was more than the advertising expenditure on the biggest food brand, Kelloggs Cornflakes (£10.9 million), more than the biggest household goods brand, Ariel Future (£9.1 million), more than Guiness, the second highest spending drinks brand (£9.35 million), and almost as much as the advertising budget for the biggest travel brand, British Airways (£12 million). By dividing the figures for ad spend per model, by those recorded by the Society for Motor Manufacturers and Traders concerning the respective new vehicle sales for 1995, Robert Dwek has recently calculated the ad spend ratio per new car sold in the UK during 1995 (Dwek, 1996, 34). According to these calculations, the biggest spender Alfa Romeo spent £1,600 on advertising for each new car sold, Volvo by the same measure spent £583 per model, Jaguar £450, CitroNn £378, Porsche £297, Vauxhall £211, Rover Group £187, and BMW £149.

If this data offers an index of the economic and industrial significance of advertising for the production and consumption of motor cars in the UK towards the end of the twentieth century, it also points to the ways in which images of motoring and cars have become part and parcel of the popular culture of modern times. Films, newspapers, television programmes, magazines, popular music and other media routinely and almost invisibly contain references to the car and to car culture. Advertisers in the modern period have often attracted criticism and controversy for their methods of persuasion and their activities are regulated by agreed and enforceable codes of conduct. The defence of their activities tends to be remarkably straight forward. 'We don't sell, we make people want to buy' is how John Hegarty, one of the directors of the leading British agency BBH, has summarised their rationale in the current period, implying a shift in modern advertising strategies away from crude or 'hard sell' attempts at direct consumer manipulation towards a more active, discerning and knowing relationship with potential buyers.

For Raymond Williams (1980), advertising was the 'magic system', fundamental to the reproduction of capitalist industries. He suggested that while advertising in general, tended to obscure the real structures and contradictions of economic life, its 'magical' properties concern the generation and mobilisation of consumption ideals and the cultural 'alchemy' involved in turning objects into culturally recognisable and desirable things. Increasingly in the modern period, we have learned not simply to buy, admire or desire objects – cars, clothes, computers etc. – but to invest them with hidden, symbolic values and to recognise them as 'things'; as signs of social respect or discernment, of style, power, security, environmental awareness and so on. You do not just buy a car, you invest in and drive a mobile signifier, something which says something about you and which comes 'wrapped' in a web of meanings and values. From the early years of the twentieth century onwards, advertisers have sought to differentiate cars into different brands and to manage their respective identities using a developing range of strategies to convert the products of the motor industry into meaningful, appealing symbols for potential purchasers.

There is a largely unresearched history of this process as it has occurred in British culture, although that history is often implicated in the popular memory of the present, for example, in nostalgic celebrations of the 'great' models and 'marques' of the British motor industry, the Jaguars, Rovers, Austins, MGs and so on and their associated values. In the current phase conditions have intensified and car manufacturers have become 'brand obsessed', as one recent commentator has put it:

> as cars become more mechanically similar, so their brand identities become more important as buying differentiators. Nowadays, there is virtually no difference in engineering quality between a Nissan and a CitroNn and a Peugeot and a Fiat (or, for that matter, a Renault and a Ford and a Vauxhall). They are virtually mechanical clones. So their badges, and all that they stand for, matter more and more ... In terms of product, the biggest difference between cars is now in their style. (Green, 1997 3)

What follows is a brief outline of some of the issues which are involved in developing an historical study of advertising the motor car in British popular culture.

Since the late nineteenth century, the design, production and marketing of motor cars in Britain has undergone massive change. Large-scale technical, economic and social changes have also had important consequences for the structure of consumer and advertising markets. The types of people or

289

consumers addressed by adverts, the types and forms of information presented in them and the media through which they have been transmitted have also changed considerably. Technical and cultural developments in systems of mass communication – from the newspaper and bill board, through film, radio and television – have extended and transformed the process of advertising in important ways.

If the forms of advertising have changed, historical research also indicates that the typical content and dynamic of advertising strategies in the twentieth century have also shifted in a number of decisive ways. For example, Pollay (1979, 1984) points to a shift from the *informational* characteristics of early advertising campaigns, organised essentially to instruct consumers about the brand characteristics of the product in question, to *transformational* approaches, which attempt to alter or reinforce consumer attitudes or values, less by rational or utilitarian description but by articulating the symbolic, cultural promise of the product and how it will 'change your life'. By the 1920s, marketing and advertising had become key mechanisms in the vital process of producing consumption, of competing in the developing domestic and overseas markets. In the 1930s, as Myers (1986) suggests, advertisers began to recognise that their previous assumptions, premised on the idea of a 'natural', pre-existing market, 'out there' for a product, had to change. Advertising began to be seen not simply as a process of 'attention grabbing', and it involved going beyond functional description of a brand, to encompass the cultivation of target markets:

> Branding meant giving the product an identity, target marketing meant selecting a suitable market, and 'positioning' the product, emphasising the qualities of the commodity most likely to appeal to the selected audience. Desire became a technical term: more important than rationality or intellect, it was perceived as the motivating force behind purchasing power. (1986, 24)

By the end of the 1950s, the post-war growth in consumer markets began to be organised around ideas of 'lifestyle' marketing. Originating in American advertising and marketing (Marchand, 1985), the projection of 'lifestyles' and allied 'market segmentation' became central principles in the organisation and construction of advertising campaigns. As Featherstone has argued, lifestyle and its research has subsequently become fundamental to consumer culture:

> it denotes individuality, self-expression, and a stylistic self-consciousness. One's body, clothes, speech, leisure pastimes, eating and drinking preferences, home, car, choice of holidays etc. are to be regarded as indicators of the individuality of taste and sense of style of

the owner/consumer. In contrast to the designation of the 1950s as an era of grey conformism, a time of *mass* consumption, changes in production techniques, market segmentation and consumer demand for a wider range of products, are often regarded as making possible greater choice (the management of which becomes and art form) [...] The implication is that we are moving towards a society without fixed status groups in which the adoption of styles of life (manifest in choice of clothes, leisure activities, consumer goods, bodily dispositions) which are fixed to specific groups have been surpassed. (1987, 55)

For Leiss, Kline and Jhally (1986), detailed historical content analysis of the general styles and strategies of advertising in magazines reveals a number of clear and distinctive phases which have shaped the development and the dynamics of advertising campaigns in the twentieth century. Their analysis allows for development of the informational – transformational frames of reference which are held to characterise long-term historical changes, and in addition provides a framework which can be applied in the analysis of specific products and market sectors – in this case – cars and motoring. The four stages which their work outlines are based on historical analysis carried out in North America, and they should not be regarded as exclusive, isolated categories. Rather, they are evolutionary periods, which sees emergent forms of advertising adding to and building upon previous, residual forms.

The first phase, which they call *Idolatry* (1890–1925), is characterised by advertising which tended to venerate products and which often as a result, put them on a pedestal. The overt selling strategy foregrounded rational appeals on behalf of the utility of the product, stressing its qualities, uses and benefits. In many adverts of the time, the product tends to be the exclusive centre of attention, often cut off from any setting or human contact. As a result, the focus tends to allow only an explanation of it and its virtues. Little or no reference is made to the user or consumer in this early and dominant type of advertising strategy.

The adverts for the 16–20 hp Rover car (circa 1907) (Fig. 1) and for 'the famous' 12 hp Rover (1914) (Fig. 2) exemplify this first phase of development well. In both cases and especially by modern standards, a simple, direct illustration of the model is accompanied by the details of its technical specifications and price. These alone were deemed sufficient according to the advertising codes of the time, to rationally inform or convince the potential purchaser. The second phase in the evolution of advertising frames that the study points to is one which sees products presented more as icons for symbolic qualities or values. They suggest that *Iconology* became a characteristic mode of advertising which emerged from the mid–1920s onwards. In this phase, the focal point of the typical advert shifts from the product as an isolated entity to encompass a setting or situation, thereby embedding the product in a symbolic context which imparts additional meanings to it. By means of allowing a setting and, to a limited extent, people to appear symbolically in a more developed visual space, this iconic stage of development does admit some address to people, to the person or the intended, implied reader/user. However, products such as cars, became embodiments of attributes and values derived largely from their settings. When people appeared in these adverts it was as very generalised typifications, part of the background or setting, not as fully autonomous individuals:

> they were often exemplars of reigning social values carrying the burden
> of society's commitment to family structure, status differentiation and
> hierarchical authority. (Leiss et al, 1986, 284)

Often and as a result, both products and persons represented in these adverts appear 'frozen' in space, in style and time.

In the examples of British car adverts from this period (Figs 6, 7, 8, 9 & 10), there are echoes or versions of these strategies which provide evidence of this phase of development and its variations. Is there not for example a suggestion in the advert for the Austin A90 Six-Westminster from 1955 (Fig. 6), that 'the hunt' is more than just a setting, and that the traditionally envied have become the envious? The masculine world of 'Giles and Charles' for instance (Fig. 7), and their 'gentlemen's agreement' over the merits of each others respective Wolseley in 1956, depicts not only a setting, but a social scenario where the dynamics and dialogue of personalised judgements and distinction as well as use intervene in, if not revolve around, the validation of the product. Giles and Charles were in fact personalised inventions for this 1956 Wolseley 6/90 campaign, which although short lived, also exemplified the emergence of the running character story – they cropped up in a number of scenarios – and the development of the serial concept in British advertising. As well as the car entering a personalised world and relationship in these types of adverts, there is also a hint of things to come in the earlier advert for the Wolseley 6/80 saloon (Fig. 8). As Stevenson (1991) has suggested, the way that the car is represented as integral to a lifestyle is a precursor of later, even 1980s, strategies for car and product promotion. The advert places the car at the heart of a symbolic social setting – the 'tennis club', 'after the game' – which is personalised and which, it is important to note, is heavily and predictably gendered. Another man, in this case a real one, Jack Brabham (fig. 9), makes a more tangible form of expert testimonial in his endorsement of the early 60s Sunbeam Alpine, based upon his world championship status. The 1955 advert for the Austin A30 Seven (fig. 10) and the person prototypes who have managed to resolve their distinctly gendered demands with its miraculous qualities also places the car at the heart of things, to the extent that modern 'family togetherness' might be thought to be impossible without its ownership. The car has become represented as an essential part of the fabric and rationale of ordinary happy social interaction; part facilitator, part lubricant, a key to admiration, improvement, mobile community and of course, economy and dependability.

The final phase identified by Leiss et al, in the development of advertisers, cultural frames for goods is called *Totemism*, a tendency which is identified as being characteristic of the post-1965 period. By using this label a direct anthropological reference is made to the significance, power and cultural processes which give totems power in pre-industrial societies. Just as totems in these settings served to articulate and represent a particular clan or group and its territory, identity, history, solidarity and difference within an overall coded system or hierarchy, so the analogy goes, cars and other products have become secular totems for lifestyles, parts of the lifestyle ensemble of modern times (Chaney, 1996). Product and brand images have become badges of group and lifestyle membership, as Pierre Bourdieu (1986) has argued, for the dynamics of 'distinction' and this requires both a creative mixing and a process of building upon previous strategies and formats.

> During the present totemistic phase the identifying features of the three preceding periods are recalled and synthesised. The product-related images are gradually freed from serving only the narrowly utilitarian qualities of the thing itself (idolatry), abstract and authoritative symbols (iconology), or a too restrictive array of interpersonal relations (narcissism). Here the utility, symbolism, and personalization are mixed and remixed under the sign of the group ... Consumption is meant to be a spectacle, a public enterprise: product-related images fulfil their totemic potential in becoming emblems for social collectivities, principally by means of their associations with lifestyles.
> (Leiss et al, 1986, 295)

In these lifestyle format adverts, a different and more holistic equilibrium is offered and implied between the product image and that which is depicted as surrounding it. It becomes one element in the overall, personalised setting, and their discussion interestingly invokes the social psychological distinction between a prototype and a stereotype. The former is based on attributions made about the personality or characteristics of a person – friendly, sensible, warm, fun-loving etc. – whereas the notion of a stereotype implies undifferentiated judgements which link individuals to groups and their social and cultural classification – in terms of class, gender, race, sexuality, age, nationality and so on (O'Sullivan et al, 1994). Lifestyle appeals blend both prototypes and stereotypes, appealing to a variety of specific social codes. They often focus on moments of open display, and are commonly closed around the depiction of a variety of leisure activities (entertaining, going out, holidaying, relaxing, motoring and so on) often caught in naturalistic, quasi-documentary style.

The advert for the MG Midget, circa 1972 (Fig. 11), provides a good example of this shift towards targeting younger lifestyles. It speaks to those 'in the know' with its ambiguous and playful message. In this case, the car and its occupant/s are not only the centre of attention of a tableau for the advert viewer, the passers-by in the picture or for the absent but implied 'mother' (his or hers?), they are represented as the epicentre, as badges for a particular, 'swinging', modern metropolitan and fashionable lifestyle and sensibility. There is a classless address and appeal in many of the adverts of this time. Whereas the imagery of pre-war motoring in Britain often invoked middle class or even aristocratic cultures, the meaning of the motor car in Britain has always been bound up with its experience and its availability, as a functioning means of private transport as well as a designed, advertised and imagined symbolic product. If the retailers and manufacturers of cars in the inter-war period geared their products and sales strategies towards a limited and rather exclusive range of consumers (O'Connell, in this volume), conditions had changed considerably by the 1960s, when as Patrick Wright has noted:

> the automobile is well within the reach of members of all social classes. By this time the advertisements have become general, or rather 'national' in their appeal. They are now addressed to everyone: the citizen as motorist. In this shift of address, the repertoire certainly goes through some changes, but the overall effect is, nevertheless, the generalisation as 'national' of cultural values which, in origin and also in their subsequent refinement, are specific to earlier bourgeois culture. (1985, 67)

While adverts for cars in the contemporary phase mix variants of all four of the earlier stages, replaying and reviewing their underlying strategies, they do so in ways which indicate for many writers a decisive shift into the post-modern conditions of current times and culture. For Davidson for instance, writing of the 1980s, a period he describes as the 'designer decade':

> What however was different about ads in the 80s was the self-consciousness with which they typified and expressed their surrounding culture. They became doubly reflective, not only in content but in form also ... The inflation in production values, the two way traffic between pop promos and movies helped to breakdown the cultural divides

294

between them, and the growth of computer graphics and special effects that only advertisers could afford to use began to challenge the production superiority of television and film. What had started out as a supermarket theory – add cultural and symbolic value to a brand – started to look like a whole view of culture. Advertising became acknowledged as being a sophisticated cultural product at a time when that was how both 'popular' and 'high' culture were being explored and consumed (Davidson, 1992, 62).

In his subsequent discussion, Davidson goes on to outline how British advertising culture changed in the 1980s, suggesting that there was a new – and politically congruent – hardness, brazenness and lack of inhibition about consumerism and lifestyle appeals which embodied the enterprise culture of the time. By the end of the 80s however, these new, unashamed consumerist ethics of self and the search for individualism began to be challenged and modified by appeals which recognised the need for some collective and social responsibilities. This was exemplified in the emergence of ecological awareness and the 'green consumer' which was to have an important impact on the ways in which cars and petrol were then and have subsequently been advertised. 'New' men and women began to appear in car ads in which they were not solely and confidently embarked on selfish missions or journeys, but were in pursuit of new, more caring consumer goals, including less pollution and environmental harmony, what the advertising industry began to regard as the use of 'us–ism' (Davidson, 1992 & Bayley, 1986 for their particular accounts of the Audi campaigns, from 'Vorsprung durch Technik' onwards).

If environmentalism and reassessments of gender posed two challenges to the brash confidence of the 1980s advertising culture, the signs of post-modernism were also to make their marks on the forms of advertising. Adverts for cars in the 1990s display these signs in their heightened use of playful parody and knowing irony, of intertextuality and seriality. These have been deployed as new languages and discourses in the images of motorised lifestyle characteristic of late twentieth-century advertising culture in Britain.

In the course of the last 100 years, it is tempting to argue in conclusion that adverts for motor cars have simply mirrored and replayed the rise and decline of certain dreams and desires, reflecting a fascination with the technologies and social relations of motorised culture in Britain. Advertising has however, always involved selection and accentuation rather than true reflection :

The automobile is much more than a means of transportation; rather, it is wholly imbued with feelings and desires that raise it to the level of a cultural symbol. Behind the gradual infiltration of the automobile into the world of our dreams lie many stories: ones of disdain for the unmendable horse, of female coquetry, of the driver's megalomania, of the sense of having a miracle parked in the drive, and of the generalised desire for social betterment. (Sachs, 1992, vii–viii)

If we have all travelled a long way from the early years of innocent appeals to simple utility or function to the quizzical or enigmatic post-modern narratives used to advertise the car in the current phase, we have also become increasingly aware of the car as a major problem in modern social life. As choked cities and clogged motorways contradict on a daily basis the earlier and recurrent visions of freedom and mobility, advertisers and car manufacturers are struggling to stay in touch. As Sachs suggests, perhaps at the end of the twentieth century we are finally approaching the end of motorised culture and the terms in which it has been represented, known and lived:

> From today's perspective, the story is not a triumphal one, replete with flags and fanfare. The history of the automobile can ultimately be read as a morality play about the withering of a historical project. The dreams are aging in our day: boredom with motorization is widespread, and contrary images are becoming evident … Today it is the personal computer, more than the internal combustion engine, that causes excitement. (Sachs, 1992, viii)

It is not at all clear, how and in what terms, cars and their advertisers will be able to transport us in the twenty-first century ahead.

Acknowledgements

Thanks are due to the following: David Edwards and Richard Brotherton at the British Motor Industry Heritage Trust; Archive Services, Gaydon, Warwick; Steve Chibnall and the 'Pulp Archive'; Amy Kieft, Jenny Rice and Susan Swann; the Research Committee, School of Humanities, De Montfort University, Leicester.

Bibliography

Bayley, S. (1986) *Sex, Drink and Fast Cars*, Faber, London.
Bourdieu, P. (1984) *Distinction: A Social Critique of the Judgement of Taste*, Routledge & Kegan Paul, London.
British Rate and Data (BRAD), *Digest: Key Facts and Trends*, February (1996).
Chaney, D. (1996) *Lifestyles*, Routledge, London.
Davidson, M. (1992) *The Consumerist Manifesto*, Routledge, London.
Dwek, R. (1996) 'Are Car Advertisers Wasting Money?', *Campaign*, 10 May.

Featherstone, M. (1987) 'Lifestyle and Consumer Culture', *Theory, Culture & Society*,4, 55–70.

Frostick, M. & Havinder, A. (1970) *Advertising and the Motor Car*, Lund Humphries, London.

Green, G. (1997) *Independent*, 11 January.

Leiss, W., Kline, S. and Jhally, S. (1986) *Social Communication in Advertising*, Methuen, London.

Marchand, R. (1985) *Advertising the American Dream: Make Way for Modernity*, University of California Press, Berkeley.

Marketing Week (1996), 'The Top 100 Advertisers', 10 May.

Mills, D. (1996) 'The Nation's Favourite Ads', *Campaign*, 15 March.

Myers, K. (1986) *Understains: The Sense and Seduction of Advertising*, Comedia, London.

O'Sullivan, T., et al (1994) *Key Concepts in Communication and Cultural Studies*, Routledge, London.

Pollay, R.W. (1979) *Information Sources in Advertising History*, Greenwood Press, Westport, Connecticut.

Pollay, R.W. (1984) 'Twentieth Century Magazine Advertising: Determinants of Informativeness', *Written Communication*, 1.

Sachs, W. (1992) *For Love of the Automobile*, University of Californis Press, Berkeley.

Stevenson, H. (1991) *Advertising British Cars of the 50s*, Haynes, London.

Williamson, J (1978) *Decoding Advertisments: Ideology and meaning in Advertising*, Marion Boyars, London

Williams, R. (1980) 'Advertising : The Magic System', *Problems in Materialism and Culture*, Verso, London.

Wright, P. (1985) *On Living in an Old Country*, Verso, London.

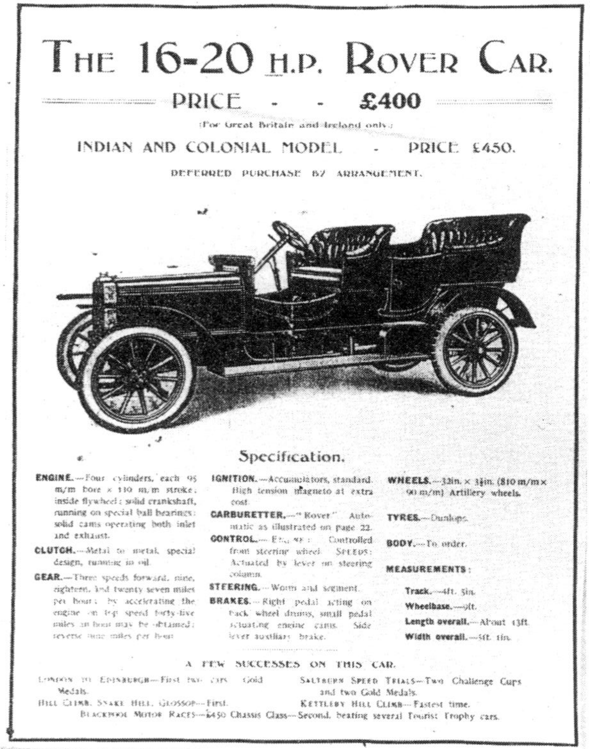

Fig 2: Advertising 'The Famous' 12 H.P. Rover, Nash's Magazine, 1914 (British Motor Industry Heritage Trust/Rover Group).

Fig 1: In technical isolation; advertising the 16–20 H.P. Rover, circa 1907 (British Motor Industry Heritage Trust/Rover Group).

Fig 4: *Cars in settings: 'Grand Society' advertising for Humber motor cars, The Sphere, 1936 (Peugot Motor Company PLC).*

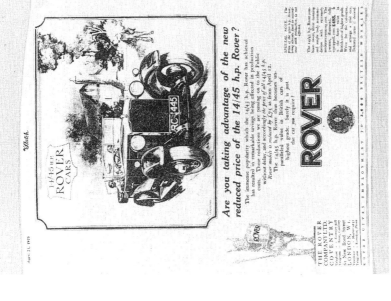

Fig 3: *Cars in settings: 'Country Touring', advertising the 14/45 H.P. Rover, The Sketch 1926 (British Motor Industry Heritage Trust/Rover Group).*

The car so many people
are so very proud to own!

AUSTIN – you can depend on it!

THE FORD V-8 "22"

£290 at Works

Fig 5: *Cars in settings; 'Under the dovecote' advertising the Ford V8, Britannia & Evem, 1937 (Ford UK).*

Fig 6: *Cars and people; 'Envied by the hunt' advertising the Austin A90 Six-Westminster, Punch, 1955 (British Motor Industry Heritage Trust/ Rover Group).*

Fig 8: *Cars and people; 'Discrimination after the game' advert for the Wolseley 6/80 and 4/44 saloons, 1955 (Heon Stevenson Collection).*

Fig 7: *Cars and people; 'Gentleman's judgment' advert for the Wolseley 4/44 and 6/90, 1956 (Heon Stevenson Collection).*

Fig 10: *Cars and people; 'Gender satisfaction' advertising the Austin A30 Seven,* Punch, 1955 *(British Motor Industry Heritage Trust/Rover Group).*

Fig 9: *Cars and people; 'Testimonial truth' advertising the Sunbeam Alpine 1.6 litre, 1960 (Heon Stevenson Collection).*

Fig 11: Cars and lifestyle; 'The swinging city' advertising the MG Midget, Punch, *1972 (British Motor Industry Heritage Trust/ Rover Group).*

Index

INDEX

INDEX

An environmentally friendly book printed and bound in England by www.printondemand-worldwide.com

PEFC Certified

This product is
from sustainably
managed forests
and controlled
sources

www.pefc.org

PEFC/16-33-415

MIX
Paper from
responsible sources
FSC® C004959

This book is made entirely of sustainable materials; FSC paper for the cover and PEFC paper for the text pages.

#0187 - 191213 - C0 - 234/156/20 [22] - CB